# THE
# Yachting
# BOOK OF
# PRACTICAL
# NAVIGATION

# THE
# Yachting
# BOOK OF
# PRACTICAL
# NAVIGATION

Stafford Campbell

 A TRITON BOOK

DODD, MEAD & COMPANY   New York

Published by Dodd, Mead & Company, Inc.
79 Madison Avenue, New York, N.Y. 10016
Distributed in Canada by
McClelland and Stewart Limited, Toronto
Manufactured in the United States of America
First Edition

Library of Congress Cataloging in Publication Data

Campbell, Stafford.
    The Yachting book of practical navigation.

    Includes index.
    1. Navigation. 2. Yachts and yachting. I. Title. VK555.C234    1984
623.89        84-18826
ISBN 0-396-08561-X

# Contents

# Contents

# Preface

*Navigation,* a word whose Latin roots mean, literally, "to drive a ship," is the process of directing the movement of a vessel from one point to another. When practiced in inshore, or "pilot" waters, it is called "coastwise navigation" or "piloting." Offshore, where the heavenly bodies are used to find the way, the process is called "celestial navigation." These two practices, as they apply to yachtsmen, are the subject of this text.

In its long history, thought by scholars to date back some six to eight thousand years, the art of navigation has almost evolved into a science; but "almost" is an important word. Nathaniel Bowditch, author of *The New American Practical Navigator,* and in the minds of many, the leading figure in modern marine navigation, often said that the science can be taught, but the art must be acquired. In this vein, the facts and techniques that I hope to impart to you in this book must be reinforced by your experience in practicing the craft in order to qualify you as a navigator.

In the organization of this text, the first chapter will introduce you to the elements of piloting, while Chapters

2–6 are devoted to the tools of the trade; those you may use for planning, those you will use on board for navigating, and those outside the vessel that contribute to guidance and safety. Chapters 7 and 8 explain the techniques involved in navigating a coastwise voyage; these merit your close study and thorough understanding, since they are the heart of the matter. Chapters 9–12 discuss special situations or evolutions you are likely to encounter in piloting, the last two describing the application of electronic calculators in coastwise navigation and some of the tricks of the piloting trade.

Chapter 13 is an introduction to celestial navigation offshore, while Chapters 14–19 explain the practice of making and plotting an actual observation of the sun, the body used most frequently. Sights of the other celestial bodies are described in Chapters 20–23, including special cases you will find useful. As in the piloting section, the final chapters describe the application of calculators to celestial navigation, and "wrinkles" for making the celestial navigator's performance better or easier.

You may already be familiar with the seaman's vocabulary, but to clarify some of the specialized navigational terms used in the text, which may be new to you, a glossary follows Chapter 26. Also, the appendices contain extracts of Chart No. 1, a compendium of the symbols and abbreviations used on United States nautical charts, and illustrations of the system of navigational aids found in United States waters; and for celestial navigators, a set of blank workforms covering the various procedures described. You may wish to familiarize yourself with these references so you can consult them as you proceed.

The primary objective of this book is to concentrate on the information and techniques of immediate, practical use to the yachtsman engaged in coastwise and celestial navigation. Should your study and experience whet your appetite for more, as well they may, two classic marine navigation texts, "Bowditch" (American Practical Navi-

*gator*, Publication No. 9, U.S. Defense Mapping Agency, Washington, D.C.) and "Dutton" (*Dutton's Navigation & Piloting*, U.S. Naval Institute Press, Annapolis, Maryland) contain a lifetime of learning and make splendid reference volumes.

Today, more and more yachtsmen are embarking on adventurous voyages; it is no longer a rarity to cross an ocean in a small boat. If you should contemplate such an undertaking yourself, you will need to have a thorough grounding in all phases of navigation. You will certainly want to include celestial in your kit, and you will find it a logical extension of piloting, which, as the order in this book indicates, should be learned first, because inshore, pilot waters are where most of the dangers exist, and where every voyage begins and ends.

Both in my function as editor of the "Practical Navigator" column in *Yachting* magazine and in this book, my aim is best expressed by John Hamilton Moore, Nathaniel Bowditch's predecessor, who, in the preface to his *New Practical Navigator* in 1796 wrote, "My grand object has been to be concise yet comprehensive, explanatory in my definitions, perspicuous in my rules and examples, and, in a word, most carefully attentive to every particular that can further the acquisition of an art that has been the object of my pursuits throughout my life."

May the art enrich your life too and add to your yachting pleasures.

# THE
# Yachting
# BOOK OF
# PRACTICAL
# NAVIGATION

# 1 | Introduction to Piloting

It's not uncommon for a yachtsman new to the sport to be a little hesitant about his ability to find his way on the water. True, there are no road signs at sea, nor are there numbered highways to follow, but if you can read a map and are familiar with a compass—the two basic tools of navigation—you will soon discover that the procedure, particularly in piloting, is really no more difficult than finding your way on land.

You will not find coastwise navigation to be an occult art; without being conscious of it you are already practicing many of the fundamentals each time you make a trip by automobile. You depart from a known location, road map in hand, and follow a prescribed route to your intended destination. You respect the traffic rules along the way and periodically confirm your progress by observing road signs, intersections, or prominent landmarks until you arrive, safe and sound, at the appointed time.

While the ocean's surface represents a much more variable environment than a paved highway, the navigational principles remain the same. Again, you depart from a known location on your chart, steer a predetermined course, check your position from time to time with reference to navigational aids or landmarks, adjust your heading as necessary to correct course errors and to avoid dangers, and arrive safely and on schedule at your destination.

The special demand on the marine navigator is for care and precision. In an automobile, if you lose your way or have mechanical difficulties, help is usually at hand, but on the water, you have to be a great deal more self-reliant. It's up to you as the navigator to see that you have all the equipment you may need on board and in good working order, and with that also goes the responsibility of knowing how to use it, so that, to the best of your ability, you will always be aware of where you are.

On shore, it's not easy to stray from the confines of the highway network, but at sea a navigator must plot his own course and determine his own position. Panic has no place in the boating scene, so the navigator should know his job well, and with the confidence that generates, be able to remain "calm, cool and collected," the hallmark of the experienced professional. To paraphrase John Curran: Eternal vigilance is the price of safety at sea.

You may have already detected the implication that planning and preparation and attention to detail go hand in hand with successful navigating. "Forehandedness" is the Navy term for anticipating situations before they occur, so that responses follow routine, thought-out procedures, rather than leading to misadventures. You will also discover in the learning process that navigation is by no means a drudgery. Quite the opposite: precise navigating can be one of the true delights in yachting.

But enough said. Let's get started by looking at the fundamental tool, the mariner's chart.

# 2 | Nautical Charts

A sailor's map is known as a "chart," and no prudent mariner ever goes to sea without one. As with any map, a nautical chart is a representation of a portion of the earth's surface, but being intended for marine navigation, it shows features not usually found on land-based maps. The principal information of interest to the navigator is the depth of the water (called "soundings"), the location and character of the shoreline or submerged dangers, the positioning of various types of devices intended as aids to navigation, and conspicuous landmarks that may help in determining his position. Charts contain a myriad of supplementary data, too, such as the type of bottom, overhead clearances, and the locations of improved channels; in fact, the modern nautical chart is a mine of information.

Much of a chart's information is presented in the form of symbols and abbreviations, and it behooves a would-be navigator to develop the ability to recognize their meanings without hesitation. A complete listing of these is contained in Chart No. 1, *Nautical Chart Symbols and Abbreviations*, an extract of which is included in Appendix I. However, it isn't a prerequisite to learn every symbol and abbreviation at the outset. Let's look instead at the kind of coastal chart you are most apt to be using, and at the information it commonly displays.

The chart segment shown in Figure 2–1 is a portion of Chart No. 12368, which covers a section of the Connecticut coast bordering Long Island Sound, a popular yachting area. First, notice that North is "up," and that the chart also includes a compass "rose" by means of which any other direction can be determined. For identifying the geographical position of any point, there is always a latitude scale at the sides and a longitude scale across the top and bottom of each conventional chart. You will remember from your school days that latitude and longitude—derived from the Latin words for breadth and length—are the coordinates for identifying all locations on earth.

You will see scattered all about the water areas a series of small numbers. These are soundings, as measured at a specified water level called the chart sounding datum. As the legend indicates, the soundings on this particular chart are shown in feet as they exist at mean low water, a widely—though not exclusively—used datum based on the average of all the low-water heights observed over a prolonged period; it is generally synonymous with low tide. Always be careful to note whether the charted depths are expressed in feet, meters, or fathoms (a fathom is six feet). Failure to do so might mean an embarrassing interlude on a sandbar waiting for the next tide to float you off.

In addition to the shoreline itself, the chart indicates a number of subsurface features that might be hazardous to a vessel. Rocks, reefs, wrecks, and underwater cables can all be found on the excerpt by their appropriate symbols. Some symbols, such as the diamond shape used for floating buoys, will be quite obvious in their meanings, as are the common abbreviations that take the place of long legends. The symbol you see indicating the lighthouse on

Greens Ledge in the chart excerpt, and the abbreviated legend describing its distinct light pattern, are typical. "Alt Fl W & R 30 sec 62ft 13M HORN" simply means that the light displayed alternates between a white flash and a red flash at an interval of 30 seconds. The light is located 62 feet above sea level and is visible at a nominal range of 13 miles. The fog signal is sounded by a horn.

Follow the improved channel on the chart inward to where man-made structures appear, and you will see that whenever bridges, overhead wires, or the like restrict the navigable waterway, the clearances are shown. We will be discussing the practice of navigating by chart in more detail later, but to start, a good exercise is to study the excerpt carefully until you can identify all of its high-lighted features and then look at a chart of your own prospective yachting area. You'll be surprised how much you can discover about your home waters, and how easy it is to orient yourself on the chart by reference to familiar landmarks. You will also begin to appreciate how essential it is always to have a correct chart at hand.

Chartmaking, as a profession, goes back many hundreds of years. In early times, sea charts were privately published and jealously guarded because the information they provided, often obtained at the cost of fortunes and lives, could be of great strategic and commercial value. By the late eighteenth century, the governments of the leading maritime nations saw the need to play an increasing role in the collection and dissemination of navigational data, and it was only natural that they started creating their own charts. Following the lead of the British Royal Navy in 1823, government charts were first made available to the general public, and with few exceptions, have been obtainable from all maritime countries ever since.

Almost all original charts published today issue from government sources. Those covering United States waters are published by the National Ocean Service (NOS), a branch of the National Oceanic and Atmospheric Admin-

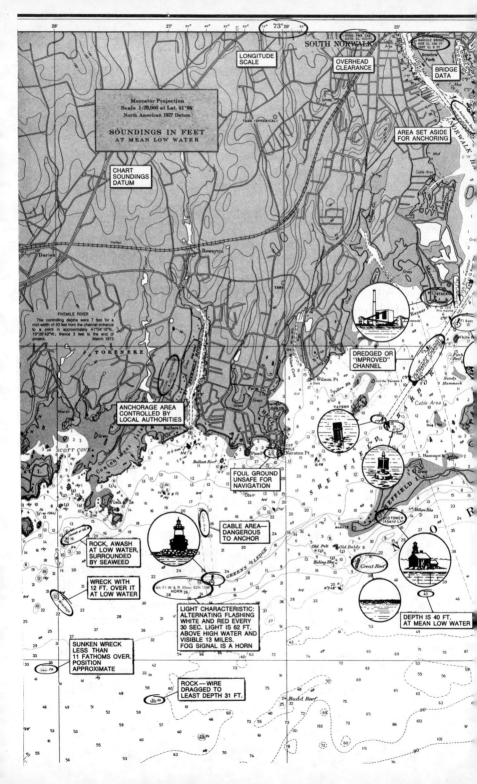

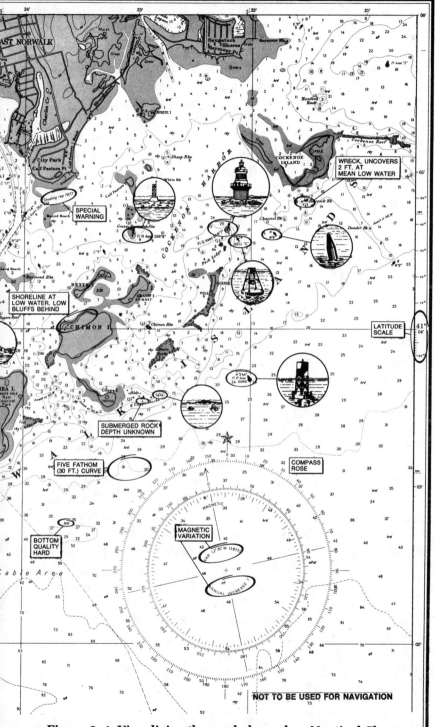

*Figure 2–1.* Visualizing the symbols used on Nautical Charts.

istration (NOAA), which is an agency of the Department of Commerce. A catalog folder of the charts and NOS publications applicable to your area, which also includes a list of the authorized sales agents in your locality, is available from the Distribution Branch (N/CG33), Riverdale, Maryland 20737. The sales agents are generally marine dealers and can also be found under "Charts—Nautical" in the Yellow Pages of your telephone book. A portion of a typical NOS catalog is shown in Figure 2–2. Note the scheme for delineating the area covered by each chart; this is used in all chart catalogs.

Catalogs of charts covering Canadian coastal and Great Lakes waters are issued by the Canadian Hydrographic Service in Ottawa, while charts of American inland rivers, not included in the NOS lists, are issued by the U.S. Army Corps of Engineers and are available from their district offices. For voyages beyond coastal waters, charts are published by the Defense Mapping Agency of the U.S. Department of Defense. The Agency issues nine area catalogs covering all the regions of the world, and a tenth volume describing their special-purpose navigational charts, tables, and nautical publications. Navigators are cautioned to use up-to-date charts and, between the acquisition of new editions, to use the DMA's *Weekly Notice to Mariners* to correct DMA, NOS, and Coast Guard charts and publications. Each Coast Guard district also issues a *Local Notice to Mariners* to advise of changes affecting the safety of navigation in that district. Yachtsmen using inshore waters not frequented by ocean-going commerce, or inside routes such as the Intracoastal Waterway, find the local notices to be their principal, if not only, source of updating information.

Charts are issued in several scale groups appropriate to the area covered. *Harbor Charts*, at scales of 1:50,000 and larger, are intended for navigation and anchorage in harbors and small waterways. The excerpt in Figure 2–1 is a Harbor Chart at a scale of 1:20,000, or about ¼ mile to the inch. *Coast Charts* carry scales from 1:50,000 to 1:150,000 and are intended for coastwise navigation inside offshore reefs and shoals, for entering bays and harbors of considerable size, and for navigating certain inland waterways. *General Charts,* with scales from 1:150,000 to 1:600,000, are for use when a vessel's course is well offshore, but when its position can be fixed by landmarks, lights, buoys, and characteristic soundings. *Sailing Charts* have scales smaller than 1:600,000 and serve as plotting charts for offshore sailing between distant coastal ports and for approaching the coast from the open ocean. The charts in all of these groups are called "conventional" charts and are published on single, unfolded sheets. *Small Craft Charts* are specially designed and folded into convenient panels for easy handling and stowage in confined quarters. This format is also particularly applicable to long, confined watercourses such as the Intracoastal Waterway, where strip panels are now replacing the conventional charts.

For the coastwise yachtsman, the choice is usually the largest-scale chart of the area, and this means the Harbor and Coast series. Small Craft Charts may be called for when there is inadequate coverage by conventional charts, or when space constraints prevail, but as long as there is adequate room in which to plot, I prefer the latter.

Offshore, most celestial navigators prefer to use plotting sheets. Known as "Position Plotting Sheets," they are published in several series by the Defense Mapping Agency and available from their agents. The use of plotting sheets is discussed in Chapter 19.

Stowage of charts is a common problem aboard small boats; to be useful they must be properly protected and at the same time immediately accessible. One of the best ways to handle conventional charts is to fold them in four parts—each about the size of an average navigation desk on a yacht—with the printed side facing out. The chart's name and number are thereby displayed for easy

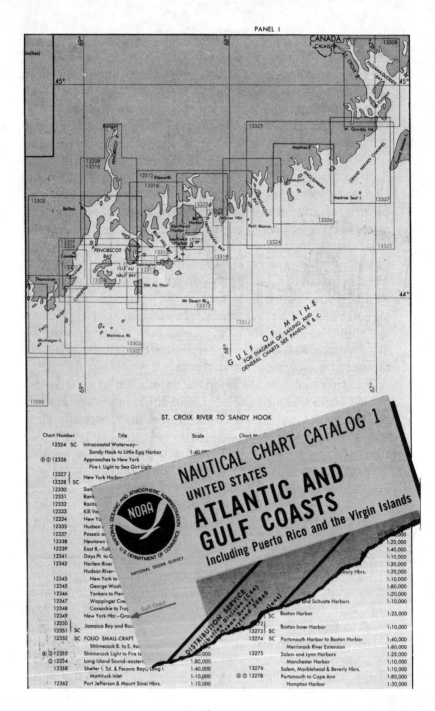

## GENERAL INFORMATION

### PURCHASE AND ISSUE

Charts and related publications as listed in this catalog may be ordered from the **Distribution Branch, (N/CG33), National Ocean Service, Riverdale, Maryland 20737,** Telephone (301) 436-6990 (Counter Sales: 6501 Lafayette Ave., Riverdale, Md., — Rm. 913, Building 1, 6001 Executive Blvd., Rockville, Md. — 439 West York St., Norfolk, Va. or from authorized sales agents.)
**Orders mailed to Riverdale, Maryland should be accompanied by a check or money order payable to NOS, Department of Commerce.** Remittance from outside of the United States should be made either by an International Money Order or by a check payable on a United States Bank.

All chart sales are final unless an error is made by this office in filling the order.

### CHART PRICES

| |
|---|
| CONVENTIONAL CHARTS (labelled in purple and blue) . . . $5.50 |
| *FOLIO SMALL-CRAFT CHARTS (labelled in green) . . . . . . . $4.75 |
| *SMALL-CRAFT (POCKET FOLD) CHARTS (labelled in green)  $3.50 |
| ALL OTHER SMALL-CRAFT CHARTS (labelled in green) . . . $4.75 |
|     Except Charts 13306 and 13310 . . . . . . . . . . . . . . . . . . . . . . . . . $5.50 |
| |
| *Identified in chart listing index. |
| All prices are subject to annual recomputation, based on cost of production, in accordance with Federal law. |

### CLASSIFICATION OF CHARTS
#### SMALL-CRAFT CHARTS

These specially designed charts are published with small craft information and are labelled in green on this catalog. They are folded into convenient panels for easy handling and storage.

#### CONVENTIONAL CHARTS

The conventional flat nautical charts are outlined in purple and blue on this catalog, and are assigned to one of the following scale groups:

HARBOR CHARTS (outlined in purple) – scales 1:50,000 and larger: They are intended for navigation and anchorage in harbors and small waterways.
COAST CHARTS (ootlined in blue) – scales from 1:50,000 to 1:150,000: They are intended for coastwise navigation inside the offshore reefs and shoals, entering bays and harbors of considerable size, and navigating certain inland waterways.
GENERAL CHARTS (outlined in blue) – scales from 1:150,000 to 1:600,000: They are for use when a vessel's course is well offshore, but when its position can be fixed by landmarks, lights, buoys, and characteristic soundings.
SAILING CHARTS (outlined in blue) – scales smaller than 1:600,000: They are plotting charts used for offshore sailing between distant coastal ports and for approaching the coast from the open ocean.
INTRACOASTAL WATERWAY (INSIDE ROUTE) CHARTS (outlined in purple) – Scale 1:40,000, embrace the inside route from Miami to Key West, Florida, and from Tampa to Anclote Anchorage, Florida.
**CAUTION:** VARIOUS SCALES ARE EMPLOYED TO PORTRAY FEATURES IN SUFFICIENT DETAIL FOR THE PURPOSE OF THE DIFFERENT CLASSES OF CHARTS. HYDROGRAPHIC INFORMATION IS NOT GENERALLY SHOWN FOR INSHORE AREAS ON SMALL-SCALE CHARTS WHERE LARGER-SCALE CHART COVERAGE IS AVAILABLE. MARINERS SHOULD ALWAYS OBTAIN LARGEST-SCALE CHART COVERAGE FOR NEAR SHORE NAVIGATION.

### NOTES, SYMBOLS, AND ABBREVIATIONS

Charts contain various types of notes placed in association with the title or in the proximity of the detail to which they refer. These notes are essential for the complete interpretation of the chart and should be thoroughly understood by the chart user. The symbols and abbreviations used on the nautical charts of the National Ocean Survey are published in booklet form as Chart No. 1 which sells for $1.50 a copy. It is recommended that the mariner familiarize himself with these symbols so that he may readily interpret all chart information.

### IMPORTANCE OF UP-TO-DATE CHARTS

The date of a chart is of vital importance to the navigator. When information becomes obsolete, *further use of the chart for navigation may be dangerous.* Natural and artificial changes, many of them critical, are occuring constantly, and it is important that navigators obtain up-to-date charts at regular intervals, and hand correct their copies for changes published in the Notices to Mariners. (See Notices to Mariners under "Published and Issued by other Federal Agencies").

Charts are revised at regular intervals. Users should consult the pamphlet "Dates of Latest Editions" for the dates of current chart editions. The pamphlet, issued quarterly, is available, free, from the Distribution Division, C44, Riverdale, Md. 20840.

Any defects found in National Ocean Survey charts should be reported to The Director, National Ocean Survey, National Oceanic and Atmospheric Administration, Rockville, Maryland 20852.

### DATES ON CHARTS

NEW EDITION: — A revision that cancels previous issues. A new edition reflects one or more changes of such importance to navigation that all previous printings are obsolete. Revisions may be based on corrections from the Notice to Mariners and/or other sources.

The date of a new edition is the date of the latest Notices to Mariners from which the chart has been corrected. The consecutive edition number and date are printed in the lower left corner of the chart.
REVISED PRINT: — A revision that does not supersede a current edition.

When the edition is revised and printed, the date of revision is shown to the right of the edition date.

### PUBLICATIONS RELATING TO NAUTICAL CHARTS
### PUBLISHED AND ISSUED BY THE NATIONAL OCEAN SURVEY
#### UNITED STATES COAST PILOTS

A series of books that cover a wide variety of information important to navigators of United States coastal, intracoastal, and Great Lakes waters. Subjects include navigation regulations, outstanding landmarks, channel and anchorages peculiarities, dangers, weather, ice, freshets, routes, pilotages and port facilities. New editions of Coast Pilots 1 through 7 are published annually. Coast Pilots 8 and 9 are published every 2 years.

*Figure 2–2.* Specimen panel from NOS Nautical Chart Catalog 1, *Atlantic and Gulf Coasts.*

identification and for filing in numerical order. With a chart catalog at hand, any single chart can then be found instantly. It is usually possible to work on a chart folded in this manner without having to unfold it—a big advantage in an open cockpit. Some yachtsmen roll their charts for stowage, in the way they are packaged for shipping, but I don't recommend this, since such charts always seem to roll back up on their own, magnifying the difficulty in plotting.

In recent years, especially as the price of individual government charts has risen, private publishers have offered collections of charts or "folios" for the more popular yachting areas. The source of the data is almost always government charts, and the original charts are sometimes reproduced in whole or part, with the scale adjusted to fit the publisher's format. Supplementary information of interest to yachtsmen may be superimposed on such chart reproductions—including calculated courses, the distances between principal points, or the location of facilities ashore—resulting in a handy and economical package if you don't mind the scale adjustment. Since the government doesn't exercise control over the production of these private folios, most carry the legend, "Not to be Used for Navigation." While I still prefer conventional charts, considering the cost of individual charts and the time and effort to keep a large inventory updated, it is easy to see why a number of yachtsmen favor the reproduced-chart folios, especially for planning a voyage in new waters.

Chartmaking itself is an interesting subject, and a brief overview may help you understand some of the conventions that the cartographers have adopted. Because navigators want to work on a flat sheet, while we live on a globe, a way had to be found to represent the round earth on flat paper. Such a representation is called a "projection," and there are a number of different projections available; however, the one most commonly used by mariners, and the basis for virtually all the charts you will use in coastwise navigation, is named the "Mercator" projection after the Flemish geographer who first published a chart embodying this principle in 1569.

Figure 2–3 illustrates the theory of the Mercator chart, the projection being developed by wrapping a flat sheet cylindrically around the earth and projecting the latitude and longitude lines upon it. In practice, the projection is expanded mathematically—a matter of technical interest, perhaps, but of little significance to the user. The out-

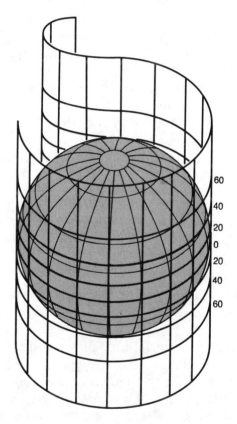

*Figure 2–3.* The Mercator Projection. One way of showing the round earth on flat paper.

standing feature of the Mercator chart is that on it, the latitude lines, which are normally parallel on earth, remain parallel, while the meridians of longitude, which actually converge as they approach the earth's poles, appear on the chart as equidistant from each other and perpendicular to the latitude lines. This means that a vessel's course, plotted as a straight line, crosses every meridian at a constant angle, permitting the course to be measured from any parallel or meridian, which is a great convenience. The only distortion in the true shape of a charted area is that the parallels of latitude appear slightly farther apart as the distance from the equator increases. In the case of Coastal and Harbor Charts this is hardly noticeable and is of no moment other than requiring, when you use the latitude scale to measure distance, that you use that portion of it as nearly as possible adjacent to the distance being measured.

As mentioned in connection with the excerpt in Figure 2–1, North on a conventional Mercator chart is "up," but in certain cases, as in the strip charts of the Intracoastal Waterway, it is not always convenient to fit the geography to the panel. In these instances, a modified Mercator form is employed. An example of this is illustrated in Figure 2–4, a portion of Chart No. 11491, where the projection has been rotated about 60° off vertical in order to show as much as possible in the limited space. It takes a little care not to become confused by this projection; the compass rose is the key. From it you can identify the latitude and longitude lines correctly and determine any intermediate direction.

Technically speaking, latitude lines—called "parallels" because they are all parallel to the equator—represent the angular distance from the equator, measured in a northward or southward direction from the earth's center, over a range of 0° to 90° of arc. Longitude lines are called "meridians" and are the angles formed at the poles between the Prime Meridian, 0°, and the position of the

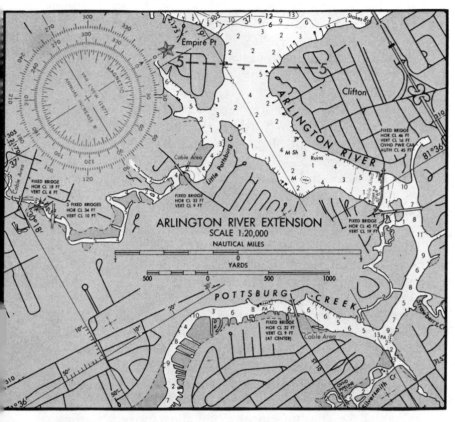

*Figure 2–4.* Panel from NOS Chart No. 11491 illustrating a Mercator projection, typical of many Small Craft Charts.

observer. By convention, longitude is measured eastward or westward from the Prime Meridian through 180°. The Prime Meridian itself is located at the Greenwich Observatory in England, where it was established by international agreement in 1884. It is observed by all maritime nations, and the longitudes on all the charts you use will relate to 0° at Greenwich. With the rectangular format and latitude/longitude scales on a Mercator chart, it's a simple matter to identify or plot any position by means of its coordinates.

*Direction* in navigation is expressed as an angle measured clockwise from North (or the ship's head, if relative direction is sought). It is measured through 360°. Thus, East becomes 90°—"090" in plotting parlance—Southwest is 225°, and so forth. In sailing-ship days, a traditional way of stating direction was by "points." There were 32 points, each 11¼° apart, and it was part of the sailor's art to be able to "box" the compass, naming all the points in order. Today, the point system, other than for identifying direction in a general way, has for all practical purposes given way to the 360° mode.

In the excerpt shown in Figure 2–1, you will have noticed that the compass rose indicates three directions simultaneously, a common convention on American charts. The outer circle, divided into 360°, measures *true* direction on the chart. The middle ring, also in degrees, indicates *magnetic* direction. (The difference between the two, known as magnetic variation, will be discussed in Chapter 5.) The innermost circle shows magnetic direction by the point system, the 32 points and 96 quarter-points being indicated, though not named, by the graduations. In coastwise navigation, courses and bearings are usually reckoned from the nearest rose (or by reference to convenient latitude or longitude lines) and plotted as a "rhumb" line—a line that makes the same angle at every meridian. We have seen that such a line plots as a straight line on a Mercator chart, and it follows that a vessel proceeding on a rhumb line maintains a constant compass heading.

*Distance* in coastwise navigation is measured, customarily, along the rhumb line. For navigational purposes, one minute of latitude on the earth's surface is considered to average 6,080 feet. It so happens that the International Nautical Mile is accepted as 6,076 feet, so, for convenience, navigators everywhere have adopted the convention that one minute of latitude equals one nautical mile. This means that instead of having to refer to a separate mileage scale, you have a ready reference to mileage in the latitude scale at either side of your chart. Remember that on a Mercator projection the spacing of the parallels changes slightly with the distance from the equator, so be sure your mileage measurement is made on the latitude scale adjacent to the distance line you are measuring. Be wary, too, of using the longitude scale for measuring mileage. The length of one minute of longitude decreases with the distance from the equator, the only place where it is equivalent to a nautical mile.

# 3 | Navigation Publications

Although we have spoken first about the essential nautical chart, there are other publications that contribute to proficient navigation. For convenience, we can divide the list into three general categories:

- Publications that are needed aboard for coastwise navigation.
- Information sources for planning a voyage.
- Reference texts for the study of navigation.

The most important publication in the first category is the *Tide Tables* for the current year. These are published annually by the National Ocean Service in four volumes covering the oceans of the world and list the predicted times and heights of high and low water relative to the chart datum for 200 reference ports, with tidal differences for some 6,000 more stations.

Using the *Tide Tables* for figuring the water level, either to compute your margin of safety over a submerged danger or under an overhead clearance, is an important, though simple, exercise. Let's look at an example illustrated in Figure 3–1. This is an excerpt from the *Tide*

*Tables, East Cost of North and South America,* the upper part (Table 1) being the daily tide predictions for Bridgeport, Connecticut, and the lower part (Table 2) being the tidal differences and other constants for twenty-one nearby stations.

You can see by inspection that on Monday, October 17, 1983, high water at Bridgeport occurs at 7:51 in the morning, and that the level will be 6.5 feet above the chart datum, which is mean low water. The succeeding low tide occurs at 1405 (2:05 P.M. on a standard clock) and will be 0.8 feet above the datum. By comparing your time with the predicted high- and low-water times, you can approximate the state of the tide, and if you desire greater accuracy, you can use Table 3, in the back of the *Tide Tables,* for this purpose.

The lower part of Figure 3–1 allows you to determine the times at which high and low water will occur at other, nearby stations. Using South Norwalk (Station No. 1241) as an example, you will see that high water will occur 10 minutes later than at Bridgeport, and low water 13 minutes later. The height of high water at South Norwalk will be 0.4 feet above the Bridgeport mark, while the low water height will be the same as at Bridgeport. The mean range between high and low water at South Norwalk is 7.1 feet (as opposed to Bridgeport's 6.7 feet), and the "spring" or extreme tides range 8.2 and 7.7 feet respectively. That is all there is to it, unless you happen to be sailing in an area that is tide-free, in which case you can dispense with the *Tide Tables* altogether.

A companion publication, related to the *Tide Tables* and similar in design, is the *Tidal Current Tables,* more popularly known simply as the *Current Tables* in order to avoid confusion. *Current Tables* are published annually by the NOS in two volumes. The excerpts in Figure 3–2 are from the volume *Atlantic Coast of North America.* The main tables, reproduced at the top of page 23, show the daily predicted times of slack water(the

BRIDGEPORT, CONN., 1983

Times and Heights of High and Low Waters

| | OCTOBER | | | | | | NOVEMBER | | | | | | DECEMBER | | | |
|---|---|---|---|---|---|---|---|---|---|---|---|---|---|---|---|---|
| | Time | Height | | Time | Height | | Time | Height | | Time | Height | | Time | Height | | Time | Height |
| Day | | | | Day | | | Day | | | Day | | | Day | | | Day | | |

| Day | h m | ft | m | Day | h m | ft | m | Day | h m | ft | m | Day | h m | ft | m | Day | h m | ft | m | Day | h m | ft | m |
|---|---|---|---|---|---|---|---|---|---|---|---|---|---|---|---|---|---|---|---|---|---|---|---|
| 1 | 0556 | 6.1 | 1.9 | 16 | 0055 | 0.8 | 0.2 | 1 | 0135 | -0.1 | 0.0 | 16 | 0140 | 0.6 | 0.2 | 1 | 0211 | -0.3 | -0.1 | 16 | 0137 | 0.4 | 0.1 |
| Sa | 1209 | 0.9 | 0.3 | Su | 0704 | 6.2 | 1.9 | Tu | 0746 | 7.1 | 2.2 | W | 0749 | 6.7 | 2.0 | Th | 0823 | 7.3 | 2.2 | F | 0749 | 6.8 | 2.1 |
| | 1823 | 6.9 | 2.1 | | 1316 | 1.1 | 0.3 | | 1408 | -0.2 | -0.1 | | 1409 | 0.5 | 0.2 | | 1451 | -0.8 | -0.2 | | 1417 | 0.0 | 0.0 |
| | | | | | 1924 | 2.0 | | | 2014 | 7.0 | 2.1 | | 2012 | 6.4 | 2.0 | | 2054 | 6.5 | 2.0 | | 2017 | 6.0 | 1.8 |
| 2 | 0052 | 0.3 | 0.1 | 17 | 0143 | 0.7 | 0.2 | 2 | 0230 | -0.4 | -0.1 | 17 | 0223 | 0.4 | 0.1 | 2 | 0302 | -0.4 | -0.1 | 17 | 0225 | 0.2 | 0.1 |
| Su | 0702 | 6.5 | 2.0 | M | 0751 | 6.5 | 2.0 | W | 0841 | 7.4 | 2.3 | Th | 0833 | 7.0 | 2.1 | F | 0913 | 7.5 | 2.3 | Sa | 0836 | 7.0 | 2.1 |
| | 1316 | 0.5 | 0.2 | | 1405 | 0.8 | 0.2 | | 1502 | -0.7 | -0.2 | | 1454 | 0.1 | 0.0 | | 1540 | -1.0 | -0.3 | | 1503 | -0.3 | -0.1 |
| | 1928 | 7.1 | 2.2 | | 2009 | 6.6 | 2.0 | | 2110 | 7.1 | 2.2 | | 2055 | 6.5 | 2.0 | | 2145 | 6.5 | 2.0 | | 2107 | 6.2 | 1.9 |
| 3 | 0154 | 0.0 | 0.0 | 18 | 0226 | 0.5 | 0.2 | 3 | 0321 | -0.6 | -0.2 | 18 | 0305 | 0.2 | 0.1 | 3 | 0350 | -0.5 | -0.2 | 18 | 0311 | 0.0 | 0.0 |
| M | 0804 | 6.9 | 2.1 | Tu | 0833 | 6.8 | 2.1 | Th | 0931 | 7.7 | 2.3 | F | 0913 | 7.2 | 2.2 | Sa | 1000 | 7.5 | 2.3 | Su | 0921 | 7.3 | 2.2 |
| | 1420 | 0.0 | 0.0 | | 1449 | 0.5 | 0.2 | | 1555 | -1.0 | -0.3 | | 1536 | -0.2 | -0.1 | | 1627 | -1.1 | -0.3 | | 1550 | -0.6 | -0.2 |
| | 2028 | 7.3 | 2.2 | | 2053 | 6.8 | 2.1 | | 2201 | 7.1 | 2.2 | | 2137 | 6.5 | 2.0 | | 2233 | 6.5 | 2.0 | | 2153 | 6.3 | 1.9 |

Time meridian 75° W.  0000 is midnight.  1200 is noon.
Heights are referred to mean low water which is the chart datum of soundings.

TABLE 2. — TIDAL DIFFERENCES AND OTHER CONSTANTS, 1983

| NO. | PLACE | POSITION | | DIFFERENCES | | | | RANGES | | Mean Tide Level |
|---|---|---|---|---|---|---|---|---|---|---|
| | | Lat. | Long. | Time | | Height | | Mean | Spring | |
| | | | | High Water | Low Water | High Water | Low Water | | | |
| | | ° ' N | ° ' W | h. m. | h. m. | ft | ft | ft | ft | ft |

on BRIDGEPORT, p.48

| NO. | PLACE | Lat. | Long. | High Water | Low Water | High Water | Low Water | Mean | Spring | Mean Tide Level |
|---|---|---|---|---|---|---|---|---|---|---|
| 1214 | Westbrook, Duck Island Roads............ | 41 16 | 72 28 | -0 23 | -0 34 | -2.6 | 0.0 | 4.1 | 4.7 | 2.0 |
| 1215 | Duck Island............................. | 41 15 | 72 29 | -0 25 | -0 37 | -2.2 | 0.0 | 4.5 | 5.2 | 2.2 |
| 1217 | Madison................................. | 41 16 | 72 36 | -0 20 | -0 32 | -1.8 | 0.0 | 4.9 | 5.6 | 2.4 |
| 1219 | Falkner Island.......................... | 41 13 | 72 39 | -0 13 | -0 27 | -1.3 | 0.0 | 5.4 | 6.2 | 2.7 |
| 1220 | Sachem Head............................. | 41 15 | 72 42 | -0 10 | -0 17 | -1.3 | 0.0 | 5.4 | 6.2 | 2.7 |
| 1221 | Money Island............................ | 41 15 | 72 45 | -0 11 | -0 25 | -1.1 | 0.0 | 5.6 | 6.4 | 2.8 |
| 1223 | Branford Harbor......................... | 41 16 | 72 49 | -0 07 | -0 20 | -0.8 | 0.0 | 5.9 | 6.8 | 2.9 |
| 1225 | New Haven Harbor entrance............... | 41 14 | 72 55 | -0 08 | -0 16 | -0.5 | 0.0 | 6.2 | 7.1 | 3.1 |
| 1227 | New Haven (city dock)................... | 41 18 | 72 55 | +0 02 | -0 03 | -0.7 | 0.0 | 6.0 | 6.9 | 3.0 |
| 1229 | Milford Harbor.......................... | 41 13 | 73 03 | -0 07 | -0 12 | -0.1 | 0.0 | 6.6 | 7.6 | 3.3 |
| 1231 | Stratford, Housatonic River............. | 41 11 | 73 07 | +0 27 | +0 59 | -1.2 | 0.0 | 5.5 | 6.3 | 2.7 |
| 1233 | Shelton, Housatonic River............... | 41 19 | 73 05 | +1 36 | +2 42 | -1.7 | 0.0 | 5.0 | 5.8 | 2.5 |
| 1235 | BRIDGEPORT.............................. | 41 10 | 73 11 | Daily predictions | | | | 6.2 | 7.7 | 3.4 |
| 1237 | Black Rock Harbor entrance.............. | 41 09 | 73 13 | -0 03 | -0 05 | +0.2 | 0.0 | 6.9 | 7.9 | 3.4 |
| 1239 | Saugatuck River entrance................ | 41 06 | 73 22 | -0 01 | -0 01 | +0.3 | 0.0 | 7.0 | 8.0 | 3.5 |
| 1241 | South Norwalk.......................... | 41 06 | 73 25 | +0 10 | +0 13 | +0.4 | 0.0 | 7.1 | 8.2 | 3.5 |
| 1243 | Greens Ledge............................ | 41 03 | 73 27 | -0 01 | -0 03 | +0.5 | 0.0 | 7.2 | 8.3 | 3.6 |
| 1245 | Stamford................................ | 41 02 | 73 33 | +0 04 | +0 06 | +0.5 | 0.0 | 7.2 | 8.3 | 3.6 |
| 1247 | Cos Cob Harbor.......................... | 41 01 | 73 36 | +0 06 | +0 09 | +0.5 | 0.0 | 7.2 | 8.3 | 3.6 |
| 1249 | Greenwich............................... | 41 01 | 73 37 | +0 02 | -0 01 | +0.7 | 0.0 | 7.4 | 8.5 | 3.7 |
| 1251 | Great Captain Island.................... | 40 59 | 73 37 | +0 01 | -0 01 | +0.6 | 0.0 | 7.3 | 8.4 | 3.6 |

*Figure 3-1.* Using the *Tide Tables*. High water occurs at Bridgeport on October 17, 1983, at 0751, with a height of 6.5 feet, and low water at 1405, 0.8 feet above the chart datum. The times and heights of high and low water at South Norwalk are shown in Table 2 as differences from the reference station.

moment between opposing tides) and the times and velocities of the maximum flood (F) and ebb (E) currents. A glance will show that on October 17, 1983, at The Race— the eastern outlet of Long Island Sound—the ebb was predicted to start at 8:19 A.M. and to reach its peak flow of 2.9 knots (a knot is one nautical mile per hour) at 11:39 A.M. The slack before the succeeding flood was predicted to occur at 2:56 P.M., with the flood current attaining its maximum velocity of 2.4 knots at 5:45 P.M.

Now let's move to Table 2 and look at the predictions for the vicinity of South Norwalk, where we have previously figured the times of the tides. At Station No. 2841, in the Norwalk River off Gregory Point, the ebb tide starts 29 minutes later than at The Race, or at 8:48 A.M. It will reach its maximum velocity half an hour after it does at The Race. The slack, or minimum flow before the flood begins, occurs at 2:44 P.M., 12 minutes before slack tide at The Race. The maximum flood will take place 21 minutes before the maximum at The Race. The current velocities at Norwalk also differ substantially from those at The Race. The ratio shown in Table 2 is two-tenths, meaning that the maximum ebb current at Norwalk will run just under 0.6 knots on the day in question, and the maximum flood current will be not quite half a knot.

If you compare both the tide and current predictions at a single location, you may discover an apparent anomaly that is not uncommon in tidal bodies with an irregular configuration, such as Long Island Sound: slack water times do not necessarily coincide with high and low tides. Using the Norwalk example, we calculated that high water occurs at 8:01 A.M., while the current isn't predicted to turn until three-quarters of an hour later. Low tide takes place at 2:18 P.M., although the flood doesn't start for another half hour.

Why is it so important to understand the current? Because of the effect it will have on the course and speed you make good through the water. In Chapter 7 we will discuss the technique of sailing through currents and the adjustments that must be made to get you to where you are going; but you can appreciate at the outset that where significant differences exist between maximum ebb and flood current velocities—such as the 8.3-knot difference at New York's Hell Gate—the state of the current is of critical interest to the navigator of a slower vessel.

If you are making a long passage, such as the length of Long Island Sound, it is somewhat tedious to figure out the predictions for one station at a time in order to see the total picture. To overcome this, the NOS has developed a series called *Tidal Current Charts*, which cover the major harbors and waterways of the United States. These come in twelve folios, each consisting of a set of eleven chartlets, which depict, by means of arrows and figures, the direction and velocity of the current for each hour of the tidal cycle. The *Current Charts* depend on the *Current Tables* (and in one of the folios, the *Tide Tables*) to determine the times of slack water at the reference station. An excerpt from the *Tidal Current Charts, Long Island Sound and Block Island Sound*, is shown in Figure 3–3. It depicts the situation in Western Long Island Sound at the time at which the ebb tide begins at The Race. You can see confirmation of what we discovered in the *Current Tables*: when the ebb begins at The Race, the current is still flooding in the Norwalk River. If space is at a premium, you may not include the *Current Charts* in your on-board inventory, but you will certainly find them useful for planning.

Some navigators prefer the privately published *Eldridge Tide and Pilot Book* (Robert Eldridge White, Boston) for tide and current information. It contains easy-to-read tables and time differences for most of the stations between Maine and Chesapeake Bay, as well as excerpts from the *Current Charts*, data from the U.S. Coast Guard *Light List*, and a store of other navigational information of interest to the yachtsman. All of this is contained in one handy volume, issued annually since 1874.

The Coast Guard *Light List* is another important on-board publication. Issued annually in five regional volumes, and available from the U.S. Government Print-

## THE RACE, LONG ISLAND SOUND, 1983

F-Flood, Dir. 295° True     E-Ebb, Dir. 100° True

### SEPTEMBER

| Day | Slack Water Time h.m. | Maximum Current Time h.m. | Vel. knots | Day | Slack Water Time h.m. | Maximum Current Time h.m. | Vel. knots |
|---|---|---|---|---|---|---|---|
| 1 Th | 0533 1155 1758 | 0232 0855 1454 2137 | 2.3F 2.5E 2.6F 3.2E | 16 F | 0132 0718 1347 1930 | 0432 1031 1650 2256 | 2.2F 2.5E 2.2F 3.0E |
| 2 F | 0056 0639 1302 1903 | 0335 1002 1555 2237 | 2.5F 2.7E 2.9F 3.5E | 17 Sa | 0225 0812 1440 2022 | 0525 1122 1739 2345 | 2.3F 2.7E 2.4F 3.2E |
| 3 Sa | 0157 0742 1406 2005 | 0437 1106 1700 2336 | 2.8F 3.2E 3.2F 3.9E | 18 Su | 0312 0858 1526 2108 | 0611 1211 1824 | 2.5F 2.9E 2.5F |

### OCTOBER

| Day | Slack Water Time h.m. | Maximum Current Time h.m. | Vel. knots | Day | Slack Water Time h.m. | Maximum Current Time h.m. | Vel. knots |
|---|---|---|---|---|---|---|---|
| 1 Sa | 0621 1251 1846 | 0314 0949 1540 2218 | 2.6F 2.9E 2.9F 3.5E | 16 Su | 0146 0733 1410 1946 | 0447 1049 1702 2311 | 2.2F 2.6E 2.2F 2.9E |
| 2 Su | 0136 0725 1356 1950 | 0418 1050 1644 2318 | 2.9F 3.4E 3.2F 3.9E | 17 M | 0233 0819 1456 2033 | 0532 1139 1745 2354 | 2.4F 2.9E 2.4F 3.1E |
| 3 M | 0233 0823 1456 2049 | 0519 1145 1745 | 3.4F 3.9E 3.6F | 18 Tu | 0315 0900 1538 2117 | 0607 1220 1824 | 2.6F 3.2E 2.6F |

---

TABLE 2. - CURRENT DIFFERENCES AND OTHER CONSTANTS, 1983

| NO. | PLACE | METER DEPTH ft | POSITION Lat. ° ' N | POSITION Long. ° ' W | TIME DIFFERENCES Min. before Flood h. m. | TIME DIFFERENCES Flood h. m. | TIME DIFFERENCES Min. before Ebb h. m. | TIME DIFFERENCES Ebb h. m. | SPEED RATIOS Flood | SPEED RATIOS Ebb | AVERAGE SPEEDS AND DIRECTIONS Minimum before Flood knots deg. | AVERAGE SPEEDS AND DIRECTIONS Maximum Flood knots deg. | AVERAGE SPEEDS AND DIRECTIONS Minimum before Ebb knots deg. | AVERAGE SPEEDS AND DIRECTIONS Maximum Ebb knots deg. |
|---|---|---|---|---|---|---|---|---|---|---|---|---|---|---|
| | LONG ISLAND SOUND Time meridian, 75°W | | | | on THE RACE, p.34 | | | | | | | | | |
| | Housatonic River | | | | | | | | | | | | | |
| 2751 | Wooster Island, 0.1 mile southwest of | 5 | 41 16.67 | 73 05.20 | +1 19 | +0 33 | +0 20 | +0 22 | 0.2 | 0.2 | 0.6 020 | | 0.0 -- | 0.7 220 |
| 2756 | Derby-Shelton Bridge, below <13> | | 41 18.73 | 73 04.78 | -- -- | -- -- | -- -- | -0 06 | -- | 0.1 | 0.0 -- | | 0.0 -- | 0.4 095 |
| 2761 | Point No Point, 2.1 miles south of | 15 | 41 06.75 | 73 07.13 | -0 30 | -0 06 | -0 08 | -0 01 | 0.4 | 0.3 | 0.0 -- | 1.3 251 | 0.0 -- | 1.2 074 |
| 2766 | Old Field Point, 1 mile east of | 15 | 40 58.47 | 73 05.80 | +3 26 | +2 31 | +2 25 | +1 56 | 0.1 | 0.2 | 0.0 -- | 0.2 105 | 0.0 -- | 0.6 308 |
| | ...do... | 22 | 40 58.47 | 73 05.80 | +2 30 | +1 54 | +2 17 | +1 44 | 0.2 | 0.2 | 0.0 -- | 0.2 110 | 0.0 -- | 0.5 297 |
| 2771 | Old Field Point, 2 miles northeast of | 15 | 41 00.23 | 73 05.70 | +0 33 | +0 13 | -0 11 | +0 58 | 0.3 | 0.3 | 0.0 -- | 1.0 266 | 0.0 -- | 1.1 097 |
| 2776 | Stratford Point, 4.3 miles south of | 40 | 41 00.23 | 73 05.70 | +0 22 | +0 08 | -0 12 | +0 41 | 0.2 | 0.2 | 0.0 -- | 0.5 236 | 0.0 -- | 0.6 081 |
| | ...do... | 15 | 41 04.77 | 73 06.67 | +0 12 | +0 19 | +0 05 | +0 14 | 0.3 | 0.3 | 0.0 -- | 1.0 254 | 0.0 -- | 1.0 075 |
| | ...do... | 60 | 41 04.77 | 73 06.67 | +0 02 | +0 06 | -0 23 | +0 15 | 0.2 | 0.2 | 0.0 -- | 0.6 291 | 0.0 -- | 0.8 078 |
| 2781 | Stratford Point, 6.1 miles south of | 15 | 41 02.97 | 73 05.80 | -0 18 | +0 03 | +0 16 | +0 30 | 0.3 | 0.2 | 0.0 -- | 1.0 267 | 0.0 -- | 0.8 080 |
| | ...do... | 51 | 41 02.97 | 73 05.80 | -0 43 | -0 31 | -0 34 | -0 12 | 0.3 | 0.2 | 0.0 -- | 0.9 279 | 0.0 -- | 0.9 087 |
| 2786 | Port Jefferson Harbor entrance | | 40 58 | 73 06 | +0 11 | +0 40 | +0 32 | +0 14 | 0.8 | 0.4 | 0.0 -- | 2.6 151 | 0.0 -- | 1.9 323 |
| 2791 | Crane Neck Point, 0.5 mile northwest of | | 40 58 | 73 10 | -0 45 | -1 24 | -1 38 | -1 34 | 0.4 | 0.3 | 0.0 -- | 1.3 256 | 0.0 -- | 1.5 016 |
| 2796 | Bridgeport Hbr. ent., btn. jetties <14> | 4 | 41 09 | 73 11 | -0 10 | -0 22 | +0 05 | -0 03 | 0.2 | 0.1 | 0.0 -- | 0.7 340 | 0.0 -- | 0.6 176 |
| 2801 | Crane Neck Point, 3.4 miles WNW of | 15 | 40 59.00 | 73 13.87 | -0 12 | +0 02 | -0 25 | +0 09 | 0.2 | 0.2 | 0.0 -- | 0.5 261 | 0.0 -- | 0.6 079 |
| 2806 | Crane Neck Point, 3.7 miles WSW of | 15 | 40 56.30 | 73 13.87 | -1 32 | -0 31 | -0 24 | -0 18 | 0.1 | 0.1 | 0.0 -- | 0.4 066 | 0.0 -- | 0.4 232 |
| 2811 | Shoal Point, 6 miles south of | 15 | 41 01.70 | 73 14.03 | +0 22 | +0 08 | +0 42 | +0 55 | 0.1 | 0.1 | 0.0 -- | 0.4 232 | 0.0 -- | 0.4 047 |
| 2816 | Pine Creek Point, 2.3 miles SSE of | 15 | 41 05.05 | 73 14.40 | -0 20 | +0 06 | +0 21 | +0 23 | 0.2 | 0.2 | 0.0 -- | 0.7 272 | 0.0 -- | 0.6 084 |
| 2821 | Saugatuck River, 0.3 mi. NW of Bluff Pt. | 15 | 41 06.27 | 73 21.92 | -0 12 | -0 41 | +0 20 | +0 10 | 0.2 | 0.1 | 0.0 -- | 0.5 265 | 0.0 -- | 0.4 080 |
| 2826 | Saugatuck R., 0.5 mile above Bluff Pt... | | 41 06 | 73 23 | Current weak and variable | | | | | | | | | |
| 2831 | Sheffield I. Tower, 1.1 miles SE of.... | 15 | 41 01.97 | 73 24.33 | +0 33 | +0 39 | +0 59 | +0 33 | 0.3 | 0.2 | 0.0 -- | 0.9 283 | 0.0 -- | 0.8 081 |
| | ...do... | 60 | 41 01.97 | 73 24.33 | -0 27 | +0 24 | +1 00 | +0 36 | 0.2 | 0.2 | 0.0 -- | 0.6 269 | 0.0 -- | 0.5 076 |
| 2836 | Sheffield I. Hbr., 0.5 mile southeast of | 12 | 41 03.32 | 73 25.25 | -2 41 | -3 54 | -3 36 | -2 12 | 0.1 | 0.1 | 0.0 -- | 0.2 229 | 0.0 -- | 0.4 042 |
| 2841 | Norwalk River, off Gregory Point... | 15 | 41 05.25 | 73 24.22 | -0 12 | -0 21 | +0 29 | +0 30 | 0.2 | 0.2 | 0.0 -- | 0.6 322 | 0.0 -- | 0.5 155 |
| 2846 | Eaton's Neck Pt., 1.3 miles north of... | 15 | 40 58.60 | 73 23.77 | +0 21 | +0 21 | +0 05 | +0 21 | 0.5 | 0.4 | 0.0 -- | 1.4 283 | 0.0 -- | 1.4 075 |
| 2851 | Eaton's Neck Pt., 1.8 miles west of... | | 40 57 | 73 26 | -1 09 | -1 01 | -0 28 | -0 29 | 0.2 | 0.1 | 0.0 -- | 0.5 199 | 0.0 -- | 0.6 068 |
| 2856 | Eaton's Neck Pt., 3 miles north of... | 15 | 41 00.38 | 73 23.80 | +0 40 | +0 30 | +0 36 | +0 17 | 0.2 | 0.3 | 0.0 -- | 0.7 253 | 0.0 -- | 0.9 046 |

*Figure 3-2.* Using the *Current Tables.* Slack water before the ebb begins occurs at The Race on October 17, 1983, at 0819. The succeeding flood begins at 1456. The maximum velocities occur at 1139 and 1745, at 2.9 and 2.4 knots respectively. The currents in the Norwalk River are shown in Table 2 as differences from the reference station.

ing Office or from most chart suppliers, the *Light List* is a compendium of the navigational aids in coastal waters. It contains key information not included on the charts, such as the time-sequencing of individual lights, descriptions of their physical structures for daytime identification,

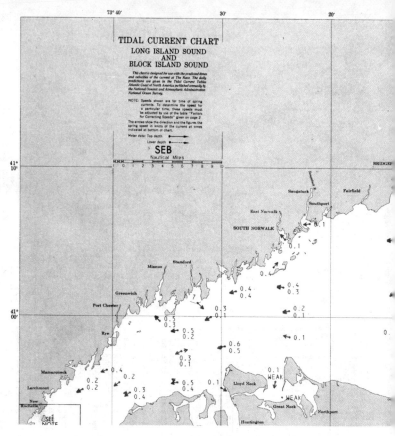

and details of fog signals. One of the features of the publication is the comprehensive explanation section in its introduction; the description of the radiobeacon system is of special interest to yachtsmen. The *Light List* is illustrated in Figure 4–1 and discussed further in Chapter 4.

You will also want to be familiar with the National Ocean Service's *United States Coast Pilots,* a series of nine area volumes designed as sailing directions for coastwise piloting. The subjects in the *Coast Pilots* include navigation regulations, descriptions of prominent landmarks, channel and anchorage peculiarities, dangers, weather, routings, pilotage requirements, port facilities, and a host of other information. By design, the *Coast Pilots* are written principally for the operators of larger vessels, but they still contain a wealth of information of

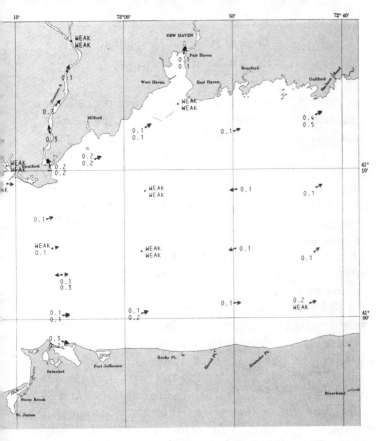

**Figure 3–3.** Excerpt from the *Tidal Current Charts, Long Island Sound and Block Island Sound,* showing currents at the time of slack water, before the ebb begins at The Race. Notice that the current is still flooding at South Norwalk, as it is at several other stations in Western Long Island Sound.

value to a yachtsman planning a cruise into an unfamiliar area, even if he chooses not to carry them aboard.

Offshore, for celestial navigation, you will need to have an almanac to provide the astronomical data for resolving your sights, and a sight reduction table for performing the mathematical operations. Most yachtsmen prefer the *Nautical Almanac,* prepared by the U.S. Naval Observatory, and DMA Pub. No. 249 for their tables. These publications are discussed further in Chapters 16 and 17, respectively.

Although not strictly part of the navigation procedure, weather reports are of concern both for planning and for safety. Today, weather predictions are as close as your radio receiver, although you may not know the schedules and frequencies. There are two useful publications to consult for this purpose: The National Oceanic and Atmospheric Administration's *NOAA Weather Radio* folder, outlining the VHF weather-radio network, which provides continuous broadcasts that can be received in most inshore waters, and *Worldwide Marine Weather Broadcasts,* published jointly by NOAA and the Navy's Weather Service Command, which extends the list offshore and to all the communication media.

The safe conduct of a voyage also implies a knowledge of the "Rules of the Road," the traffic laws designed to prevent collisions between ships at sea. The navigation requirements for vessels navigating the high seas as well as inland waters of the United States are contained in the publication *Navigation Rules,* issued by the Coast Guard. Because there is no margin for error in our increasingly congested waterways, knowledge and correct application of the navigation rules must be part of every navigator's skills.

In the planning department, there is a wide variety of cruising guides, many privately published, covering most of the popular yachting areas. A number of these are excellent, and you may find it useful to carry key volumes aboard. These guides come in two types: those that provide yachtsmen with sailing directions especially tailored to their needs—*A Cruising Guide to the New England Coast* (Dodd, Mead & Company, New York), one of the first and best, is a good example—and those that emphasize shore facilities and accept advertising, such as the *Waterway Guide* (Waterway Guide, Inc., Annapolis, Maryland) and the *Boating Almanacs* (Boating Almanac,

Inc., Severna Park, Maryland). In certain areas like the Bahamas, government charts and sailing directions are not sufficiently detailed for the yachtsman's needs, and publications like the *Yachtsman's Guide to the Bahamas* (Tropic Isle Publishers, Coral Gables, Florida) are extremely useful.

The selection of a cruising guide is highly subjective. Many prefer those like Wilensky's *Long Island Sound* (Snug Harbor Publishing, Stamford, Connecticut) that lead you by the hand in a thoroughly researched and lively style into a concentrated cruising area; others prefer only a facility listing. Your own selection will be based on your personal tastes and the coverage available for your area. One thing is certain, however: because the situation is changing rapidly and constantly in the exploding yachting scene, it is almost impossible to maintain a complete, up-to-date inventory of available guides. A more practical approach is to acquire the latest edition of a guide at the time of, and for the specific area of, your projected cruise and to keep your old guides in your navigation library for planning and reference between voyages.

On the subject of libraries, every student of navigation will want to have either or both of the classic reference texts mentioned in the Introduction to this book. First and foremost is "Bowditch," *American Practical Navigator*, available through most of the sales agents of the Defense Mapping Agency. Called the epitome of navigation, which it truly is, it was originally published by Nathaniel Bowditch (1773–1838) of Salem, Massachusetts, one of the outstanding mathematicians of his day. The copyright was acquired by the U.S. Navy Hydrographic Office in 1868, after some 66 years of successful publication, and the work has continued through seventy editions in the century-and-a-half of its existence. In 1972, the Defense Mapping Agency assumed the responsibility for the *American Practical Navigator*, which it has reissued in two volumes, separating the tables from the text in order to accommodate new material on the latest devices and techniques.

*Dutton's Navigation & Piloting* is now in its thirteenth edition. Originally prepared in 1926 by Commander Benjamin Dutton of the United States Navy, it gained widespread recognition as the Naval Academy's primary teaching text for many years. Like "Bowditch," "Dutton" is encyclopedic in scope and a fine reference volume.

The perennial problem on any small boat is stowage space, both for charts and other publications. A method of folding and indexing charts has been described in Chapter 2, and you will probably take with you only those applicable to the voyage at hand. The same remarks apply to publications; if you are short of space, leave the planning and reference volumes at home and carry only those you expect to consult at sea. Since the combined weight of "Bowditch" and "Dutton" is some thirteen pounds, and since you will be actively navigating rather than studying at sea, the suggestion is probably self-evident.

# 4 | Aids to Navigation

An aid to navigation has been defined as "any device external to a craft, designed to assist in determination of position of the craft, or of a safe course, or to warn of dangers"; in short, anything established to assist the navigator in the safe conduct of his voyage. Such devices may be large or small, fixed or floating, lighted or unlighted, and may or may not emit sound. Even electronic aids like radiobeacons and Loran are considered part of the broad category commonly called "navaids."

The vast majority of navaids are government-established and maintained. In the United States the task falls to the Coast Guard. We benefit from the most extensive system of navigational aids in the world, with some 50,000 installations in American waters, over half of which are floating devices. The Coast Guard *Light List*, mentioned in Chapter 3, is the "bible" of navaids in the United States, and the navigator should be familiar with its format and content. An extract from one of its pages is shown in Figure 4–1, and the typical navaids that are highlighted are illustrated in Figures 4–2, 4–3, and 4–4 and appear on the chart excerpt in Chapter 2.

Aids to navigation, as their definition suggests, are

| (1) | (2) Name | (3) Location | | (4) Nominal Range | (5) Ht. above water | (6) Structure | | (7) | |
|---|---|---|---|---|---|---|---|---|---|
| No. | Characteristic | Lat. N. | Long. W. | | | Ht. above ground | Daymark | Remarks | Year |

**Saugatuck River**

| | | | | | | | | | |
|---|---|---|---|---|---|---|---|---|---|
| | — Buoy 20 | In 8 feet | | | | Red nun | | Red reflector. | |
| | — Buoy 22 | In 7 feet | | | | Red nun | | Red reflector. | |
| | — Buoy 24 | In 8 feet | | | | Red nun | | Red reflector. | |
| | — Buoy 26 | In 8 feet | | | | Red nun | | Red reflector. | |
| | — Buoy 27 | In 8 feet | | | | Black can | | Green reflector. | |
| | — Buoy 29 | In 8 feet | | | | Black can | | Green reflector. | |

**Norwalk**
(Chart 12368)
NORWALK EAST APPROACH

| | | | | | | | | | |
|---|---|---|---|---|---|---|---|---|---|
| | — Buoy 2 | In 22 feet | | | | Red nun | | Red reflector. | |
| | | 41 04.4 | 73 20.8 | | | | | | |
| | — Buoy 4 | In 13 feet, marks southwest end of rock reef at Channel Rock. | | | | Red nun | | Red reflector. | |
| | — Bell Buoy 5 | In 13 feet | | | | Black | | | |
| 1172 | PECK LEDGE LIGHT 7 | In 7 feet, on south side of east entrance to Cockenoe Island Harbor. | | 6 | | SG on white conical tower, middle part brown, on black cylindrical pier. | | | 1906—1933 |
| | Fl. G., 4s | 41 04.6 | 73 22.1 | | | | | | |
| 1173 | GRASSY HAMMOCK LIGHT 8 | On rocks, north side of channel. | | 5 | 26 | TR on skeleton tower | | | 1901—1968 |
| | Fl. R., 4s | 41 04.6 | 73 23.0 | | | | | | |
| | — Buoy 9 | In 8 feet, on point of shoal north of Betts Island. | | | | Black can | | Green reflector. | |
| | — Buoy 11 | In 8 feet, off end of shoal northeast of Raymond Rocks. | | | | Black can | | Green reflector. | |

SHEFFIELD ISLAND HARBOR

| | | | | | | | | | |
|---|---|---|---|---|---|---|---|---|---|
| | Noroton Point Buoy 1A | In 16 feet, at east end of 12-foot shoal. | | | | Black can | | Green reflector. | |
| | Noroton Point Buoy | In 14 feet, on south-west side of shoal. | | | | Red and black horizontal bands; nun. | | Red reflector. | |
| | Norwalk Channel Entrance Buoy 1. | In 10 feet | | | | Black can | | Green reflector. | |
| | Tavern Island Buoy | In 7 feet, marks south side of rock, south-west of island. | | | | Red and black horizontal bands; nun. | | Red reflector. | |

NORWALK CHANNEL     Channel buoys located 30 to 50 feet outside channel limit.

| | | | | | | | | | |
|---|---|---|---|---|---|---|---|---|---|
| 1173.31 | Lighted Buoy 2 | In 12 feet | | 5 | | Red | | Replaced by nun buoy if endangered by ice. | |
| | Fl. W., 4s | | | | | | | | |
| | — Buoy 3 | In 12 feet | | | | Black can | | Green reflector. | |
| 1173.32 | Lighted Buoy 4 | In 12 feet | | 3 | | Red | | Replaced by nun buoy if endangered by ice. | |
| | Fl. R., 4s | | | | | | | | |
| | — Buoy 5 | In 12 feet | | | | Black can | | Green reflector. | |
| | — Buoy 7 | In 7 feet | | | | Black can | | Green reflector. | |
| | — Buoy 8 | In 12 feet, 75 feet outside channel limit. | | | | Red nun | | Red reflector. | |
| 1174 | — LIGHT 10 | In 9 feet, 200 yards north of rock, southeast of Keyser Point. | | 6 | 27 | TR on skeleton tower | | | 1901—1968 |
| | Fl. W., 4s | | | | | | | | |
| 1175 | MANRISSA ISLAND SOUTHERLY LIGHT | On dock, west side of slip. | | | 15 | | | Private aid. | 1960 |
| | F. G. | | | | | | | | |

**Figure 4–1.** Excerpt from the *Light List.* Key aids to navigation in the Norwalk, Connecticut area are listed. The highlighted entries are typical navaids illustrated in succeeding figures.

located strategically for purposes of position finding, as is the case with major lighthouses; or to keep the navigator clear of dangers—which is the principal role of Grassy Hammock Light; or to mark routes, as do the buoys at the entrance to Norwalk Channel. The rationale behind the positioning of an aid is usually obvious.

The first category of visual aids comprises the large light structures located along the seacoast and at important harbor entrances. They go back as far as 700 B.C. in Egypt, their main purpose being to position the navigator approaching from far offshore. Lighthouses can be identified by their light characteristics, which can be found on the chart and in the *Light List;* by their physical appearance, which is also described in the *Light List;* or by their fog or radiobeacon signals, which are found in the same source. Figure 4–2 shows three common types of lighthouses: the ones located at Peck Ledge, on Sheffield Island (abandoned), and on Greens Ledge. Compare the appearance of the Peck Ledge lighthouse with the description given in the *Light List* excerpt in Figure 4–1. At one time, almost all lighthouses were manned, but today, lighthouse-keeping is a thing of the past, and all but a few are operated without resident personnel.

Beacons have always been unmanned and are, in effect, miniature lighthouses. Easier to maintain than floating navaids, they are placed on banks and ledges, often to mark isolated dangers. Grassy Hammock Light, found in the *Light List* excerpt and illustrated in Figure 4–3, is a typical example. On beacons in key locations, electrically operated horns or mechanical bells are sometimes installed to signal their presence during periods of low visibility. Major lighthouses, on the other hand, always have sound devices of the greatest intensity, to maximize the limit of their usefulness. A sound signal may be produced by a horn, siren, whistle, mechanical bell, or diaphone (often a two-toned sound), and is usually aimed toward the most critical sector. The type of sound apparatus is

PECK LEDGE LIGHT

SHEFFIELD ISLAND (abandoned)

GREENS LEDGE LIGHT

*Figure 4–2.* Three types of lighthouses in the waters surrounding the Norwalk Islands.

*Figure 4–3.* Grassy Hammock Light (No. 1173). Flashing red every 4 seconds, 26 feet above the water, it is visible for 5 miles.

shown in the chart legend, while the nature of the signal is found in the "Remarks" column of the *Light List.*

Floating navaids first appeared during the Golden Age of Discovery in fifteenth- and sixteenth-century Europe. In America, the private placement of navigation buoys dates from the early 1700s; the first integrated system was established in the Delaware River in 1767. Congress enacted legislation providing for federal administration of the navaid system in 1789, and the navigator has been the clear beneficiary.

Floating aids may be divided into three convenient groups: un*lighted, sound,* and *lighted* types. Many larger buoys combine two or more of these characteristics. In the *unlighted* category, distinctly shaped, cylindrical "cans" and conical-topped "nuns" predominate, while spherical shapes are used as midchannel, or "safe water" marks in the U.S. lateral system as it is currently being modified. Examples of common cans and nuns are illustrated in Figure 4–4 (a) and (b), and each of these is highlighted for reference in the *Light List* excerpt in Figure 4–1. We will describe the system of numbering,

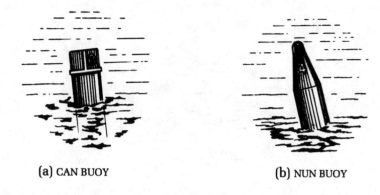

(a) CAN BUOY

(b) NUN BUOY

(c)  FLATTOP BELL BUOY

(d)  SMALL LIGHTED
CHANNEL BUOY

(e) LARGE LIGHTED BUOY,
OPEN SOUND

*Figure 4–4.* **Various types of standard navigation buoys found in the Norwalk Islands and approaches.**

coloring, and deploying buoys in a moment, but first, let's look at those fitted with audible devices or lights.

*Sound* buoys are equipped with bells, four-toned gongs, or whistles, normally activated by wave action. They may be lighted or unlighted, but like most lighted buoys they cannot be differentiated by shape, as cans and nuns may, but only by color, number, or signal characteristic. The "flattop," unlighted bell buoy "5," located in Norwalk East Approach and shown in Figure 4–4 (c), is a typical sound buoy. Because all but a very few audible buoys depend upon wave action to function (those few, in critical locations where the sea is usually calm, may employ an electrical sounding device), you must not assume that a buoy is not in place simply because you can't hear it.

*Lighted* navaids are a very important group and are located at key points throughout the buoyage system. The lights exhibited may be red, green, or white, or for special purpose buoys, yellow. Red is reserved for red navaids or for horizontally banded marks where the preferred course leaves it to starboard. Green is for green (or black) aids, or for banded marks to be left, preferably, to port. A white light has no lateral significance and is used predominantly on midchannel marks—eventually to become its exclusive use.

In addition to its color, the characteristic rhythm of a light is also indicative of the purpose of the buoy on which it is displayed. Flashing, occulting (a periodic light in which the period of darkness is less than the period of light), equal interval, or quick-flashing rhythms are all used in our lateral system for port- and starboard-hand marks, the quick-flashing variety indicating special caution as in the case of a sharp bend in a channel, or to mark obstructions or wrecks. One category of short-interval lights, designated "Interrupted Quick Flashing," which displays a group of quick flashes at regular intervals, is presently used on horizontally banded buoys to mark channel junctions or dangers that can be passed safely on either side, although this application is gradually being phased out in favor of "Composite Group Flashing," in which the number of flashes alternates between groups. A flashing white light displaying the Morse Code letter "A" (·—) appears exclusively on vertically striped, midchannel buoys marking fairways or traffic-separation zones.

Figure 4–4 (d) and (e) shows two typical examples of lighted buoys. The smaller one (d) is red and marks the entrance to Norwalk Channel, as indicated in the *Light List* (Figure 4–1), and the larger one (e) is Norwalk Harbor Lighted Buoy "24A," an important mark on the north side of Long Island Sound off the Norwalk Islands.

Besides its primary characteristics, a buoy may incorporate secondary devices to aid in its identification. Reflective bands or shapes, and names, letters, or numbers may be applied, and many navaids, including those shown in Figure 4–4, are designed to work as radar reflectors in order to extend the distance at which they can be located. A few major marks are fitted with radar transponders (called Racon) extending their location range still farther, and some of the largest navigational buoys, particularly those that have replaced key lightships, may include an automatic radiobeacon.

A uniform system of buoy identification and a consistent pattern of placement are important in fulfilling the primary mission of floating navaids. There are two such systems in use throughout the world: the *lateral* system, like the one found in American and Canadian waters; and the *cardinal* system, which prevails in a number of European countries. A few nations use elements of both systems. The principal difference in the two systems is that buoys in the lateral system are positioned to indicate the locations of dangers relative to the course to be followed, whereas those in the cardinal system are situated to indicate the direction of a hazard relative to the buoy itself.

In the American lateral system, the arrangement of floating navaids as well as their colors, shapes, numbers, and lights are predicated on an approach from the open sea. Along the coasts, a clockwise direction is considered to be "from seaward." The extract of Chart No. 1 in Appendix II describes our lateral system as applied in various waters, illustrating the types of marks used and their appropriate chart symbols.

In brief, when approaching from seaward, buoys to be left to starboard are red ("red, right, returning"), with even numbers increasing as you proceed. Port-hand marks are green or black, and odd-numbered, with their numbers increasing similarly. Horizontally banded marks at danger points or at channel junctions indicate the preferred passing side by the color of their topmost band. Midchannel buoys are vertically striped, and, like junction buoys, if identified, it will be by letter instead of number. Where bell and gong buoys mark main channels, it is customary to locate bells to starboard and gongs to port, although the rule is not inviolate.

In accordance with an agreement between maritime nations reached in 1982 by the International Association of Lighthouse Authorities (IALA), certain modifications to the traditional U.S. buoyage system are being undertaken by our Coast Guard. The objective will be to make systems around the world more alike and less confusing to international mariners, and the planned date for completion is 1989.

The principal changes in our waters are that the color green will eventually replace black on all port-hand aids, and their lights will show green only—starboard-hand aids will remain red with red lights. Red-and-white will gradually replace black-and-white as the color of midchannel marks, and unlighted fairway buoys will be replaced by a spherical shape. The characteristic of lighted midchannel aids will remain the Morse "A" signal, with white lights being used exclusively for that purpose, while a spherical, red topmark will be added to assist in daytime identification. All special purpose navaids are to become yellow in color, using buoy shapes appropriate to their placement within the system. When lighted, they will display yellow only. During the transition period, don't be misled if the color or light characteristic of a buoy is not exactly as indicated on your chart; it has probably been changed before the chart was corrected, but its placement is most likely the same.

Markers used on the Intracoastal Waterway and on rivers in the Western United States represent exceptions to the regular lateral system, although the differences are minor. In the river system, midchannel buoys are not used, while in the Intracoastal Waterway, where "from seaward" means proceeding from north and east toward south and west, red triangular shapes and green square shapes are used on daymarks to indicate the proper passing side. Where the Intracoastal and other waterways coincide, the same distinctive shapes are repeated in yellow patches to minimize confusion over which is the ICW and which is another channel using the same watercourse.

On both rivers and the Intracoastal Waterway, and to a lesser extent in other coastal waters, range markers may be used to provide the mariner with directional guidance for indicating the centerline of an improved channel or the safe route across an obstructed area. Range markers may be lighted or not and often are of distinctive colors. If lighted, they may exhibit highly directional beams and special colors or characteristics, to avoid confusing them with other navaids in the vicinity. Understanding the use of a fixed range, such as the one illustrated in Figure 4–5, is easy. Since the rear range marker is always higher than the front one, the objective is to maneuver in such a way as to bring the rear one directly over its lower, forward counterpart. In the illustration, the navigator at position A alters course to the right to align the range markers, while the navigator at position B must come left to bring them in line. Having arrived at position C, the vessel is steered to keep the range "closed" until a point is reached where the channel turns onto the next leg.

Audible and visual navaids are not, as we have mentioned, the only government-maintained aids to navigation. The use of radiobeacons—the most widely used electronic aids—and Loran (from Long Range Navigation) is growing rapidly in the coastal zones. The radiobeacon system is designed to meet three objectives: to provide a nearly continuous, two-position-line capability to a distance of at least 50 miles offshore; to provide working ranges of up to 150 miles at certain key locations for approaching from far offshore; and to provide continuous, low-powered guidance for inshore navigation. The national system consists of more than 200 marine radiobeacons, each transmitting a characteristic identifying signal. The sites of these beacons and their transmitting frequencies are generally indicated on the charts. Further details about individual stations, as well as an excellent treatment of the scope, method of operation, and limita-

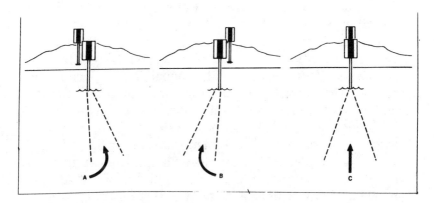

*Figure 4–5.* Using a range. The navigator at A must adjust his course to the right, and at B to the left in order to center on the range as in C.

tions of the system, are given in the *Light List*. The excerpt from the *Light List* shown in Figure 4–6 illustrates the radiobeacon system and the coverage it provides for coastwise navigation. More about its use will be discussed in Chapter 6.

Loran is another electronic system that works in all kinds of weather, 24 hours a day. It was developed during World War II at the Massachusetts Institute of Technology and, at the conclusion of hostilities, was made available to civilian users under the name "Loran-A." During the late 1950s and early 1960s, rapid advances in electronic technology made possible substantial improvements in the system, resulting in a greater effective range and increased accuracy. The improved system was called "Loran-C," and the benefits it offered, coupled with the development of low-cost shipboard receivers, have brought Loran-C to the recreational boating community. The older system has now been replaced and Loran-C coverage is available throughout the coastal waters of the contiguous 48 states, the Great Lakes, and most of Alaska and Hawaii.

The Loran system is based on chains of from three to five land-based transmitting stations, each separated from the other by several hundred miles. Within a chain, one station is designated as the master station (M) and the others as secondary stations, Whiskey (W), Xray (X), Yankee (Y), or Zulu (Z). The radio signal from a secondary station is synchronized precisely with that of the master, and the navigator's on-board receiver measures the minute difference in time that it takes for a simultaneous signal to arrive from each pair of transmitters. This time difference, called the "TD," is measured in microseconds (millionths of a second) and displayed as a readout on the receiver. Conventional charts of scales of 1:80,000 and smaller—comprising all of the sailing and general charts and most of the larger-area coast charts—are overlaid with a lattice of Loran-C time-difference lines identified

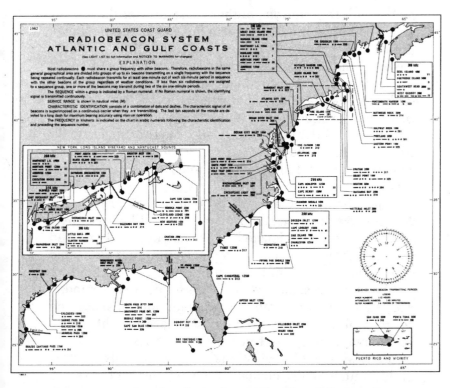

*Figure 4–6.* Chartlet from the *Light List* showing the radiobeacon system on the Atlantic and Gulf Coasts.

by their TD readings. Each of these lines represents all of the points at which the TDs from any pair of master and secondary stations will be the same; it is, in effect, a line of position. The use of these lines in position finding will be discussed in Chapter 8. Given an understanding of its limitations, Loran-C is an extremely useful all-weather navigational aid.

There are still other electronic devices serving as navaids, such as Omega, Decca, and satellite systems, but their cost, complexity, and energy requirements are generally beyond the practical limits of the coastwise yachtsman. Descriptions of these systems, for those who have a technical interest in them, may be found in "Bowditch" and "Dutton." An emerging satellite network, known as the Global Positioning System (GPS-NAVSTAR), with extraordinary accuracy in all weather anywhere on earth, is under development by the military. It is expected to become available for civilian use by the end of the decade, and if the price and energy requirements can be brought within the practical limits of yachtsmen, GPS may well become the future choice among electronic navaids.

Radar, the acronym for Radio Detection And Ranging, does not exactly fit the definition of a navaid with respect to being externally located. It is, however, interrelated with the system, since many navigation aids are fitted with radar reflectors or Racon transponders, which return a characteristic signal when triggered by a ship's radar. Although the cost of radar equipment and its space and energy requirements restrict its use to larger yachts, it can be a tremendous aid in times of reduced visibility.

In any system of navigational aids as extensive as that of the United States, changes are inevitable, not only as a result of international agreement such as the 1982 IALA convention, but also because of improvements in equipment, new or different navigation patterns, changing hydrography, or reductions or consolidations to meet cost constraints. The normal changes in floating navaids include buoys being replaced by others of different characteristics or by fixed aids; buoys being renumbered or relocated to keep up with shifting channels; or buoys being removed because they are no longer judged essential for safe navigation. Changes—even planned ones—present a problem both to the government and the user, the difficulty usually arising in timely notification of the boating public. Theoretically, all changes are reported in advance in the *Notice to Mariners*, and the affected charts are promptly corrected to reflect any change, but the mills of bureaucracy grind slowly, and the charts and publications you acquire today often do not indicate changes made very recently. The lesson is clear: It is risky ever to rely blindly on any single aid to navigation. While our navaid system is remarkably reliable—probably the most reliable in the world—the marine environment is much more hostile than its onshore counterpart, and a good navigator, even with the latest charts aboard, must constantly be on the alert for marks damaged, removed, or displaced by severe weather, aids recently relocated or renumbered as part of an improvement program, or faulty light or sound characteristics resulting from the technical failure that can occasionally happen even in a system as well maintained as ours.

# 5 | The Magnetic Compass

One thing all navigators agree upon is that the single most important instrument on board is the ship's compass. Because it is indispensable, many yachtsmen make a practice of carrying a second one as a backup, often using a convenient hand-held model for this purpose. While the magnetic concept dates back a thousand years, modern yacht compasses owe their lineage to Lord Kelvin's developments in the late nineteenth century. Today, all small-boat compasses are based on Kelvin's principles, and, properly adjusted, are instruments of remarkable accuracy and dependability. Your compass merits your understanding and care; with both, it will be your reliable guide across the trackless waters.

A marine compass has four main components: the binnacle, the bowl, the card, and the lubber's line. The binnacle is the base or stand in which the compass is housed, while the bowl is the body in which the compass card is mounted. The card is the movable, graduated element that indicates geographic direction. The lubber's line is affixed to the bowl and serves as the index against which the card is read. In a portable, hand-bearing compass, the binnacle and bowl are combined for convenient holding, and a prism arrangement permits viewing both the card and the observed body at the same time.

Modern compass cards are usually graduated in degrees, although a few, often for decorative purposes, also show the point system of the old sailing-ship days. We will deal strictly with the degree scale. In seagoing phraseology, degrees are conventionally expressed as three-digit numbers, with zeros added where necessary. Thus, 2° is spoken of as "zero-zero-two," 20° as "zero-two-zero," and 200° as "two-zero-zero," continuing around the 360° card. The identifying terms "compass" (C), "magnetic" (M), or "true" (T) may be appended when necessary to avoid ambiguity. True direction, you may recall, is relative to the geographic poles; magnetic is the direction indicated by the earth's magnetic field; and compass is the reading of the particular instrument. We'll talk about this further in a moment.

A compass used for steering is read at the lubber's line, which has been prealigned with the fore-and-aft axis of the vessel. The reading represents the vessel's compass heading. Bearings, which are the direction of one terrestrial point from another, can be measured with a steering compass either by pointing the ship's head (and the lubber's line) directly at the object, or, less accurately but more conveniently, by sighting the object across the center of the card while the vessel maintains its course. The best way of taking bearings from a small boat is to sight with a compass that is entirely independent of the vessel's steering instrument.

Magnetic compasses operate on the principle of aligning the magnets that govern the card with the earth's magnetic field; North on the card points to the North Magnetic Pole. It is sometimes difficult to explain to neophyte helmsmen that the ship's head, represented by the lubber's line, moves about the card, while the card itself maintains a steady alignment with respect to magnetic North, since this is just the opposite of a landsman's compass with its floating needle instead of a floating card.

Since the magnetic poles are some distance from the earth's true geographic poles and are subject to a slow drift over a period of years, it can be expected that there will be a discrepancy between true North and the direction in which the compass points. This angular difference, and any additional divergence caused by the vessel's own magnetic field, add up to the "compass error." This error can be reckoned by its two components, which are called "variation" and "deviation." Variation is the difference between true and magnetic direction and is normally stated in the upper legend at the center of the compass rose on the chart of the particular locality. An example, excerpted from the chart of the Norwalk Islands area, is shown in Figure 5–1. Here the variation is seen as 12°30' West. The annual change is stated in the lower legend at the center of the rose, and—as in this case, where it is only one minute—is negligible if the chart is of recent date. The variation changes with location throughout the world. In coastal waters of the continental United States, it may range from 20° West to 20° East, but it can reach 60° or more as the geographic poles are approached. There is nothing a navigator can do about compensating for magnetic variation except to determine the correct value for his operating area and to apply it correctly when figuring courses and bearings.

Deviation, the difference between the correct magnetic direction and the actual compass reading, is a function of a vessel's own magnetism and can be minimized by the proper stowage of equipment and competent compass adjustment. Certain ship's gear, such as the engine, is permanently fixed, and its magnetic influence is constant. Items such as portable radios, flashlights, and knives, on the other hand, can create a temporary but unrecognized aberration should they find their way into a compass's

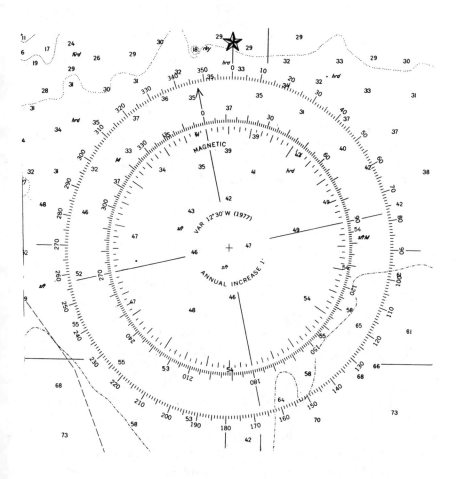

*Figure 5–1.* The Compass Rose from a typical NOS chart. The upper legend at the center of the rose shows the magnetic variation for the area; the lower legend the annual change, here negligible. The outer ring of graduations represents *true* direction, the inner ring *magnetic*. The innermost graduations are in the old-fashioned point system.

magnetic field. The best practice, therefore, is always to stow gear with magnetic properties in the same location, as far as practicable from the compass, and to keep all movable magnetic articles out of its field when underway. Six feet is generally a safe distance from a typical yacht compass.

Where a constant deviation exists, it can be minimized by using correcting magnets; these are commonly mounted within the compass housing and act to neutralize the vessel's magnetic effect. In this manner, deviation can be reduced to negligible, though seldom completely to zero, on most yachts with well-designed compasses. The process is called "adjusting" a compass and is best done by a qualified professional.

In adjusting the compass on a small vessel, a typical procedure is to place her on a northerly heading at a known location and read the compass bearing of a distant charted object whose magnetic direction from the observer's location has been predetermined from the chart. The difference between the observed compass bearing and the predetermined magnetic bearing is the deviation on the northerly heading. Half that deviation is then removed by adjusting the athwartship correcting magnet. The vessel is then headed East and the same process repeated, correcting half the error with the fore-and-aft magnet. Next, the heading is altered to South and, again, half the remaining error is removed with the same corrector as for North. Finally, heading West, half the error found on this course is eliminated with a fore-and-aft adjustment. The entire routine may be repeated several times to reduce the deviation to an absolute minimum.

A professional uses a wide series of headings—a process known as "swinging ship"—to recheck a compass he has compensated and then prepares a table for the navigator's permanent reference, listing the deviation, if any, at regular intervals, usually every 15° around the compass. A typical deviation table might show one column for the magnetic heading, a second column for the corresponding deviation, and a third for the compass reading, so that corrections can be readily determined when needed. In taking bearings, it is important to remember that the degree of deviation is always a function of the ship's heading, and not of the direction of the bearing.

Careful navigators make a practice of checking their compasses at the beginning of each season, after any changes have been made in the vessel or her stowage, or at the outset of an important voyage. Less formal checks can also be made any time you are on the water, either by comparison with another compass of proven accuracy— such as a good hand-bearing compass; by steering on charted ranges or predetermined courses between fixed points; by taking the bearings of distant objects from known positions; or, if you have a celestial navigator aboard, by taking the bearing or "azimuth" of the sun at a known time, a procedure described in Chapters 18 and 23.

Now that we have discussed compass error, how does a navigator apply the necessary corrections? You have seen that the error is separated into two parts: variation, the difference between true and magnetic direction; and deviation, the difference between the magnetic and compass bearing. A classic sailor's wrinkle for remembering this relationship is the phrase: "Can Dead Men Vote Twice?" As you can see in the box, the first letters of each word reveal the key.

| CAN | DEAD | MEN | VOTE | TWICE? |
|-----|------|-----|------|--------|
| O | E | A | A | R |
| M | V | G | R | U |
| P | I | N | I | E |
| A | A | E | A | |
| S | T | T | T | |
| S | I | I | I | |
| | O | C | O | |
| | N | | N | |

Since converting from compass to true represents a decreasing error, the process is called "correcting," and the rule for applying either variation or deviation in this case is: Correcting, add easterly. In the opposite direction, converting from true to magnetic or compass, the process is called "uncorrecting," and the rule is the reverse: Uncorrecting, add westerly. Naturally, you must know whether the variation and deviation are easterly or westerly, and, if this is not indicated on your chart or deviation table, you can determine it by remembering that if magnetic direction in degrees is less than true, or if compass is less than magnetic, the error is easterly. "East reads least" is the popular mnemonic.

As an example, a compass heading of 113°, corrected for a 3° easterly deviation, becomes a magnetic heading of 116°. If the variation is 12° West, the true heading corrects to 104°. You could also have taken the net of the 3° easterly deviation and the 12° westerly variation, resulting in a 9° West total compass error. That figure, applied to the 113° compass heading, yields the true heading, 104°. Going the opposite way, if your charted course is 104° true and the variation is 12° West, this variation is added to the true course to produce the magnetic course of 116°. Then, if the deviation is 3° East, instructions are given to the helmsman to steer a compass course of 113°. Fortunate is the navigator whose vessel has negligible deviation. He has only to apply variation with the proper sign when going back and forth between his steering compass reading—the same as magnetic in this case—and his true direction. Since the chart's compass rose provides magnetic as well as true direction, if you can disregard deviation you can take your readings right off the chart in either mode.

In practice, a navigator plots his course on the chart, converts it to the equivalent compass heading, and gives his instructions to the helmsman. A prudent practitioner, however, checks again after his vessel has steadied on her new heading, in order to make certain that the helmsman is steering the desired course, that its relationship to the geographic situation and nearby navaids is reasonable, and that the compass corrections have been applied in the correct manner. Human errors are often more significant than compass errors.

# 6 | Piloting Tools

Besides the essential charts and publications and a reliable compass, there are several other items that should be on board for effective piloting. If you include equipment designed to aid or enhance the navigator's performance, the list can become extensive, limited only by available space, budgetary considerations, and personal preference. It has been said that today's luxury becomes tomorrow's necessity, and this observation can certainly be applied to navigation equipment; but where, at any moment, the dividing line lies between essential and desirable is highly subjective. For convenience, let's consider the on-board equipment for coastwise navigation in four arbitrary categories: plotting instruments, measuring apparatus, positioning devices, and communication equipment. The techniques for operating each type of equipment will be discussed in the chapters that follow.

Next to his trusty pencil, the navigator's most frequently used plotting device is his protractor. Strictly speaking, a protractor is a scale for measuring angles, while a plotter is a device for measuring and plotting courses and bearings on a chart. In the yachting vernacular, however, the two terms are used interchangeably to describe the standard plotting tools. While navigators agree universally on the importance of a good compass, there are almost as many opinions as there are practitioners when it comes to selecting the ideal plotting instrument.

Plotters fall into two general categories: those that require reference to the compass rose on the chart, and those that require reference only to latitude or longitude lines. In the first group are devices such as parallel rules (Figure 6–1, top), which are used to transfer direction from anywhere on a chart to the compass rose or vice versa. The same result can be achieved with two right triangles, by means of a protractor fitted with parallel rollers, or with a clear plastic sheet with parallel lines ruled on it. A feature of all these types of plotters is that they can refer to either the magnetic or the true compass rose, thereby simplifying the application of variation.

The second group of plotting instruments, which don't require reference to the compass rose, consist of a protractor combined with a fixed or movable straightedge. An example of the fixed straightedge type of instrument is the Power Squadron's USPS Course Plotter, shown in the center of Figure 6–1. This instrument is similar to the familiar aircraft plotter, from which it evolved. In use, the straightedge is aligned with the course or bearing, the bull's-eye is centered over any convenient parallel or meridian, and the true direction is read at the intersection of the parallel or meridian line on the applicable protractor scale. The handy size and absence of moving parts, and the feature of not having to use the compass rose—which may not even appear on the open panel of a folded chart—make it popular with small-boat navigators. If you have to interchange true and magnetic readings, however, you will have to do the arithmetic yourself.

Single-arm protractors, an example of which is illustrated at the bottom of Figure 6–1, consist of a movable straightedge pivoted at the center of a protractor. They are admirably suited to coastwise piloting, and are my

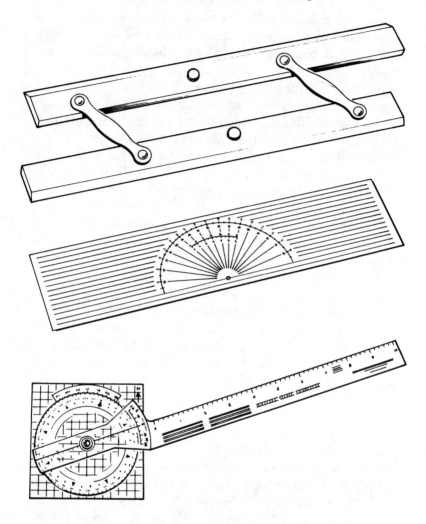

*Figure 6–1.* Plotting Tools commonly used by yachtsmen. Parallel Rules, USPS Course Plotter, Single-Arm Protractor.

personal choice. To use one, the straightedge is lined up with the course or bearing, and the circular protractor is rotated until one of its cross-hatched lines is parallel with any latitude or longitude line. The true direction is read at the main index, and many instruments provide an auxiliary scale for converting to magnetic direction if you prefer not to do it by mental arithmetic. The better single-arm devices are constructed of strong, clear plastic; about one-sixteenth of an inch thick represents a good compromise between strength and flexibility. The protractor part should be at least five to six inches in diameter, and its circumference should be graduated in one-degree increments for easy reading. Some models have an inner rose showing the traditional compass points. This lends a salty appearance, but it is really more decorative than useful if you are accustomed to using the modern 360° system. The crosshairs inscribed on the protractor portion are essential to its operation and should be neither too far apart—a quarter-inch is about the ideal spacing—nor difficult to read through the plastic. Most single-arm protractors come with long arms; seventeen inches is common. If you have to work, as many yacht navigators do, on folded charts in a confined space, you may want to shorten the arm by lopping a few inches off its outer end. It's a lot more convenient that way, and it doesn't affect the operation of the instrument. One important quality to look for is a ruggedly constructed, noncorrosive center pivot, so that the single moving part will always move when you want it to.

There are scores of versions of each type of plotting device, but the ultimate instrument is the universal drafting machine. A standard engineering draftsman's tool ashore, it is used widely in Navy and Merchant Marine big-ship navigation. A drafting machine consists of a straightedge attached to a protractor in such a manner that either part can be rotated independently. The drafting machine is fastened to a surface on which the chart being used has been fixed. After the protractor ring has been lined up with the compass rose, the straightedge may be used to plot, measure, or transfer the direction of a line anywhere on the chart, thus combining the best features of a single-arm protractor and parallel rules. A standard-size drafting machine requires space for its operation and care in its maintenance; not easy on a yacht. Adaptations more suitable to the yachting environment are offered by several manufacturers, but these devices also require careful maintenance.

The best advice in selecting your own plotting device is to choose a type that is easy for you to understand and work with, and one that is suited to your operating environment. Then, you should practice with it under all conditions until its operation becomes second nature to you. The middle of a complicated piloting exercise is not the time to be introduced to new instruments and unfamiliar techniques.

Another key navigation instrument is the divider. Taking its name from its original use by draftsmen in dividing a line into equal parts, and later adopted for measuring lengths on mechanical drawings, the versatile divider has become an essential tool for the marine navigator as well. Known in nautical terminology as a "pair of dividers," or simply, "dividers," the device has a number of practical uses in addition to its most common one as a means of measuring distance on a chart.

Dividers come in several types, two of which, commonly found aboard yachts, are illustrated in Figure 6–2. The draftsman's dividers on the left are preferred by most professional navigators, and with a little practice, they can be manipulated easily with one hand. The model on the right, sometimes called a "yachtsman's" or "one-hand" divider, has a number of adherents among small-boat sailors because it can withstand a little rougher treatment. Personal preferences aside, either variety can be used for a wide range of exercises in marine navigation.

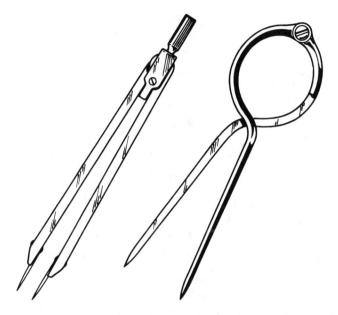

*Figure 6–2.* Two types of dividers commonly used by yachtsmen. Draftsman's Dividers (left) and Yachtsman's Dividers (right).

Besides figuring distance, which is done by placing one point on each end of a line and transferring that measurement to the chart legend or adjacent latitude scale, dividers can also be used to solve time, rate, and distance computations through a logarithmic scale that appears on plotting sheets and on some charts. They can also be used in place of a draftsman's compass—although an inexpensive, student compass is handy to have aboard—for stepping off the arc of visibility of a light, or for solving current problems, all of which we will be discussing in later chapters.

In the special-purpose category of plotting instruments is the station pointer, also known as a three-arm protractor. It is illustrated in Figure 6–3. Although the station

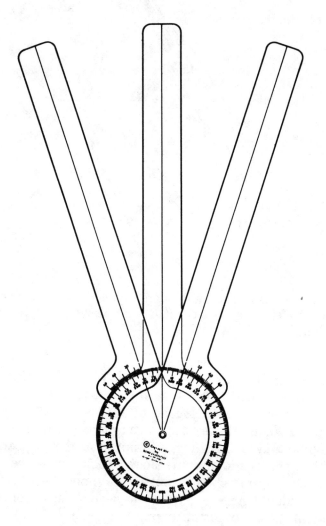

*Figure 6–3.* A Three-Arm Protractor or Station Pointer used for the rapid solution of a three-point fix, a procedure described in Chapter 8.

pointer can be used in an emergency as a single-arm protractor, its primary purpose is for position-fixing from horizontal angles, a specialized procedure discussed in Chapter 8.

"Lead, log, and lookout" were bywords of the ancient mariners, and the information they convey is no less important to small-boat navigating today. The instruments available now may be a far cry from their forerunners, but the collection and use of their data follow time-honored patterns. Traditionally, depth was measured by means of a marked line, the lead weight at the end often being "armed" with tallow to sample the quality of the bottom. This is still the most foolproof way to determine depth, especially in the relatively shallow inshore passages frequented by yachts. But while many navigators keep a lead line aboard as a backup, we live in the electronic age, and today there are many excellent and economical depth-monitoring instruments. The specific configuration of the model you choose, be it digital or flashing light, indicating or recording or both, is a question of personal preference and what best fits your boat. Most important is to select an instrument that will give accurate information and dependable service in your use, because you will probably call on your depth finder not only as a safety device but also as a navigational aid.

The speed of a vessel through the water, and, by the application of time, the distance traveled, is another measurement of interest to a navigator. Speed was originally calculated with a "log"—a floating object thrown overboard from the forward part of a ship and timed as it passed through a measured distance alongside. Four hundred years or so ago, someone had the bright idea of attaching a line to the object; the line could then be paid out and measured, and the device could be used repeatedly. Eventually, the log line was knotted at predetermined intervals, so that the number of knots paid out in a given time indicated the ship's speed. This original "log" is the ancestor of modern instruments that measure speed through the water, and the "knot" has come to mean a speed of one nautical mile per hour. One never says "knots per hour," incidentally, unless talking about an acceleration rate; the expression would be redundant and " 'lubberly."

There is a wide choice of mechanical and electronic devices for measuring boat speed and distance traveled. Some are simple and some extremely sophisticated, but all can measure with much greater accuracy than was ever possible with the old-fashioned log. New models with new features appear at each boat show and are constantly improving. Again, the choice is subjective; even a basic model will provide the minimum information you need. You may recognize that a device that measures only speed can be used with a stopwatch to determine distance, and vice versa. That same stopwatch, if you carry one, may also prove useful for timing the sequences of lighted navaids or fog signals or for "running your time" when navigating in fog, as explained in Chapter 9.

The "lookout" portion of the mariner's credo involves not only visual observation—the most important safety device on the ship—but also measurement for position-finding. For observation, a good pair of binoculars is an invaluable aid to the lookout. Probably best suited to the needs of a small yacht, and representing a good compromise between magnifying power, field size, light-gathering ability, weight, and bulk is the 7 × 50 glass, the standard for deck officers in the Navy. The "7" stands for the magnifying power, and 7-power is about the maximum practical in a hand-held glass. The "50" means that the objective lens is 50 mm in diameter; good because it allows a wide field, provides excellent light-gathering characteristics, and doesn't make the package too unwieldy. In piloting, glasses are particularly useful for spotting and identifying aids to navigation, onshore objects, or the intentions of approaching vessels. Binoculars with good light-gathering qualities are a godsend in sorting things out during twilight. Some navigators prefer to keep a separate, personal pair, adjusted to their own eyesight, so they are available for instant use when the occasion arises.

In determining direction, there is the ship's compass by which to steer, and as we discussed, bearings can be measured across it if it is suitably located. It is often more practical, however, to have a second, hand-bearing compass aboard for the independent and direct measurement of bearings. It can also serve as a backup for the steering compass. Hand-bearing compasses come in a variety of styles, the traditional variety in a configuration resembling Liberty's torch, and newer models shaped like hockey pucks. Some are lighted, some not, but all allow you to view an object across a floating compass card and read the magnetic bearing simultaneously.

While not in a class with compasses and depth finders, there are other optical devices that can serve the coastwise navigator. For example, the distance from an object can be measured with an optical range finder, a stadimeter, or with the celestial navigator's sextant when the object is visible and the sea state suitable, although the practice is infrequent in normal yacht piloting.

As for positioning devices, today's yachtsman is again the beneficiary of the electronic age. The three principal electronic aids to navigation, which were discussed in Chapter 4, are radiobeacons, Loran transmitters, and radar systems. Radio direction-finders, which are tuned to receive signals from the radiobeacon system, lack the precision of Loran or radar, but are the most widely used radio aids because they are modestly priced, relatively uncomplicated to use, compact and self-contained, and usually accurate enough for a yachtsman's piloting needs. A radio direction-finder operates by means of a characteristic signal transmitted by a radiobeacon on the low-frequency band from a charted location. The shipboard receiver identifies the sending station by its signal, and by rotating a directional antenna to the null (minimum signal) point, the bearing of the sending station can be found and plotted on the chart.

Three common types of radio direction-finding apparatus are used on small boats. The first has a manually rotated antenna, integral with the set, with an index, like the compass lubber line, aligned with the vessel's fore-and-aft axis. The navigator tunes the receiver to the appropriate radiobeacon, rotates the antenna to the null point, and reads the relative bearing—the bearing relative to the ship's head—at the index. The vessel's heading at the moment the reading is made is then applied to the relative bearing to arrive at the compass bearing for plotting.

Much easier to use is a second type of radio direction-finder, which has a separate, hand-held antenna. Like a hand-bearing compass, it can be used to read the bearing directly when the null point is determined. A bearing accuracy of ± 3° can be obtained with a good set of this type and a proficient operator. The third variety is called an automatic direction-finder, or ADF, and works like an aircraft set, performing the antenna rotation electronically and displaying the bearing of the radiobeacon on a dial. Automatic sets, as might be expected, are more expensive than manual radio direction-finders, and yachtsmen moving into this price bracket may turn to Loran instead.

Loran-C, with the many technical improvements that have been made in both the system and the user equipment, and the competitive pricing evidenced in its rapidly expanding market, is now practical for all but the smallest boats. It is already approaching radio direction-finding in the number of shipboard installations and has been designated as the principal government-provided radionavigation system for the coastal zones of the United States and the Great Lakes. Loran sets can be had that display time-difference readings alone; others convert two or more TD readings into latitude and longitude, and the more expensive ones add some of the sophisticated features that modern electronic microprocessors can provide. Although not without minor limitations, Loran-C receivers that offer latitude and longitude readouts are the most popular with yacht navigators.

Radar is beyond the scope of smaller yachts, but where it is installed, it is a piloting tool of great value. Developed during World War II, radar works by means of short bursts of electrical energy focused by a highly directional antenna. When the bursts intercept an object, a small amount of the radio energy "bounces" back to the receiver, and since the receiver measures the time-delay between the emitted and the returned signal, and senses the position of the rotating antenna, it can translate the result into the range and bearing of the target and display it on a circular screen as a blip. By scanning continuously, radar can literally "see" everything above water level of consequence to the navigator, regardless of the visibility. The reason more radars aren't installed aboard yachts has only to do with space requirements—the antenna must be at least three feet in diameter and must be located as high above the deck as possible—with the energy requirements of the system, which are high, and with the cost. There is no argument about its usefulness.

The last category of on-board equipment includes communication devices which, while not immediately involved in the navigation procedure, can and do supply information that contributes to the safe conduct of a voyage. A navigator today relies on his radio for such things as weather reports, notices of dangers to navigation, time signals, inlet conditions, bridge-opening communications, and, if in distress, for timely assistance. Most modern boats are equipped with very-high-frequency (VHF) transceivers, a few smaller ones with citizen's band (CB) sets, and those that are expected to range offshore with single-sideband or, in increasing numbers, with ham radios.

Like all on-board equipment, any device, and especially an electronic device, is useful only if it is available when needed, works properly, and is understood by the operator. While this may sound obvious, it is surprising how often the opposite is the case, particularly in an infrequently used yacht. The moral is to be deliberate in the selection of your piloting tools, to acquire only those you can really use, see to their proper stowage and maintenance on board, and above all, to learn to use them well before the safety of your ship depends on it. These are your responsibilities as a navigator.

# 7 | Dead Reckoning

There has long been speculation about the origin of the term "dead reckoning." Bowditch concluded that it stemmed from the early use of the log which, relative to the vessel's movement, was "dead" in the water. Other historians, however, maintain that it is merely a shortened form of "deduced reckoning," the estimating of a vessel's track after taking into account the effects of wind and current. Regardless of the version you prefer, dead reckoning in modern navigation has come to mean the process of locating a position from the courses and distances traveled since the last known point. The location so determined is called the "dead-reckoning position," or "DR." If you are proceeding through a current of known direction and velocity, you may also take its effect into account in reckoning your position; however, modern terminology prefers to identify such a position as an "estimated position," or "EP."

The vast majority of navigators derive their dead-reckoning positions graphically; that is, by plotting each successive course and distance on the chart. The special advantage of this method in coastal waters is that it enables a navigator to visualize the relationship between his projected track and any marks or hazards along the route.

It is also possible to locate a DR position mathematically, by a procedure called "traverse sailing." The technique for doing this is described later in this chapter, and the method for doing it on an electronic calculator is explained in Chapter 11.

You will recall that the Mercator projection used in nautical charts is designed for easy plotting; a course line is drawn as a straight line crossing all the meridians at the same angle, and distances are readily determined from the adjacent latitude scale. For his plot, a navigator simply lays down the course from the point of departure, using any convenient plotting instrument, and steps off the appropriate distance along it with the dividers.

Precise navigation requires careful plotting, which includes neat and accurate labeling. It is customary to indicate courses above the track line, expressing them in the form of three-digit numbers following the prefix "C." As with the spoken description, zeros are added where necessary. For example, a course of 45° will be labeled "C045." Speeds are shown below the line, following the prefix "S." Unless otherwise indicated by a suffix—such as an "M" after the course digits, to designate magnetic—courses and bearings are assumed to be true, and speeds to be in knots. Times are normally expressed in four-digit numbers, using the 24-hour clock; thus, 4:00 A.M. appears as 0400, and 2:48 P.M. becomes 1448.

Figure 7–1 shows a correctly labeled DR plot in which the course is 116° magnetic, the speed 6 knots, and the DR position advanced to 10 minutes after noon. Some navigators prefer to use a half-circle at the DR or to run the DR label diagonally, to avoid possible confusion with a fix, which is a position determined without reference to a previous position, usually derived from the intersection of two or more lines of position. An EP is sometimes marked with a small square for the same purpose. Most important, however, is labeling the plot clearly, consis-

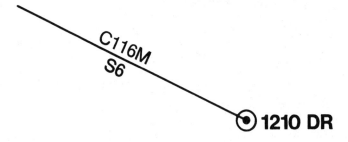

*Figure 7–1.* Labeling the plot. The course is shown above the line with an appropriate prefix and suffix, and the speed below the line. The dead-reckoning position is labeled with the time.

tently, and promptly. It will go a long way in eliminating error.

To review this essential technique, let's examine a practical example that you can follow on the chart reproduction in Figure 7–2. A navigator has departed from his favorite fishing ground at the western end of a four-fathom bank just south of the Norwalk Islands. His depth finder confirmed that he was located over a 27-foot-deep spot. Getting underway at noon, he set his course at 116° magnetic and plotted it on the chart from the point of departure. His boat's speed, measured by log, was 6 knots, and after 10 minutes of steaming, he calculated the distance run as exactly 1 nautical mile. Many such calculations can be performed mentally; however, a slide-rule device or calculator can be used if preferred. The distance run was stepped off along the course line with dividers that had been set at 1 mile (1 minute on the latitude scale), and the resulting DR position at 1210 was labeled on the plot.

Next, the navigator changed course to 084° M and reduced his speed to 5 knots. Running on this course for 6

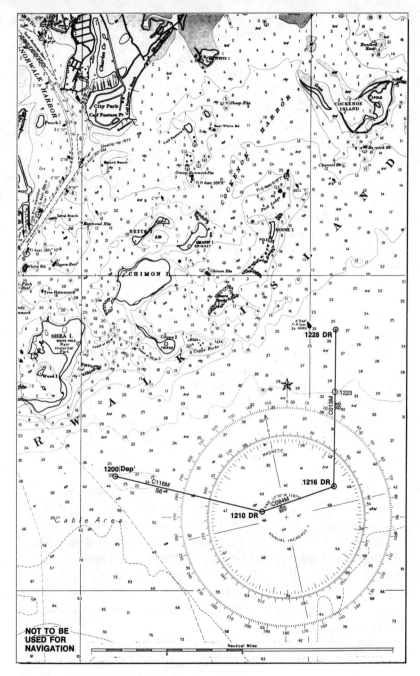

**Figure 7–2. The Dead-Reckoning Plot.**

minutes, he plotted his new track on the chart and stepped off the half-mile he calculated he had traveled during the period. This point became the 1216 DR position shown in Figure 7–2. Altering course once more, this time to 013° M, and maintaining his 5-knot speed, the navigator headed for a planned rendezvous in the vicinity of Gong Buoy "24A." At 1223, the depth finder indicated that the vessel had crossed the five-fathom (30-foot) curve, confirming its approximate position at that time. At 1228, the navigator reckoned he had traveled 1 mile on his final leg and marked his 1228 DR on the chart. Spotting the gong buoy off his port beam, he knew that his DR position was substantially correct.

In this example, you will see that the navigator chose to use magnetic courses on his plot, the common practice aboard yachts. He could have converted the magnetic directions into true directions, either by reference to the compass rose, had he been plotting by that method, or by mentally applying the local variation, as discussed in Chapter 5. In either case, the plot would have been identical; only the course labeling would have been different.

The water you sail through, particularly where tidal conditions exist, is constantly in motion. This has the effect of altering the speed or direction you actually make good over the bottom and introduces a corresponding error in the dead-reckoning position calculated by applying the courses steered and distances run through the water from the last known position. A DR position, therefore, must always be considered to be inexact: an approximate point, surrounded by an "area of uncertainty." Since the effect of current is proportional to time, it follows that the longer the time elapsed since your last fix, the greater will be the area of uncertainty about your DR position.

In nautical terminology, "current" consists of all the influences that act to divert a vessel, lumped together; this includes the horizontal motion resulting from the rise and fall of the tide (tidal current) and the motion caused by other natural phenomena or by an element of the earth's general circulatory system, such as the Gulf Stream. While any current you experience may stem from causes known or unknown, the important thing for the practical navigator is to be able to make a reasonable estimate of the direction in which it is flowing—its "set"—and its velocity, or "drift." He will then be able to calculate the effect of the current on his dead-reckoning position, or determine the combination of course and speed needed to make good his intended track.

Estimating the current is not an exact science and requires experience, but several sources are available to help you in the task. One is the *Tidal Current Tables* discussed in Chapter 3. Additionally, some nautical charts give an indication of the area currents by means of arrows and symbols. If you are an experienced mariner, you may also find the *Tide Tables* helpful, since you can often make an educated guess about the velocity and direction of a current by knowing the predicted times and heights of high and low water and the configuration of the adjacent coastline. An alert navigator can improve his estimate by careful observation of the water flowing past anchored boats, navigational buoys, or even lobster pots. When running between marks on a course, a vessel's deviation from the planned track is another useful indication of the current's strength and effect. With a little practice, the set and drift can be estimated with some accuracy, and it is this accuracy that determines the validity of your subsequent current-sailing solutions.

There are three common situations, or cases, in current sailing:

- When the course steered, the speed through the water, and the set and drift of the current are known, and you wish to find the course made good and the speed made good.

- When the course to be made good, the vessel's speed through the water, and the current's set and drift are known, and you wish to find the course to steer and the speed made good over the intended track.
- When the course to be made good, the speed to be made good, and the set and drift are known, and you wish to find the course to steer and the required speed to be made through the water.

The solution to a given current problem can be obtained in several ways: by calculator (as explained in Chapter 11); by tables, such as *Bowditch*, Table 3; by mechanical devices, similar in concept to the aircraft pilot's wind-correction computer; or by graphic solution, the method often used by yachtsmen. Let's examine a typical current-sailing problem that exemplifies the first case, and review the steps in its graphic solution.

A small powerboat is steering a course of 073° at a speed of 6.3 knots by its log. The current is setting toward 155° with a drift rate of 2 knots. What will be the course and speed made good? The answer can be obtained by constructing a current triangle, illustrated in Figure 7–3, the three sides of which depict, respectively, the course and speed registered by the vessel, the set and drift of the current, and the course and speed actually made good. When used in this way, the sides of the triangle are called

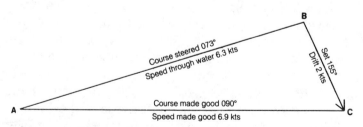

*Figure 7–3.* **The current triangle, illustrating the relationship between its component parts.**

"vectors"—which are simply straight lines whose orientation represents direction and whose length represents magnitude. You can construct such a vector diagram right on the chart.

Referring to the illustration, **A** represents the point of departure, the line from **A** to **B** is the course steered, and the length of **AB** is the speed through the water. Without any current, point **B** would be the dead-reckoning position one hour after departure. However, there is a current, represented by the line **BC,** the direction of which depicts the set, and the length of which is the drift. By constructing the current vector from **B**—the DR position—we arrive at **C,** which becomes the estimated position, or EP. You can now see that the remaining side of the triangle, **AC,** depicts the actual movement of the vessel from its point of departure to the estimated position. The direction of line **AC** is the course made good, 090°, while its length indicates the actual speed made good, 6.9 knots. It doesn't make any difference in this case whether the directions are true or magnetic, just as long as you are consistent throughout.

The second current-sailing case arises when a navigator has selected a course to be made good through a known current and the speed at which he expects to travel through the water. This provides one element of each of two sides of the current triangle; the navigator must then find the missing elements of the two sides: the course to be steered and the speed that will actually be made good over the planned track. Figure 7–4 illustrates the geometry of the situation and shows the graphic solution—which, you will notice, is a little trickier than the solution in the first case. It is easiest to construct this vector diagram right on the compass rose of the chart, as has been done in the illustration, following a four-step sequence:

1. Draw the course to be made good, here 090° true, from the center of the rose, **C,** making it of indefinite

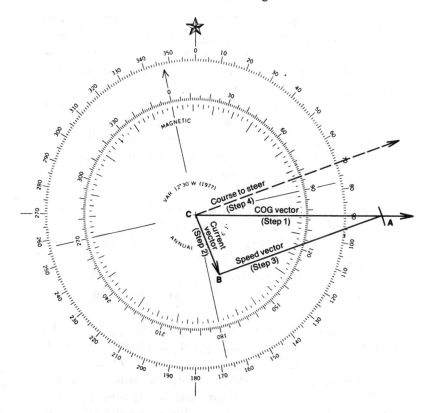

*Figure 7–4.* **Constructing a Current Diagram on a compass rose. Plotting the COG, current, and speed vectors produces the course to steer and the speed made good.**

length. We'll call this the COG vector (for "course over the ground").

2. Draw a line from the center of the rose in the direction of the current's set, say 158°, and of a length, **CB**, representing the drift, here 3 knots. Any convenient scale may be used for this, the current vector.

3. Using the same scale used for the current vector in step 2, set the dividers at the expected speed

through the water—8 knots in this example—and, with one point at **B,** swing the other point around to determine the point of intersection, **A,** of this speed vector with the COG vector constructed in step 1.

4. Measure the direction of the speed vector, **BA,** on the compass rose to determine the course to steer, 070° true, and measure the length of the COG vector, **CA,** using the same scale as in steps 2 and 3. This will give the speed that will be made good, 8.6 knots, over the intended track.

If you wish to check this for yourself, you can simply substitute the course to steer, 070° at 8 knots, and the new current set and drift, 158° at 3 knots, in a current triangle of the type described in the first case given above, and arrive at the course that will be made good, 090°, and the speed that will be made good, 8.6 knots, thereby proving your answer.

Occasionally, a navigator may wish to specify both the course and speed to be made good, and needs to find the course to steer and the speed required through a known current to accomplish his objective. This solution is quite similar to that in case 1, except that the current triangle is constructed in the reverse order. From the starting point, **A,** the side **AC** is drawn first, in the direction of the intended track, with its length representing the speed to be made good over that track. From **C,** a second vector is drawn in the direction opposite to the current's set, with its length, **CB,** being equal to the drift. When this is done, the direction of side **AB,** which connects the ends of the two previously constructed vectors, will be the course to steer, and its length will indicate the speed that the vessel must travel through the water.

The mathematical name for the procedure we have been using is "vector arithmetic," and although we have chosen to solve the sample problems graphically, it is perfectly possible to solve them by math alone. Even if you are not a mathematics buff, you may find it interesting to understand the principles involved.

Any point can be located relative to another point by either of two coordinate systems illustrated in Figure 7–5. The course and distance from the starting point are identified as the "polar" coordinates, and point **A** may be said to be located at distance **D** from starting point **P**, along course line **PA**, which is so many degrees **(Cn)** from North. At the same time, point **A** can be located by its "rectangular" coordinates: the distance **e**, east or west of point **P**, and the distance **n**, north or south of **P**. In essence, the line **PA** can be described as a vector, with **e** and **n** as its rectangular components or equivalents.

As an example, a course of due North, 000°, at 10 knots is the equivalent of zero knots in an east/west direction, and 10 knots along a north/south line. A vector 10 units long in the direction 032° (the vector **PA** in Figure 7–5) is

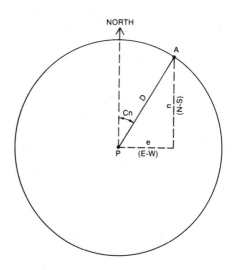

*Figure 7–5.* Polar and Rectangular Coordinates. Point **A** can be located either by the course angle Cn and distance D, or by the EW component e and the NS component n.

the polar equivalent of 5.3 units east and 8.5 units north in the rectangular system. In combining vectors arithmetically, the polar coordinates of each vector are converted to their rectangular equivalents, the algebraic (net) sum of the north/south and east/west components is obtained, and the result is reconverted into the polar coordinate system. The vectors you deal with can be parts of a current triangle, or even a series of courses and distances sailed by dead reckoning.

In dead reckoning, however, the advantage of the graphic determination of a DR position usually outweighs any convenience that vector arithmetic may offer, although there are a few special circumstances in which the latter might be considered. In a sailboat tacking to windward on a large number of short courses, where voluminous chart work is required, or in lifeboat navigation, where a chart may be unavailable, the vector arithmetic solution, called "traverse sailing," can be useful for determining a DR position. As a practical example, look at Figure 7–6. The three legs, **AB, BC,** and **CD** of the course

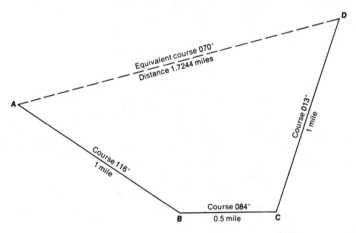

*Figure 7–6.* Traverse Sailing. The algebraic sum of the vectors AB, BC, and CD is equivalent to the direct course and distance, vector AD.

are those sailed in our earlier dead-reckoning exercise illustrated in Figure 7–2. Suppose, however, that you wanted to find the direct course and distance from **A** to **D** without measuring it on your chart. The mathematical alternative is to transform each of the courses and distances into their rectangular equivalents, find the net sum, and convert that back into the polar-coordinate equivalent course and speed. The table below shows the arithmetic involved.

| Course, Distance | NS Component | EW Component |
|---|---|---|
| 116°, 1.0 nautical miles | −0.44 nm (S) | +0.90 nm (E) |
| 084°, 0.5 nautical miles | +0.05 nm (N) | +0.50 nm (E) |
| 013°, 1.0 nautical miles | +0.97 nm (N) | +0.22 nm (E) |
| Net total: | +0.58 nm (N) | +1.62 nm (E) |

Polar-coordinate equivalent:
070°, 1.72 nautical miles

Where does one find the polar-coordinate equivalents of a set of rectangular coordinates, and vice versa? Easy; any calculator that has a polar-rectangular conversion capability can produce them in seconds, or you can use a traverse table such as "Bowditch," Table 3.

If, in the same problem, the latitude and longitude of the point of departure are known, and you wish to find the geographical coordinates of the destination, you follow a similar procedure. The net north/south component of the course vector can be applied directly to the latitude (since 1 minute of latitude is everywhere the equivalent of 1 nautical mile); however, determination of the longitude requires another step. Since the length of a minute of longitude decreases as the meridians converge toward the poles, it is necessary to apply a factor that depends on the latitude in order to transfer the net east/west component into minutes of longitude. This, too, can be done by computation or by using "Bowditch," Table 3, but after experimenting with these math procedures, you will probably agree that for typical piloting the graphic solution is preferable.

There is another facet of sailing geometry that is of special interest to the racing yachtsman: How far can he afford to deviate from the course he is sailing in order to gain extra boat-speed? Again, the problem can be solved graphically or mathematically, although in this case the latter may be the more advantageous approach. Figure 7–7 illustrates the geometry involved. Assuming that the intended track is from **A** to **C,** any deviation from the direct course (shown here in 5° increments) will pass through the appropriate point on line **BB,** increasing the total distance traveled in proportion to the angle of devia-

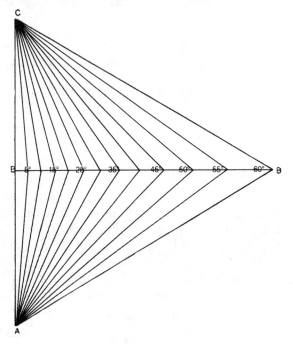

*Figure 7–7.* The geometry of course deviation, illustrating the extra distance traveled.

tion. As an example, if the deviation is 60°, the diagram shows that you would actually be sailing two sides of an equilateral triangle, or exactly twice the direct distance between **A** and **C**. To make such a maneuver worthwhile, your boat-speed would have to be more than doubled.

The extra-distance problem can be solved by the use of dividers on a diagram like the one in Figure 7–7, or by applying the trigonometric formula:

Total Distance = Direct Distance × Secant of Angle of Deviation

The most practical way for dealing with the situation aboard a racing yacht, however, is to precompute a handy

| TACKING DOWNWIND | |
|---|---|
| Deviation | Boat-speed must increase by more than |
| 5° | 1% |
| 10° | 2% |
| 15° | 4% |
| 20° | 7% |
| 25° | 10% |
| 30° | 15% |

| TACKING UPWIND (vs. normal 45° deviation) | |
|---|---|
| Additional deviation | Boat-speed must increase by more than |
| 1° | 2% |
| 3° | · 6% |
| 5° | 10% |
| 7° | 15% |
| 9° | 20% |
| 11° | 27% |
| 13° | 33% |
| 15° | 42% |

table, such as the one on page 79 that shows how much your boat-speed must increase at various angles of deviation in order to make a diversion profitable.

In the final analysis, dead reckoning is only a process of positioning yourself by keeping track of where and how far you have come from a known starting point. While a DR position can't always be expected to be exact, it will be as good as the information you use and the care with which you apply it. While the methods you choose are subject to personal preference, it is essential to gain all the experience you can in the technique of reckoning and plotting, so that you can learn to judge the accuracy of your own work with confidence. That is still the art in the science of navigation.

# 8 | Position Finding in Piloting

Although a vessel's probable position has been established by dead reckoning, the navigator should seek every opportunity to confirm or correct that position by an independent "fix," determined without reference to a previous position. Most frequently, a fix is obtained from two or more "lines of position," an important concept that you should understand thoroughly. A line of position, or "LOP," is defined as "a line on some point of which a vessel may be presumed to be located as a result of observation or measurement." In other words, at the time of observation, you are somewhere on that LOP, although you may not know exactly where at the moment.

Landsmen are in the habit of relating location to specific points, such as "next to the red schoolhouse" or "under the clock." Sometimes, however, they may use lines of position unconsciously. A person on a street corner, for example, might say, "I'm under the sign at the corner of Fifth Avenue and Forty-second Street," thinking of it as a specific spot. But if this person were to consider Fifth Avenue as one line of position (he is, actually, somewhere on Fifth Avenue), and Forty-second

Street as another (because he is also somewhere on Forty-second Street), his location has been pinpointed at the one place where it is possible to be on both lines at the same time, the point where they intersect—his fix.

Lines of position in coastwise navigation may be obtained from a variety of sources and in a variety of ways, although bearings on fixed objects are the most common way of obtaining them. As in dead reckoning, the geometry of a fix can be resolved mathematically, as will be discussed in Chapter 11, but here again, the graphic solution, obtained by plotting on the chart, is usually the most practical. In inshore waters, plotting is also the safest method, since it shows the vessel's proximity to navigational hazards and can be less confusing and error-prone in a fast-moving piloting exercise.

Bearings, as we have seen, can be taken either by observation across the steering compass—if it is suitably located—or, more conveniently, with a compass dedicated to the purpose. Bearings are measured clockwise from the reference direction through 360° and are spoken of, or written in, three digits, just like compass readings. For bearings taken by compass, the usual reference direction is North—and often magnetic North, since magnetic compasses are universal aboard yachts. It is also possible, although more cumbersome, to take relative bearings, using the ship's head as the reference direction. The line of position for plotting is then figured by applying the relative bearing to the vessel's heading at the moment of measurement.

Figure 8–1 depicts an observer in a small boat, using a hand-bearing compass to take the bearings of two charted objects, a lighthouse and a conspicuous building ashore. The line of position to the lighthouse runs 312° true, while the building bears 036°. Since the vessel is on both position lines simultaneously, its fix must be where the lines intersect. Because the two harbor buoys shown in the figure just happen to form natural ranges on each

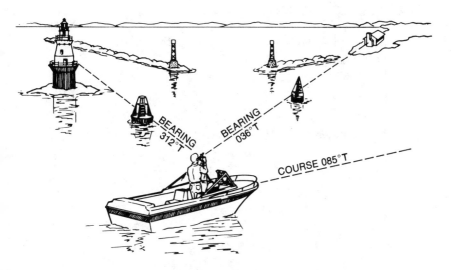

*Figure 8–1.* Observer taking bearings of terrestrial objects with a hand-bearing compass.

bearing, they provide a convenient double-check on the position lines, and since all of the elements of the two ranges appear on the chart (Figure 8–2), it would have been possible to plot the lines without reference to the compass direction. Notice that the spread between the two bearings selected is close to the ideal right angle (90°), minimizing the position error that could result from small inaccuracies in observing or plotting the bearings. It is good practice to avoid fixes that depend on position lines which intersect at less than 30°, unless no better lines are available.

Having taken a round of bearings, the navigator plots them immediately on the chart (Figure 8–2), using the same tools and techniques as in the dead-reckoning plot. Each line of position, or the useful portion of it near the vessel's location, has been drawn from the charted object

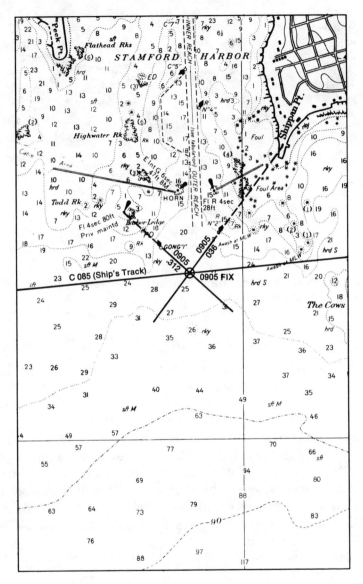

*Figure 8–2.* A plot of the fix obtained in Figure 8–1 from two intersecting lines of position.

in the direction *opposite* to the bearing—the "reciprocal" direction. The reason for this is that the bearing is taken from seaward, but plotted from the object. The navigator has chosen to use true direction on this particular plot, but he could equally well have used magnetic direction; only the labels would have changed. Notice the labeling scheme, with time above and direction from seaward below each of the bearing lines. This is standard practice, and used throughout this book; however, some navigators, with a view to maintaining an uncluttered plot, will omit part of the label when there is no possibility of confusion about the time of the observation or the source and direction of the position line. Since the fix in Figure 8–2 is clearly the result of the simultaneous bearings of two objects observed at 9:05 A.M., the position-line labels might have been left out without detracting from the plot. The best rule, however, is always to label completely if there is any chance of future question.

Besides using the compass bearings of terrestrial objects, there are other ways of obtaining lines of position. We have mentioned the use of ranges, in which a line can be constructed through two objects on a chart without requiring a compass reading. Position lines can also be obtained electronically, from bearings determined by radio direction-finder, by Loran, or by radar. Although the technique for deriving a position line with any given type of apparatus is a function of the apparatus and its operation, the utilization of the line is the same as with any other LOP.

Loran position lines are unique in that they are not straight lines. Representing the locus of all points receiving a signal from two transmitting stations at a constant time difference, these "lines" take the shape of hyperbolic curves. The portion of the curve that lies in the vicinity of a vessel's position can be identified on the chart and used in conjunction with another Loran line or a line obtained by any other means to produce a fix. Most Loran receivers are designed to track two or more pairs of stations, and display two or more time-difference LOPs. The more sophisticated sets, and the ones gaining rapid popularity with yachtsmen, not only track multiple TD lines, but also convert their fixes electronically into latitude and longitude readings. One word of caution, however; if the LOPs intersect at a relatively small angle, small errors in their measurement may displace the fix from its true position without your being aware of it. One reason for the measurement error is that radio signals travel at slightly different speeds across land and across water. Unless the receiver is specially compensated, this can introduce a small misreading in the TD and a resulting error in the LOP. In the highest quality Loran receivers, this so-called "secondary phase factor" is compensated for, and the National Ocean Service is embarked on a program to apply this correction to the lattices on charts. Nonetheless, it is always sound practice to confirm Loran positions with other means at your disposal, since electronic equipment in the marine environment is never totally immune to aberration.

Another type of position line is one derived from a "distance-off" measurement. Such a line is actually the circumference of a circle whose radius is the distance from a charted object. It is plotted with a draftsman's compass, placing the point on the charted object and scribing the appropriate portion of the arc in the area in which the vessel is presumed to be located. If a bearing and a distance-off reading can be obtained simultaneously on the same object (radar does just this, but you can do it visually, too), you have in effect two intersecting lines of position and, by definition, a fix. Figure 8–3 illustrates a case in which the range, **D,** from a conspicuous flagpole was measured at 10:30 A.M. to be 2.1 miles. At the same time, the bearing was found to be 075° true. Where the two lines of position cross is the 1030 fix.

In addition to radar ranging, there are several ways

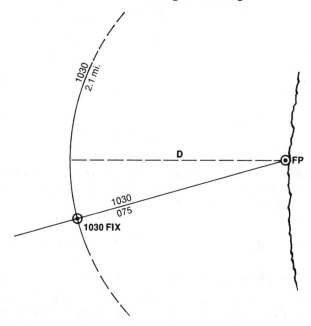

*Figure 8–3.* A line of position from a distance-off measurement is the circumference of a circle whose radius, D, is the distance-off. The intersection of this circumference line with a line of position from a simultaneous bearing produces a fix.

to measure distance-off visually, requiring one form or another of optical instrument. Most frequently found aboard small boats are optical range-finders, which measure distance, the way your eyes do, by the angle of convergence between the lines of sight to an object from two separated lenses; and sextants, which measure the angular height of an object (Figure 8–4), or angular length of a baseline, of known dimension. Stadimeters, which operate similarly to sextants, are common on naval vessels but are not often seen on yachts. The hand-held range-finders are most accurate for short distances (50 to 1000 yards), while sextants are practical from a half to several miles,

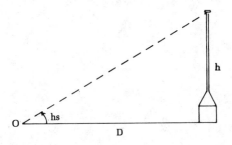

*Figure 8–4.* The sextant angle, hs, between the top and base of a flagpole of known height, h. The angle measured is used to determine the distance-off, D.

depending on the dimension of the object or baseline measured.

Used in the conventional, vertical position, a sextant measures an angle by bringing the top of an observed object to the visible horizon, or to the object's waterline if it is within the horizon. The navigator must correct the reading for the index error of the sextant, if any, and for the height of eye above the water at the time of observation. The correction for eye height, called the "dip" (D), may be found in the Dip table in the *Nautical Almanac*, which is reproduced in Figure 8–5, or in the similar table in "Bowditch," Appendix F. Alternatively, the D-correction can be found by the formula:

$$\text{Dip (in minutes)} = 0.97 \sqrt{\text{Height of eye (in feet)}}$$

The dip correction is always negative; thus, for a height of eye of 9 feet, D is $-2.9'$.

The corrected sextant angle, in degrees and minutes, and the difference in feet between the height of the object and the observer's height of eye, are entered into "Bowditch," Table 9, "Distance by Vertical Angle," and the distance-off is read out directly. If the base of the observed object is within the distance to the visible horizon, Table

## DIP

| Ht. of Eye | Corrⁿ | Ht. of Eye | Ht. of Eye | Corrⁿ | | Ht. of Eye | Corrⁿ | Ht. of Eye | Ht. of Eye | Corrⁿ |
|---|---|---|---|---|---|---|---|---|---|---|
| m | | ft. | m | ′ | | m | | ft. | m | ′ |
| 2·4 | −2·8 | 8·0 | 1·0 − 1·8 | | | 9·9 | −5·6 | | 6 − 2·4 | |
| 2·6 | −2·9 | 8·6 | 1·5 − 2·2 | | | 10·3 | −5·7 | 33·9 | 8 − 2·7 | |
| 2·8 | −3·0 | 9·2 | 2·0 − 2·5 | | | 10·6 | −5·8 | 35·1 | 10 − 3·1 | |
| 3·0 | −3·1 | 9·8 | 2·5 − 2·8 | | | 11·0 | −5·9 | 36·3 | See table | |
| 3·2 | −3·2 | 10·5 | 3·0 − 3·0 | | | 11·4 | −6·0 | 37·6 | ← | |
| 3·4 | −3·3 | 11·2 | See table | | | 11·8 | −6·1 | 38·9 | | |
| 3·6 | −3·4 | 11·9 | ← | | | 12·2 | −6·2 | 40·1 | ft. ′ | |
| 3·8 | −3·5 | 12·6 | | | | 12·6 | −6·3 | 41·5 | 70 − 8·1 | |
| 4·0 | −3·6 | 13·3 | m ′ | | | 13·0 | −6·4 | 42·8 | 75 − 8·4 | |
| 4·3 | −3·7 | 14·1 | 20 − 7·9 | | | 13·4 | −6·5 | 44·2 | 80 − 8·7 | |
| 4·5 | −3·8 | 14·9 | 22 − 8·3 | | | 13·8 | −6·6 | 45·5 | 85 − 8·9 | |
| 4·7 | −3·9 | 15·7 | 24 − 8·6 | | | 14·2 | −6·7 | 46·9 | 90 − 9·2 | |
| 5·0 | −4·0 | 16·5 | 26 − 9·0 | | | 14·7 | −6·8 | 48·4 | 95 − 9·5 | |
| 5·2 | −4·1 | 17·4 | 28 − 9·3 | | | 15·1 | −6·9 | 49·8 | | |
| 5·5 | −4·2 | 18·3 | | | | 15·5 | −7·0 | 51·3 | 100 − 9·7 | |
| 5·8 | −4·3 | 19·1 | 30 − 9·6 | | | 16·0 | −7·1 | 52·8 | 105 − 9·9 | |
| 6·1 | −4·4 | 20·1 | 32 − 10·0 | | | 16·5 | −7·2 | 54·3 | 110 − 10·2 | |
| 6·3 | −4·5 | 21·0 | 34 − 10·3 | | | 16·9 | −7·3 | 55·8 | 115 − 10·4 | |
| 6·6 | −4·6 | 22·0 | 36 − 10·6 | | | 17·4 | −7·4 | 57·4 | 120 − 10·6 | |
| 6·9 | −4·7 | 22·9 | 38 − 10·8 | | | 17·9 | −7·5 | 58·9 | 125 − 10·8 | |
| 7·2 | −4·8 | 23·9 | | | | 18·4 | −7·6 | 60·5 | | |
| 7·5 | −4·9 | 24·9 | 40 − 11·1 | | | 18·8 | −7·7 | 62·1 | 130 − 11·1 | |
| 7·9 | −5·0 | 26·0 | 42 − 11·4 | | | 19·3 | −7·8 | 63·8 | 135 − 11·3 | |
| 8·2 | −5·1 | 27·1 | 44 − 11·7 | | | 19·8 | −7·9 | 65·4 | 140 − 11·5 | |
| 8·5 | −5·2 | 28·1 | 46 − 11·9 | | | 20·4 | −8·0 | 67·1 | 145 − 11·7 | |
| 8·8 | −5·3 | 29·2 | 48 − 12·2 | | | 20·9 | −8·1 | 68·8 | 150 − 11·9 | |
| 9·2 | −5·4 | 30·4 | ft. ′ | | | 21·4 | | 70·5 | 155 − 12·1 | |
| 9·5 | −5·5 | 31·5 | 2 − 1·4 | | | | | | | |
| | | 32·7 | 4 − 1·9 | | | | | | | |

*Figure 8–5.* The Dip Table from the *Nautical Almanac.* The correction to the sextant reading for all heights of eye between 8.6 and 9.2 feet is −2.9′.

22—the instructions for its use are contained in the same volume—is entered instead.

For the small-boat navigator without "Bowditch" Table 9 but with a hand-held scientific calculator, a shortcut solution when relatively close to an object can be found by multiplying the charted height in feet by 0.00016 and dividing that product by the tangent of the sextant angle corrected only for index error. The answer will be the distance-off in nautical miles and is reasonably accurate for angles greater than 0° 20′ and distances within 4 miles.

Horizontal sextant angles are of a very high order of accuracy and can be used when precise position-fixing is required. The line of position is obtained independently of compass direction, it being necessary only to measure the angular difference between the bearings to two objects. In this procedure, the sextant is held horizontally, mirror side up, and the leftmost of a pair of charted objects is viewed as the horizon while the right-hand object is brought to it.

Figure 8–6 illustrates a graphic method of deriving a single line of position from a pair of charted objects, and it can be performed right on the chart. In this example, the horizontal angle between objects **A** and **B,** as measured by sextant, is 73°. First, a line is drawn on the chart in any convenient direction toward your approximate position from either of the objects. Next, a protractor is used to locate mythical point **P,** where the angle between the line you have drawn and a line to the second object is exactly 73°. The third step is to locate the center of the circle passing through the two charted objects and point **P.** This is done by constructing the perpendicular bisectors of any two sides of the triangle **APB.** A perpendicular bisector, in case you have forgotten, is constructed by setting a draftsman's compass to any length greater than half the distance between the two selected points and scribing arcs on each side of the connecting line. The line joining the two intersections of these arcs is the perpendicular bisector.

In Figure 8–6 we arbitrarily selected the sides **AB** and **BP** to bisect, but any two sides would do. From the intersection point of the bisectors, which is the center of the

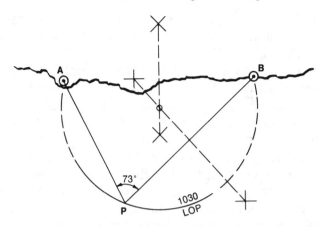

*Figure 8–6.* Obtaining a line of position from a horizontal angle. Point P is found by plotting the observed angle between the bearings to A and B. The center of a circle is determined from the intersection of the perpendicular bisectors of sides AB and BP. The arc line of position is the circumference of the circle.

circle, that part of the circumference that we will use as our line of position is drawn, with a radius equal to the distance to any of the three points: **A, B,** or **P.** As you are already aware, the resulting line of position can be combined with any others to produce a fix.

Carrying this technique a step further, if a third charted object can be identified, and the horizontal angles between the center object and each of the other two objects can be measured at the same time, a simultaneous fix, called a "three-point fix," can be obtained. In the example in Figure 8–7, the angle measured at 1030 between objects **A** and **C** is 51°, and between **A** and **B**, 28°. Two lines of position have been derived from that information, and their intersection is the 1030 fix. Notice that the fix has been obtained without regard to compass direction—the special feature of this technique. Had compass bearings of each of the three objects been available, the navigator could have plotted them, and they would have intersected at the same point.

A fast and easy way to obtain a three-point fix is with the three-arm protractor or "station pointer" that was mentioned in Chapter 6, a model of which is shown in Figure 6–3. The left and right, movable arms are set to the respective sextant angles, left and right of the fixed, center arm. Then, by trial and error, the protractor is moved about the chart so that the hairlines on the three arms pass through the three objects. At that position, the fix is located at the center hole of the protractor. In selecting objects for three-point fixes, the best results are obtained when the angles are of the order of 30° or more, and the nearer they are equal, the better. The only situation to look out for is one in which all three objects and the observer are on or near the circumference of the same circle. This case is called a "revolver," and the fix becomes indeterminate. It is easy enough to avoid, simply by mak-

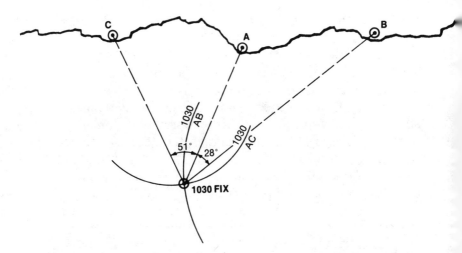

*Figure 8–7.* The intersection of two lines of position from the two horizontal angles, AB and AC, produces a three-point fix.

ing sure that the center object is nearest the observer. Sextant angles are seldom used on small boats to the extent that compass bearings are, but if you have a sextant aboard and seek high-precision position-fixing, such as is required by hydrographic surveyors, the technique is useful to know.

Regardless of how you derive your fix, it is probably a more reliable position than your DR position, and so it is common practice to start your DR plot anew from the fix and carry it forward until the next fix. An estimate of the current affecting your track can also be made at the time of a fix by comparing the DR position with the fix. The direction of the offset is the set of the current, while the distance divided by the elapsed time is the drift.

As a review of the piloting procedures, let's continue the practical exercise started in Figure 7–2, which is carried forward in Figure 8–8. Following a series of courses and speeds, we had tracked the vessel from its noon departure to the 1228 DR position in the vicinity of Gong Buoy "24A." At this point the navigator found that he had the buoy and the tripod on Copps Island in range and, at the same time, the pole on the south end of Goose Island bore 330° M. Plotting these two lines of position, he established his 1228 fix and restarted the DR plot from there. Although he noticed that the current had offset his track slightly in the earlier legs, the navigator found, in consulting his current table, that the time of slack water before the next flood began was near, and he therefore elected not to make any adjustment in setting his new course for the east entrance of Cockenoe Harbor.

After changing course to 001° M, the vessel's speed was increased to 6 knots and the DR track projected to the next turning point, which the navigator estimated he would reach at 1239. As he proceeded on course he observed, just before his ETA (estimated time of arrival), that he passed about midway between the bell and nun buoys at the channel entrance, confirming again that his vessel was approximately on track. The depth finder—which, you will recall, had been used at 1223 to establish the time of crossing the five-fathom curve—was kept running as a further check against straying off course and into shoal water.

At 1239, a bearing was taken on Peck Ledge Light, reading 236° M, and next on Grassy Hammock Rocks Beacon, at 269° M. The navigator correctly observed Peck Ledge first, since its bearing was changing more rapidly. The 1239 fix coincided with the DR, indicating that the estimate of course, speed, and current had been correct. The course was then changed to 264° M, heading for Can Buoy "9" and, respecting the channel speed limit, the speed was reduced to 5 knots.

A check on the track was provided when the Grassy Hammock Beacon was passed close aboard in a 9-foot depth, and both course and speed were reconfirmed when Can "9" was reached at 1251, the estimated time of arrival. Shaping his course for the next turning point, the navigator instructed the helmsman to steer 279° M. At 1256, bearings were taken on Beacons "14" and "11," in that order, and the lines of position plotted to produce the 1256 fix. From that point, the course was altered to 315° M, heading directly for Can Buoy "13" on the west side of the Norwalk Entrance Channel. Arriving in midchannel at 1259, the navigator turned northeast and, leaving the red marks to starboard and the black to port, followed the improved channel to a point opposite Can "19," from where he entered the South Anchorage Basin to anchor.

There are several points particularly worth noting in this exercise. While floating navaids were observed, and in two cases used as turning marks, the fixes depended upon stationary objects, so that the navigator's position

*Figure 8–8.* (Right) Piloting: a continuing plot of a dead-reckoning track, confirmed or corrected by frequent fixes from departure at 1200 to arrival at entrance channel at 1259.

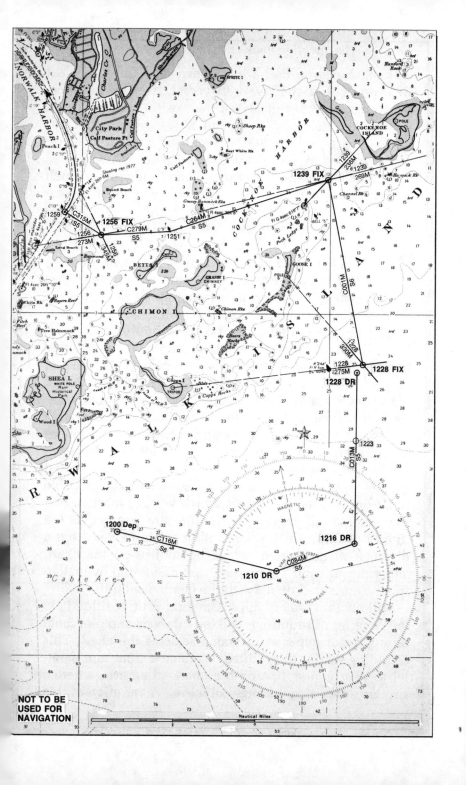

Nautical Miles

was reliable even had a buoy been off-station. In clear weather, with a shallow-draft vessel, it might not have been necessary to follow the track with such precision nor to take as many fixes. But if we assume that our navigator's vessel drew 7 feet, and the visibility was reduced by patchy fog, the detail and precision would be essential. This is the important area of judgment, which contributes so much to the successful practice of navigation.

At times, as might be the case in sailing along a relatively featureless coast, you may be able to identify only a single object suitable for observation and can, as a consequence, get only one line of position. What then? You can't derive a conventional fix from a single position line, but such a line can still be used in a number of constructive ways. One of these is by taking a simultaneous reading of the depth finder. You will recall that in our piloting exercise, Figure 8–8, the navigator checked the time he crossed the five-fathom curve, 1223, as a confirmation of his speed along his track. Again, in the vicinity of Grassy Hammock Beacon, the depth reading backed up his rough positional check. Quite often, and especially if the bottom contours are irregular, it is possible to plot a single line of position and estimate from a depth sounding (corrected for the state of the tide when necessary) the probable point on the position line at which you are located. In a like manner, although opportunities are less frequent, a line of position (in the form of an arc) obtained from a distance-off measurement can be scribed on the chart, and your probable location on that line found by matching the measured depth with the charted soundings.

Still another way of approximating your position is to take a series of soundings at fixed intervals and plot them on a strip of paper at the same scale as the chart. This sounding strip is then "fitted" to an area along and parallel to your course line on the chart, in an area where a similar series of soundings coincides. A variation of this procedure, which works satisfactorily when the bottom contours are regular, is to sail along a constant-depth curve, maintaining the depth by maneuvering your vessel. Then, the intersection of a single visual bearing with the appropriate depth curve on the chart indicates your probable position.

A single position line, if at right angles to your course, can tell you whether your speed over the bottom is causing you to run ahead of or behind your reckoned position. A bearing ahead or astern can tell you whether you are to the right or left of your intended course. Ranges, formed by two objects in line, make ideal leading marks for this purpose.

While not of the quality of a conventional fix, approximate positions derived from a single line of position and other reliable information that can be applied are almost always better than a dead-reckoning position alone. Although it is not common practice to replot the DR track from such a position, it is important to take cognizance of the improved estimate so that your projected course between fixes does not lead you into danger.

Sometimes it is not as important to know where you are as it is to know where you are *not*. This involves the practice of using a single line as a danger bearing or danger angle. As an example, Figure 8–9 shows a submerged, unmarked reef rising so steeply from the bottom that soundings alone will not give sufficient warning as it is approached. The reef, between you and a point marked with a high tower, is about 0.8 miles from the tower and practically on your course. A danger bearing is plotted from the tower, just clearing the reef, and is measured on the chart as 357°. Your observed bearing of the tower is 002°, but you are not certain exactly how far along the track you are. You can see that as long as the observed bearing remains greater than the danger bearing, you are in safe water. By continuing to head for the tower on course 002°, you will clear the obstruction.

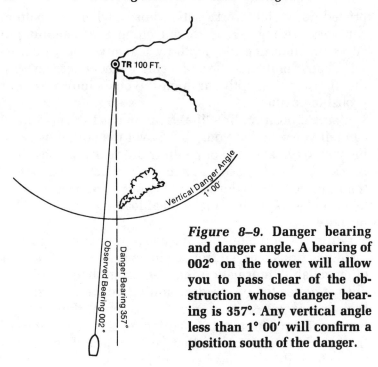

*Figure 8–9.* Danger bearing and danger angle. A bearing of 002° on the tower will allow you to pass clear of the obstruction whose danger bearing is 357°. Any vertical angle less than 1° 00′ will confirm a position south of the danger.

It is also possible, though less frequently practicable, to precompute a vertical danger angle, in this case 1° 00′. Then, by measuring the vertical angle of the tower with a sextant as you approach, you know you will be south of the reef and in deep water as long as the sextant angle is less than the vertical danger angle.

A frequently used method for utilizing lines of position is a "running fix," a position determined by the intersection of single lines of position taken at different times and advanced (or "retired") to a common time. Figure 8–10 illustrates the principle and technique. Proceeding on course 290° at 5 knots, the navigator plots a line of position from Beacon **A,** which bears 028° at eleven o'clock. One hour later, the bearing on **A** is taken again and is 075°. The 1100 line is advanced the distance traveled along the course—in this case, 5 miles in the hour elapsed—and the advanced line is drawn parallel to the original line at the point of advance. The intersection of the plotted 1200 line, and the 1100 line advanced to 1200, is the 1200 running fix.

Restarting the plot, the navigator next gets a single bearing of Beacon **B,** 357°, at 1330. This position line is crossed with the 1200 bearing on **A,** which has been advanced 7.5 miles along the course line—the distance traveled in the elapsed time—producing a running fix

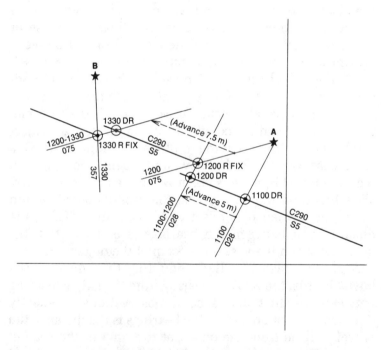

*Figure 8–10.* **The Running Fix. The 1200 running fix is produced by the intersection of the 1200 bearing on A and the 1100 bearing on A advanced to 1200. The 1330 running fix is produced by the intersection of the 1330 bearing on B and the 1200 bearing on A advanced to 1330.**

from single bearings of *two* objects taken at different times, just as the first fix was produced by two bearings of the *same* object taken at different times.

Position lines obtained by any means can be combined in a running fix. Do notice the form of labeling the lines to avoid confusion; the advanced (or retired) lines are always identified with the time at which they were observed followed by the time to which they were adjusted. As you will readily understand, a running fix is only as accurate as the estimate of the course and distance over which the line of position is transferred. As a consequence, it is desirable to use as short a time interval as practical, allowing for an adequate "spread" (30° or more if possible) between the intersecting lines. If course or speed changes occur during the elapsed period between bearings, the position line is moved, just like the vessel, along the actual track. Just be sure to construct the advanced position line exactly parallel with the original.

There are several special cases in which the information derived from successive bearings of a single object can be used without having to plot a fix on the chart. One such case occurs with "bow and beam" bearings, in which the first bearing is taken when the object is exactly 45° ("broad on the bow") from the vessel's heading, and the second when it is exactly 90° ("abeam"). Then, the distance run between the bearings is equal to the distance-off when the vessel is abeam of the object.

A second case is called "doubling the angle on the bow." In this, the relative bearing from the ship's heading between the first and second observations is exactly doubled. The run between the bearings is the distance the vessel will be from the object at the time of the second bearing. Other such relationships can be determined and solved mathematically but, because it is quite difficult to make all of the precise measurements when aboard a small boat, and especially since by plotting on the chart the navigator can better visualize his position in relation to his surroundings, the graphic method for establishing running fixes is almost universally preferred.

As you review this important chapter, you'll see that we are constantly dealing with lines. Mariners use them to plot the course from departure to destination, to avoid hazards, to get their bearings from range or other marks, and even to plot bottom contours when navigating by depth sounder. The emphasis in all of these is on the word "line," a term that reflects the experienced navigator's thinking.

# 9 | Navigation at Night and in Fog

Piloting at night imposes additional demands on the navigator's skill. The relationship of near and distant geographical features on which you rely, consciously or unconsciously, during the day cannot be discerned—except, to a degree, by radar. Instead, reliance must be placed on lighted navigational aids and careful piloting. In coastwise navigation at night, it is particularly important to follow definite courses from point to point and to maintain a meticulous plot, so that you have a good estimate of your position at all times.

Fortunately, most of the coastal areas visited by yachtsmen are well provided with lighted navaids. The light characteristics of major installations are indicated on the chart and detailed in the *Light List*. Distinctive color and light combinations are used on installations in close proximity, so as to avoid confusion.

The distance at which a light may first be seen depends not only on its intensity, but also on the prevailing atmospheric conditions and the earth's curvature. There are three frames of reference for expressing the visual range. *Nominal* range is the range indicated in the *Light List* (Figure 4–1) and in the chart legend (Figure 2–1). It is strictly a function of the light's intensity and represents the maximum distance the light may be seen in clear weather, without regard to the earth's curvature. *Luminous* range is the greatest distance that the light may be seen under the existing conditions of visibility, again without regard to curvature. *Geographic* range is the calculated distance at which the light may be viewed by an observer at a given elevation, taking into account the earth's curvature, but without considering the nominal or luminous ranges.

Chart legends used to show light ranges as the lesser of the nominal range or the geographic range for a standard height of eye of 15 feet, but the practice is yielding to the universal listing of nominal range alone. As a result, the estimating of a light's visual range under the circumstances in which you observe it requires a small computation. Given the nominal range, you first estimate the luminous range by means of the luminous range diagram in the *Light List* (or in Bowditch), which gives the parameters for various atmospheric conditions from exceptionally clear to dense fog. Next, by adding the respective distances to the horizon from the elevated light source and from the observer's height of eye, you can determine the geographic range for comparison. The lesser of the luminous or geographic ranges will be the maximum distance at which you can expect to see the light. The formula for figuring the horizon distances in your calculation is given in Chapter 11, page 126, but if you prefer, you can use the *Light List's* geographic range table or a similar table in Bowditch. In any event, there are other circumstances, such as abnormal refraction, background loom from city lights, and so forth, that make the determination of exact range problematical. The distance you figure, therefore, should always be dealt with as an approximation.

It is a good idea, if you are making for a light some distance away, to draw an arc on the chart at the probable visible range and estimate the time of arrival at the inter-section of the arc with your course. If the night is clear and the light of proper intensity, it should appear on the horizon close to the appointed time. Sometimes, if you are waiting nervously for a light to appear, the flash or its loom may be spotted a little earlier by elevating your vantage point. If there is a sea running when you first pick up a light on the horizon, watch it for a moment before you make a positive identification. A "flashing" light may turn out to be a fixed light of another vessel disappearing and reappearing with the swells. When the light's charac-teristic is clearly identifiable, your stopwatch may be use-ful if you can't estimate the time sequence with sufficient accuracy.

Channel markers, including all the lighted, floating navaids, display light characteristics consistent with their color and placement within the buoyage system. The extract of Chart 1 in the appendix illustrates this use, and the aids, themselves, are included in the *Light List* and identified on the chart by symbol and abbreviated legend. As discussed in Chapter 4, the lighting scheme within our buoyage system is in the process of being streamlined—to confine red to red aids, green to green, and to display white lights only on safe water buoys, and yellow on special purpose marks—so don't be surprised during the transition if you should find a situation in which the actual and charted characteristics don't agree exactly.

A special class of inshore navigational aid, particularly useful at night, is the lighted range marker. Usually located at harbor entrances or to mark the centerline of a channel, lighted range markers occur in pairs, with the rear light higher than the front one. Normally, the marker lights are displayed by the same structures used for ranges in the daytime, and they may exhibit highly direc-tional beams, or special colors or characteristics, to pre-vent confusion with other lighted aids nearby.

In a congested area, it is not uncommon to see a number of flashing lights at the same time. This can be quite confusing, especially against the backdrop of a brightly lighted area ashore. Here again a careful plot and a reliable compass come to your rescue. If you know approximately where you are and have a good bearing on the light, you will probably be able to identify it quickly and easily. Otherwise, it may be necessary to approach the mark closely enough for visual identification—not always an ideal practice in restricted waters.

You should remind yourself frequently to avoid total reliance on lights, and especially those on minor navaids. Most major installations have backup systems to take over if the main light fails, but smaller buoys do not. While the record of dependability is excellent, lights do occasionally exhibit faulty characteristics, or go out altogether. If you are confident of your plot, you will probably find the buoy anyway or, if it is equipped with a sound device, hear it before you arrive. Many marks have reflective material applied to facilitate spotting and identifying by searchlight. A pair of binoculars with good light-gathering power, like the standard Navy 7 × 50's, makes the job easier, although there is still no substitute for precise plotting.

Electronic aids may also offer a major assist at night. Away from shore, coastal radiobeacons provide lines of position from which a fix can be derived, while inshore, low-powered beacons, often placed strategically at harbor entrances, may be "homed" on (by orienting the radio direction-finder antenna dead ahead and altering the vessel's course to the null) until a point is reached at which lighted aids appear.

Loran yields lines of position that are usually more precise than those obtained by radio direction-finder. Radar is, of course, the most valuable electronic tool in confined areas. Not only can it spot navigational aids and distinctive geographical features, but it can also produce range and bearing information for position-fixing. Radar really comes into its own in its primary application: collision avoidance at night or during periods of reduced visibility.

It takes practice to spot, identify, and determine the orientation and relative movement of other ships at sea. The navigator should be familiar with the lights required on various classes of vessels (referring, if necessary, to the *Navigation Rules* described in Chapter 3). It is always a good procedure, upon seeing the lights of an approaching vessel, to start taking a series of bearings to ascertain whether it will pass ahead, is opening with your course, or, if the bearing remains steady, is on a collision course with you. It is still better practice, if the other ship is a big one, to keep out of its way entirely—it is required by law in confined waters. A large ship simply may not be able to see you, much less avoid you when she does. A cardinal rule for a small-boat navigator is *never* to pass ahead of a larger, powered vessel unless you are absolutely certain of your position and his intentions.

The navigator's relatively comfortable world changes completely when fog shuts in. Gone is any visual reference to the shore and, in thick fog, only those objects that can be approached within a few yards may ever be seen. Geographical orientation becomes difficult, if not downright confusing, and dependence on instruments is the order of the day. Precise information about your vessel's position and movement is vital, and the maintenance of a first-class plot is more important than ever. If you have not yet developed confidence through experience in your instruments and your piloting ability, you would be well advised to postpone venturing forth in a fog until you have that confidence, since it will be an unnerving experience if not a hazardous one.

But navigators do venture forth, and with safety, when the fundamentals have been mastered. Fog is not a condition to be feared, although it does command the utmost respect from the entire ship's company, as well as the total attention of the navigator. That attention rightfully starts *before* fog is encountered, with checking and re-checking the compass, depth finder, speed or distance measuring instruments, and any other electronic equipment aboard, during periods of good visibility. With the careful plot you should have been running you will also have a point of departure should fog suddenly close in.

Approaching a landfall in fog, a navigator may be able to utilize RDF bearings or Loran lines for positioning or, as in night navigation, to maneuver into a position that would place a floating navaid, preferably audible, between him and a radiobeacon. Except for radar, which is the best device to have aboard under these circumstances, the depth finder or lowly lead line may be the best indicator of approaching danger if the bottom contour is cooperative.

From a known position, a navigator in fog usually sets his course in legs as short as possible, often hopping from buoy to buoy even if it extends his total distance. The course and the speed, which should be moderated in fog to the extent that you can stop or maneuver within your range of visibility, must be monitored precisely, and each mark must be positively identified before proceeding to the next. A good procedure, called "running your time," is to precalculate your estimated time of arrival at each mark, taking into account your best estimate of the effect of the current. Then, by the watch, you can determine when you have "run your time" and stop, look, and listen, or circle slowly until you see or hear the aid you are seeking. If you miss finding a mark promptly in hazardous waters, or if you become otherwise unsure of your position, the only sensible alternatives are to consider anchoring or turning offshore until conditions improve. Most beginners seem to be reluctant to do this, presumably because the sanctuary of a cozy, shoreside berth appears irresistible, but the seasoned navigator does not hesitate to choose one of the safer, though temporarily less comfortable, alternatives. I've never met a good navigator who, in retrospect, regretted that choice.

Aside from electronic instrumentation and your plot, audible navigational aids are the best source of positioning information in fog. The characteristics of major fog signals are given in the *Light List*, and you may use your stopwatch to identify them positively. The type of audible device installed on the lesser aids is indicated on the chart, but caution should be exercised in relying on any floating aid, since those devices that depend on wave action may not—as noted in Chapter 4—sound at all in calm water. Upwind, sounds are notoriously hard to hear and to pinpoint in bearing.

The navigator in fog must be alert to everything—bells, whistles, motor noises, the cry of gulls on a ledge, the sound of breaking waves; yes, even barking dogs ashore— that might contribute to his estimate of his position. Current flow around buoys or other anchored objects is particularly to be noted since, at the moderated speed used in fog, the effect of the current will be more pronounced than it is at normal cruising speeds. The depth finder, if available, should be kept going continuously, since the observation of the changing bottom contours adds to the navigator's information. Sometimes it is safe to approach a bold shore, and if this can be done from the lee side, the fog may "scale up" just enough to provide a momentary glimpse of the shoreline.

The wear and tear on the nerves notwithstanding, the most serious danger in fog, and especially in crowded, commercial waterways, is the danger of collision with another vessel. Having your radar reflector in place is of help, and with radar itself aboard you can probably proceed with safety. Otherwise, the best course, if you have a choice, may be to avoid the confrontation altogether until conditions improve. After all, you wouldn't cross Times Square by choice while blindfolded.

The fog signals you should make, as well as those required of other types of vessels, are part of the *Navigation Rules*. Large commercial vessels are usually meticulous in sounding their required fog signals; many smaller vessels and yachts, unfortunately, are not. As a consequence, you must never relax your guard in fog. Stay alert, listen carefully, and be safe.

# 10 | Anchoring

The technique of dropping an anchor is generally considered to be one of the rudiments of seamanship, and almost every coastwise voyage involves anchoring; yet it often seems to be handled in a haphazard manner even if the voyage preceding it has been conducted with care. A competent navigator can play an important role in the when, where, and how of the process.

When to anchor is a question usually answered by the skipper and suggests a snug anchorage at the completion of a passage, or the natural ending to an exhilarating day's sail; but an experienced navigator may recommend other times, too. Should you, as the navigator of a low-powered auxiliary vessel, anticipate your arrival at a tide race like New York's Hell Gate at the beginning of a foul tide, it is smart to find an anchorage and wait for the current to turn fair—as was the practice in the old sailing-ship days. In a similar vein, if the estimated time of arrival at a particular bridge coincides with restricted operating hours, or if passage beneath the bridge is limited to certain stages of the tide because of the overhead clearance, anchoring may again be the safest and most efficient tactic.

One of the most difficult admissions for any navigator to make, even to himself, is that he is lost, or at least disoriented and unsure of his position. Should this happen in a fog or at night, dropping the anchor should always be considered as a primary alternative to forging ahead. Under the stress of picking your way through dangerous waters, and the discomfort brought on by darkness and fatigue, not to mention the dungeon-like feeling of a pea-soup fog, the human tendency is to press on even though it may be far safer to anchor and wait for conditions to improve. Obviously, this alternative is most practical—and desirable—in the relatively shallow waters in which most coastwise navigation takes place. Farther offshore, or wherever there is known to be adequate sea room, you have the other option of turning seaward and standing away from the dangers, although you must have a good idea of your position to do this safely. It is always sound to remember the ancient seaman's adage, "When in doubt, anchor"; there are bound to be opportunities to apply it in any modern yacht that cruises adventurously.

Where to anchor is another decision in which the navigator can contribute both to the safety of the vessel and the comfort of her crew. If shelter from wind and wave or from a strong current is the aim, and particularly if storm conditions are anticipated, the navigator, with his charts and publications, should be the best source of information as to the quality of an anchorage from the viewpoint of protection offered by the adjacent land and the nature of the holding ground. Having helped select the area, the navigator is also in the position to select the safest approach route, often a challenge in reduced visibility, requiring the most precise piloting of the voyage. Once inside the anchorage, the final decision about where to set the hook with relation to other moored vessels is influenced by the state of the tide and its predicted rise and fall, the expected strength and direction of the wind and current—all information supplied by the navigator.

It is common in naval anchorages and major commercial ports to designate areas in which vessels may anchor, and in many instances specific berths are assigned within these areas. With the ever-increasing activity in popular yachting centers, the practice of designating anchorages for small boats may become more and more prevalent. Receiving a berth assignment is one thing, locating the berth precisely and anchoring within it is another. The most practical way to accomplish this is first to identify the exact location of the assigned berth on your chart and to establish bearings from it to prominent charted objects on the shore. If natural ranges can be found, so much the better. One line is selected as the approach bearing, and the other, as nearly as possible at right angles to the first, as the drop bearing. A typical situation is illustrated in Figure 10–1. Here the navigator finds an approach bearing formed by a church steeple in range with an elevated tank, and the drop bearing as another natural range consisting of a prominent dock and a flagpole. Had ranges not been available, compass bearings would have served as well if not as conveniently. Turning onto the approach bearing, the vessel is steered along that line until the drop bearing is reached and the anchor set.

After anchoring, either in a prescribed berth or in one of his own choosing, the navigator should make certain that the anchor is well set and not dragging. This is done by taking and recording the bearings of fixed objects, which can be rechecked periodically, or, if the berth is a designated one, by taking the bearings of the same objects or ranges used for the approach and drop. A convenient shortcut method for a yacht that has anchored independently, or has picked up a strange mooring, is to identify one or two natural ranges ashore, which in this case do not have to be objects that appear on the chart, and to use these, as long as they remain steady, to ensure that the vessel hasn't shifted from the spot where she anchored. The process is an application of the principles of position finding, but under the easier conditions that apply to a stationary vessel.

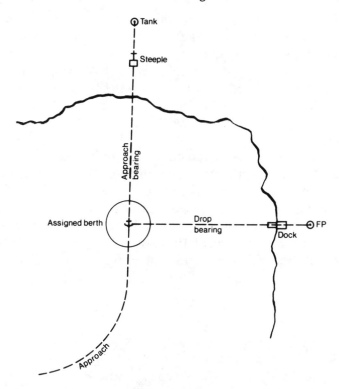

*Figure 10–1.* A vessel's approach to an assigned berth is made by following an approach bearing until the pre-established drop bearing is reached. The same bearings may be used to ensure that the vessel remains within her berth.

How to anchor may be primarily an exercise in seamanship, but here again the navigator can offer a strong assist. Knowledge of the state and range of the tide, for example, is essential if a yacht's draft makes the question of adequate water depth at all critical. Then, too, there is the question of selecting the scope—the ratio between the length of the anchor line and the depth of the water—which may be vital in avoiding dragging after the anchor is set. The holding power of an anchor is influenced by the angle of pull, a flatter angle generally giving a better set. This can be seen in Figure 10–2. If the boat at **(b)** in the lower figure has anchored with 42 feet of line in 6 feet of water at low tide, its conservative 7:1 scope provides a relatively flat angle of pull and a reliable set. But should the tide rise 8 feet, to position **(a)** in the lower figure, that same 42-foot anchor line will provide only a very marginal 3:1 scope.

At the same time, as the upper part of Figure 10–2 illustrates, if the length of the anchor line remains constant while the water depth changes with the tide, the amount of swinging room changes significantly. This must be taken into account in any crowded anchorage, and a compromise reached between the desired scope and the room available in which to swing. In order to reach a sound

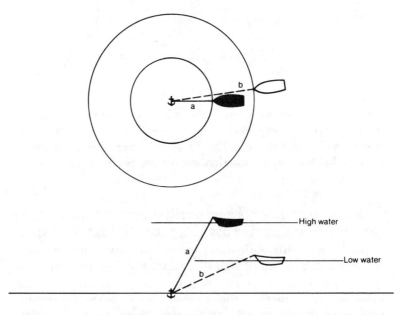

*Figure 10–2.* The rise and fall of the tide creates a significant difference both in the angle of pull at the bottom and in the boat's swinging circle.

decision in a critical situation, it may be necessary to determine the state of the tide from the *Tide Tables*, and the exact water depth by using a hand lead line or an accurate depth finder. If you use the latter, remember that its transducer may be several feet below the waterline, and that the readings may have to be adjusted to get an absolute measurement.

Another matter in which the navigator can help is in the type of set selected. If the holding ground is questionable, as indicated by the bottom characteristic shown on the chart, he may suggest a particular type of anchor; the "lightweight" anchors that are superb in sand or mud, for example, are notoriously poor in kelp. Similarly, if the anchorage is a tideway, it is often good judgment to set two anchors, one with and one against the current (Figure 10–3a), so that when the flow reverses, the load will be taken by the upstream anchor and the other will not break out and have to reset itself. If a vessel is to be moored alongside a channel, and the area outside the channel shoals rapidly—typical of a body like the Intracoastal Waterway—a fore-and-aft version of a two-anchor set (Figure 10–3b) may be necessary to keep from grounding or from swinging into the fairway.

Another type of anchoring configuration, often used if a storm is anticipated, involves setting a second anchor, as illustrated in Figure10–3c, in the direction from which the storm winds or seas are expected to come, while lying to the first one set for the prevailing conditions. Then, as in a reversing current, the danger of dragging and trying to reset an anchor under storm conditions is greatly reduced. Obviously, storm warnings call for the heaviest ground tackle and the best anchoring technique available. A two-hook set can also be helpful in dealing with the short-scope problem in today's typically crowded anchorage. Usually the anchors are placed at a 90°-angle, as illustrated in Figure 10–3d, reducing the swinging room and amount of yawing about that is characteristic of most

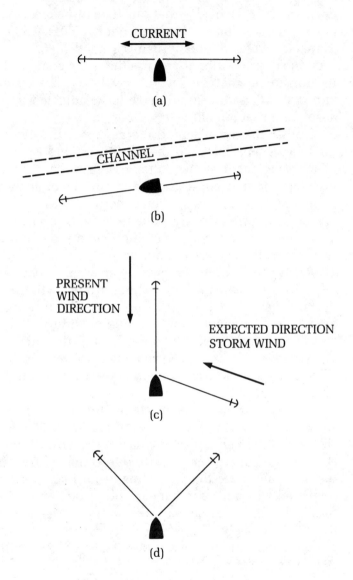

*Figure 10–3.* Various configurations of two-anchor sets: (a) In a tideway; (b) Fore-and-aft mooring alongside a shoaling channel edge; (c) Anticipating a storm wind; (d) In a crowded anchorage.

yachts at anchor, and doubling the security against unexpected dragging.

In selecting an anchorage in a popular locale, it is always tempting to choose one of the Special Anchorage Areas designated on the chart. One of the advantages of this is that the anchor lights required by the *Navigation Rules* do not have to be displayed. On the other hand, most Special Anchorage Areas are crowded with permanent moorings during the yachting season, and in the off months, the remains of old mooring tackle may well foul your anchor. Increasingly, the preferred anchorages may be found to be fully occupied, and a well-prepared navigator should always have alternatives in mind. Because a yacht may actually spend as much of her life at anchor as she does underway, safe anchoring may be as important to her security as is safe piloting.

# 11 | Piloting by Calculator

Navigation, as you have seen, is a mathematical science, based mainly on the precepts of geometry and trigonometry. While graphic methods of solution are traditional, and in many cases are advantageous, mathematical solutions are equally possible. Historically, when graphic methods were not used, the navigator used tables and diagrams to eliminate the tedious and time-consuming computations that were necessary, but the electronic age has changed all this. With the advent of miniaturized circuitry and the development of small calculators, even the most complex computations can be done in seconds, and many navigators have found a calculator to be a useful adjunct.

The first problem facing a navigator who wants to take advantage of the new technology, however, is the basic one of selecting the most practicable instrument for his needs. Since the multiplicity of calculators now available encompasses such a wide range of performance—not to mention price—some understanding of the choices is desirable before you start shopping. The best way to go about this is first to identify the types of problems you expect your calculator to solve, and then to review the equipment that can handle them. In other words, what should be the combination of functions or features of the calculator you acquire?

To guide you toward an answer, Figure 11–1 classifies the mathematical level of various types of navigation problems, with examples of each. The third column of the table lists the calculator functions used in the solution, and the fourth, the symbols on the calculator keyboard that are typically used to represent these functions. One or more of the functions listed may be required in the computation. To solve a problem involving sextant corrections, for example, you would want the sexagesimal/decimal conversion feature in addition to the arithmetic functions required for the time-speed-distance level of computation. One point that should be clarified, however, is that the listings in the table are not absolute. That is to say, it may be entirely possible to solve certain problems without having to use all of the listed functions, although doing so may be much more cumbersome. On the other hand, some solutions may be made still easier or quicker with a greater number of calculator features. The objective of Figure 11–1 is to suggest the minimum practical functions for solving a problem with a minimum number of keystrokes. Where a keypunch sequence is performed automatically, as in the more sophisticated programmable calculators, the number of steps may not be as important, but in the manual models, on which almost everyone learns, features that contribute to the shortest solution will be those you will want.

A fact to keep in mind in your selection process is that most calculators, except for those prewired expressly for navigation, are designed for a wide range of problem-solving, of which navigational exercises are only one small part. As a consequence, a general-purpose calculator with features for handling the more complex navigation exercises will generally have the capability to solve a vast number of nonnavigational problems, and

| Level of Navigation Problem | Examples of Type | Incremental Calculator Functions | Typical Keyboard Symbols |
|---|---|---|---|
| Arithmetic | Time-Speed-Distance | Four arithmetic functions | $+$  $-$  $\times$  $\div$ |
| | Horizon Distance, Vertical Angles | Squares and square roots | $x^2$  $\sqrt{x}$ |
| | Sextant Corrections | Sexagesimal/Decimal conversions, Change-sign key | DMS  $+/-$ or CHS |
| Vector Arithmetic | Current Sailing (Course and Speed Made Good), Traverse Sailing | Register Exchange, Polar/Rectangular coordinate conversion, Two addressable memories, capable of register arithmetic | x↔y  $P \rightarrow R$  STO |
| Trigonometry | Current Sailing (Course to Steer), Distance-off by Two Bearings | Natural trigonometric functions and inverse functions | sin  cos  tan |

*Figure 11–1.* Desirable Functions in a Navigation Calculator.

will very likely offer some functions that will never be used in navigation. Adding further to the possibility of confusion is calculator terminology, not yet standardized in the industry, evidenced by the differing symbols or names used to identify similar functions.

Calculators are offered in several basic categories.

Should you plan to confine your use to arithmetic applications, a simple four-function (add, subtract, multiply, and divide) model is all you need. As the complexity of your navigation problems increases, you can advance to the next calculator "plateau"—represented by the "slide-rule," or scientific models that offer the capability of performing trigonometric and other higher operations. Many calculators of this type have such additional features as coordinate-conversion capabilities or multiple memories that can store intermediate data in a long calculation, saving duplicate keystrokes and considerable time.

In essence, the solution of any calculator problem consists of a sequence of keypunches. The fewer of these the operator has to perform, the shorter the time required, and, usually, the smaller the chance for error. Accordingly, as the complexity of the problems and the corresponding number of keystrokes increases (often into the hundreds), calculator manufacturers meet the challenge with the category of instruments called "preprogrammed" and "programmable." These adhere to exactly the same mathematical principles as their less sophisticated kin, but their features save the operator many keystrokes.

The preprogrammed group is capable of performing many sequences with the depression of a single key. Most scientific calculators have at least some preprogrammed functions, such as square roots or the value of $\pi$, while other, special-purpose models may be "hard-wired" to perform complex sequences, such as great-circle computations or other navigational specialties. Such special-purpose instruments may be of particular interest to the yachtsman who uses his calculator exclusively for the solution of a preselected set of navigation problems; they are discussed in more detail later.

Among general-purpose calculators, the programmable group is the ultimate in sophistication and versatility. Their outstanding feature is the ability to accept an entire keystroke sequence for storage in a program memory before the solution begins. The operator has only to enter the initial data and start the program, which then steps through the prearranged keystroke routine internally. This is a particularly attractive feature for anyone who must repeatedly solve multiple-step problems, and explains why this kind of instrument is seen more and more frequently in the navigation departments of large ships.

The programmable category is further subdivided into two types. The first acquires its program when the operator punches the keystroke sequence into a program memory, which, after the variable data have been entered, is engaged to complete the computation. Only one program at a time can be handled by these "keyboard-programmable" instruments, and it is lost when another program replaces it or, with the exception of a few models that can retain a sequence, when the calculator is turned off.

The most advanced of the programmable calculators is the type that can store keystroke sequences on a magnetic tape or modular chip. These are referred to as "fully programmable," or, more properly, as "card- or chip-programmed" calculators. On some models the operator can even create his own programs to be stored permanently on magnetic strips. In operation, a program is selected, fed into the calculator's program memory, and the variable input data introduced. The calculator then steps through the preset sequence automatically, displaying the solution in a matter of seconds. These fully programmable instruments have the greatest potential for reducing computation time, and the least opportunity for error.

After having decided on the level of capability you want in your hand-held calculator, you have still one more choice to make—the choice between the two competing logics, or "languages," that modern calculators employ. The two are called "algebraic logic" (or "entry"), and "Reverse Polish Notation" (RPN). The difference in operation between these two forms of address is discussed below. Hewlett-Packard, one of the first companies to achieve widespread distribution of scientific calculators, employs RPN, while most of the other manufacturers today use algebraic logic. In my opinion, for the types of problems normally encountered by a practicing navigator, the logic employed by a particular calculator is less important than its list of functions. As a result, the decision in selecting the form of logic is primarily subjective—which form of address you can work with most readily. More important is the choice of a well-made instrument capable of withstanding the rigors of shipboard life. An inoperative calculator, regardless of its features, is less than useless.

"Hard-wired" or "dedicated" navigational computers, as they are known, represent a special category, and one that is evolving rapidly. These instruments are preprogrammed to handle a range of navigation exercises, usually including complex celestial solutions. In the more sophisticated models, there is even a prompting system that calls for inputs and tags the answer in the display. Approaching a truly automatic navigation system, they have particular appeal to a yachtsman who performs the more elaborate operations only intermittently.

Having considered the selection of a calculator for navigation, let's look at the operating techniques as they apply to some common navigational problems. Although no two makes or models are exactly alike, the principles are the same. It is important, however, first to understand the difference between the two logic systems described earlier, which manifests itself mainly in the order in which the keys for adding, subtracting, multiplying, and dividing are pressed during the solution of a problem. A short example will help to explain this difference. In algebraic logic, a simple arithmetic exercise would be keypunched in the following sequence, $\boxed{2}$ $\boxed{\times}$

⎡3⎤   ⎡=⎤ , and, at the press of the "equals" key, the answer, 6, would appear in the display. In RPN, so named after the Polish logician who developed the system, the same problem would be solved by pressing ⎡2⎤ , then ⎡ENTER⎤ , to enter it, then ⎡3⎤   ⎡×⎤ . When the "times" sign, ⎡×⎤ , is pressed, the answer, 6, is shown in the display. Incidentally, the display is also known as the "x-register" in calculator parlance, to distinguish it from the "y-register," which is the working register within the machine.

You can see that for simple problems the number of keystrokes is not materially different between the two systems. Only in complex exercises, especially those with multiple levels of parentheses, does the difference in logic become significant. In virtually all navigation problems that difference is not of major consequence. It is more important that you are comfortable with the logic system you select and develop facility in using it.

Returning to the keyboard, you will find that special-function keys are almost always clustered at the top, but here the similarity ends. In order to remain within overall size limits and still have a keyboard of practical operating dimensions, the physical number of keys is limited, most manufacturers having settled on thirty-five to forty-five. In order to accommodate more functions than there are keys, secondary functions—and in the case of the more powerful calculators, tertiary functions—may be assigned to individual keys. These are brought into use by first pressing a function-change key, which is identified by various symbols according to the manufacturer's choice. I can only emphasize the requirement that you understand all the functions you have available and the scheme employed for handling multifunction keys on your chosen instrument.

As an example of a special-function operation, consider the conversion of an angular measurement expressed in degrees, minutes, and seconds (the sexagesimal system) to degrees expressed in whole and decimal numbers (the decimal system)—a step necessary in applying sextant corrections by calculator. You can perform the operation arithmetically by means of the formula:

$$\text{Degrees} + \left( \frac{\text{Minutes} \times 60 + \text{Seconds}}{3600} \right)$$

pressing the individual keys in the proper sequence. But since this is an operation that is repeated frequently in navigation, the calculator you have selected may have the special sexagesimal-to-decimal conversion function, making the interchange possible with the press of a single key.

Regardless of the keyboard involved, the solution of any problem on a calculator is accomplished by first identifying the mathematical formula that applies, and then, according to the form of logic used by the instrument, by establishing a keypunch sequence, or "program," to solve it. Sometimes there is more than one formula that can be applied, and often there is more than one keystroke sequence that can be used to solve a given problem. That choice is up to you, but it will often be dictated by the program that produces your answer in the fewest possible steps.

Let's review some examples of the various types of navigation problems outlined in Figure 11–1 that you can try on your calculator. The formula expressing the relationship between time, speed, and distance is:

$$\text{Time} \times \text{Speed} = \text{Distance}$$

Given any two of the quantities in this equation, you can solve for the third. To find out how far you will travel in, say, 3 hours at 5 knots, simply multiply three times five to obtain the answer, 15 nautical miles. Conversely, to find

out how long it will take to reach a destination 15 miles
away by steaming at 5 knots, the distance is divided by
the speed to obtain the time, 3 hours. Fuel consumption,
and similar problems for which an arithmetic relationship can be established, may be worked with a similar
keyboard sequence, and this can be done quickly and
easily, even though the numbers or their decimal parts
may be large.

The distance to an observer's horizon is found by the
formula:

$$\text{Distance (nautical miles)} = 1.15\sqrt{\text{Height of eye (feet)}}$$

To solve this by calculator, enter the height of eye, obtain
its square root (usually by a single keystroke), and multiply that by the constant, 1.15, to produce the distance in
nautical miles. Thus, at an elevation of 6 feet, the observer's horizon will be 2.817 miles away.

Right triangles are used in the solutions to many navigation problems. The relationship between the sides is
expressed by the classic Pythagorean theorem:

$$a^2 + b^2 = c^2$$

Then, if you know the lengths of any two sides of the
triangle, you can find the third, and if your calculator
handles squares and square roots at a single keystroke,
the answer can be found almost instantaneously.

Sextant corrections, and any problem that involves the
arithmetic combination of values expressed in degrees,
minutes, and seconds, require that the equivalent in decimal notation be determined first, the mathematical operation then performed, and the answer reconverted to
the sexagesimal system. As discussed, if your calculator
has the capability of making this conversion internally,
you will save many keystrokes.

The concept of vector arithmetic has been explained in

Chapter 7. If your calculator has the capability of making rapid conversions between polar and rectangular coordinates, it will offer an ideal solution to a current-sailing problem such as that illustrated in Figure 7–3. The process consists of entering the course and speed into the x- and y-registers, placing them in proper order by means of the x-y register-exchange key, and finding the equivalent, rectangular components of the course and speed vector by means of the conversion key. The process is repeated for the current vector, and the two sets of rectangular components are then added algebraically. The net totals, again in the proper order in the x- and y-registers, are reconverted to the polar coordinates of the vector that represents the course and speed made good.

A mathematical traverse is performed in much the same manner. Each segment of the traverse is broken down into its rectangular equivalents, as has been done in the box on page 77 for the traverse illustrated in Figure 7-6. The algebraic sums of the equivalents are then calculated, and these sums are converted back to the polar coordinates of the course and distance.

The second type of current problem, illustrated in Figure 7–4, can be solved by a calculator that has natural trigonometric functions: the sines, cosines, and tangents of angles. The formula reads:

$$\text{Course to Steer} = \text{COG} - \sin^{-1}\left(\frac{\sin(\text{set} - \text{COG}) \times \text{drift}}{\text{boat-speed}}\right)$$

where COG represents the course to be made good and the boat-speed is the vessel's speed through the water. If you wish to find the actual speed made good along the intended track, a second formula applies:

$$\text{Speed Made Good} =$$

$$\cos(\text{set} - \text{COG}) \times \text{drift} + \sqrt{\text{boat-speed}^2 - \text{drift}^2 + [\cos(\text{set} - \text{COG}) \times \text{drift}]^2}$$

Here a combination of trigonometric functions and squares and square roots is used, and you will have to decide for yourself if it represents any time saving over the graphic solution described in Chapter 7.

Another piloting exercise that is often solved graphically also lends itself to a trigonometric solution on a scientific-level calculator: a distance-off determination by successive bearings on the same object. Figure 11–2 illustrates an example in which a navigator on course 090° takes a bearing of a fixed object from point **A**, reading 055°, and then, having run a distance of 1.2 miles to point **B**, takes another reading of the same object, now bearing 020°. How far will he be from the object at the second bearing, **B**, and what will the distance-off be when the object is abeam at point **C**?

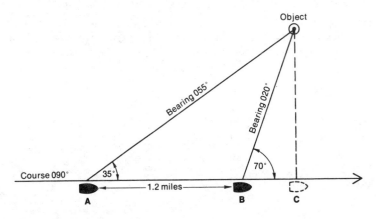

*Figure 11–2.* Distance off by two bearings, same object.

A formula for the solution to the first problem is:

$$\text{Distance-off at } b_2 = \frac{\text{Distance run} \times \sin (\text{course} - b_1)}{\sin (b_1 - b_2)}$$

where $b_1$ and $b_2$ are the first and second bearings, respectively. Experienced navigators may recognize this example as the classic, special case called "doubling the angle on the bow" (from 35° to 70° relative) and can confirm that in this example the distance-off is equal to the distance run, or 1.2 miles.

To find the distance-off when the object is abeam, a second calculation is made by the formula:

$$\text{Distance-off abeam} =$$
$$\text{Distance-off at } b_2 \times \text{Sin} (b_2 - \text{course} + 180°)$$

In our example, your calculator will quickly compute the distance-off abeam as being 1.1276 miles.

The examples that have been given in this chapter are only representative of the many types of navigation problems you can solve on an electronic calculator; the final list is limited only by your ingenuity in setting up the problem and your calculator technique in solving it. If you move on to the more complex exercises in celestial navigation, the potential time saving may make your calculator prove its worth even more. Piloting problems, such as those we have reviewed, are an excellent way to get a grounding in calculator science and practical experience in calculator use.

# 12 | Wrinkles in Piloting

A "wrinkle" in nautical parlance is any innovative idea for performing a task better or more easily—a "trick of the trade." In the navigational art, there are a number of these practical hints that even a novice can use effectively, and, as experience is gained through practice, there will be others he will discover on his own.

Probably the most understated of the strategems of the professional navigator is the concern with planning and preparation; the "forehandedness" described in Chapter 1. Checking to see that all of the charts and publications needed for a voyage are up-to-date and aboard is an obvious first step; but plotting courses and figuring the times of tide changes are among the other tasks that can be accomplished before leaving the dock, and under more comfortable circumstances than are likely to prevail once the vessel is under way. It is always a good idea on your own boat—and essential if you assume the navigator's duties on someone else's—to try out all the navigation equipment before you depart. Many an unsettling experience can be avoided if, in case conditions deteriorate unexpectedly, the navigator is familiar beforehand with the method of operation and the reliability of the equipment he may be counting on to bring him home safely.

Once under way, a well-prepared navigator will be ever alert to the surrounding scene, especially where changes are taking place. Noticing the current flow around buoys, the direction of smoke rising ashore, the movement of clouds—all the sights and sounds that add to his store of information—contributes in a major way to the effectiveness of his performance. The so-called "seaman's eye" is just that, and the ability to notice, to estimate, and to judge from the phenomena around you is the reward for constant and thoughtful observation.

There is a legitimate process called "eyeball navigation" that is akin to the seaman's eye. It involves such things as noting the color of the water—a good indication of the depth in tropical areas; finding objects to provide ranges or to act as leading marks; or observing the actions of other vessels preceding you, all of which may confirm or correct the information gathered from your more formal efforts.

As the voyage progresses, the practical navigator takes advantage of every opportunity to check his dead reckoning. Looking back as well as ahead is helpful in detecting drift from the intended track. Using the depth finder regularly helps confirm the position estimate or warns of impending danger. Checking off the buoys as they are passed eliminates confusion in a busy waterway and provides an opportunity to note any changes you discover, so as to make the return voyage easier. In reduced visibility it is good to plan your course so that it intercepts buoys at frequent intervals. These are all commonsense practices, yet it is easy for a casual novice to overlook them, thus making his own job harder.

A chart is a bird's-eye view of the area in which you are sailing. Learning to project yourself onto its surface and to envision the surroundings as seen from that vantage point is a wrinkle that takes practice but is well worth the effort. A corollary is the habit of going on deck after you have completed your chartwork, to see if the situation is as you expected it to be. There is simply no substitute for a thoughtful and observant navigator.

We have discussed currents and how experienced navigators take advantage of them to make the most efficient use of time and fuel. You will also want to reckon with cross-track drift, which can get you into trouble if you are not wary. One way of determining the natural leeway made by a boat under sail is to observe the angle between its heading and its wake. Another trick, if you haven't predetermined the proper course to steer, is to take a bearing on a leading mark ashore—or better still to find a natural range—and adjust your heading by eye until the bearing remains steady.

Estimating the current direction and velocity from a moving vessel is never easy, although you can learn a lot by observing the current flow past stationary objects or by noticing the current's effect on your progress along a given track. If you can't get the information from the current tables  but are aware of the state of the tide, you may be able to make an adequate approximation. If you think of the coastline as the edge of a large basin that fills and drains with the tide, a study of your chart and a little imagination may give you a good hint about the probable direction and possibly even the strength of the current.

Knowledge of the state of the tide is useful in other ways, too. When entering a strange harbor or an area where the charted depths appear to be critical, it is a good idea to plan your initial approach for mid-tide and while the tide is still flooding. "Half-tide and rising" was the early explorers' rule for entering an unfamiliar area  and is a practical rule for today's adventurous yachtsman. At mid-tide you will probably have a comfortable margin over the chart datum, even if minor shoaling has taken place since the chart was published, but best of all, if you run aground while proceeding slowly, the rising tide will enable you to float off.

In earlier chapters, we discussed the advent of the electronic age and its benefit to yacht navigation, particularly with respect to Loran, radio direction-finders, and calculators. The speed, accuracy, and all-weather capability of these modern devices are admirable, and they are extremely useful as long as the navigator knows that all the components are operating properly and understands their limitations clearly enough to be able to evaluate his results with confidence. Let's look at two examples that illustrate these points.

In Figure 12–1, the lines of position $A_1$ and $B_1$ are those derived from two time-difference readings on a Loran receiver. Because the signal had traveled partly over land and partly over water, a small error—the "secondary phase factor"—was introduced, and the true readings should have produced the lines $A_2$ and $B_2$. Add to this the fact that the LOPs intersect at a shallow angle—remember that an angle of less than 30° is to be avoided, if possible, even in terrestrial bearings—and you can see the area of uncertainty that is created. The navigator unaware of the anomaly can easily rely on an incorrect fix. This may not represent a serious problem out at sea, but it can be critical in confined pilot waters.

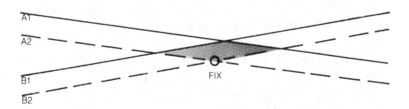

*Figure 12–1.* Small errors in LOPs, combined with small angles of intersection, can be a source of incorrect positioning when using Loran.

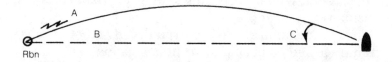

*Figure 12–2.* An RDF signal (A) follows a great-circle course, but may be plotted as a rhumb line, B, on a Mercator chart. A correction must be made for the angle, C, or the LOP will be in error.

Figure 12–2 illustrates a problem common to radio direction-finders. A radio signal travels by a great-circle course, **A,** while it is plotted on a conventional Mercator chart as a straight rhumb line, **B.** If the radiobeacon is at short range, the difference is unimportant, but if you are located at some distance east or west of the station, especially at high latitudes, a correction must be made to offset the angle **C** since it can otherwise lead to a significant error in your line of position.

You should recognize that calculators, like all electronic instruments, are delicate devices, while the environment on a small boat at sea is anything but ideal. A place must be found where your instrument will be least exposed to shock and moisture when it is in use, and where it can be properly protected when not in use. One way to protect the calculator is to provide a holder fastened to a convenient place on the chart table, allowing you to work the instrument with one hand, and preventing it from going adrift. Remember, too, to bring spare batteries if the calculator is not connected to the ship's power supply; a dead calculator is a liability.

Before starting any voyage during which you rely on a calculator for navigation, it is smart to review the programs you expect to use, and if they are new to you, or if you are rusty in the procedures, to test yourself with several dry runs. Underlying every calculator operation is the fact that the instrument is only a processing device. It can neither think for you nor can it expand your knowledge. This demands that you be thoroughly grounded in the principles of navigation and use your calculator as a means of facilitating computations, not as a shortcut to mastery of the subject. It must also be recognized that no matter how sophisticated an electronic instrument is, it can never be absolutely immune to failure. As a consequence, a prudent navigator always carries any necessary tables and essential backup equipment and knows how to use them if the need arises. Make sure you rank among the prudent.

As a final bit of advice, you should know that there comes a time in every navigator's career when he is uncertain of his results, and it can happen most readily when one is fatigued. This is the time for a cool head to prevail; not the time to panic or to forge ahead blindly. Good judgment requires that you take your time, go back over your work carefully, and determine if you have made a mistake in your calculations, or whether you may have failed to follow the procedures correctly. If you are ever unsure of the procedures, it will be worthwhile to review the applicable chapters in this book, or if you are having difficulty with the tables, don't overlook their excellent explanation sections.

As my old Navy chief used to say after every instruction session, "When all else fails, try reading the directions."

# 13 | Introduction to Celestial Navigation

"What can be more difficult than to guide a ship when only water and heaven may be seen?" So said the distinguished Spanish geographer, Martín Cortés, in the introduction to his celebrated navigational work in 1551. But times have changed; we live in the late twentieth century, and with the technical developments that have taken place since Cortés's day, celestial navigation has now become as easy as piloting. Finding one's way on the open sea by means of the heavenly array is, in fact, a logical extension of the technique of coastwise piloting, the most notable difference being that celestial bodies are constantly in motion relative to the observer, while charted, terrestrial objects remain stationary.

Why should one learn celestial navigation in these modern times? Aren't we living in the electronic age, where position finding is supposed to be a mere matter of pushing buttons? It is true that, within their limits, some of the marvelous new devices, such as radio direction-finders, or Loran, or satellite navigators, may be as useful offshore as they are in coastal waters, but it is equally true that, like any electronic device, they can never be entirely immune to failure, particularly in the environment of a yacht at sea. Celestial navigation, being self-contained and dependent only on the navigator, therefore remains as the ultimate backup—the one method that will bring you home when all else fails. At the same time, there is an extraordinary personal satisfaction in knowing that you can pinpoint your position at sea, using similar tools and sighting the same sun, moon, and stars as did the great navigators of history. For many of us, that satisfaction is reason enough to rely on celestial as our primary means of offshore navigation.

This section of the book begins with the assumption that you are thoroughly familiar with the fundamentals of piloting, particularly those described in Chapters 7 and 8. At the first point you become at all uncertain, it is recommended that you review your piloting before proceeding further. In addition to the charts, protractor, and dividers you have used in piloting, there are a few more tools needed for celestial navigation: a sextant for making an observation, a watch for timing it, and an almanac and sight-reduction table for converting the sight into a line of position.

The system taught here (based upon the *Nautical Almanac* and DMA Pub. No. 249) is the fastest and easiest tabular system that is available today. Its accuracy is entirely compatible with that of observations made from a yacht, and the speed of solution, in the hands of a capable navigator, is comparable to that of a manual calculator. The most sophisticated calculators—those programmed specifically to solve celestial problems—may be still faster, and for those interested, we will explore their use as a substitute for the tables, in Chapter 25. Always remember, however, that calculators possess the same frailties as other delicate electronic instruments, and every prudent navigator should acquire a thorough understanding of the tabular method as a precautionary measure in case of equipment failure.

There are two basic approaches to learning celestial navigation. Traditionally, the theory of celestial mechanics was mastered first, and only then did the practical experience begin. The opposite approach, and the one I prefer, is to start with practical exposure—picking up the sextant and making an actual observation—and then, after having learned the technique, you can review the underlying theory if you're interested. I subscribe to the principle that one doesn't have to understand the theory of the internal-combustion engine to be able to drive an automobile; that practical experience is much more important. Accordingly, Chapters 14–19 are devoted to the practice of taking and solving a sun sight—just as you would do it aboard a yacht—and that process is extended, in Chapters 20–22, to include the moon, the planets, and the stars. Chapter 24 contains a brief overview of celestial theory, but if you need still more background to satisfy you, the classic texts, "Bowditch" and "Dutton," which were mentioned in the preface, are excellent for reference.

In piloting, besides plotting the course and keeping track of the dead-reckoning position, you took bearings on fixed objects, such as lighthouses and prominent landmarks, and plotted those observations as lines of position on your chart. You will recall that the intersection of two or more position lines produced a fix, independent of any previous position, and that lines of position obtained by radio direction-finder, radar, Loran, or other electronic means could be used in exactly the same manner as, and in conjunction with, lines obtained visually.

You are well on your way to taking the mystery out of celestial navigation when you realize that the result of a celestial observation is simply another line of position, and that the lines obtained by this method are no different then any other position lines and can be used in all the same ways.

So, leaving the theory until later, let's review the six easy steps that are involved, from the time you select the celestial body you will "shoot," to the plotting of the resulting line of position on your chart or plotting sheet.

- Making the sextant observation
- Taking the time of the sight
- Extracting data from the almanac
- Calculating the computed altitude
- Determining intercept and azimuth
- Plotting the line of position

In celestial navigation, as in any specialized human activity, practitioners have built up a vocabulary over the years, which is often unintelligible to a layman. But don't despair; I'll give you a working definition of the more frequently used terms as we go along, and for ready reference, there is a glossary at the back of the book. Many of the standard terms also appear in abbreviated form, and a list of the most common abbreviations is given on pages 140–141 and repeated in the glossary.

## Abbreviations Commonly Used in Celestial Navigation

| | |
|---|---|
| **a** | Altitude difference, or intercept |
| **aλ** | Assumed longitude |
| **aL** | Assumed latitude |
| **A** | Away |
| **AP** | Assumed position |
| **corr** | Correction to a tabulated value |
| **d** | Declination hourly change, or tabular altitude differential |
| **D** | Dip; correction for observer's height of eye |
| **Dec (dec)** | Declination of a celestial body |
| **DR** | Dead reckoning (position) |
| **GHA (gha)** | Greenwich hour angle |
| **GMT** | Greenwich mean time |
| **GP** | Geographical position (of a celestial body on earth) |
| **ha (App. Alt.)** | Apparent altitude |
| **hs** | Sextant altitude |
| **Hc** | Computed altitude |
| **Ho** | Observed altitude |
| **H.P.** | Horizontal parallax |
| **IC** | Index correction |

| | |
|---|---|
| **incr** | Incremental value |
| **L** | Lower limb |
| **LAN** | Local apparent noon |
| **LHA** | Local hour angle |
| **Mer Pass** | Meridian passage (time of) |
| **R** | Refraction corrections |
| **SHA** | Sidereal hour angle |
| **T** | Toward |
| **Tab** | Tabular value |
| **U** | Upper limb |
| **UTC** | Coordinated universal time |
| *v* | Small, variable corrections |
| **W** | Watch time |
| **z** | Zenith distance |
| **Z** | Uncorrected azimuth angle |
| **ZD** | Zone description |
| **Zn** | True azimuth |
| ♈ | First point of Aries (Vernal Equinox) |
| ° | Degrees |
| ′ | Minutes (of arc) |

# 14 | Sextant Observation: The Sun

The sextant observation is the one part of the celestial process in which the navigator's personal skill plays an essential role in its success, and this is especially true when the sight is made from the bouncing deck of a small boat. It has been said that the rest of the procedure has been reduced to "telephone-book arithmetic," which I can leave to you to judge, but becoming proficient in using a sextant is a question of practice—a true case of learning by doing.

A great deal has been written about the subtleties of selecting a sextant, but I have been able to achieve acceptable results with a plastic, lifeboat sextant, as well as with a brass instrument made in the mid-1800s for the clipper-ship trade. I have navigated halfway around the world with a Navy Mark 2 from World War II and have sailed the other half with a modern C. Plath, which is one of the finest available. My conclusion is that you can get a sound grounding in the fundamentals with almost any workable instrument, and your final selection can wait until you have accumulated enough practice to be able to make a personal judgment.

All modern marine sextants are similar in concept, based on the double-reflecting-mirror precept first suggested by Sir Isaac Newton in 1700. The principal parts are illustrated in Figure 14–1.

The purpose of the sextant is to make precise measurements of the altitude (the angular distance above the horizon) of a celestial body. The actual measuring is done by sighting the horizon through the clear portion of the horizon mirror, and then, by adjusting the sextant's movable index arm, the reflected image of the observed body is brought into coincidence with the horizon line. The altitude is read in whole degrees on the scale of the main arc, or limb, and in fractional parts by means of the auxiliary scale—on the model illustrated, on the micrometer drum.

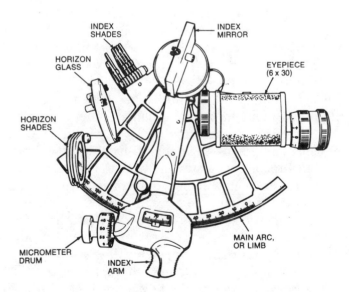

*Figure 14–1.* **The Principal Parts of a Modern Marine Sextant.**

Sextants come with two varieties of horizon glasses: the conventional, half-silvered kind, in which the horizon is viewed through the clear half, and the body's reflected image in the mirrored half; and the new "whole-horizon" glass, in which the entire surface is both transparent and reflective, like a one-way mirror. Modern sextants are equipped with two sets of shades. The index shades are essential in an observation of the sun, because the intensity of the reflected image can cause injury to the unprotected eye. The horizon shades are designed to reduce the glare if the horizon appears to be too bright, thereby aiding the task of taking precise measurements.

Whatever model you choose, remember that your sextant is a precision optical instrument, and proper care is a key to its performance. The two main enemies of a sextant aboard a yacht are the damp, salt-laden atmosphere, and exposure to physical shock. While the risk of damage can never be eliminated entirely, it can be substantially reduced by keeping the instrument protected from salt spray, to the extent possible, and by always returning it to its case, and stowing the case securely between sights. I suggest to beginners that they treat their sextants like fine china; then they will be ready to perform properly when needed.

Let's start first with a simple sun sight, probably the sight you will take more often than all others combined. This is not to discourage you in any way from trying the other celestial bodies—in fact, your technique will profit by it—but I recommend starting with the sun and learning it well, since it will be your constant companion. Let's assume we are off the New England coast on a fine, clear summer day, say, June 8, 1984, and you have come on deck just before noon to take your first sight. Holding the sextant in your right hand, swing down the darkest of the index shades, and, looking through the eyepiece, sight the horizon through the horizon glass. Then, moving the index arm with your left hand, bring the reflected image of the sun in the mirrored portion of the horizon glass down to the horizon line at which you have been aiming. Shifting your left hand to the micrometer drum, or to other means of fine adjustment, bring the sun's bottom edge—its "lower limb"—into exact coincidence with the visible horizon.

You will find that it takes less time to do it than to tell about it, but an experienced navigator will take a second or two more to rotate the sextant about the line of sight to the horizon, simply to make sure that the reflected image is at the very lowest part of its apparent arc, and that the sextant is being held absolutely vertically. Figure 14–2

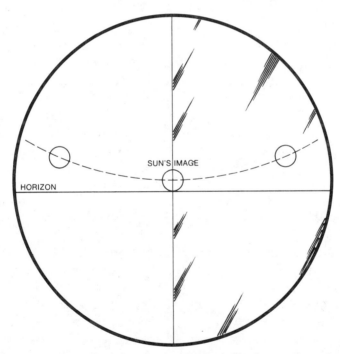

*Figure 14–2.* Rocking the Sextant. The sun's image appears to describe an arc in the horizon glass when the sextant is rotated about the line of sight to the horizon. The correct altitude is measured at the lowest point of the arc.

illustrates the technique, known as rocking the sextant. This is how the sun's image would appear in a circular horizon glass as the sextant is being rocked. The instrument will be exactly vertical at the lowest part of the arc described, and that is the point where the altitude measurement should be made. Some sextants are equipped with a prism device attached to the horizon glass, giving the observer an indication if the instrument is not being held correctly, but however you check it, the altitude will be incorrectly high if the sight is not taken· in a true vertical plane.

Traditionally, sextant altitudes are expressed in degrees (°), minutes ('), and tenths of minutes. The angular measurement from the horizon to your zenith, directly overhead, is 90°00'. There are 60 minutes of arc in each whole degree, and 60 seconds in each minute, although tenths of minutes are more commonly used in celestial navigation. You shouldn't have any difficulty reading your sextant, but to avoid careless errors, it's always a good idea to read the whole degrees first from the main arc, and then the minutes and any fractions from the micrometer drum or vernier. The sextant illustrated in Figure 14–3, set for the hypothetical sun sight you have just taken, reads 69° on the main arc, 48' on the micrometer drum, and 0.5' on its vernier. The sextant altitude is, therefore, 69°48.5', or, as it is abbreviated by navigators, 69–48.5.

Having determined the sextant altitude (hs), it must be corrected for such things as errors that might be inherent in the instrument, the difference between the line of sight to your visible horizon and the true horizontal, and for the bending of light rays as they travel through the earth's atmosphere; small corrections, to be sure, but important for accuracy in your sight calculations. The first correction, called the index correction (IC), is necessary because even the finest sextant cannot be expected to stay in perfect adjustment. IC is determined before or

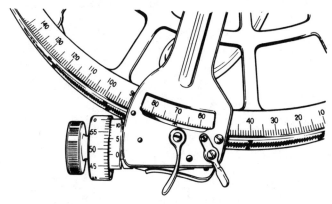

*Figure 14–3.* **Reading the Sextant. Whole degrees are read from the main arc, or limb; minutes and tenths from the micrometer drum or vernier. The reading illustrated is 69° 48.5'.**

after taking a sight by setting the index arm at zero degrees and aiming the sextant at the horizon. The horizon line may appear to be slightly offset between the clear and the reflecting portions of the horizon glass. Using the fine adjustment, the horizon line is brought back into coincidence, and the sextant read. The correction needed to bring that reading back to zero is the index correction. It is good practice to check the IC each time a sextant is used, but one check will suffice for a simultaneous series of sights. In our exercise, let's say that you checked your sextant just before shooting the sun and found that when the horizon line was exactly straight the instrument read 2.4', not zero. Then, IC is minus 2.4', the amount necessary to bring the reading back to zero.

The second correction is for dip (D). This is to compensate for the slight difference in the angle between the true horizontal and the line of sight to the horizon as you view it from your elevated position on deck. The effect of dip is to cause the measured altitude to be too high, so that the correction, based on the observer's height of eye

## ALTITUDE CORRECTION TABLES 10°-90°—SUN, STARS, PLANETS

| OCT.—MAR. SUN APR.—SEPT. | | | | | | STARS AND PLANETS | | | | DIP | | | | | |
|---|---|---|---|---|---|---|---|---|---|---|---|---|---|---|---|
| App. Alt. | Lower Limb | Upper Limb | App. Alt. | Lower Limb | Upper Limb | App. Alt. | Corrⁿ | App. Alt. | Additional Corrⁿ | Ht. of Eye | Corrⁿ | Ht. of Eye | Corrⁿ | Ht. of Eye | Corrⁿ |
| | | | | | | | | | **1984** | m | | ft. | | m | |
| 9 34 | 10·8 | 21 5 | 9 39 | 10·6 | 21 2 | 9 56 | 5·3 | | **VENUS** | 2·4 | 2·8 | 8·0 | 8·6 | 1·0 — 1·8 | |
| 9 45 | 10·9 | 21 4 | 9 51 | 10·7 | 21 1 | 10 08 | 5·2 | | Jan. 1-Dec. 12 | 2·6 | 2·9 | 8·6 | 9·2 | 1·5 — 2·2 | |
| 9 56 | 11·0 | 21 3 | 10 03 | 10·8 | 21 0 | 10 20 | 5·1 | | | 2·8 | 3·0 | 9·2 | 9·8 | 2·0 — 2·5 | |
| 10 08 | 11·1 | 21 2 | 10 15 | 10·9 | 20 9 | 10 33 | 5·0 | | 0 | 3·0 | 3·1 | 9·8 | 10·5 | 2·5 — 2·8 | |
| 10 21 | 11·2 | 21 1 | 10 27 | 11·0 | 20 8 | 10 46 | 4·9 | 60 | + 0·1 | 3·2 | 3·2 | 10·5 | | 3·0 — 3·0 | |
| 10 34 | 11·3 | 21 0 | 10 40 | 11·1 | 20 7 | 11 00 | 4·8 | | Dec. 13-Dec. 31 | 3·4 | 3·3 | 11·2 | | See table | |
| 10 47 | 11·4 | 20 9 | 10 54 | 11·2 | 20 6 | 11 14 | 4·7 | | | 3·6 | 3·4 | 11·9 | | | |
| 11 01 | 11·5 | 20 8 | 11 08 | 11·3 | 20 5 | 11 29 | 4·6 | 0 | | 3·8 | 3·5 | 12·6 | | m | |
| 11 15 | 11·6 | 20 7 | 11 23 | 11·4 | 20 4 | 11 45 | 4·5 | 41 | + 0·2 | 4·0 | 3·6 | 13·3 | | 20 — 7·9 | |
| 11 30 | 11·7 | 20 6 | 11 38 | 11·5 | 20 3 | 12 01 | 4·4 | 76 | + 0·1 | 4·3 | 3·7 | 14·1 | | 22 — 8·3 | |
| 11 46 | 11·8 | 20 5 | 11 54 | 11·6 | 20 2 | 12 18 | 4·3 | | | 4·5 | 3·8 | 14·9 | | 24 — 8·6 | |
| 12 02 | 11·9 | 20 4 | 12 10 | 11·7 | 20 1 | 12 35 | 4·2 | | | 4·7 | 3·9 | 15·7 | | 26 — 9·0 | |
| 12 19 | 12·0 | 20 3 | 12 28 | 11·8 | 20 0 | 12 54 | 4·1 | | **MARS** | 5·0 | 4·0 | 16·5 | | 28 — 9·3 | |
| 12 37 | 12·1 | 20 2 | 12 46 | 11·9 | 19 9 | 13 13 | 4·0 | | Jan. 1-Mar. 4 | 5·2 | 4·1 | 17·4 | | | |
| 12 55 | 12·2 | 20 1 | 13 05 | 12·0 | 19 8 | 13 33 | 3·9 | | | 5·5 | 4·2 | 18·3 | | 30 — 9·6 | |
| 13 14 | 12·3 | 20 0 | 13 24 | 12·1 | 19 7 | 13 54 | 3·8 | 0 | | 5·8 | 4·3 | 19·1 | | 32 — 10·0 | |
| 13 35 | 12·4 | 19 9 | 13 45 | 12·2 | 19 6 | 14 16 | 3·7 | 60 | + 0·1 | 6·1 | 4·4 | 20·1 | | 34 — 10·3 | |
| 13 56 | 12·5 | 19 8 | 14 07 | 12·3 | 19 5 | 14 40 | 3·6 | | Mar. 5-Apr. 24 | 6·3 | 4·5 | 21·0 | | 36 — 10·6 | |
| 14 18 | 12·6 | 19 7 | 14 30 | 12·4 | 19 4 | 15 04 | 3·5 | | | 6·6 | 4·6 | 22·0 | | 38 — 10·8 | |
| 14 42 | 12·7 | 19 6 | 14 54 | 12·5 | 19 3 | 15 30 | 3·4 | 0 | | 6·9 | 4·7 | 22·9 | | | |
| 15 06 | 12·8 | 19 5 | 15 19 | 12·6 | 19 2 | 15 57 | 3·3 | 41 | + 0·2 | 7·2 | 4·8 | 23·9 | | 40 — 11·1 | |
| 15 32 | 12·9 | 19 4 | 15 46 | 12·7 | 19 1 | 16 26 | 3·2 | 76 | + 0·1 | 7·5 | 4·9 | 24·9 | | 42 — 11·4 | |
| 15 59 | 13·0 | 19 3 | 16 14 | 12·8 | 19 0 | 16 56 | 3·1 | | Apr. 25-June 15 | 7·9 | 5·0 | 26·0 | | 44 — 11·7 | |
| 16 28 | 13·1 | 19 2 | 16 44 | 12·9 | 18 9 | 17 28 | 3·0 | | | 8·2 | 5·1 | 27·1 | | 46 — 11·9 | |
| 16 59 | 13·2 | 19 1 | 17 15 | 13·0 | 18 8 | 18 02 | 2·9 | 0 | | 8·5 | 5·2 | 28·1 | | 48 — 12·2 | |
| 17 32 | 13·3 | 19 0 | 17 48 | 13·1 | 18 7 | 18 38 | 2·8 | 34 | + 0·3 | 8·8 | 5·3 | 29·2 | | | |
| 18 06 | 13·4 | 18 9 | 18 24 | 13·2 | 18 6 | 19 17 | 2·7 | 60 | + 0·2 | 9·2 | 5·4 | 30·4 | | ft. | |
| 18 42 | 13·5 | 18 8 | 19 01 | 13·3 | 18 5 | 19 58 | 2·6 | 80 | + 0·1 | 9·5 | 5·5 | 31·5 | | 2 — 1·4 | |
| 19 21 | 13·6 | 18 7 | 19 42 | 13·4 | 18 4 | 20 42 | 2·5 | | June 16-Aug. 27 | 9·9 | 5·6 | 32·7 | | 4 — 1·9 | |
| 20 03 | 13·7 | 18 6 | 20 25 | 13·5 | 18 3 | 21 28 | 2·4 | 0 | | 10·3 | 5·7 | 33·9 | | 6 — 2·4 | |
| 20 48 | 13·8 | 18 5 | 21 11 | 13·6 | 18 2 | 22 19 | 2·3 | 41 | + 0·2 | 10·6 | 5·8 | 35·1 | | 8 — 2·7 | |
| 21 35 | 13·9 | 18 4 | 22 00 | 13·7 | 18 1 | 23 13 | 2·2 | 76 | + 0·1 | 11·0 | 5·9 | 36·3 | | 10 — 3·1 | |
| 22 26 | 14·0 | 18 3 | 22 54 | 13·8 | 18 0 | 24 11 | 2·1 | | Aug. 28-Dec. 31 | 11·4 | 6·0 | 37·6 | | See table | |
| 23 22 | 14·1 | 18 2 | 23 51 | 13·9 | 17 9 | 25 14 | 2·0 | 0 | | 11·8 | 6·1 | 38·9 | | | |
| 24 21 | 14·2 | 18 1 | 24 53 | 14·0 | 17 8 | 26 22 | 1·9 | 60 | + 0·1 | 12·2 | 6·2 | 40·1 | | ft. | |
| 25 26 | 14·3 | 18 0 | 26 00 | 14·1 | 17 7 | 27 36 | 1·8 | | | 12·6 | 6·3 | 41·5 | | 70 — 8·1 | |
| 26 36 | 14·4 | 17 9 | 27 13 | 14·2 | 17 6 | 28 56 | 1·7 | | | 13·0 | 6·4 | 42·8 | | 75 — 8·4 | |
| 27 52 | 14·5 | 17 8 | 28 33 | 14·3 | 17 5 | 30 24 | 1·6 | | | 13·4 | 6·5 | 44·2 | | 80 — 8·7 | |
| 29 15 | 14·6 | 17 7 | 30 00 | 14·4 | 17 4 | 32 00 | 1·5 | | | 13·8 | 6·6 | 45·5 | | 85 — 8·9 | |
| 30 46 | 14·7 | 17 6 | 31 35 | 14·5 | 17 3 | 33 45 | 1·4 | | | 14·2 | 6·7 | 46·9 | | 90 — 9·2 | |
| 32 26 | 14·8 | 17 5 | 33 20 | 14·6 | 17 2 | 35 40 | 1·3 | | | 14·7 | 6·8 | 48·4 | | 95 — 9·5 | |
| 34 17 | 14·9 | 17 4 | 35 17 | 14·7 | 17 1 | 37 48 | 1·2 | | | 15·1 | 6·9 | 49·8 | | | |
| 36 20 | 15·0 | 17 3 | 37 26 | 14·8 | 17 0 | 40 08 | 1·1 | | | 15·5 | 7·0 | 51·3 | | 100 — 9·7 | |
| 38 36 | 15·1 | 17 2 | 39 50 | 14·9 | 16 9 | 42 44 | 1·0 | | | 16·0 | 7·1 | 52·8 | | 105 — 9·9 | |
| 41 08 | 15·2 | 17 1 | 42 31 | 15·0 | 16 8 | 45 36 | 0·9 | | | 16·5 | 7·2 | 54·3 | | 110 — 10·2 | |
| 43 59 | 15·3 | 17 0 | 45 31 | 15·1 | 16 7 | 48 47 | 0·8 | | | 16·9 | 7·3 | 55·8 | | 115 — 10·4 | |
| 47 10 | 15·4 | 16 9 | 48 55 | 15·2 | 16 6 | 52 18 | 0·7 | | | 17·4 | 7·4 | 57·4 | | 120 — 10·6 | |
| 50 46 | 15·5 | 16 8 | 52 44 | 15·3 | 16 5 | 56 11 | 0·6 | | | 17·9 | 7·5 | 58·9 | | 125 — 10·8 | |
| 54 49 | 15·6 | 16 7 | 57 02 | 15·4 | 16 4 | 60 28 | 0·5 | | | 18·4 | 7·6 | 60·5 | | | |
| 59 23 | 15·7 | 16 6 | 61 51 | 15·5 | 16 3 | 65 08 | 0·4 | | | 18·8 | 7·7 | 62·1 | | 130 — 11·1 | |
| 64 30 | 15·8 | 16 5 | 67 17 | 15·6 | 16 2 | 70 11 | 0·3 | | | 19·3 | 7·8 | 63·8 | | 135 — 11·3 | |
| 70 12 | 15·9 | 16 4 | 73 16 | 15·7 | 16 1 | 75 34 | 0·2 | | | 19·8 | 7·9 | 65·4 | | 140 — 11·5 | |
| 76 26 | 16·0 | 16 3 | 79 43 | 15·8 | 16 0 | 81 13 | 0·1 | | | 20·4 | 8·0 | 67·1 | | 145 — 11·7 | |
| 83 05 | 16·1 | 16 2 | 86 32 | 15·9 | 15 9 | 87 03 | 0·1 | | | 20·9 | 8·1 | 68·8 | | 150 — 11·9 | |
| 90 00 | | | 90 00 | | | 90 00 | 0·0 | | | 21·4 | | 70·5 | | 155 — 12·1 | |

App. Alt. = Apparent altitude = Sextant altitude corrected for index error and dip.

*Figure 14–4.* **Example of Altitude Correction Tables from the *Nautical Almanac*.**

above the surface, is always negative. The value of the D-correction is taken from the DIP column in the almanac's altitude correction tables, an example of which is shown in Figure 14–4.

The altitude tables are of a type called critical tables; that is, a table in which a single value is tabulated for all readings between limiting entry values. Referring to the excerpt from the dip table in Figure 14–5, for your height of eye at the time of your sun sight, which, let's assume, was 9 feet, the D-correction would be –2.9', the correction for all heights of eye between 8.6 and 9.2 feet.

Taking the net total of the IC and D-corrections, and applying that to the sextant altitude, you arrive at an intermediate value called apparent altitude (ha). This value is then used to find the third and final altitude correction, the refraction, or R-correction. In our example, the IC of –2.4', and the D-correction of –2.9' total –5.3', which, when applied to the hs of 69°48.5', produces an ha of 69°43.2'.

| DIP | | | | |
|---|---|---|---|---|
| Ht. of Eye | Corrⁿ | Ht. of Eye | Ht. of Eye | Corrⁿ |
| m | | ft. | m | |
| 2·4 | 2·8 | 8·0 | 1·0 | 1·8 |
| 2·6 | | 8·6 | 1·5 | 2·2 |
| 2·8 | 2·9 | 9·2 | 2·0 | 2·5 |
| 3·0 | 3·0 | 9·8 | 2·5 | 2·8 |
| 3·2 | 3·1 | 10·5 | 3·0 | 3·0 |
| 3·4 | 3·2 | 11·2 | See table |  |
| 3·6 | 3·3 | 11·9 |  |  |
| 3·8 | 3·4 | 12·6 |  |  |
| 4·0 | 3·5 | 13·3 | m | |
| 4·3 | 3·6 | 14·1 | 20 | 7·9 |
| 4·5 | 3·7 | 14·9 | 22 | 8·3 |
| 4·7 | 3·8 | 15·7 | 24 | 8·6 |
|  | 3·9 |  | 26 | 9·0 |

*Figure 14–5.* Excerpt from the DIP table showing the D-correction of –2.9' for a height of eye of 9 feet.

To determine the final altitude correction, enter the SUN column of the almanac tables, a portion of which is shown in Figure 14–6. Strictly speaking, the almanac designers have lumped several corrections together, all of which depend on the apparent altitude, so, for conven-

**ALTITUDE CORRECTION TABLES 10°-90°**

| OCT.—MAR. | **SUN** | APR.—SEPT. | | | |
|---|---|---|---|---|---|
| App. Alt. | Lower Limb | Upper Limb | App. Alt. | Lower Limb | Upper Limb |
| 9 34 | + 10·8 | − 21·5 | 9 39 | + 10·6 | − 21·2 |
| 9 45 | + 10·9 | − 21·4 | 9 51 | + 10·7 | − 21·1 |
| 9 56 | + 11·0 | 21·3 | 10 03 | + 10·8 | 21·0 |
| 10 08 | + 11·1 | 21·2 | 10 15 | + 10·9 | − 20·9 |
| 10 21 | + 11·2 | 21·1 | 10 27 | + 11·0 | 20·8 |
| 10 34 | + 11·3 | − 21·0 | 10 40 | + 11·1 | 20·7 |
| 10 47 | + 11·4 | − 20·9 | 10 54 | + 11·2 | − 20·6 |
| 11 01 | + 11·5 | − 20·8 | 11 08 | + 11·3 | 20·5 |
| 11 15 | + 11·6 | − 20·7 | 11 23 | + 11·4 | 20·4 |
| 11 30 | + 11·7 | − 20·6 | 11 38 | + 11·5 | − 20·3 |
| 11 46 | + 11·8 | 20·5 | 11 54 | + 11·6 | − 20·2 |
| 43 59 | + 15·3 | − 17·0 | 45 31 | + 15·1 | 16·7 |
| 47 10 | + 15·4 | − 16·9 | 48 55 | + 15·2 | − 16·6 |
| 50 46 | + 15·5 | − 16·8 | 52 44 | + 15·3 | − 16·5 |
| 54 49 | + 15·6 | − 16·7 | 57 02 | + 15·4 | − 16·4 |
| 59 23 | + 15·7 | − 16·6 | 61 51 | + 15·5 | − 16·3 |
| 64 30 | + 15·8 | 16·5 | 67 17 | + 15·6 | − 16·2 |
| 70 12 | + 15·9 | 16·4 | 73 16 | + 15·7 | 16·1 |
| 76 26 | + 16·0 | − 16·3 | 79 43 | + 15·8 | 16·0 |
| 83 05 | + 16·1 | − 16·2 | 86 32 | + 15·9 | − 15·9 |
| 90 00 | | | 90 00 | | |

App. Alt. = Apparent altitude = Sextant altitude corrected for index error and dip.

*Figure 14–6.* **Portion of the *Nautical Almanac*'s Altitude Correction Tables, showing an R-correction of + 15.6′ to an observation of the sun's lower limb in June, at an apparent altitude of 69°43.2′.**

ience, we can deal with them all as a single correction. Having shot the sun in June, enter the APR.-SEPT. column under "Lower Limb," and with the ha of 69°43.2′, find the R-correction of +15.6′ between the appropriate critical values. Notice that we were careful to use the lower-limb values; had we brought the upper limb (the top of the sun's disc) to the horizon, the correction would have been −16.2′ for the same apparent altitude—a substantial difference if one is in error. Adding the +15.6′-correction to our apparent altitude, we have determined the "observed altitude" (Ho)—in our case, 69°58.8′—which we will set aside while we proceed with the next three steps.

Every navigator worth his salt keeps a workbook, and one handy way to do this is with standardized forms that provide headings for prompting, and boxes for recording figures as they are obtained, thus providing both a permanent record and a regular routine, which reduces the chance of error. There are as many variations of workforms as there are navigators, and you will eventually find forms that suit you best. The Appendix contains blank workbook forms that I have found to be most useful, and all the practical examples in this book have been worked out on those forms. If we had been keeping one with the data we have accumulated until now, it would look like this:

| DATE | June 8, 1984 |
|------|--------------|
| BODY | Sun ☾ |
| hs | 69– 48.5 |
| IC | – 2.4 |
| D | – 2.9 |
| ha | 69– 43.2 |
| R | + 15.6 |
| Ho | 69 – 58.8 |

The symbol ☉ indicates that the observation was of the sun's lower limb, and you will see all the other pertinent values and algebraic totals that were entered as we went along. We will continue with the form as we move on to the next step, taking the time of the sight.

# 15 | Timing the Sight

In navigating through coastal waters, timing a bearing to the nearest minute is usually good enough, because the vessel is moving relatively slowly, and the landmarks are fixed. In celestial observations, however, the bodies from which position lines are derived are constantly in motion with respect to the earth, and accurate positioning requires timing to the nearest *second*. In an exercise like your sun sight, for example, being 1 minute off in time could mean being up to 15 miles off in position.

Historically, the difficulty in obtaining accurate time was the navigator's nemesis, but the advent of electronic watches, and the availability of radio time signals anywhere in the world, make it an easy matter today. Time, in fact, has enjoyed the most rapid technological advance of any part of the navigational art. Clock time, actually a measure of the earth's rotation, was first reckoned in terms of celestial phenomena, then later by mechanical means, and today, with extraordinary precision, by using the vibrations of atoms as the regulator.

Although we still relate time to the sun's apparent movement, the development of accurate clocks showed that that movement, due to variations in the earth's rotation, is not uniform. As a consequence, a fictitious "mean sun" is imagined to be moving westward at a constant 15 degrees per hour, averaging out the irregularities so that we can measure time in a consistent manner. In our civil lives in North America, we divide that average 24-hour day into two 12-hour segments, A.M. (ante meridian) and P.M. (post meridian), to distinguish between events occurring before or after noon. In many parts of the world, and universally for navigational purposes, the 24-hour clock is used, and time is expressed as four digits, such as 0705 for 7:05 A.M., or 1645 for 4:45 P.M.

For convenience, most people like to think of the sun rising and setting at prescribed times wherever they are, but if a single, universal time were used, the phenomena would occur at different times in each location. So, a series of time zones was established, in which geographical regions adopted a common standard time more nearly representative of solar time in their area. Starting in 1883, with the adoption by the railroads of four time zones for the continental United States, the scheme is now used worldwide. The zones are generally established at 15° intervals (representing 1 hour's movement of the mean sun) centered at Greenwich, England, where 0° longitude was established by international agreement. Each time zone is identified by a "zone description" (ZD), which is expressed as the number of whole hours that must be applied to the local zone time to obtain the correct time at Greenwich. Figure 15–1 lists the 24 zones and their prescribed limits and zone descriptions. In some instances, boundaries may be arbitrarily adjusted to conform to local custom, or, as in the case of daylight saving time, an area may choose to keep the time of the adjacent zone to their east. The standard times kept in various places or countries are listed in the almanac.

| ZONE | ZD | SUFFIX |
|------|----|--------|
| Time Zones, Zone Descriptions, and Suffixes | | |
| 7½°W. to   7½°E. ......... | 0 | Z |
| 7½°E. to  22½°E. ......... | − 1 | A |
| 22½°E. to  37½°E. ......... | − 2 | B |
| 37½°E. to  52½°E. ......... | − 3 | C |
| 52½°E. to  67½°E. ......... | − 4 | D |
| 67½°E. to  82½°E. ......... | − 5 | E |
| 82½°E. to  97½°E. ......... | − 6 | F |
| 97½°E. to 112½°E. ......... | − 7 | G |
| 112½°E. to 127½°E. ......... | − 8 | H |
| 127½°E. to 142½°E. ......... | − 9 | I |
| 142½°E. to 157½°E. ......... | −10 | K |
| 157½°E. to 172½°E. ......... | −11 | L |
| 172½°E. to 180° ........... | −12 | M |
| 7½°W. to  22½°W. ....... | + 1 | N |
| 22½°W. to  37½°W. ....... | + 2 | O |
| 37½°W. to  52½°W. ....... | + 3 | P |
| 52½°W. to  67½°W. ....... | + 4 | Q |
| 67½°W. to  82½°W. ....... | + 5 | R |
| 82½°W. to  97½°W. ....... | + 6 | S |
| 97½°W. to 112½°W. ....... | + 7 | T |
| 112½°W. to 127½°W. ....... | + 8 | U |
| 127½°W. to 142½°W. ....... | + 9 | V |
| 142½°W. to 157½°W. ....... | +10 | W |
| 157½°W. to 172½°W. ....... | +11 | X |
| 172½°W. to 180° ........... | +12 | Y |

*Figure 15–1.* **Time Zones and their Zone Descriptions from Bowditch,** *American Practical Navigator,* **Table 36.**

It is the normal practice at sea to set the ship's clocks to the time of the zone in which you are sailing, advancing or retarding them by an hour as you move from zone to zone. Thus, in Longitude 75°W, with a normal ZD of +5, 7 A.M. is the equivalent of noon in Greenwich. During the summer months, when daylight saving time is in effect, the ZD for the 75°W-zone advances to +4, so 0700 then is only 1100 in Greenwich.

As a convention, the time at Greenwich has been adopted as the universal time for celestial navigation. The almanac presents all of its astronomical data in terms of Greenwich mean time (GMT), although that can, of course, be converted to any local time by applying the zone description. Present-day technology has, to an extent, outstripped historical convention, and with the exceptional accuracy of atomic clocks, it has been discovered that time based on the mean sun is no longer exact. So, a new term, *coordinated universal time* (UTC), more closely tied to the earth's actual rotation, is used by technicians, and is the basis for the Bureau of Standards' radio time-broadcasts. UTC, as broadcast, may vary by a fraction of a second from Greenwich mean time as used in the almanac, but for practical purposes, celestial navigators can use the two times interchangeably.

Since the almanac data are presented in terms of Greenwich mean time, using the 24-hour clock, I find it easiest to set a digital watch to GMT, so that the exact time of a sight can be read out directly. Whenever possible, experienced navigators try to check a timepiece daily by radio time-ticks, and if it is a simple matter to reset it, the watch can always display the correct time. If you don't choose to keep Greenwich time on your watch, or if you don't wish to reset it, you can simply compare its reading with the correct time, make a note of the error, and apply the necessary correction when you record the time of your sight.

At sea, unless you are fortunate enough to have a fellow crew member to read the time and record it for you, you have to time your sights yourself. I have found it handiest in that circumstance to move my watch to the inside of my left wrist, or to hold it in the palm of my left hand, and then, at the instant that the reflected image touches the horizon, I glance first at the watch time and record it and then read the sextant at my convenience.

Returning now to our practical example, let's assume that you have your watch time (W) set to GMT, and that a recent time-tick showed it to be right on the second; zero correction needed. Say, also, that you took your sight just before noon, local time, and your watch read 15 hours, 56 minutes, 51 seconds. Adding this information to your workbook, the form to date would look like this:

| DATE | June 8, 1984 |
|------|--------------|
| BODY | Sun ☉ |
| hs | 69 – 48.5 |
| IC | –2.4 |
| D | –2.9 |
| ha | 69 – 43.2 |
| R | + 15.6 |
| Ho | 69 – 58.8 |
| W | 15 – 56 – 51 |
| corr | 0 0 |
| GMT | 15 – 56 – 51 |

With this GMT, 15–56–51, and the date, June 8, 1984, you are now ready to enter the almanac.

# 16 | The Almanac

You have already been introduced to the *Nautical Almanac* when you used its altitude correction tables in Chapter 14. Now it is time to turn to its daily pages to establish the sun's precise position in the sky at the time of your sight. The almanac contains all the astronomical data a navigator needs to proceed with the solution of his sight, as well as a wealth of auxiliary and planning information, and an excellent explanatory section.

There are two choices of almanacs: the *Nautical Almanac*, which is published in a single volume for each calendar year; and the *American Air Almanac*, which is issued in semiannual editions. Both are prepared by the United States Naval Observatory and are published by the Government Printing Office. Although some years ago there was an argument for the simplicity and presentation of the *Air Almanac*, the *Nautical Almanac* has since adopted a straightforward, convenient format, and I prefer it, not only for the single-volume aspect, but also for its auxiliary information specifically oriented to the marine navigator. All the examples in this book have been worked with the use of the *Nautical Almanac*.

The two pieces of information that you need from the almanac for your sun sight are the Greenwich hour angle (GHA) and declination (Dec) of the sun at the exact time of the observation. GHA and declination are the coordinates, corresponding to longitude and latitude on earth, of a body on the celestial sphere whose location we must pinpoint in order to derive a line of position. The celestial sphere? It doesn't actually exist; it is just an imaginary sphere, concentric with the earth and with the earth at its center, which provides a convenient matrix for locating celestial bodies, all of which are presumed to be projected on it, just as they are on the dome of a planetarium. The earth's rotation from west to east causes the apparent westward movement of the bodies on the celestial sphere—an easy way to conceptualize the relative motion between the earth and the heavenly bodies. The Greenwich hour angle is the angular distance measured westward from the meridian of Greenwich, 0°, as is West longitude. Declination, like latitude, is the angular distance north (or south) of the celestial equator. The relationship between the horizontal coordinates, GHA, longitude, and local hour angle (a measurement we will discuss later in this chapter) is illustrated in Figure 16–1.

Proceeding with the sun sight, the almanac is opened to the daily pages for June 8, where the astronomical data for all the navigational bodies are displayed for a 3-day period. We are presently interested in the right-hand page, or "sun side," a reproduction of which is shown in Figure 16–2. Notice that GHA and Dec are presented for each whole hour of Greenwich mean time. Figure 16–3 is an enlargement of the portion of the table applicable to your sun sight. If you look down the SUN column to the hour of GMT at which the sight was taken (remember, in Chapter 15, that the Greenwich mean time was 15–56–51), you will see opposite 15$^h$ a GHA of 45°14.1′, and a Dec of 22°54.0′ North. You have to adjust both of these

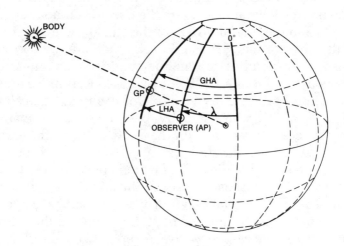

*Figure 16–1.* The Relationship between Horizontal Coordinates. Greenwich hour angle, GHA, is measured westward from the Greenwich meridian, 0°, to the meridian of the celestial body; GP, geographical position, represents the point on Earth directly beneath the body. Longitude, λ, is measured West (or East) from Greenwich to the observer. Local hour angle, LHA, is measured West from the observer to the celestial body.

values for the 56 minutes and 51 seconds of time remaining, and, in the case of the Greenwich hour angle, this is done by turning to the yellow *Increments and Corrections* tables in the back of the almanac. An excerpt of the table for 56 minutes is shown in Figure 16–4. Descending the SUN column, look opposite 51ˢ to find the sun's GHA increment of 14°12.8'. This is added to the tabular value for 15 hours from the daily page to produce the GHA for 15–56–51 of 59°26.9'.

The adjustment for declination is even easier. By inspection of Figure 16–3, you can see that the declina-

1984 JUNE 8, 9, 10 (FRI., SAT., SUN.) 117

| G.M.T. | SUN G.H.A. | Dec. | MOON G.H.A. | v | Dec. | d | H.P. |
|---|---|---|---|---|---|---|---|
| 8 00 | 180 15.9 N22 50.6 | | 70 23.2 11.5 N | 2 23.8 11.5 59.3 | | | |
| 01 | 195 15.8 | 50.9 | 84 53.7 11.5 | 2 08.3 11.5 59.3 | | | |
| 02 | 210 15.7 | 51.1 | 99 24.2 11.5 | 1 52.8 11.5 59.3 | | | |
| 03 | 225 15.5 ·· | 51.3 | 113 54.7 11.6 | 1 37.3 13.6 59.3 | | | |
| 04 | 240 15.4 | 51.5 | 128 25.3 11.5 | 1 21.7 11.5 59.3 | | | |
| 05 | 255 15.3 | 51.8 | 142 55.8 11.5 | 1 06.2 13.5 59.3 | | | |
| 06 | 270 15.2 N22 52.0 | | 157 26.3 11.6 N | 0 50.7 13.5 59.3 | | | |
| 07 | 285 15.1 | 52.2 | 171 56.9 11.6 | 0 35.2 15.6 59.3 | | | |
| 08 | 300 14.9 | 52.4 | 186 27.5 11.5 | 0 19.6 13.5 59.3 | | | |
| F 09 | 315 14.8 ·· | 52.6 | 200 58.0 11.6 N | 0 04.1 15.6 59.3 | | | |
| R 10 | 330 14.7 | 52.9 | 215 28.6 11.6 S | 0 11.5 13.5 59.3 | | | |
| I 11 | 345 14.6 | 53.1 | 229 59.2 11.5 | 0 27.0 15.5 59.3 | | | |
| D 12 | 0 14.5 N22 53.3 | | 244 29.7 11.6 S | 0 42.5 13.5 59.3 | | | |
| A 13 | 15 14.3 | 53.5 | 259 00.3 11.6 | 0 58.0 13.6 59.3 | | | |
| Y 14 | 30 14.2 | 53.7 | 273 30.9 11.5 | 1 13.6 15.5 59.3 | | | |
| 15 | 45 14.1 ·· | 54.0 | 288 01.4 11.6 | 1 29.1 13.5 59.3 | | | |
| 16 | 60 14.0 | 54.2 | 302 32.0 11.5 | 1 44.6 13.5 59.3 | | | |
| 17 | 75 13.9 | 54.4 | 317 02.5 11.6 | 2 00.1 13.4 59.3 | | | |
| 18 | 90 13.7 N22 54.6 | | 331 33.1 11.5 S | 2 15.5 13.5 59.3 | | | |
| 19 | 105 13.6 | 54.8 | 346 03.6 11.6 | 2 31.0 13.5 59.3 | | | |
| 20 | 120 13.5 | 55.0 | 0 34.2 11.5 | 2 46.5 15.4 59.2 | | | |
| 21 | 135 13.4 ·· | 55.2 | 15 04.7 11.5 | 3 01.9 13.6 59.2 | | | |
| 22 | 150 13.3 | 55.4 | 29 35.2 11.5 | 3 17.3 15.4 59.2 | | | |
| 23 | 165 13.1 | 55.7 | 44 05.7 11.5 | 3 32.7 15.4 59.2 | | | |
| 9 00 | 180 13.0 N22 55.9 | | 58 36.2 11.4 S | 3 48.1 15.3 59.2 | | | |
| 01 | 195 12.9 | 56.1 | 73 06.6 11.5 | 4 03.4 15.4 59.2 | | | |
| 02 | 210 12.8 | 56.3 | 87 37.1 11.4 | 4 18.8 15.3 59.2 | | | |
| 03 | 225 12.7 ·· | 56.5 | 102 07.5 11.4 | 4 34.1 15.2 59.2 | | | |
| 04 | 240 12.5 | 56.7 | 116 37.9 11.4 | 4 49.3 15.3 59.2 | | | |
| 05 | 255 12.4 | 56.9 | 131 08.3 11.4 | 5 04.6 15.2 59.2 | | | |
| 06 | 270 12.3 N22 57.1 | | 145 38.7 11.4 S | 5 19.8 15.2 59.2 | | | |
| 07 | 285 12.2 | 57.3 | 160 09.1 11.3 | 5 35.0 15.2 59.2 | | | |
| S 08 | 300 12.0 | 57.5 | 174 39.4 11.3 | 5 50.2 15.1 59.2 | | | |
| A 09 | 315 11.9 ·· | 57.7 | 189 09.7 11.3 | 6 05.3 15.1 59.2 | | | |
| T 10 | 330 11.8 | 57.9 | 203 40.0 11.3 | 6 20.4 15.1 59.2 | | | |
| U 11 | 345 11.7 | 58.1 | 218 10.3 11.2 | 6 35.5 13.0 59.1 | | | |
| R 12 | 0 11.6 N22 58.3 | | 232 40.5 11.2 S | 6 50.5 15.0 59.1 | | | |
| D 13 | 15 11.4 | 58.5 | 247 10.7 11.2 | 7 05.5 14.9 59.1 | | | |
| A 14 | 30 11.3 | 58.7 | 261 40.9 11.2 | 7 20.4 14.9 59.1 | | | |
| Y 15 | 45 11.2 ·· | 58.9 | 276 11.1 11.1 | 7 35.3 14.9 59.1 | | | |
| 16 | 60 11.1 | 59.1 | 290 41.2 11.1 | 7 50.2 14.8 59.1 | | | |
| 17 | 75 10.9 | 59.3 | 305 11.3 11.0 | 8 05.0 14.7 59.1 | | | |
| 18 | 90 10.8 N22 59.5 | | 319 41.3 11.1 S | 8 19.7 14.8 59.1 | | | |
| 19 | 105 10.7 | 59.7 | 334 11.4 11.0 | 8 34.5 14.6 59.1 | | | |
| 20 | 120 10.6 22 59.9 | | 348 41.4 10.9 | 8 49.1 14.6 59.1 | | | |
| 21 | 135 10.4 23 00.1 | | 3 11.3 10.9 | 9 03.7 14.6 59.1 | | | |
| 22 | 150 10.3 | 00.3 | 17 41.2 10.9 | 9 18.3 14.5 59.0 | | | |
| 23 | 165 10.2 | 00.5 | 32 11.1 10.9 | 9 32.8 14.5 59.0 | | | |
| 10 00 | 180 10.1 N23 00.7 | | 46 41.0 10.8 S | 9 47.3 14.4 59.0 | | | |
| 01 | 195 10.0 | 00.9 | 61 10.8 10.8 | 10 01.7 14.3 59.0 | | | |
| 02 | 210 09.8 | 01.0 | 75 40.6 10.7 | 10 16.0 14.3 59.0 | | | |
| 03 | 225 09.7 ·· | 01.2 | 90 10.3 10.7 | 10 30.3 14.2 59.0 | | | |
| 04 | 240 09.6 | 01.4 | 104 40.0 10.6 | 10 44.5 14.2 59.0 | | | |
| 05 | 255 09.5 | 01.6 | 119 09.6 10.7 | 10 58.7 14.1 59.0 | | | |
| 06 | 270 09.3 N23 01.8 | | 133 39.3 10.5 S11 12.8 14.0 58.9 | | | | |
| 07 | 285 09.2 | 02.0 | 148 08.8 10.6 | 11 26.8 14.0 58.9 | | | |
| 08 | 300 09.1 | 02.2 | 162 38.4 10.4 | 11 40.8 13.9 58.9 | | | |
| S 09 | 315 09.0 ·· | 02.4 | 177 07.8 10.5 | 11 54.7 13.8 58.9 | | | |
| U 10 | 330 08.8 | 02.6 | 191 37.3 10.4 | 12 08.5 13.8 58.9 | | | |
| N 11 | 345 08.7 | 02.7 | 206 06.7 10.3 | 12 22.3 13.7 58.9 | | | |
| D 12 | 0 08.6 N23 02.9 | | 220 36.0 10.3 S12 36.0 13.6 58.9 | | | | |
| A 13 | 15 08.5 | 03.1 | 235 05.3 10.2 | 12 49.6 13.6 58.9 | | | |
| Y 14 | 30 08.3 | 03.3 | 249 34.5 10.3 | 13 03.2 13.6 58.9 | | | |
| 15 | 45 08.2 ·· | 03.5 | 264 03.8 10.1 | 13 16.6 13.4 58.8 | | | |
| 16 | 60 08.1 | 03.6 | 278 32.9 10.1 | 13 30.0 13.3 58.8 | | | |
| 17 | 75 08.0 | 03.8 | 293 02.0 10.1 | 13 43.3 13.3 58.8 | | | |
| 18 | 90 07.8 N23 04.0 | | 307 31.1 10.0 S13 56.6 13.1 58.8 | | | | |
| 19 | 105 07.7 | 04.2 | 322 00.1 9.9 | 14 09.7 13.1 58.8 | | | |
| 20 | 120 07.6 | 04.4 | 336 29.0 9.9 | 14 22.8 13.0 58.8 | | | |
| 21 | 135 07.5 ·· | 04.5 | 350 57.9 9.9 | 14 35.8 12.9 58.8 | | | |
| 22 | 150 07.3 | 04.7 | 5 26.8 9.8 | 14 48.7 12.8 58.7 | | | |
| 23 | 165 07.2 | 04.9 | 19 55.6 9.7 | 15 01.5 12.7 58.7 | | | |
| | S.D. 15.8 d 0.2 | | S.D. 16.2 | 16.1 | 16.0 | | |

| Lat. | Twilight Naut. | Civil | Sunrise | Moonrise 8 | 9 | 10 | 11 |
|---|---|---|---|---|---|---|---|
| N 72 | ☐ | ☐ | ☐ | | | | ▬ |
| N 70 | ☐ | ☐ | ☐ | 14 03 | 16 22 | 18 59 | ▬ |
| 68 | ☐ | ☐ | ☐ | 14 01 | 16 09 | 18 27 | 21 38 |
| 66 | //// | //// | 00 33 | 14 00 | 15 59 | 18 04 | 20 27 |
| 64 | //// | //// | 01 41 | 13 58 | 15 50 | 17 46 | 19 51 |
| 62 | //// | //// | 02 15 | 13 57 | 15 43 | 17 32 | 19 26 |
| 60 | //// | 01 04 | 02 40 | 13 56 | 15 37 | 17 20 | 19 06 |
| N 58 | //// | 01 47 | 02 59 | 13 55 | 15 32 | 17 10 | 18 49 |
| 56 | //// | 02 15 | 03 15 | 13 55 | 15 27 | 17 01 | 18 36 |
| 54 | 00 59 | 02 36 | 03 29 | 13 54 | 15 23 | 16 54 | 18 24 |
| 52 | 01 38 | 02 53 | 03 41 | 13 53 | 15 20 | 16 47 | 18 14 |
| 50 | 02 04 | 03 07 | 03 51 | 13 53 | 15 16 | 16 41 | 18 05 |
| 45 | 02 47 | 03 36 | 04 13 | 13 52 | 15 13 | 16 35 | 17 57 |
| N 40 | 03 17 | 03 58 | 04 31 | 13 51 | 15 07 | 16 23 | 17 40 |
| 35 | 03 40 | 04 16 | 04 46 | 13 50 | 15 02 | 16 14 | 17 26 |
| 30 | 03 58 | 04 31 | 04 58 | 13 50 | 14 57 | 16 06 | 17 14 |
| 20 | 04 26 | 04 55 | 05 20 | 13 49 | 14 53 | 15 58 | 17 04 |
| N 10 | 04 48 | 05 15 | 05 38 | 13 48 | 14 46 | 15 46 | 16 47 |
| 0 | 05 07 | 05 33 | 05 56 | 13 47 | 14 41 | 15 35 | 16 31 |
| S 10 | 05 24 | 05 50 | 06 13 | 13 46 | 14 35 | 15 23 | 16 17 |
| 20 | 05 39 | 06 07 | 06 31 | 13 45 | 14 30 | 15 15 | 16 03 |
| 30 | 05 55 | 06 25 | 06 51 | 13 44 | 14 24 | 15 05 | 15 49 |
| 35 | 06 04 | 06 36 | 07 04 | 13 43 | 14 20 | 14 53 | 15 32 |
| 40 | 06 13 | 06 47 | 07 17 | 13 43 | 14 14 | 14 46 | 15 22 |
| 45 | 06 23 | 07 00 | 07 34 | 13 42 | 14 09 | 14 38 | 15 11 |
| S 50 | 06 34 | 07 16 | 07 54 | 13 42 | 14 05 | 14 29· | 14 58 |
| 52 | 06 40 | 07 23 | 08 04 | 13 41 | 13 59 | 14 19 | 14 42 |
| 54 | 06 45 | 07 31 | 08 14 | 13 40 | 13 56 | 14 13 | 14 35 |
| 56 | 06 51 | 07 40 | 08 27 | 13 40 | 13 53 | 14 08 | 14 27 |
| 58 | 06 58 | 07 50 | 08 41 | 13 40 | 13 50 | 14 02 | 14 18 |
| S 60 | 07 05 | 08 01 | 08 58 | 13 39 | 13 47 | 13 56 | 14 08 |
| | | | | 13 39 | 13 43 | 13 48 | 13 56 |

| Lat. | Sunset | Twilight Civil | Naut. | Moonset 8 | 9 | 10 | 11 |
|---|---|---|---|---|---|---|---|
| N 72 | ☐ | ☐ | ☐ | 01 44 | 01 15 | ▬ | ▬ |
| N 70 | ☐ | ☐ | ☐ | 01 42 | 01 20 | 00 57 | ▬ |
| 68 | ☐ | ☐ | ☐ | 01 40 | 01 25 | 01 10 | 00 50 |
| 66 | 23 32 | //// | //// | 01 38 | 01 29 | 01 20 | 01 09 |
| 64 | 22 19 | //// | //// | 01 36 | 01 33 | 01 29 | 01 25 |
| 62 | 21 45 | //// | //// | 01 35 | 01 36 | 01 36 | 01 38 |
| 60 | 21 20 | 22 56 | //// | 01 34 | 01 38 | 01 43 | 01 49 |
| N 58 | 20 20 | 22 13 | //// | 01 33 | 01 41 | 01 49 | 01 59 |
| 56 | 20 44 | 21 45 | //// | 01 32 | 01 43 | 01 54 | 02 07 |
| 54 | 20 30 | 21 23 | 23 02 | 01 31 | 01 45 | 01 58 | 02 15 |
| 52 | 20 18 | 21 06 | 22 22 | 01 31 | 01 46 | 02 03 | 02 22 |
| 50 | 20 07 | 20 51 | 21 55 | 01 30 | 01 48 | 02 07 | 02 28 |
| 45 | 19 45 | 20 23 | 21 12 | 01 29 | 01 51 | 02 15 | 02 41 |
| N 40 | 19 28 | 20 00 | 20 42 | 01 27 | 01 54 | 02 22 | 02 52 |
| 35 | 19 13 | 19 43 | 20 19 | 01 26 | 01 57 | 02 28 | 03 02 |
| 30 | 19 00 | 19 28 | 20 01 | 01 25 | 01 59 | 02 33 | 03 10 |
| 20 | 18 39 | 19 03 | 19 32 | 01 24 | 02 03 | 02 43 | 03 25 |
| N 10 | 18 20 | 18 43 | 19 10 | 01 22 | 02 06 | 02 51 | 03 38 |
| 0 | 18 03 | 18 25 | 18 51 | 01 20 | 02 09 | 02 59 | 03 50 |
| S 10 | 17 46 | 18 09 | 18 35 | 01 19 | 02 12 | 03 06 | 04 02 |
| 20 | 17 28 | 17 52 | 18 19 | 01 17 | 02 16 | 03 15 | 04 15 |
| 30 | 17 07 | 17 33 | 18 03 | 01 15 | 02 20 | 03 24 | 04 30 |
| 35 | 16 55 | 17 23 | 17 54 | 01 14 | 02 22 | 03 30 | 04 38 |
| 40 | 16 41 | 17 11 | 17 45 | 01 13 | 02 24 | 03 36 | 04 48 |
| 45 | 16 24 | 16 58 | 17 35 | 01 12 | 02 27 | 03 43 | 05 00 |
| S 50 | 16 04 | 16 42 | 17 24 | 01 10 | 02 31 | 03 52 | 05 14 |
| 52 | 15 55 | 16 35 | 17 19 | 01 09 | 02 32 | 03 56 | 05 21 |
| 54 | 15 44 | 16 27 | 17 13 | 01 08 | 02 34 | 04 01 | 05 28 |
| 56 | 15 32 | 16 18 | 17 07 | 01 07 | 02 36 | 04 06 | 05 36 |
| 58 | 15 17 | 16 09 | 17 01 | 01 06 | 02 38 | 04 12 | 05 46 |
| S 60 | 15 01 | 15 57 | 16 53 | 01 05 | 02 41 | 04 18 | 05 57 |

| | SUN | | | MOON | | | |
|---|---|---|---|---|---|---|---|
| Day | Eqn. of Time 00ʰ | 12ʰ | Mer. Pass. | Mer. Pass. Upper | Lower | Age | Phase |
| 8 | 01 04 | 00 58 | 11 59 | 19 58 | 07 33 | 09 | |
| 9 | 00 52 | 00 46 | 11 59 | 20 47 | 08 22 | 10 | ◐ |
| 10 | 00 41 | 00 35 | 11 59 | 21 37 | 09 12 | 11 | |

**Figure 16–2.** Typical daily page from the *Nautical Almanac* for sun and moon.

| 1984 JUNE 8, | | | | | | | |
|---|---|---|---|---|---|---|---|
| | **SUN** | | **MOON** | | | | |
| G.M.T. | G.H.A. | Dec. | G.H.A. | v | Dec. | d | H |
| | ° ′ | ° ′ | ° ′ | ′ | ° ′ | ′ | |
| **8** 00 | 180 15.9 | N22 50.6 | 70 23.2 | 11.5 | N 2 23.8 | 15.5 | 5′ |
| 01 | 195 15.8 | 50.9 | 84 53.7 | 11.5 | 2 08.3 | 15.5 | 5′ |
| 02 | 210 15.7 | 51.1 | 99 24.2 | 11.5 | 1 52.8 | 15.5 | 5′ |
| 03 | 225 15.5 ·· | 51.3 | 113 54.7 | 11.6 | 1 37.3 | 15.6 | 5′ |
| 04 | 240 15.4 | 51.5 | 128 25.3 | 11.5 | 1 21.7 | 15.5 | 5′ |
| 05 | 255 15.3 | 51.8 | 142 55.8 | 11.5 | 1 06.2 | 15.5 | 5′ |
| 06 | 270 15.2 | N22 52.0 | 157 26.3 | 11.6 | N 0 50.7 | 15.5 | 5′ |
| 07 | 285 15.1 | 52.2 | 171 56.9 | 11.6 | 0 35.2 | 15.6 | 5′ |
| 08 | 300 14.9 | 52.4 | 186 27.5 | 11.5 | 0 19.6 | 15.5 | 5′ |
| F 09 | 315 14.8 ·· | 52.6 | 200 58.0 | 11.6 | N 0 04.1 | 15.6 | 5′ |
| R 10 | 330 14.7 | 52.9 | 215 28.6 | 11.6 | S 0 11.5 | 15.5 | 5′ |
| I 11 | 345 14.6 | 53.1 | 229 59.2 | 11.5 | 0 27.0 | 15.5 | 5′ |
| D 12 | 0 14.5 | N22 53.3 | 244 29.7 | 11.6 | S 0 42.5 | 15.5 | 5′ |
| A 13 | 15 14.3 | 53.5 | 259 00.3 | 11.6 | 0 58.0 | 15.6 | 5′ |
| Y 14 | 30 14.2 | 53.7 | 273 30.9 | 11.5 | 1 13.6 | 15.5 | 5′ |
| 15 | 45 14.1 ·· | 54.0 | 288 01.4 | 11.6 | 1 29.1 | 15.5 | 5′ |
| 16 | 60 14.0 | 54.2 | 302 32.0 | 11.5 | 1 44.6 | 15.5 | 5′ |
| 17 | 75 13.9 | 54.4 | 317 02.5 | 11.6 | 2 00.1 | 15.4 | 5′ |
| 18 | 90 13.7 | N22 54.6 | 331 33.1 | 11.5 | S 2 15.5 | 15.5 | 5′ |
| 19 | 105 13.6 | 54.8 | 346 03.6 | 11.6 | 2 31.0 | 15.5 | 5′ |
| 20 | 120 13.5 | 55.0 | 0 34.2 | 11.5 | 2 46.5 | 15.4 | 5′ |
| 21 | 135 13.4 ·· | 55.2 | 15 04.7 | 11.5 | 3 01.9 | 15.4 | 5′ |
| 22 | 150 13.3 | 55.4 | 29 35.2 | 11.5 | 3 17.3 | 15.4 | 5′ |
| 23 | 165 13.1 | 55.7 | 44 05.7 | 11.5 | 3 32.7 | 15.4 | 5′ |
| **9** 00 | 180 13.0 | N22 55.9 | 58 36.2 | 11.4 | S 3 48.1 | 15.3 | 5′ |
| 01 | 195 12.9 | 56.1 | 73 06.6 | 11.5 | 4 03.4 | 15.4 | 5′ |

*Figure 16–3.* Excerpt from the *Nautical Almanac* showing astronomical data for the sun on June 8, 1984. At 15ʰ GMT, the sun's GHA is 45°14.1′. The Dec at 15ʰ is N22°54.0′, and at 16ʰ, N22°54.2′.

tion of the sun on June 8 is increasing slowly, at a rate of 0.2′ per hour. Since the time of your sight was almost at 16 hours, a +0.2′ correction would apply, and the resulting declination would read 22°54.2′ North. Although this arithmetical interpolation can be made easily by eye, you should be aware that while the declination in this particular example was both northerly and increasing, that is not always the case, and one must be careful in applying

## 56ᵐ INCREMENTS AND CORRECTIONS

| 56ᵐ | SUN PLANETS | ARIES | MOON | v or Corrⁿ d | v or Corrⁿ d | v or Corrⁿ d |
|---|---|---|---|---|---|---|
| s | ° ′ | ° ′ | ° ′ | ′ ′ | ′ ′ | ′ ′ |
| 00 | 14 00·0 | 14 02·3 | 13 21·7 | 0·0 0·0 | 6·0 5·7 | 12·0 11·3 |
| 01 | 14 00·3 | 14 02·6 | 13 22·0 | 0·1 0·1 | 6·1 5·7 | 12·1 11·4 |
| 02 | 14 00·5 | 14 02·8 | 13 22·2 | 0·2 0·2 | 6·2 5·8 | 12·2 11·5 |
| 03 | 14 00·8 | 14 03·1 | 13 22·4 | 0·3 0·3 | 6·3 5·9 | 12·3 11·6 |
| 04 | 14 01·0 | 14 03·3 | 13 22·7 | 0·4 0·4 | 6·4 6·0 | 12·4 11·7 |
| 05 | 14 01·3 | 14 03·6 | 13 22·9 | 0·5 0·5 | 6·5 6·1 | 12·5 11·8 |
| 06 | 14 01·5 | 14 03·8 | 13 23·2 | 0·6 0·6 | 6·6 6·2 | 12·6 11·9 |
| 07 | 14 01·8 | 14 04·1 | 13 23·4 | 0·7 0·7 | 6·7 6·3 | 12·7 12·0 |
| 08 | 14 02·0 | 14 04·3 | 13 23·6 | 0·8 0·8 | 6·8 6·4 | 12·8 12·1 |
| 09 | 14 02·3 | 14 04·6 | 13 23·9 | 0·9 0·8 | 6·9 6·5 | 12·9 12·1 |
| 45 | 14 11·3 | 14 13·6 | 13 32·5 | 4·5 4·2 | 10·5 9·9 | 16·5 15·5 |
| 46 | 14 11·5 | 14 13·8 | 13 32·7 | 4·6 4·3 | 10·6 10·0 | 16·6 15·6 |
| 47 | 14 11·8 | 14 14·1 | 13 32·9 | 4·7 4·4 | 10·7 10·1 | 16·7 15·7 |
| 48 | 14 12·0 | 14 14·3 | 13 33·2 | 4·8 4·5 | 10·8 10·2 | 16·8 15·8 |
| 49 | 14 12·3 | 14 14·6 | 13 33·4 | 4·9 4·6 | 10·9 10·3 | 16·9 15·9 |
| 50 | 14 12·5 | 14 14·8 | 13 33·7 | 5·0 4·7 | 11·0 10·4 | 17·0 16·0 |
| 51 | 14 12·8 | 14 15·1 | 13 33·9 | 5·1 4·8 | 11·1 10·5 | 17·1 16·1 |
| 52 | 14 13·0 | 14 15·3 | 13 34·1 | 5·2 4·9 | 11·2 10·5 | 17·2 16·2 |
| 53 | 14 13·3 | 14 15·6 | 13 34·4 | 5·3 5·0 | 11·3 10·6 | 17·3 16·3 |
| 54 | 14 13·5 | 14 15·8 | 13 34·6 | 5·4 5·1 | 11·4 10·7 | 17·4 16·4 |
| 55 | 14 13·8 | 14 16·1 | 13 34·9 | 5·5 5·2 | 11·5 10·8 | 17·5 16·5 |
| 56 | 14 14·0 | 14 16·3 | 13 35·1 | 5·6 5·3 | 11·6 10·9 | 17·6 16·6 |
| 57 | 14 14·3 | 14 16·6 | 13 35·3 | 5·7 5·4 | 11·7 11·0 | 17·7 16·7 |
| 58 | 14 14·5 | 14 16·8 | 13 35·6 | 5·8 5·5 | 11·8 11·1 | 17·8 16·8 |
| 59 | 14 14·8 | 14 17·1 | 13 35·8 | 5·9 5·6 | 11·9 11·2 | 17·9 16·9 |
| 60 | 14 15·0 | 14 17·3 | 13 36·1 | 6·0 5·7 | 12·0 11·3 | 18·0 17·0 |

*Figure 16–4.* Excerpt from the *Increments and Corrections* tables, showing an increment of 14°12.8′ to the sun's GHA for 56 minutes, 51 seconds of time.

a correction in the right direction. Because you are working with values obtained from a variety of sources, it is a good idea to enter each figure promptly in your workbook to avoid error. For our present exercise, the workform should now look like this:

| DATE | June 8, 1984 |
|------|--------------|
| BODY | Sun ☉ |
| hs | 69- 48.5 |
| IC | - 2.4 |
| D | - 2.9 |
| ha | 69 - 43.2 |
| R | + 15.6 |
| Ho | 69 -58.8 |
| W | 15 -56 -51 |
| corr | 0 0 |
| GMT | 15 -56 -51 |
| gha | 45 -14.1 |
| incr | 14 -12.8 |
| GHA | 59 -26.9 |
| | |
| Dec | 22 - 54.2 N |

Next, you must determine the sun's local hour angle (LHA) for your sight. LHA is the same sort of measurement as GHA, except that it originates at the observer's local meridian, not at the prime meridian at Greenwich (Figure 16–1). The determination is made by applying the observer's longitude to the Greenwich hour angle previously calculated. For convenience, a longitude is selected near your dead-reckoning position, such that LHA will work out to a whole degree, thereby eliminating one interpolation in the sight reduction table. The selected longitude is called the assumed longitude, and is abbreviated aλ. Since the sun's apparent movement is toward the west, you will subtract the assumed longitude from the GHA if the longitude is West, and add the longitude to the GHA if the longitude is East. Figure 16–1 will help you understand this relationship, but it may be still easier just to remember the simple formula:

$$\text{LHA} = \text{GHA} \begin{array}{l} -\text{West} \\ +\text{East} \end{array} \text{Longitude}$$

For our practical example, let's arbitrarily establish your DR, or dead-reckoning position, at the time of your sun sight at 40°43′N, 70°14′W. Since the GHA worked out to be 59°26.9′, a convenient assumed longitude nearby, one which would make the local hour angle come out to a whole degree, would be 70°26.9′W. Following the rule for applying the assumed longitude to the GHA, the 70°26.9′ should be subtracted from the GHA, but, as you will have already noticed, the GHA is smaller than the assumed longitude; what do we do? Checkmate? Not at all. This is just an example of the occasional case in which West longitude exceeds GHA; you simply add 360° to the Greenwich hour angle and proceed from there. Should you ever find yourself in East longitudes, and the sum of the GHA and the assumed longitude exceeds 360°, the correct LHA is found by subtracting 360° from the total. In our example, by adding 360° to GHA, and then subtracting the assumed longitude, the LHA works out to 349°. Entering this, and an assumed latitude, aL, of 41° N—the nearest whole degree to your DR latitude—your workbook should look like this:

| DATE | June 8, 1984 |
|------|--------------|
| BODY | Sun ☉ |
| hs | 69 - 48.5 |
| IC | - 2.4 |
| D | - 2.9 |
| ha | 69 - 43.2 |
| R | + 15.6 |
| Ho | 69 - 58.8 |
| W | 15 - 56 - 51 |
| corr | 00 |
| GMT | 15 - 56 - 51 |
| gha | 45 - 14.1 |
| incr | 14 - 12.8 |
| GHA | 59 - 26.9 |
|  | 360 |
|  | 419 - 26.9 |
| aλ | - 70 - 26.9 |
| LHA | 349 |
| Dec | 22 - 54.2 N |
| aL | 41    N |

You have now established both the coordinates of your assumed position, AP, which will be needed for the sixth and final step, plotting the line of position. In our exercise these are:

$$aL \quad 41°N$$
$$a\lambda \quad 70°26.9'W$$

You also have the three values needed to enter the sight reduction table, the next step in the celestial procedure.

$$LHA \quad 349°$$
$$Dec \quad 22°54.2'N$$
$$aL \quad 41°N$$

# 17 Calculating Computed Altitude

The fourth step in the six-step process of deriving a line of position from an observation of a celestial body is to calculate what the altitude of the body would have measured had you been exactly at the assumed position. That "computed altitude" (Hc) can then be compared with the altitude observed (Ho) to determine the observer's true location in relation to the assumed position. The calculation, which involves the solution of a spherical triangle, can be performed by the traditional methods of spherical trigonometry, but if the name doesn't frighten you the work required will. The mathematics were so burdensome, in fact, before the advent of electronic calculators, that for two centuries navigators devoted their efforts to the development of tables for simplifying the solution. As a result, inspection tables for sight reduction were born, and virtually all celestial navigators use them today, if not as their primary means, certainly as their ultimate backup. The solution by calculator is discussed in Chapter 25, but first you should become thoroughly familiar with the tabular method, the one we will use to complete our practice sight.

There are a number of sight reduction tables that have appeared over the years, and, like fishermen with their lures, each navigator has his favorite. Some continue to use the old table known as Dreisonstok (Pub. No. 208), which first appeared over fifty years ago and still finds its way into print from time to time, while others prefer Ageton (Pub. No. 211), because it is so compact. Many merchant mariners still use Pub. No. 214, which was the Navy standard during World War II and was the forerunner of the modern inspection tables, although it has now been superceded by Pub. No. 229, *Sight Reduction Tables for Marine Navigation,* and Pub. No. 249, *Sight Reduction Tables for Air Navigation.* Both of these latter tables are currently being published by the Defense Mapping Agency (DMA) and are available through DMA-authorized sales agents.

Which sight reduction table is for you? You have the choice between the completeness and precision of Pub. No. 229, or the speed and simplicity of Pub. No. 249. I recommend the latter to yachtsmen, because it is easier to learn, cheaper to buy, quicker to use, and its accuracy is entirely consistent with the accuracy that can be expected in observations made from a small boat at sea. In any case, once you learn how Pub. No. 249 works, it is not hard to learn the other table; they are quite similar in concept. Don't be misled by the "Air Navigation" in the title of Pub. No. 249; the tables are completely compatible with the *Nautical Almanac* and have found widespread acceptance among marine navigators.

---

**Figure 17–1.** Selected page from   Volume III, Pub. No. 249, *Sight Reduction Tables for Air Navigation.* Much in favor with yachtsmen, Pub. No. 249 is the quickest and easiest to use of all sight reduction tables.

N. Lat. {LHA greater than 180°....Zn=Z / LHA less than 180°....Zn=360−Z}

| LHA | 15° Hc d Z | 16° Hc d Z | 17° Hc d Z | 18° Hc d Z | 19° Hc d Z | 20° Hc d Z | 21° Hc d Z | 22° Hc d Z | 23° Hc d Z | 24° Hc d Z | 25° Hc d Z | 26° Hc d Z | 27° Hc d Z | 28° Hc d Z | 29° Hc d Z | LHA |
|---|---|---|---|---|---|---|---|---|---|---|---|---|---|---|---|---|
| 0 | 6400 60 180 | 6500 60 180 | 6600 60 180 | 6700 60 180 | 6800 60 180 | 6900 60 180 | 7000 60 180 | 7100 60 180 | 7200 60 180 | 7300 60 180 | 7400 60 180 | 7500 60 180 | 7600 60 180 | 7700 60 180 | 7800 60 180 | 360 |
| 1 | 6359 60 178 | 6459 60 178 | 6559 60 178 | 6659 60 178 | 6759 60 178 | 6859 60 177 | 6959 60 177 | 7059 60 177 | 7159 60 177 | 7259 60 177 | 7359 60 177 | 7459 60 177 | 7559 59 176 | 7658 60 176 | 7758 60 176 | 359 |
| 2 | 6357 59 175 | 6456 60 176 | 6556 60 175 | 6656 60 175 | 6756 60 175 | 6856 60 175 | 6956 60 174 | 7056 60 174 | 7155 60 174 | 7255 60 174 | 7355 60 174 | 7455 59 173 | 7554 60 173 | 7653 60 173 | 7753 60 172 | 358 |
| 3 | 6352 60 173 | 6452 60 173 | 6556 60 173 | 6651 60 173 | 6751 60 173 | 6850 60 172 | 6950 60 172 | 7050 59 172 | 7150 59 171 | 7249 59 171 | 7348 60 170 | 7448 59 170 | 7547 59 169 | 7746 59 168 | 7745 59 168 | 357 |
| 4 | 6346 60 171 | 6446 59 171 | 6545 60 171 | 6645 59 170 | 6744 60 170 | 6844 59 170 | 6943 59 169 | 7042 59 169 | 7141 59 168 | 7240 59 168 | 7339 59 167 | 7438 60 167 | 7537 59 166 | 7636 56 165 | 7734 58 164 | 356 |
| 5 | 6338 60 169 | 6438 59 168 | 6537 59 168 | 6636 59 168 | 6735 59 168 | 6735 59 168 | 7032 59 166 | 7131 59 165 | 7230 58 165 | 7328 57 164 | 7426 58 163 | 7524 56 162 | 7622 56 161 | 7720 57 160 | 7816 55 159 | 355 |
| 6 | 6329 59 167 | 6428 58 167 | 6527 59 166 | 6625 58 166 | 6823 59 165 | 6922 58 164 | 7021 58 163 | 7118 59 163 | 7217 57 162 | 7314 56 161 | 7412 57 160 | 7509 57 159 | 7506 55 158 | 7643 54 156 | 7637 53 154 | 354 |
| 7 | 6318 59 165 | 6417 58 165 | 6415 59 164 | 6614 58 163 | 6712 58 163 | 6810 58 162 | 6908 58 161 | 7006 58 161 | 7104 57 160 | 7201 57 159 | 7258 57 158 | 7355 57 157 | 7552 56 155 | 7547 54 154 | 7643 54 152 | 353 |
| 8 | 6305 59 163 | 6404 58 162 | 6502 58 162 | 6500 58 161 | 6858 57 160 | 6855 58 160 | 6853 57 159 | 6950 57 158 | 7047 57 157 | 7144 56 156 | 7240 56 155 | 7236 56 154 | 7432 56 152 | 7526 55 151 | 7621 52 149 | 352 |
| 9 | 6251 58 161 | 6349 58 160 | 6447 59 159 | 6544 59 159 | 6642 57 159 | 6739 57 157 | 6836 56 156 | 6930 57 155 | 7029 56 154 | 7125 55 153 | 7220 55 152 | 7315 55 151 | 7410 53 149 | 7503 53 148 | 7556 52 146 | 351 |
| 10 | 6235 58 159 | 6333 57 158 | 6430 57 157 | 6527 57 157 | 6524 54 156 | 6720 57 155 | 6817 55 153 | 6913 55 153 | 7008 55 151 | 7103 55 151 | 7158 54 149 | 7252 53 148 | 7345 53 146 | 7438 52 145 | 7530 50 143 | 350 |
| 11 | 6238 57 157 | 6335 57 156 | 6412 55 155 | 6508 57 154 | 6605 55 154 | 6700 54 153 | 6756 55 152 | 6851 53 150 | 6946 54 150 | 7040 54 148 | 7134 53 147 | 7227 53 146 | 7320 52 144 | 7412 49 142 | 7501 49 140 | 349 |
| 12 | 6159 57 155 | 6256 56 154 | 6352 56 153 | 6448 55 152 | 6544 55 151 | 6639 55 151 | 6734 54 149 | 6828 54 148 | 6922 54 148 | 7016 52 146 | 7108 53 145 | 7201 51 143 | 7252 50 141 | 7342 49 139 | 7431 48 137 | 348 |
| 13 | 6139 56 153 | 6235 56 152 | 6331 55 152 | 6426 55 150 | 6521 55 149 | 6616 54 147 | 6804 54 147 | 6700 54 146 | 6852 52 145 | 6945 52 143 | 7041 51 142 | 7132 51 140 | 7223 49 139 | 7313 47 137 | 7401 46 135 | 347 |
| 14 | 6118 55 151 | 6213 55 150 | 6308 55 149 | 6404 55 148 | 6457 54 147 | 6551 54 146 | 6645 53 145 | 6738 52 144 | 6830 52 143 | 6922 51 141 | 7013 50 140 | 7103 49 138 | 7153 48 136 | 7240 47 134 | 7327 45 132 | 346 |
| 15 | 6055 55 149 | 6150 55 148 | 6245 54 147 | 6339 53 146 | 6432 54 145 | 6526 52 144 | 6618 52 143 | 6710 52 142 | 6802 51 140 | 6853 50 139 | 6943 49 137 | 7032 48 136 | 7120 47 134 | 7207 45 132 | 7252 43 130 | 345 |
| 16 | 6031 55 147 | 6126 54 146 | 6219 54 145 | 6313 53 144 | 6406 54 144 | 6459 52 143 | 6551 52 141 | 6642 52 140 | 6733 50 139 | 6823 50 138 | 6912 48 135 | 7000 47 134 | 7047 44 132 | 7133 44 130 | 7217 43 128 | 344 |
| 17 | 6006 54 146 | 6100 54 145 | 6153 53 144 | 6246 52 143 | 6338 52 142 | 6430 51 140 | 6521 51 139 | 6612 50 138 | 6702 49 136 | 6751 48 135 | 6839 47 133 | 6926 46 132 | 7012 45 130 | 7057 44 128 | 7141 42 126 | 343 |
| 18 | 5940 53 144 | 6035 53 143 | 6126 52 142 | 6218 52 141 | 6310 51 140 | 6400 51 138 | 6451 50 137 | 6541 49 136 | 6630 48 135 | 6718 48 133 | 6805 46 131 | 6852 45 129 | 6937 44 128 | 7021 42 126 | 7104 41 124 | 342 |
| 19 | 5913 52 142 | 6005 52 141 | 6057 52 140 | 6149 51 139 | 6240 51 138 | 6330 50 137 | 6420 49 135 | 6509 49 134 | 6557 47 133 | 6645 46 131 | 6731 45 130 | 6817 44 128 | 6901 42 126 | 6944 41 124 | 7025 39 122 | 341 |
| 20 | 5845 51 141 | 5936 52 140 | 6028 51 138 | 6119 50 137 | 6209 50 136 | 6259 49 135 | 6348 48 134 | 6436 47 132 | 6523 47 131 | 6610 46 129 | 6656 44 128 | 6740 44 126 | 6824 42 124 | 6906 41 122 | 6947 39 120 | 340 |
| 21 | 5815 51 139 | 5906 51 138 | 5957 50 137 | 6047 50 136 | 6137 49 135 | 6226 48 133 | 6314 48 132 | 6402 47 131 | 6449 45 129 | 6535 45 128 | 6619 44 126 | 6703 43 124 | 6746 41 123 | 6827 40 121 | 6907 38 118 | 339 |
| 22 | 5744 50 137 | 5836 50 136 | 5926 49 135 | 6015 49 134 | 6104 49 133 | 6153 47 132 | 6240 47 131 | 6327 46 129 | 6413 45 128 | 6458 44 126 | 6542 44 124 | 6625 42 123 | 6707 41 121 | 6748 39 119 | 6827 37 117 | 338 |
| 23 | 5714 50 136 | 5804 49 135 | 5853 49 134 | 5942 48 133 | 6031 47 131 | 6118 47 130 | 6205 47 129 | 6251 45 128 | 6337 44 126 | 6421 44 124 | 6505 42 123 | 6547 41 121 | 6628 40 119 | 6708 38 117 | 6746 37 115 | 337 |
| 24 | 5642 49 134 | 5731 49 133 | 5820 49 132 | 5909 47 131 | 5956 47 130 | 6043 47 129 | 6130 45 127 | 6215 45 126 | 6300 44 124 | 6344 42 123 | 6426 42 121 | 6508 41 119 | 6548 39 118 | 6628 38 116 | 6705 36 114 | 336 |
| 25 | 5609 49 133 | 5658 48 132 | 5746 48 131 | 5834 47 130 | 5921 47 128 | 6008 45 127 | 6053 45 126 | 6138 44 124 | 6222 43 123 | 6305 42 122 | 6347 41 120 | 6428 40 118 | 6508 39 116 | 6547 37 115 | 6624 35 113 | 335 |
| 26 | 5535 49 132 | 5624 48 130 | 5712 47 129 | 5759 46 128 | 5845 46 127 | 5931 45 126 | 6016 45 124 | 6101 43 123 | 6144 42 122 | 6226 42 120 | 6308 40 119 | 6348 39 117 | 6427 36 115 | 6505 37 113 | 6542 34 111 | 334 |
| 27 | 5501 48 130 | 5549 47 129 | 5636 47 128 | 5724 47 127 | 5809 45 126 | 5854 45 124 | 5939 43 123 | 6022 43 122 | 6105 42 120 | 6147 41 119 | 6228 40 117 | 6308 38 116 | 6346 37 114 | 6423 36 113 | 6459 35 110 | 333 |
| 28 | 5426 47 129 | 5513 47 128 | 5600 46 127 | 5646 46 125 | 5732 44 124 | 5816 44 123 | 5900 44 122 | 5944 42 120 | 6026 41 119 | 6107 41 117 | 6147 39 116 | 6226 38 114 | 6304 37 112 | 6341 36 111 | 6417 33 109 | 332 |
| 29 | 5351 46 128 | 5438 47 127 | 5524 45 126 | 5609 46 124 | 5654 44 123 | 5738 44 122 | 5822 42 120 | 5904 42 119 | 5946 41 117 | 6026 39 116 | 6106 39 115 | 6144 38 113 | 6221 36 112 | 6259 35 110 | 6334 33 108 | 331 |
| 30 | 5314 47 126 | 5401 45 125 | 5446 45 124 | 5531 45 123 | 5616 43 122 | 5659 43 120 | 5742 42 119 | 5824 41 118 | 5905 41 116 | 5946 39 115 | 6025 38 113 | 6103 37 112 | 6140 36 110 | 6216 34 109 | 6250 33 107 | 330 |
| 31 | 5237 46 125 | 5323 45 124 | 5408 45 123 | 5453 44 122 | 5537 43 120 | 5620 42 119 | 5702 42 118 | 5744 41 117 | 5825 39 115 | 5904 39 114 | 5943 37 112 | 6020 36 111 | 6057 35 109 | 6133 34 107 | 6207 32 106 | 329 |
| 32 | 5200 45 124 | 5245 45 123 | 5330 44 122 | 5414 44 120 | 5458 42 119 | 5540 42 118 | 5622 41 117 | 5703 40 115 | 5744 39 114 | 5823 38 113 | 5901 37 111 | 5938 36 110 | 6014 34 108 | 6049 33 107 | 6122 31 105 | 328 |
| 33 | 5122 45 123 | 5207 44 122 | 5251 44 120 | 5335 43 119 | 5418 42 118 | 5500 42 117 | 5542 40 116 | 5622 40 114 | 5702 39 113 | 5741 38 111 | 5819 37 110 | 5856 35 109 | 5931 35 108 | 6006 33 105 | 6039 32 104 | 327 |
| 34 | 5044 44 121 | 5128 44 120 | 5213 43 119 | 5256 43 118 | 5338 42 117 | 5420 41 116 | 5501 40 114 | 5541 39 113 | 5620 38 112 | 5658 37 110 | 5736 36 109 | 5812 35 108 | 5848 34 106 | 5923 32 105 | 5955 30 103 | 326 |
| 35 | 5005 44 120 | 5049 43 119 | 5132 43 118 | 5215 42 117 | 5257 42 116 | 5339 40 115 | 5419 40 113 | 5459 39 112 | 5538 38 111 | 5616 37 109 | 5729 35 108 | 5808 34 106 | 5838 33 105 | 5838 33 103 | 5911 31 102 | 325 |
| 36 | 4926 43 119 | 5009 43 118 | 5052 42 117 | 5135 41 116 | 5217 41 114 | 5257 40 113 | 5337 39 112 | 5416 38 111 | 5455 38 109 | 5533 37 108 | 5610 35 107 | 5646 33 106 | 5722 33 104 | 5756 31 103 | 5826 30 101 | 324 |
| 37 | 4846 43 118 | 4929 42 117 | 5012 42 116 | 5054 41 115 | 5135 41 114 | 5216 39 113 | 5255 39 110 | 5334 39 110 | 5413 37 109 | 5450 36 107 | 5526 36 106 | 5602 34 104 | 5637 32 103 | 5710 32 102 | 5742 30 100 | 323 |
| 38 | 4806 43 117 | 4849 42 116 | 4931 41 115 | 5012 41 114 | 5053 41 113 | 5134 39 112 | 5213 39 110 | 5252 38 109 | 5330 37 108 | 5407 36 106 | 5443 35 105 | 5518 34 104 | 5552 32 102 | 5625 32 101 | 5657 30 99 | 322 |
| 39 | 4725 43 116 | 4808 42 115 | 4850 41 114 | 4931 40 113 | 5011 40 112 | 5051 39 110 | 5130 39 109 | 5209 38 108 | 5247 37 107 | 5323 36 105 | 5359 35 104 | 5434 33 103 | 5508 33 101 | 5541 32 100 | 5612 31 98 | 321 |
| 40 | 4644 42 114 | 4726 42 114 | 4808 41 113 | 4849 40 112 | 4929 40 111 | 5009 39 110 | 5048 38 108 | 5126 37 107 | 5203 37 106 | 5240 36 104 | 5315 35 103 | 5350 33 102 | 5423 33 100 | 5456 32 99 | 5528 30 98 | 320 |
| 41 | 4603 42 114 | 4645 41 113 | 4726 41 112 | 4807 40 111 | 4847 40 110 | 4926 38 109 | 5005 38 108 | 5042 37 106 | 5119 36 105 | 5156 35 104 | 5231 34 102 | 5305 34 101 | 5339 32 99 | 5411 32 99 | 5443 30 97 | 319 |
| 42 | 4522 41 113 | 4604 41 112 | 4645 40 111 | 4724 40 110 | 4804 39 109 | 4843 39 108 | 4921 38 107 | 4959 36 105 | 5035 36 104 | 5111 35 103 | 5146 35 102 | 5220 33 100 | 5254 32 99 | 5326 32 97 | 5358 30 96 | 318 |
| 43 | 4440 41 112 | 4522 41 111 | 4602 40 110 | 4642 39 109 | 4721 39 108 | 4800 38 107 | 4838 38 106 | 4915 37 104 | 4952 36 103 | 5027 35 102 | 5102 34 101 | 5136 33 99 | 5209 32 98 | 5241 30 97 | 5313 30 95 | 317 |
| 44 | 4358 41 111 | 4439 40 110 | 4519 40 109 | 4559 39 108 | 4638 39 108 | 4716 39 106 | 4754 37 105 | 4831 36 104 | 4907 36 102 | 4943 35 101 | 5018 33 100 | 5051 33 99 | 5124 32 97 | 5156 31 96 | 5228 29 95 | 316 |
| 45 | 4315 41 110 | 4356 40 109 | 4436 39 108 | 4515 39 107 | 4554 38 106 | 4632 38 105 | 4710 37 104 | 4747 36 103 | 4823 35 102 | 4858 35 100 | 4933 33 99 | 5006 33 98 | 5039 32 96 | 5111 31 95 | 5142 30 94 | 315 |
| 46 | 4233 40 109 | 4313 40 108 | 4353 39 107 | 4432 38 106 | 4511 38 106 | 4549 38 105 | 4626 37 103 | 4703 35 102 | 4738 36 101 | 4814 34 100 | 4848 34 98 | 4922 32 97 | 4954 32 96 | 5026 31 94 | 5057 30 93 | 314 |
| 47 | 4150 40 109 | 4230 40 108 | 4310 39 107 | 4349 39 106 | 4427 38 105 | 4505 37 104 | 4542 36 103 | 4618 36 101 | 4654 35 100 | 4729 34 99 | 4804 33 98 | 4837 32 96 | 4909 32 95 | 4941 31 94 | 5012 30 92 | 313 |
| 48 | 4107 40 108 | 4147 39 107 | 4226 39 106 | 4305 39 105 | 4343 38 104 | 4421 37 103 | 4458 36 102 | 4534 36 101 | 4610 34 99 | 4644 34 98 | 4718 33 97 | 4751 33 96 | 4824 31 94 | 4855 30 93 | 4927 29 92 | 312 |
| 49 | 4024 39 107 | 4103 39 106 | 4142 38 105 | 4221 38 104 | 4259 37 104 | 4337 37 102 | 4412 37 102 | 4449 35 100 | 4524 35 99 | 4559 34 98 | 4633 33 96 | 4706 32 95 | 4738 31 94 | 4809 30 92 | 4841 30 91 | 311 |
| 50 | 3940 40 106 | 4020 39 105 | 4059 38 104 | 4137 37 103 | 4215 37 102 | 4252 37 101 | 4328 36 100 | 4404 36 99 | 4440 34 98 | 4514 34 96 | 4548 33 95 | 4621 33 94 | 4654 31 93 | 4725 31 92 | 4756 30 90 | 310 |
| 51 | 3857 39 105 | 3936 39 104 | 4015 38 103 | 4053 37 102 | 4131 37 101 | 4207 37 100 | 4244 36 99 | 4320 35 98 | 4354 34 97 | 4429 34 96 | 4502 33 95 | 4535 32 93 | 4607 31 92 | 4640 31 91 | 4711 30 90 | 309 |
| 52 | 3813 39 104 | 3852 38 103 | 3930 38 102 | 4008 38 101 | 4046 37 100 | 4122 36 99 | 4159 36 99 | 4235 35 97 | 4309 34 96 | 4343 33 95 | 4417 33 94 | 4450 32 92 | 4522 31 91 | 4555 30 90 | 4625 30 89 | 308 |
| 53 | 3729 39 104 | 3808 38 103 | 3846 38 101 | 3924 38 100 | 4001 36 100 | 4037 36 99 | 4114 36 98 | 4150 35 96 | 4225 34 95 | 4258 33 94 | 4332 33 93 | 4404 32 91 | 4436 31 90 | 4509 30 89 | 4540 30 88 | 307 |
| 54 | 3645 39 103 | 3724 38 102 | 3802 37 101 | 3839 37 100 | 3916 37 99 | 3953 36 98 | 4029 35 97 | 4105 35 96 | 4140 34 95 | 4214 33 94 | 4247 33 92 | 4319 32 91 | 4351 31 90 | 4424 30 89 | 4455 30 88 | 306 |
| 55 | 3601 38 102 | 3639 38 101 | 3717 38 100 | 3755 37 99 | 3832 36 98 | 3908 36 97 | 3944 36 96 | 4020 34 95 | 4054 34 94 | 4129 33 93 | 4202 32 92 | 4235 32 91 | 4307 32 89 | 4339 31 88 | 4410 30 87 | 305 |
| 56 | 3516 39 101 | 3555 38 100 | 3633 37 99 | 3710 37 98 | 3747 36 98 | 3823 36 97 | 3859 36 96 | 3935 35 94 | 4010 34 93 | 4043 33 93 | 4117 33 91 | 4150 31 90 | 4222 31 89 | 4254 31 88 | 4325 30 86 | 304 |
| 57 | 3432 38 101 | 3510 38 100 | 3548 37 99 | 3625 37 98 | 3702 36 97 | 3738 35 96 | 3814 35 95 | 3849 35 94 | 3924 34 92 | 3958 33 92 | 4032 32 91 | 4104 32 89 | 4137 31 88 | 4208 30 87 | 4240 29 86 | 303 |
| 58 | 3347 38 100 | 3426 37 99 | 3503 37 98 | 3540 36 97 | 3617 36 96 | 3653 35 95 | 3728 35 94 | 3804 35 93 | 3838 33 92 | 3912 33 91 | 3946 32 90 | 4019 31 89 | 4052 31 88 | 4123 30 86 | 4154 30 85 | 302 |
| 59 | 3303 38 99 | 3341 37 98 | 3418 37 97 | 3455 37 96 | 3533 35 96 | 3608 36 94 | 3644 35 93 | 3719 34 92 | 3753 33 91 | 3828 32 90 | 3900 33 89 | 3934 31 88 | 4006 31 87 | 4038 30 85 | 4108 30 84 | 301 |
| 60 | 3218 38 98 | 3256 37 97 | 3333 37 96 | 3410 37 95 | 3447 36 94 | 3523 35 94 | 3558 35 93 | 3633 34 92 | 3707 34 91 | 3742 32 89 | 3814 32 88 | 3849 32 87 | 3921 31 86 | 3953 30 85 | 4024 30 84 | 300 |
| 61 | 3133 38 98 | 3211 37 97 | 3247 37 96 | 3324 37 95 | 3401 36 94 | 3437 35 93 | 3512 35 92 | 3547 34 91 | 3621 34 90 | 3655 33 89 | 3729 32 88 | 3803 31 86 | 3835 31 85 | 3908 30 84 | 3938 29 83 | 299 |
| 62 | 3048 38 97 | 3126 37 96 | 3203 37 95 | 3240 36 94 | 3317 36 93 | 3352 35 92 | 3427 34 91 | 3502 34 90 | 3536 33 89 | 3610 33 88 | 3644 32 87 | 3717 32 86 | 3749 31 85 | 3822 30 84 | 3852 29 82 | 298 |
| 63 | 3003 38 96 | 3041 37 95 | 3118 37 94 | 3155 37 93 | 3232 35 93 | 3307 35 92 | 3342 34 90 | 3416 34 90 | 3450 33 88 | 3524 32 87 | 3557 32 86 | 3631 31 85 | 3703 31 84 | 3736 29 83 | 3806 29 82 | 297 |
| 64 | 2918 38 95 | 2956 37 94 | 3033 36 93 | 3110 37 93 | 3147 36 92 | 3222 35 91 | 3257 34 90 | 3331 34 89 | 3405 33 88 | 3438 32 86 | 3511 32 85 | 3545 31 84 | 3617 31 83 | 3649 30 82 | 3720 29 81 | 296 |
| 65 | 2833 37 95 | 2910 37 94 | 2948 37 93 | 3024 37 92 | 3101 35 91 | 3137 35 90 | 3212 35 89 | 3247 34 88 | 3320 33 87 | 3356 34 86 | 3430 33 85 | 3503 32 84 | 3535 31 83 | 3608 30 82 | 3639 29 81 | 295 |
| 66 | 2748 37 94 | 2825 36 93 | 2903 37 92 | 2939 37 91 | 3016 36 90 | 3051 35 89 | 3126 35 89 | 3201 34 88 | 3235 33 87 | 3308 34 85 | 3342 33 84 | 3415 32 83 | 3448 31 82 | 3520 30 81 | 3551 29 80 | 294 |
| 67 | 2703 37 93 | 2740 37 92 | 2817 37 91 | 2854 37 90 | 3030 36 89 | 3106 35 88 | 3141 35 88 | 3215 34 87 | 3249 33 86 | 3223 34 85 | 3256 33 84 | 3330 32 83 | 3402 31 82 | 3435 29 81 | 3505 29 79 | 293 |
| 68 | 2617 38 93 | 2655 36 91 | 2732 36 90 | 2808 37 89 | 2845 36 88 | 2921 35 88 | 2956 34 87 | 3030 34 86 | 3104 33 85 | 3137 34 84 | 3211 33 83 | 3244 31 82 | 3316 31 81 | 3349 29 80 | 3418 29 78 | 292 |
| 69 | 2532 37 92 | 2609 37 91 | 2646 37 90 | 2723 36 89 | 2759 35 88 | 2834 36 87 | 2910 35 86 | 2945 34 85 | 3018 33 84 | 3052 33 83 | 3125 33 83 | 3158 32 82 | 3230 31 80 | 3302 30 79 | 3332 29 78 | 291 |

S. Lat. {LHA greater than 180°....Zn=180−Z / LHA less than 180°....Zn=180+Z}

Calculating Computed Altitude    169    **LAT 41°**

**N. Lat.** {LHA greater than 180° ........ Zn=Z / LHA less than 180° .......... Zn=360−Z}   **LAT 41° DECLINATION**

| LHA | 15° Hc | d | Z | 16° Hc | d | Z | 17° Hc | d | Z | 18° Hc | d | Z | 19° Hc | d | Z | 20° Hc | d | Z |
|---|---|---|---|---|---|---|---|---|---|---|---|---|---|---|---|---|---|---|
| | ° ′ | ′ | ° | ° ′ | ′ | ° | ° ′ | ′ | ° | ° ′ | ′ | ° | ° ′ | ′ | ° | ° ′ | ′ | ° |
| 0 | 64 00 | +60 | 180 | 65 00 | +60 | 180 | 66 00 | +60 | 180 | 67 00 | +60 | 180 | 68 00 | +60 | 180 | 69 00 | +60 | 180 |
| 1 | 63 59 | 60 | 178 | 64 59 | 60 | 178 | 65 59 | 60 | 178 | 66 59 | 60 | 178 | 67 59 | 60 | 178 | 68 59 | 60 | 177 |
| 2 | 63 57 | 59 | 176 | 64 56 | 60 | 176 | 65 56 | 60 | 175 | 66 56 | 60 | 175 | 67 56 | 60 | 175 | 68 56 | 60 | 175 |
| 3 | 53 52 | 60 | 173 | 64 52 | 60 | 173 | 65 52 | 59 | 173 | 66 51 | 60 | 173 | 67 51 | 60 | 173 | 68 51 | 59 | 172 |
| 4 | 63 46 | 60 | 171 | 64 46 | 59 | 171 | 65 45 | 60 | 171 | 66 45 | 59 | 170 | 67 44 | 60 | 170 | 68 44 | 59 | 170 |
| 5 | 63 38 | +60 | 169 | 64 38 | +59 | 169 | 65 37 | +59 | 168 | 66 36 | +59 | 168 | 67 35 | +59 | 168 | 68 34 | +59 | 167 |
| 6 | 63 29 | 59 | 167 | 64 28 | 59 | 167 | 65 27 | 59 | 166 | 66 26 | 59 | 166 | 67 25 | 58 | 165 | 68 23 | 59 | 165 |
| 7 | 63 18 | 59 | 165 | 64 17 | 58 | 164 | 65 15 | 59 | 164 | 66 14 | 58 | 163 | 67 12 | 58 | 163 | 68 10 | 58 | 162 |
| 8 | 63 05 | 59 | 163 | 64 04 | 58 | 162 | 65 02 | 58 | 162 | 66 00 | 53 | 161 | 66 58 | 57 | 160 | 67 55 | 58 | 160 |
| 9 | 62 51 | 58 | 161 | 63 49 | 58 | 160 | 64 47 | 57 | 159 | 65 44 | 58 | 159 | 66 42 | 57 | 158 | 67 39 | 57 | 157 |
| 10 | 62 35 | +58 | 159 | 63 33 | +57 | 158 | 64 30 | +57 | 157 | 65 27 | +57 | 157 | 66 24 | +56 | 156 | 67 20 | +57 | 155 |
| 11 | 62 18 | 57 | 157 | 63 15 | 57 | 156 | 64 12 | 56 | 155 | 65 08 | 57 | 154 | 66 05 | 55 | 154 | 67 00 | 56 | 153 |
| 12 | 61 59 | 57 | 155 | 62 56 | 56 | 154 | 63 52 | 56 | 153 | 64 48 | 56 | 152 | 65 44 | 55 | 151 | 66 39 | 55 | 151 |
| 13 | 61 39 | 56 | 153 | 62 35 | 56 | 152 | 63 31 | 55 | 151 | 64 26 | 55 | 150 | 65 21 | 55 | 149 | 66 16 | ·· | 148 |
| 14 | 61 18 | 55 | 151 | ···· | 55 | 150 | 63 08 | ·· | ·· | | | 148 | 64 57 | ·· | ··· | | | |

*Figure 17–2.* Excerpt from Pub. No. 249, Volume III, showing the values for Latitude 41°N, Declination 22°N, and LHA 349° to be: Hc 68°51′, $d+55′$, Z 151°.

DMA Pub. No. 249 is issued in three volumes: Volume I is for selected stars and is discussed in Chapter 22; Volume II, for latitudes 0°–39°, and Volume III, for latitudes 40°–89°, provide for the reduction of sights of the sun, moon, and planets, and for sights of stars whose declination is within the range 0°–29°. Volume I is updated every five years—we will be using Epoch 1985.0 for our examples—but Volumes II and III remain the same and are simply reprinted from time to time.

For reducing our sun sight, we will need Volume III, which covers our 41° assumed latitude. Open the table to the pages for 41° and select the one that covers the declination we calculated, 22°54.2′. Since both the declination and the assumed latitude were North, their name is the same, so we want the page entitled, "Lat.41° Declination (15°–29°) <u>Same</u> Name as Latitude." An illustration of the appropriate page, greatly reduced in size, is seen in Figure 17–1. To follow our practical exercise, an enlarged

# (15°-29°) SAME NAME AS LATITUDE

| 21° | | | 22° | | | Hc | Z | LHA |
|---|---|---|---|---|---|---|---|---|
| Hc | d | Z | Hc | d | Z | | | |
| ° ′ | ′ | ° | ° ′ | ′ | ° | ° ′ | ° | ° |
| 70 00 | +60 | 180 | 71 00 | +60 | 180 | 72 | 180 | 360 |
| 69 59 | 60 | 177 | 70 59 | 60 | 177 | 71 | 176 | 359 |
| 69 56 | 60 | 175 | 70 56 | 59 | 174 | 71 | 172 | 358 |
| 69 50 | 60 | 172 | 70 50 | 60 | 172 | 71 5 | 168 | 357 |
| 69 43 | 59 | 169 | 70 42 | 59 | 169 | 71 41 | 164 | 356 |
| 69 33 | +59 | 167 | 70 32 | +59 | 166 | 71 31 | 50 | 355 |
| 69 22 | 58 | 164 | 70 20 | 58 | 163 | 71 18 | 56 | 354 |
| 69 08 | 58 | 161 | 70 06 | 58 | 161 | 71 04 | 52 | 353 |
| 68 53 | 57 | 159 | 69 50 | 57 | 158 | 70 47 | 49 | 352 |
| 68 36 | 56 | 156 | 69 32 | 57 | 156 | 70 2′ | 146 | 351 |
| 68 17 | +56 | 154 | 69 13 | +55 | 153 | 70 C | 143 | 350 |
| 67 56 | 55 | 152 | 68 51 | 55 | 151 | 69 4 | 140 | 349 |
| 67 34 | 54 | 149 | 68 28 | 54 | 148 | 69 2. | 137 | 348 |
| 67 10 | 54 | 147 | 68 04 |  |  | 68 5. | 13. |  |

excerpt of a portion of this page is shown in Figure 17–2.

Descending the LHA column—in this case, at the right-hand side of the table—find the value of the local hour angle we had previously calculated: 349°. Then, in the column under the whole degree of declination, 22°, find, opposite LHA, the computed altitude, Hc; here, 68° 51′. Note this, along with the values for d, the tabulated difference per degree of declination, and Z, the azimuth angle, both of which we will come to in a moment. The computed altitude from the table, Tab Hc, was for the whole degree of declination, so it must now be adjusted to include the remaining 54.2′. This can be done by multiplying the tabular difference, d, from the table (+55′) by the incremental declination in fractional degrees (54.2/60), and applying the product, +49.7′, to the tabular Hc. Even easier, use Table 5, *Correction to Tabulated Altitude for Minutes of Declination*, which is found at the back of the sight reduction tables. Figure 17–3

TABLE 5.—Correction to Tabulated Altitude for Minutes of Declination

| 30 | 31 32 33 | 34 35 36 | 37 38 39 | 40 41 42 | 43 44 45 | 46 47 48 | 49 50 51 | 52 53 54 | 55 56 57 | 58 59 60 | d /' |
|---|---|---|---|---|---|---|---|---|---|---|---|
| 0 | 0 0 0 | 0 0 0 | 0 0 0 | 0 0 0 | 0 0 0 | 0 0 0 | 0 0 0 | 0 0 0 | 0 0 0 | 0 0 0 | 0 |
| 0 | 1 1 1 | 1 1 1 | 1 1 1 | 1 1 1 | -1 1 1 | 1 1 1 | 1 1 1 | 1 1 1 | 1 1 1 | 1 1 1 | 1 |
| 1 | 1 1 1 | 1 1 1 | 1 1 1 | 1 1 2 | 1 1 2 | 2 2 2 | 2 2 2 | 2 2 2 | 2 2 2 | 2 2 2 | 2 |
| 2 | 2 2 2 | 2 2 2 | 2 2 2 | 3 3 3 | 2 2 2 | 3 3 3 | 2 2 3 | 3 3 3 | 3 3 3 | 3 3 3 | 3 |
| 2 | 2 2 2 | 2 2 2 | 2 3 3 | 3 3 3 | 3 3 3 | 3 3 3 | 3 3 3 | 3 4 4 | 4 4 4 | 4 4 4 | 4 |
| 2 | 3 3 2 |  |  | 2 | 3 3 4 | 4 4 |  |  |  |  |  |

| ... | ... | 27 28 29 | 30 30 ... | ... | ... | 37 38 38 | 39 40 41 | 42 ... ... | ... 45 46 | 46 47 48 | 48 |
|---|---|---|---|---|---|---|---|---|---|---|---|
| 24 | 25 26 27 | 28 29 29 | 30 31 32 | 33 33 34 | 35 36 37 | 38 38 39 | 40 41 42 | 42 43 44 | 45 46 47 | 47 48 49 | 49 |
| 25 | 26 27 28 | 28 29 30 | 31 32 32 | 33 34 35 | 36 37 38 | 38 39 40 | 41 42 42 | 43 44 45 | 46 47 48 | 48 49 50 | 50 |
| 26 | 26 27 28 | 29 30 31 | 31 32 33 | 34 35 36 | 37 37 38 | 39 40 41 | 42 42 43 | 44 45 46 | 47 48 48 | 49 50 51 | 51 |
| 26 | 27 28 29 | 29 30 31 | 32 33 34 | 35 36 36 | 37 38 39 | 40 41 42 | 42 43 44 | 45 46 47 | 48 49 49 | 50 51 52 | 52 |
| 26 | 27 28 29 | 30 31 32 | 33 34 34 | 35 36 37 | 38 39 40 | 41 42 42 | 43 44 45 | 46 47 48 | 49 49 50 | 51 52 53 | 53 |
| 27 | 28 29 30 | 31 32 32 | 33 34 35 | 36 37 38 | 39 40 40 | 41 42 43 | 44 45 46 | 47 48 49 | 50 50 51 | 52 53 54 | 54 |
| 28 | 28 29 30 | 31 32 33 | 34 35 36 | 37 38 38 | 39 40 41 | 42 43 44 | 45 46 47 | 48 49 50 | 51 52 53 | 54 55 55 | 55 |
| 28 | 29 30 31 | 32 33 34 | 35 35 36 | 37 38 39 | 40 41 42 | 43 44 45 | 46 47 48 | 49 50 51 | 52 53 54 | 55 56 56 | 56 |
| 28 | 29 30 31 | 32 33 34 | 35 36 37 | 38 39 40 | 41 42 43 | 44 45 46 | 47 48 48 | 49 50 51 | 52 53 54 | 55 56 57 | 57 |
| 29 | 30 31 32 | 33 34 35 | 36 37 38 | 39 40 41 | 42 43 44 | 44 45 46 | 47 48 49 | 50 51 52 | 53 54 55 | 56 57 58 | 58 |
| 30 | 30 31 32 | 33 34 35 | 36 37 38 | 39 40 41 | 42 43 44 | 45 46 47 | 48 49 50 | 51 52 53 | 54 55 56 | 57 58 59 | 59 |

*Figure 17–3.* Excerpt from Table 5, Pub. No. 249, showing a correction of 50′ for *d* of 55′ and incremental minutes of declination, 54.

shows a portion of Table 5 by which we can figure the altitude adjustment.

Enter the heading of Table 5 with the value of *d* from the main table: here, +55′. Descend the vertical column to the entry opposite the minutes of declination: in our example, 54 is the nearest whole minute. The correction (+50′) is then applied to the tabular Hc of 68°51′, resulting in a computed altitude—the altitude as it would have been measured at the assumed position—of 69°41′. In our example, the value of *d* was positive as indicated by the + sign in the main table, but if the value is negative, it will be so designated. Always be careful to observe the proper sign in applying the correction to the tabular Hc.

Your workbook, with the additional entries from the sight reduction table, is now almost complete and should look like this:

| | |
|---|---|
| DATE | June 8, 1984 |
| BODY | Sun ☉ |
| hs | 69-48.5 |
| IC | -2.4 |
| D | -2.9 |
| ha | 69-43.2 |
| R | +15.6 |
| Ho | 69-58.8 |
| W | 15-56-51 |
| corr | 00 |
| GMT | 15-56-51 |
| gha | 45-14.1 |
| incr | 14-12.8 |
| GHA | 59-26.9 |
| | 360 |
| | 419-26.9 |
| aλ | -70-26.9 |
| LHA | 349 |
| Dec | 22-54.2 N |
| aL | 41    N |
| Tab. Hc | 68-51 |
| corr | +50 |
| Hc | 69-41.0 |

# 18 | Altitude Difference and Azimuth

Step five is very brief. The first part is determining the difference between the computed altitude, Hc, just obtained from the sight reduction table, and the observed altitude, Ho, which you had worked out in Chapter 14. The difference between Ho and Hc is called the altitude difference or "intercept," and is abbreviated "a." In the case of our sun sight, the difference between our Ho of 69° 58.8′ and Hc of 69°41.0′ is 17.8′.

For our plot we will need to recognize which of the altitudes we compared was the larger. This will tell us whether the intercept will be drawn from our assumed position in the direction of the azimuth—"toward"—or on the reciprocal bearing—"away." The rule states: Ho greater, toward; Hc greater, away. Since, in our example, the observed altitude was the greater, the intercept will be plotted toward the azimuth direction. There are two mnemonics that sailors use to remember the rule. "Hogtied" (Ho greater, toward) and "Coast Guard Academy" (C greater, away).

You will recall that earlier you noted Z in the main

table to be 151°. Following the rules shown in the corner of the table, you can see that in North latitude, when the LHA is greater than 180°, Zn, which is the abbreviation for azimuth, or true bearing, is equal to Z. Since our sun sight was taken in North latitude, and since the local hour angle was 349°, or greater than 180°, the true bearing of the sun from the assumed position was 151°. Incidentally, this same true azimuth can be used in comparison with a simultaneous compass bearing, as discussed in Chapter 5, to check for compass error at sea.

We now have in hand all the data to complete the workbook for the sight. In its final form, it looks like this:

| | |
|---|---|
| DATE | June 8, 1984 |
| BODY | Sun ☉ |
| hs | 69 - 48.5 |
| IC | - 2.4 |
| D | - 2.9 |
| ha | 69 - 43.2 |
| R | + 15.6 |
| Ho | 69 - 58.8 |
| W | 15 - 56 - 51 |
| corr | 00 |
| GMT | 15 - 56 - 51 |
| gha | 45 - 14.1 |
| incr | 14 - 12.8 |
| GHA | 59 - 26.9 |
| | 360 |
| | 419 - 26.9 |
| aλ | - 70 - 26.9 |
| LHA | 349 |
| Dec | 22 - 54.2 N |
| aL | 41      N |
| Tab. Hc | 68 - 51 |
| corr | + 50 |
| Hc | 69 - 41.0 |
| Ho | 69 - 58.8 |
| a | 17.8 T |
| Zn | 151° |

For review, let's restate our practical exercise in textbook terms so that you can retrace all the steps in the completed workform. It is important that you can do this, because in the chapters to follow, in which we explore sights of the moon, planets, and stars, it is assumed you are familiar with the basic process, and the emphasis is on the small procedural differences.

A navigator in DR position Latitude 40°43′N, Longitude 70°14′W, makes an observation of the sun's lower limb at 15:56:51, Greenwich mean time, on June 8, 1984. The sextant altitude reads 69°48.5′, and the sextant has an index correction of –2.4′. The height of eye is 9 feet. Find the intercept (a), whether it is toward (T) or away (A), and the true azimuth (Zn).
(Answer: a = 17.8′T; Zn = 151°; Plot from AP 41°N, 70°26.9′W)

With the intercept and azimuth now in hand, we are ready to turn to the plot to construct the line of position that we have derived from the observation of the sun.

# 19 | Plotting the Line of Position

The sixth and final step in the celestial procedure is to plot the line of position resulting from your sextant observation and subsequent calculations. Figure 19–1 illustrates the method as it applies to our sun sight. The ship's track, properly labeled with the course and speed, has been entered earlier on the plot, and the dead-reckoning position advanced to local noon. Since the actual observation was made three minutes before noon, it wasn't necessary to establish a separate DR since the vessel had only moved about 800 yards during the interval.

Using your workbook to supply the necessary data, you first locate and label the assumed position, AP. Because we had selected a whole degree of latitude, it is an easy matter to pinpoint the assumed position right on the latitude line at the appropriate longitude; ours, you will recall, was 70°26.9′W. Next, the intercept you calculated, 17.8′, is set on your dividers—a minute measured on the adjacent latitude scale is equivalent to a nautical mile on the chart—and the distance is stepped off along

# POSITION PLOTTING SHEET

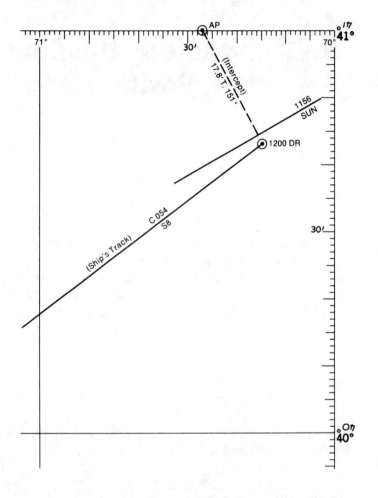

*Figure 19–1.* Plotting the line of position from a sextant observation. The intercept is stepped off from the assumed position toward (or away from, when called for) the direction of the true azimuth. A perpendicular line is constructed at the end of the intercept; this is the line of position.

the azimuth line. Your workbook shows that the true azimuth was 151°, and since Ho was greater than Hc, the intercept is stepped off *toward* the direction 151°. At the end of the intercept, a line is drawn perpendicular to the azimuth, and that is your line of position. A simple way to construct this perpendicular is by means of a draftsman's right triangle, laying the triangle at the end of the intercept while holding your protractor or parallel rules along the azimuth line. The reason why the line is drawn at right angles to the azimuth is because the position line is actually part of the circumference of a huge circle, a circle so large that a tangential line at the point where the radius intersects the circumference is virtually coincident with the circumference and is a great deal easier to construct. We will discuss this further in Chapter 24.

Now that the line of position has been established on the plot, the necessary labels should be added promptly to avoid any chance of confusion. The common practice is to show the time of the observation above the position line, and the body observed below it, as has been done in Figure 19–1. Your celestial line can be crossed with other position lines from simultaneous visual, electronic, or celestial observations to produce a fix, and, like any other position line, it can be advanced or "retired" (navigator's lingo for retarded) to create a running fix in the same manner as you learned in piloting in Chapter 8. The celestial technique is reviewed in Chapter 26, but it should be remembered in establishing any fix, and especially one where celestial lines are used, that it is good practice not to rely on position lines that intersect at less than 30 degrees, unless no better lines are available.

Whether to use a plotting sheet or a chart for your plot is largely a matter of personal preference. When I am well offshore, I prefer a plotting sheet like the 960 series (formerly 3000–Z) published by the Defense Mapping Agency and illustrated in Figure 19–1. These plotting sheets use a Mercator projection like most nautical charts, have a scale of 4 inches to one degree of longitude, and are of a convenient dimension (17 × 22 inches) for the average yacht navigation station. You can, of course, use a chart equally well, provided the scale is not too small, and I find this particularly useful when I am nearing land and may have the opportunity to cross my celestial position lines with those from terrestrial or electronic observations.

That is really all there is to the procedure for solving a sun sight, and most other celestial operations follow a similar pattern. The use of a standardized workform, as we have done for the sun, makes the process easy, and, as we explore the other navigational bodies, think in terms of the procedure you learned for the sun, and it will be easy to recognize the few exceptions.

# 20 | The Moon

Since time immemorial, the moon has had an undeservedly poor reputation among navigators. I suspect that this is because of the moon's relative nearness to the earth, its changing size, and its irregular motion, all of which made sights of the moon much more laborious to reduce and thus intensified the navigator's already burdensome existence. The natural response, perhaps, was simply to avoid the confrontation.

With today's almanac and modern inspection tables, there is no longer any justification for concern over moon sights; in fact, they can be particularly useful at times. Quite often, one of the moon's limbs is sufficiently well defined during daylight hours to permit simultaneous observations of the moon and the sun for an immediate fix, and because of the moon's luminosity, sights at twilight may be possible while the horizon is still comparatively bright, producing results superior to those from any of the lesser bodies. During World War II, submarine navigators, using sextant eyepieces with exceptional light-gathering ability, were able to take moon sights when they surfaced at night, and occasionally, star sights over the moon-illuminated horizon. If you decide to try this yourself, let me caution that it is sometimes difficult to separate the true horizon from a false horizon that often appears under a low moon, so judge your results accordingly.

The best way to introduce yourself to moon observations is, as in the case of the sun, to work through a practical example. You will be glad to know that our procedure for working a moon sight is quite similar to that for the sun, using the same six basic steps, with only a few exceptions that I will point out as we proceed. Let's assume that you are the navigator, and some five hours after you took your sun line, your vessel has moved to a DR position at Latitude 41°08′N, Longitude 69°31′W, in the vicinity of Nantucket Shoals. At Greenwich mean time 20:57:09 on June 8, 1984, you make an observation of the moon's upper limb at a sextant altitude of 22°50.6′. A time-tick shows your watch to be 1 second slow; the index correction is still −2.4′, and the height of eye, 9 feet.

As in the case of your sun line, it is easiest to work with a standardized workform, and the one for the moon requires only minor changes from the one with which you are already familiar. Here is the moon sight in our practical example in completed form; we will walk through the steps one at a time, so you can follow each one.

A sextant observation of the moon is made in exactly the same way as for the sun, bringing either the lower or upper limb (whichever is best defined and will produce the better sight) down to tangency with the horizon. The corrections for index error and dip also follow the sun procedure to obtain the apparent altitude, but then, to correct the apparent altitude, ha, to the observed altitude, Ho, you must use the moon tables inside the _back_ cover of the _Nautical Almanac_, an example of which is seen in Figure 20–1.

In the first part of the workform, the index correction of −2.4′, and the dip correction for a 9-foot height of eye—

| DATE | June 8, 1984 |
|---|---|
| BODY | Moon ☾ |
| hs | 22-50.6 |
| IC | -2.4 |
| D | -2.9 |
| ha | 22-45.3 |
| R | +61.5 |
| H.P.  IH.P. | +4.6  59.1 |
| (-30') | -30.0 |
| Ho | 23-21.4 |
| W | 20-57-09 |
| corr | +01 |
| GMT | 20-57-10 |
| gha  v | 0-34.2  11.5 |
| incr | 13-38.4 |
| v corr | 11.0 |
| GHA | 14-23.6 |
|  | +360 |
|  | 374-23.6 |
| aλ | -69-23.6 |
| LHA | 305 |
| dec  d | 2-46.5  14.1 |
| d corr | +14.8 |
| Dec | 3-01.3 S |
| a L | 41 N |
| Tab Hc | 23-27.0 |
| corr | -01 |
| Hc | 23-26.0 |
| Ho | 23-21.4 |
| a | 4.6 A |
| Zn | 117° |

found in the dip table to be −2.9′—are applied to the sextant altitude, hs, to obtain the apparent altitude, ha, of 22°45.3′. To convert ha to Ho, you then enter the main body of the table, which presents the correction in two parts. The first, or R-correction, is taken from the upper half of the table by descending the column in which the

# ALTITUDE CORRECTION TABLES 0°–35°—MOON

| App. Alt. | 0°–4° Corrⁿ | 5°–9° Corrⁿ | 10°–14° Corrⁿ | 15°–19° Corrⁿ | 20°–24° Corrⁿ | 25°–29° Corrⁿ | 30°–34° Corrⁿ | App. Alt. |
|---|---|---|---|---|---|---|---|---|
| 00 | 0° 33.8 | 5° 58.2 | 10° 62.1 | 15° 62.8 | 20° 62.2 | 25° 60.8 | 30° 58.9 | 00 |
| 10 | 35.9 | 58.5 | 62.2 | 62.8 | 62.1 | 60.8 | 58.8 | 10 |
| 20 | 37.8 | 58.7 | 62.2 | 62.8 | 62.1 | 60.7 | 58.8 | 20 |
| 30 | 39.6 | 58.9 | 62.3 | 62.8 | 62.1 | 60.7 | 58.7 | 30 |
| 40 | 41.2 | 59.1 | 62.3 | 62.8 | 62.0 | 60.6 | 58.6 | 40 |
| 50 | 42.6 | 59.3 | 62.4 | 62.7 | 62.0 | 60.6 | 58.5 | 50 |
| 00 | 1° 44.0 | 6° 59.5 | 11° 62.4 | 16° 62.7 | 21° 62.0 | 26° 60.5 | 31° 58.5 | 00 |
| 10 | 45.2 | 59.7 | 62.4 | 62.7 | 61.9 | 60.4 | 58.4 | 10 |
| 20 | 46.3 | 59.9 | 62.5 | 62.7 | 61.9 | 60.4 | 58.3 | 20 |
| 30 | 47.3 | 60.0 | 62.5 | 62.7 | 61.9 | 60.3 | 58.2 | 30 |
| 40 | 48.3 | 60.2 | 62.5 | 62.7 | 61.8 | 60.3 | 58.2 | 40 |
| 50 | 49.2 | 60.3 | 62.6 | 62.7 | 61.8 | 60.2 | 58.1 | 50 |
| 00 | 2° 50.0 | 7° 60.5 | 12° 62.6 | 17° 62.7 | 22° 61.7 | 27° 60.1 | 32° 58.0 | 00 |
| 10 | 50.8 | 60.6 | 62.6 | 62.6 | 61.7 | 60.1 | 57.9 | 10 |
| 20 | 51.4 | 60.7 | 62.6 | 62.6 | 61.6 | 60.0 | 57.8 | 20 |
| 30 | 52.1 | 60.9 | 62.7 | 62.6 | 61.6 | 59.9 | 57.8 | 30 |
| 40 | 52.7 | 61.0 | 62.7 | 62.6 | 61.5 | 59.9 | 57.7 | 40 |
| 50 | 53.3 | 61.1 | 62.7 | 62.6 | 61.5 | 59.8 | 57.6 | 50 |
| 00 | 3° 53.8 | 8° 61.2 | 13° 62.7 | 18° 62.5 | 23° 61.5 | 28° 59.7 | 33° 57.5 | 00 |
| 10 | 54.3 | 61.3 | 62.7 | 62.5 | 61.4 | 59.7 | 57.4 | 10 |
| 20 | 54.8 | 61.4 | 62.7 | 62.5 | 61.4 | 59.6 | 57.4 | 20 |
| 30 | 55.2 | 61.5 | 62.8 | 62.5 | 61.3 | 59.6 | 57.3 | 30 |
| 40 | 55.6 | 61.6 | 62.8 | 62.4 | 61.3 | 59.5 | 57.2 | 40 |
| 50 | 55.9 | 61.6 | 62.8 | 62.4 | 61.2 | 59.4 | 57.1 | 50 |
| 00 | 4° 56.4 | 9° 61.7 | 14° 62.8 | 19° 62.4 | 24° 61.2 | 29° 59.3 | 34° 57.0 | 00 |
| 10 | 56.7 | 61.8 | 62.8 | 62.3 | 61.1 | 59.3 | 56.9 | 10 |
| 20 | 57.1 | 61.9 | 62.8 | 62.3 | 61.1 | 59.2 | 56.9 | 20 |
| 30 | 57.4 | 61.9 | 62.8 | 62.3 | 61.0 | 59.1 | 56.8 | 30 |
| 40 | 57.7 | 62.0 | 62.8 | 62.2 | 60.9 | 59.1 | 56.7 | 40 |
| 50 | 57.9 | 62.1 | 62.8 | 62.2 | 60.9 | 59.0 | 56.6 | 50 |

| H.P. | L U | L U | L U | L U | L U | L U | L U | H.P. |
|---|---|---|---|---|---|---|---|---|
| 54.0 | 0.3 0.9 | 0.3 0.9 | 0.4 1.0 | 0.5 1.1 | 0.6 1.2 | 0.7 1.3 | 0.9 1.5 | 54.0 |
| 54.3 | 0.7 1.1 | 0.7 1.2 | 0.7 1.2 | 0.8 1.3 | 0.9 1.4 | 1.1 1.5 | 1.2 1.7 | 54.3 |
| 54.6 | 1.1 1.4 | 1.1 1.4 | 1.1 1.4 | 1.2 1.5 | 1.3 1.6 | 1.4 1.7 | 1.5 1.8 | 54.6 |
| 54.9 | 1.4 1.6 | 1.5 1.6 | 1.5 1.6 | 1.6 1.7 | 1.6 1.8 | 1.8 1.9 | 1.9 2.0 | 54.9 |
| 55.2 | 1.8 1.8 | 1.8 1.8 | 1.9 1.9 | 1.9 1.9 | 2.0 2.0 | 2.1 2.1 | 2.2 2.2 | 55.2 |
| 55.5 | 2.2 2.0 | 2.2 2.0 | 2.3 2.1 | 2.3 2.1 | 2.4 2.2 | 2.4 2.3 | 2.5 2.4 | 55.5 |
| 55.8 | 2.6 2.2 | 2.6 2.2 | 2.6 2.3 | 2.7 2.3 | 2.7 2.4 | 2.8 2.4 | 2.9 2.5 | 55.8 |
| 56.1 | 3.0 2.4 | 3.0 2.5 | 3.0 2.5 | 3.0 2.5 | 3.1 2.6 | 3.1 2.6 | 3.2 2.7 | 56.1 |
| 56.4 | 3.4 2.7 | 3.4 2.7 | 3.4 2.7 | 3.4 2.7 | 3.5 2.8 | 3.5 2.9 | 3.5 2.9 | 56.4 |
| 56.7 | 3.7 2.9 | 3.7 2.9 | 3.8 2.9 | 3.8 2.9 | 3.8 3.0 | 3.8 3.0 | 3.9 3.0 | 56.7 |
| 57.0 | 4.1 3.1 | 4.1 3.1 | 4.1 3.1 | 4.1 3.1 | 4.2 3.1 | 4.2 3.2 | 4.2 3.2 | 57.0 |
| 57.3 | 4.5 3.3 | 4.5 3.3 | 4.5 3.3 | 4.5 3.3 | 4.5 3.4 | 4.6 3.4 | 4.6 3.3 | 57.3 |
| 57.6 | 4.9 3.5 | 4.9 3.5 | 4.9 3.5 | 4.9 3.5 | 4.9 3.5 | 4.9 3.5 | 4.9 3.6 | 57.6 |
| 57.9 | 5.3 3.8 | 5.3 3.8 | 5.2 3.8 | 5.2 3.7 | 5.2 3.7 | 5.2 3.7 | 5.2 3.7 | 57.9 |
| 58.2 | 5.6 4.0 | 5.6 4.0 | 5.6 4.0 | 5.6 3.9 | 5.6 3.9 | 5.6 3.9 | 5.6 3.9 | 58.2 |
| 58.5 | 6.0 4.2 | 6.0 4.2 | 6.0 4.2 | 6.0 4.2 | 6.0 4.1 | 5.9 4.1 | 5.9 4.1 | 58.5 |
| 58.8 | 6.4 4.4 | 6.4 4.4 | 6.4 4.4 | 6.3 4.4 | 6.3 4.3 | 6.3 4.3 | 6.2 4.2 | 58.8 |
| 59.1 | 6.8 4.6 | 6.8 4.6 | 6.7 4.6 | 6.7 4.6 | 6.7 4.5 | 6.6 4.5 | 6.6 4.4 | 59.1 |
| 59.4 | 7.2 4.8 | 7.1 4.8 | 7.1 4.8 | 7.1 4.8 | 7.0 4.7 | 7.0 4.7 | 6.9 4.6 | 59.4 |
| 59.7 | 7.5 5.1 | 7.5 5.0 | 7.5 5.0 | 7.5 5.0 | 7.4 4.9 | 7.3 4.8 | 7.2 4.7 | 59.7 |
| 60.0 | 7.9 5.3 | 7.9 5.3 | 7.9 5.2 | 7.8 5.2 | 7.8 5.1 | 7.7 5.0 | 7.6 4.9 | 60.0 |
| 60.3 | 8.3 5.5 | 8.3 5.5 | 8.2 5.4 | 8.2 5.4 | 8.1 5.3 | 8.0 5.2 | 7.9 5.1 | 60.3 |
| 60.6 | 8.7 5.7 | 8.7 5.7 | 8.6 5.7 | 8.6 5.6 | 8.5 5.5 | 8.4 5.4 | 8.2 5.3 | 60.6 |
| 60.9 | 9.1 5.9 | 9.0 5.9 | 9.0 5.9 | 8.9 5.8 | 8.8 5.7 | 8.6 5.6 | 8.5 5.4 | 60.9 |
| 61.2 | 9.5 6.2 | 9.4 6.1 | 9.4 6.1 | 9.3 6.0 | 9.2 5.9 | 9.1 5.8 | 8.9 5.6 | 61.2 |
| 61.5 | 9.8 6.4 | 9.8 6.3 | 9.7 6.3 | 9.7 6.2 | 9.5 6.1 | 9.4 5.9 | 9.2 5.8 | 61.5 |

## DIP

| Ht. of Eye (m) | Corrⁿ | Ht. of Eye (ft) | Ht. of Eye (m) | Corrⁿ | Ht. of Eye (ft) |
|---|---|---|---|---|---|
| 2.4 | 2.8 | 8.0 | 9.5 | 5.5 | 31.5 |
| 2.6 | 2.9 | 8.6 | 9.9 | 5.6 | 32.7 |
| 2.8 | 3.0 | 9.2 | 10.3 | 5.7 | 33.9 |
| 3.0 | 3.1 | 9.8 | 10.6 | 5.8 | 35.1 |
| 3.2 | 3.2 | 10.5 | 11.0 | 5.9 | 36.3 |
| 3.4 | 3.3 | 11.2 | 11.4 | 6.0 | 37.6 |
| 3.6 | 3.4 | 11.9 | 11.8 | 6.1 | 38.9 |
| 3.8 | 3.5 | 12.6 | 12.2 | 6.2 | 40.1 |
| 4.0 | 3.6 | 13.3 | 12.6 | 6.3 | 41.5 |
| 4.3 | 3.7 | 14.1 | 13.0 | 6.4 | 42.8 |
| 4.5 | 3.8 | 14.9 | 13.4 | 6.5 | 44.2 |
| 4.7 | 3.9 | 15.7 | 13.8 | 6.6 | 45.5 |
| 5.0 | 4.0 | 16.5 | 14.2 | 6.7 | 46.9 |
| 5.2 | 4.1 | 17.4 | 14.7 | 6.8 | 48.4 |
| 5.5 | 4.2 | 18.3 | 15.1 | 6.9 | 49.8 |
| 5.8 | 4.3 | 19.1 | 15.5 | 7.0 | 51.3 |
| 6.1 | 4.4 | 20.1 | 16.0 | 7.1 | 52.8 |
| 6.3 | 4.5 | 21.0 | 16.5 | 7.2 | 54.3 |
| 6.6 | 4.6 | 22.0 | 16.9 | 7.3 | 55.8 |
| 6.9 | 4.7 | 22.9 | 17.4 | 7.4 | 57.4 |
| 7.2 | 4.8 | 23.9 | 17.9 | 7.5 | 58.9 |
| 7.5 | 4.9 | 24.9 | 18.4 | 7.6 | 60.5 |
| 7.9 | 5.0 | 26.0 | 18.8 | 7.7 | 62.1 |
| 8.2 | 5.1 | 27.1 | 19.3 | 7.8 | 63.8 |
| 8.5 | 5.2 | 28.1 | 19.8 | 7.9 | 65.4 |
| 8.8 | 5.3 | 29.2 | 20.4 | 8.0 | 67.1 |
| 9.2 | 5.4 | 30.4 | 20.9 | 8.1 | 68.8 |
| 9.5 | | 31.5 | 21.4 | | 70.5 |

### MOON CORRECTION TABLE

The correction is in two parts; the first correction is taken from the upper part of the table with argument apparent altitude, and the second from the lower part, with argument H.P., in the same column as that from which the first correction was taken. Separate corrections are given in the lower part for lower (L) and upper (U) limbs. All corrections are to be added to apparent altitude, but 30' is to be subtracted from the altitude of the upper limb.

For corrections for pressure and temperature see page A4.

For bubble sextant observations ignore dip, take the mean of upper and lower limb corrections and subtract 15' from the altitude.

App. Alt. = Apparent altitude = Sextant altitude corrected for index error and dip.

**Figure 20–1.** Moon altitude correction tables from the *Nautical Almanac*. Note that all corrections are additive, but that 30' must be subtracted from observations of the moon's upper limb.

degrees of apparent altitude appear, to the reading opposite the minutes of ha. Interpolation, if any is necessary,
can be done by eye. In our example, descending the
column headed 20°–24°, under 22° and opposite 40' you
will see the value 61.5'. Since this value remains the
same for all minutes between 40' and 50', no interpolation is needed, and so, for our apparent altitude of
22°45.3', the R-correction is 61.5'.

The second, or H.P.-correction, is for horizontal parallax. Horizontal parallax is the difference in altitude between that measured from the observer's position on the
earth's surface, and that measured from the center of the
earth. A correction for H.P. is necessary only for moon
sights; all the other celestial bodies are far enough away
to make the correction negligible. The amount of the H.P.-
correction is found by descending the same column as for
the first, R-correction, into the lower half of the table—
under the heading L, for lower limb, or U, for upper
limb—to the reading opposite the value for H.P., which
you will find in the daily pages of the almanac as will be
described momentarily. In our moon sight, we had chosen to use the upper limb for our observation, and the
horizontal parallax had been found in the almanac to be
59.2'. Descending the 20°–24° column in Figure 20–1,
under the U-heading, you can see that the value for an
H.P.of 59.1' would be 4.5', and for an H.P. of 59.4', it
would be 4.7'. Interpolating by eye, you arrive at an H.P.-
correction of 4.6' for our H.P. of 59.2' as entered on the
workform.

Both of the moon-table corrections are added to the
apparent altitude, but in the case of observations of the
moon's upper limb, 30' must be subtracted from the total.
Accordingly, when our R-, H.P.-, and upper-limb corrections are all applied to the apparent altitude of 22°45.3',
the resulting observed altitude, Ho, becomes 23°21.4'.

As in the procedure for our sun sight, the observed
altitude is set aside while we turn to the almanac for the

needed astronomical data. It is here, when you open to
the appropriate daily page to find the moon's Greenwich
hour angle and declination (Figure 20–2), that you will
find, in the moon's fifth column opposite the nearest hour
of Greenwich mean time, the H.P. (59.2′). This is the
value that is used for the second half of the altitude
correction, and you will notice that I have included a
small box in which to record it on my suggested
workform.

A moon sight is timed in exactly the same way as in
an observation of the sun or any other celestial body, at
the instant the reflected image of the body appears to
touch the horizon. In our June 8 practical example, the

### 1984 JUNE 8, 9, 10 (FRI., SAT., SUN.)

| G.M.T. | SUN | | MOON | | | |
|---|---|---|---|---|---|---|
| | G.H.A. | Dec. | G.H.A. | v | Dec. | d H.P. |
| **8** 00 | 180 15.9 | N22 50.6 | 70 23.2 | 11.5 | N 2 23.8 | 15.5 59.3 |
| 01 | 195 15.8 | 50.9 | 84 53.7 | 11.5 | 2 08.3 | 15.5 59.3 |
| 02 | 210 15.7 | 51.1 | 99 24.2 | 11.5 | 1 52.8 | 15.5 59.3 |
| 03 | 225 15.5 | ·· 51.3 | 113 54.7 | 11.6 | 1 37.3 | 15.6 59.3 |
| 04 | 240 15.4 | 51.5 | 128 25.3 | 11.5 | 1 21.7 | 15.5 59.3 |
| 05 | 255 15.3 | 51.8 | 142 55.8 | 11.5 | 1 06.2 | 15.5 59.3 |
| 06 | 270 15.2 | N22 52.0 | 157 26.3 | 11.6 | N 0 50.7 | 15.5 59.3 |
| 07 | 285 15.1 | 52.2 | 171 56.9 | 11.6 | 0 35.2 | 15.6 59.3 |
| 08 | 300 14.9 | 52.4 | 186 27.5 | 11.5 | 0 19.6 | 15.5 59.3 |
| F 09 | 315 14.8 | ·· 52.6 | 200 58.0 | 11.6 | N 0 04.1 | 15.6 59.3 |
| R 10 | 330 14.7 | 52.9 | 215 28.6 | 11.6 | S 0 11.5 | 15.5 59.3 |
| I 11 | 345 14.6 | 53.1 | 229 59.2 | 11.5 | 0 27.0 | 15.5 59.3 |
| D 12 | 0 14.5 | N22 53.3 | 244 29.7 | 11.6 | S 0 42.5 | 15.5 59.3 |
| A 13 | 15 14.3 | 53.5 | 259 00.3 | 11.6 | 0 58.0 | 15.6 59.3 |
| Y 14 | 30 14.2 | 53.7 | 273 30.9 | 11.5 | 1 13.6 | 15.5 59.3 |
| 15 | 45 14.1 | ·· 54.0 | 288 01.4 | 11.6 | 1 29.1 | 15.5 59.3 |
| 16 | 60 14.0 | 54.2 | 302 32.0 | 11.5 | 1 44.6 | 15.5 59.3 |
| 17 | 75 13.9 | 54.4 | 317 02.5 | 11.6 | 2 00.1 | 15.6 59.3 |
| 18 | 90 13.7 | N22 54.6 | 331 33.1 | 11.5 | S 2 15.5 | 15.5 59.3 |
| 19 | 105 13.6 | 54.8 | 346 03.6 | 11.6 | 2 31.0 | 15.5 59.3 |
| **20** | 120 13.5 | 55.0 | 0 34.2 | 11.5 | 2 46.5 | 15.4 59.2 |
| 21 | 135 13.4 | ·· 55.2 | 15 04.7 | 11.5 | 3 01.9 | 15.4 59.2 |
| 22 | 150 13.3 | 55.4 | 29 35.2 | 11.5 | 3 17.3 | 15.4 59.2 |
| 23 | 165 13.1 | 55.7 | 44 05.7 | 11.5 | 3 32.7 | 15.4 59.2 |

*Figure 20–2.* **Excerpt from the** *Nautical Almanac* **showing
astronomical data for the moon on June 8, 1984, at 20ʰ GMT.**

watch again was set to Greenwich mean time, and it read 20:57:09 at the moment of the observation. In this case, however, we will assume that we had found, by an earlier radio time-tick, that our watch was reading 1 second slow, and so, as it shows in the workform, 1 second was added to correct the GMT of the observation to 20:57:10.

The almanac's daily page, an excerpt of which is shown in Figure 20–2, is entered in the same way as you did for the sun, except, of course, you use the MOON columns. In our example, the tabular Greenwich hour angle of 0°34.2′ is found opposite the hours of GMT; here, 20$^h$. Similarly, the increment for the 57 minutes and 10 seconds of time is found in the yellow *Increments and Corrections* table in the back of the almanac (Figure 20–3); be careful again to use the MOON column. In the case of the moon, there is a small, additional increment called the *v*-correction, which takes into account the excesses in the moon's irregular movement over the constant rate used in the increment table. The value of *v* is found in the second column of moon data (Figure 20–2); at 20 hours Greenwich mean time on June 8, it is 11.5′, and a box has been provided on the workform to record it. Returning to the body of the workform, the first GHA increment of 13° 38.4′ (for 57$^m$10$^s$), and the small *v*-increment, found in the columns at the right of Figure 20–3 to be 11.0′ for a *v*-value of 11.5′, are added to the tabular Greenwich hour angle to obtain the final GHA for our observation: 14° 23.6′.

The declination of the moon is found opposite the hour of observation in the third of the moon's daily-page columns, as seen in Figure 20–2. At 20 hours GMT, it is 2° 46.5′S. While this declination figure can be adjusted for minutes and seconds of time by inspection, as you did for the sun, it is usually quicker and easier to note the value for *d* (which represents the hourly change in declination) in the fourth column of the moon data and enter that value in the increment table in the same way as you did

INCREMENTS AND CORRECTIONS 57ᵐ

| 57 | SUN PLANETS | ARIES | MOON | v or Corr d | v or Corr d | v or Corr d |
|---|---|---|---|---|---|---|
| s | ° ' | ° ' | ° ' | ' ' | ' ' | ' ' |
| 00 | 14 15·0 | 14 17·3 | 13 36·1 | 0·0 0·0 | 6·0 5·8 | 12·0 11·5 |
| 01 | 14 15·3 | 14 17·6 | 13 36·3 | 0·1 0·1 | 6·1 5·8 | 12·1 11·6 |
| 02 | 14 15·5 | 14 17·8 | 13 36·5 | 0·2 0·2 | 6·2 5·9 | 12·2 11·7 |
| 03 | 14 15·8 | 14 18·1 | 13 36·8 | 0·3 0·3 | 6·3 6·0 | 12·3 11·8 |
| 04 | 14 16·0 | 14 18·3 | 13 37·0 | 0·4 0·4 | 6·4 6·1 | 12·4 11·9 |
| 05 | 14 16·3 | 14 18·6 | 13 37·2 | 0·5 0·5 | 6·5 6·2 | 12·5 12·0 |
| 06 | 14 16·5 | 14 18·8 | 13 37·5 | 0·6 0·6 | 6·6 6·3 | 12·6 12·1 |
| 07 | 14 16·8 | 14 19·1 | 13 37·7 | 0·7 0·7 | 6·7 6·4 | 12·7 12·2 |
| 08 | 14 17·0 | 14 19·3 | 13 38·0 | 0·8 0·8 | 6·8 6·5 | 12·8 12·3 |
| 09 | 14 17·3 | 14 19·6 | 13 38·2 | 0·9 0·9 | 6·9 6·6 | 12·9 12·4 |
| 10 | 14 17·5 | 14 19·8 | 13 38·4 | 1·0 1·0 | 7·0 6·7 | 13·0 12·5 |
| 11 | 14 17·8 | 14 20·1 | 13 38·7 | 1·1 1·1 | 7·1 6·8 | 13·1 12·6 |
| 12 | 14 18·0 | 14 20·3 | 13 38·9 | 1·2 1·2 | 7·2 6·9 | 13·2 12·7 |
| 13 | 14 18·3 | 14 20·6 | 13 39·2 | 1·3 1·2 | 7·3 7·0 | 13·3 12·7 |
| 14 | 14 18·5 | 14 20·9 | 13 39·4 | 1·4 1·3 | 7·4 7·1 | 13·4 12·8 |
| 15 | 14 18·8 | 14 21·1 | 13 39·6 | 1·5 1·4 | 7·5 7·2 | 13·5 12·9 |
| 16 | 14 19·0 | 14 21·4 | 13 39·9 | 1·6 1·5 | 7·6 7·3 | 13·6 13·0 |
| 17 | 14 19·3 | 14 21·6 | 13 40·1 | 1·7 1·6 | 7·7 7·4 | 13·7 13·1 |
| 18 | 14 19·5 | 14 21·9 | 13 40·3 | 1·8 1·7 | 7·8 7·5 | 13·8 13·2 |
| 19 | 14 19·8 | 14 22·1 | 13 40·6 | 1·9 1·8 | 7·9 7·6 | 13·9 13·3 |
| 20 | 14 20·0 | 14 22·4 | 13 40·8 | 2·0 1·9 | 8·0 7·7 | 14·0 13·4 |
| 21 | 14 20·3 | 14 22·6 | 13 41·1 | 2·1 2·0 | 8·1 7·8 | 14·1 13·5 |
| 22 | 14 20·5 | 14 22·9 | 13 41·3 | 2·2 2·1 | 8·2 7·9 | 14·2 13·6 |
| 23 | 14 20·8 | 14 23·1 | 13 41·5 | 2·3 2·2 | 8·3 8·0 | 14·3 13·7 |
| 24 | 14 21·0 | 14 23·4 | 13 41·8 | 2·4 2·3 | 8·4 8·1 | 14·4 13·8 |
| 25 | 14 21·3 | 14 23·6 | 13 42·0 | 2·5 2·4 | 8·5 8·1 | 14·5 13·9 |
| 26 | 14 21·5 | 14 23·9 | 13 42·3 | 2·6 2·5 | 8·6 8·2 | 14·6 14·0 |
| 27 | 14 21·8 | 14 24·1 | 13 42·5 | 2·7 2·6 | 8·7 8·3 | 14·7 14·1 |
| 28 | 14 22·0 | 14 24·4 | 13 42·7 | 2·8 2·7 | 8·8 8·4 | 14·8 14·2 |
| 29 | 14 22·3 | 14 24·6 | 13 43·0 | 2·9 2·8 | 8·9 8·5 | 14·9 14·3 |
| 30 | 14 22·5 | 14 24·9 | 13 43·2 | 3·0 2·9 | 9·0 8·6 | 15·0 14·4 |
| 31 | 14 22·8 | 14 25·1 | 13 43·4 | 3·1 3·0 | 9·1 8·7 | 15·1 14·5 |
| 32 | 14 23·0 | 14 25·4 | 13 43·7 | 3·2 3·1 | 9·2 8·8 | 15·2 14·6 |
| 33 | 14 23·3 | 14 25·6 | 13 43·9 | 3·3 3·2 | 9·3 8·9 | 15·3 14·7 |
| 34 | 14 23·5 | 14 25·9 | 13 44·2 | 3·4 3·3 | 9·4 9·0 | 15·4 14·8 |
| 35 | 14 23·8 | 14 26·1 | 13 44·4 | 3·5 3·4 | 9·5 9·1 | 15·5 14·9 |
| 36 | 14 24·0 | 14 26·4 | 13 44·6 | 3·6 3·5 | 9·6 9·2 | 15·6 15·0 |
| 37 | 14 24·3 | 14 26·6 | 13 44·9 | 3·7 3·5 | 9·7 9·3 | 15·7 15·0 |
| 38 | 14 24·5 | 14 26·9 | 13 45·1 | 3·8 3·6 | 9·8 9·4 | 15·8 15·1 |
| 39 | 14 24·8 | 14 27·1 | 13 45·4 | 3·9 3·7 | 9·9 9·5 | 15·9 15·2 |
| 40 | 14 25·0 | 14 27·4 | 13 45·6 | 4·0 3·8 | 10·0 9·6 | 16·0 15·3 |
| 41 | 14 25·3 | 14 27·6 | 13 45·8 | 4·1 3·9 | 10·1 9·7 | 16·1 15·4 |
| 42 | 14 25·5 | 14 27·9 | 13 46·1 | 4·2 4·0 | 10·2 9·8 | 16·2 15·5 |
| 43 | 14 25·8 | 14 28·1 | 13 46·3 | 4·3 4·1 | 10·3 9·9 | 16·3 15·6 |
| 44 | 14 26·0 | 14 28·4 | 13 46·5 | 4·4 4·2 | 10·4 10·0 | 16·4 15·7 |
| 45 | 14 26·3 | 14 28·6 | 13 46·8 | 4·5 4·3 | 10·5 10·1 | 16·5 15·8 |
| 46 | 14 26·5 | 14 28·9 | 13 47·0 | 4·6 4·4 | 10·6 10·2 | 16·6 15·9 |
| 47 | 14 26·8 | 14 29·1 | 13 47·3 | 4·7 4·5 | 10·7 10·3 | 16·7 16·0 |
| 48 | 14 27·0 | 14 29·4 | 13 47·5 | 4·8 4·6 | 10·8 10·4 | 16·8 16·1 |
| 49 | 14 27·3 | 14 29·6 | 13 47·7 | 4·9 4·7 | 10·9 10·4 | 16·9 16·2 |
| 50 | 14 27·5 | 14 29·9 | 13 48·0 | 5·0 4·8 | 11·0 10·5 | 17·0 16·3 |
| 51 | 14 27·8 | 14 30·1 | 13 48·2 | 5·1 4·9 | 11·1 10·6 | 17·1 16·4 |
| 52 | 14 28·0 | 14 30·4 | 13 48·5 | 5·2 5·0 | 11·2 10·7 | 17·2 16·5 |
| 53 | 14 28·3 | 14 30·6 | 13 48·7 | 5·3 5·1 | 11·3 10·8 | 17·3 16·6 |
| 54 | 14 28·5 | 14 30·9 | 13 48·9 | 5·4 5·2 | 11·4 10·9 | 17·4 16·7 |
| 55 | 14 28·8 | 14 31·1 | 13 49·2 | 5·5 5·3 | 11·5 11·0 | 17·5 16·8 |
| 56 | 14 29·0 | 14 31·4 | 13 49·4 | 5·6 5·4 | 11·6 11·1 | 17·6 16·9 |
| 57 | 14 29·3 | 14 31·6 | 13 49·7 | 5·7 5·5 | 11·7 11·2 | 17·7 17·0 |
| 58 | 14 29·5 | 14 31·9 | 13 49·9 | 5·8 5·6 | 11·8 11·3 | 17·8 17·1 |
| 59 | 14 29·8 | 14 32·1 | 13 50·1 | 5·9 5·7 | 11·9 11·4 | 17·9 17·2 |
| 60 | 14 30·0 | 14 32·4 | 13 50·4 | 6·0 5·8 | 12·0 11·5 | 18·0 17·3 |

**Figure 20–3.** Excerpt from the *Nautical Almanac's Increments and Corrections* tables indicating the GHA increment for 57ᵐ10ˢ, and the appropriate *v* and *d* corrections.

for the v-increment. In our example, the d-correction at 57 minutes for a d-value of 15.4' is 14.8'. When this correction is applied to the tabular declination, the final declination for 20ʰ57ᵐ10ˢ GMT becomes 3°01.3'S. Unlike the v-increment, which is always additive, it is necessary to check whether the declination is increasing or decreasing (in our example, it is the former), so that you apply the d-correction with the proper sign.

With the extra altitude adjustment, the additional hour-angle correction, and, if you wish, using the d-correction to adjust the declination, the special treatment of a moon sight is now complete. For clarity, I have described each step in detail, but you will soon find that with a workform and a little practice the few extra requirements of a moon sight quickly become routine. The remaining steps in deriving the moon's line of position are identical with the procedure you followed with the sun.

Having obtained the Greenwich hour angle, you must next apply your assumed longitude (selecting it to come out to a whole degree) to arrive at the local hour angle. The DR position in our example is 69°31'W, so 69°23.6'W would be appropriate for an assumed longitude, but, as in the case of our sun sight, aλ is larger than GHA, so 360° must be added to the GHA before the subtraction (required, you will remember, because the longitude is West) can take place. The workform shows the calculations resulting in a local hour angle of 305°. We now have the LHA (305°), the declination (3°01.3'S), and assume a latitude (41°) near our DR latitude of 41°08'N, the three values needed to enter the sight reduction table. An excerpt of the applicable page from Pub. No. 249, Volume III, is shown in Figure 20–4. Note that since the declination is South, while the assumed latitude is North, the table headed "Declination Contrary Name to Latitude" has been selected.

In the same manner as for the sun, enter the column

| N. Lat. LHA greater than 180°......... Zn=Z  LHA less than 180°......... Zn=360−Z | DECLINATION (0°–14°) | CONTRARY NAME TO LATITUDE | LAT 41° |

| HA | 0° Hc | d | Z | 1° Hc | d | Z | 2° Hc | d | Z | 3° Hc | d | Z | 4° Hc | d | Z | 5° Hc | d | d | Z | 13° Hc | d | Z | 14° Hc | d | Z | LHA |
|---|---|---|---|---|---|---|---|---|---|---|---|---|---|---|---|---|---|---|---|---|---|---|---|---|---|---|---|
| 69 | 15 42 | 41 | 104 | 15 01 | 41 | 105 | 14 19 | 41 | 106 | 13 38 | 41 | 106 | 12 57 | 42 | 107 | 12 15 | 41 | 42 | 113 | 06 40 | 43 | 114 | 05 57 | 42 | 114 | 291 |
| 68 | 16 25 | 41 | 105 | 15 44 | 41 | 106 | 15 03 | 41 | 106 | 14 22 | 42 | 107 | 13 40 | 42 | 108 | 12 58 | 4? | 42 | 114 | 07 21 | 43 | 114 | 06 38 | 43 | 115 | 292 |
| 67 | 17 09 | 41 | 106 | 16 28 | 42 | 106 | 15 46 | 41 | 107 | 15 05 | 42 | 108 | 14 23 | 42 | 109 | 13 41 | 42 | 43 | 114 | 08 02 | 43 | 115 | 07 19 | 43 | 116 | 293 |
| 66 | 17 53 | 42 | 106 | 17 11 | 41 | 107 | 16 30 | 42 | 108 | 15 48 | 42 | 109 | 15 06 | 42 | 109 | 14 24 | ? | 43 | 115 | 08 43 | 43 | 116 | 08 00 | 43 | 117 | 294 |
| 65 | 18 36 | -42 | 107 | 17 54 | -41 | 108 | 17 13 | -42 | 109 | 16 31 | -42 | 109 | 15 49 | -43 | 110 | 15 06 | − | -43 | 116 | 09 24 | 44 | 117 | 08 40 | -43 | 117 | 295 |
| 64 | 19 19 | 42 | 108 | 18 37 | 42 | 109 | 17 55 | 42 | 109 | 17 13 | 42 | 110 | 16 31 | 43 | 111 | 15 48 | 4 | 43 | 117 | 10 04 | 44 | 117 | 09 20 | 43 | 118 | 296 |
| 63 | 20 02 | 42 | 109 | 19 20 | 42 | 109 | 18 38 | 43 | 110 | 17 56 | 43 | 111 | 17 13 | 42 | 112 | 16 31 | 4. | 44 | 117 | 10 44 | 44 | 118 | 10 00 | 44 | 119 | 297 |
| 62 | 20 45 | 42 | 109 | 20 03 | 43 | 110 | 19 21 | 43 | 111 | 18 38 | 43 | 112 | 17 55 | 43 | 112 | 17 12 | 43 | 44 | 118 | 11 24 | 44 | 119 | 10 40 | 44 | 119 | 298 |
| 61 | 21 28 | 43 | 110 | 20 45 | 42 | 111 | 20 03 | 43 | 112 | 19 20 | 43 | 112 | 18 37 | 43 | 113 | 17 54 | 43 | 4 | 119 | 12 04 | 45 | 119 | 11 19 | 43 | 120 | 299 |
| 60 | 22 10 | -42 | 111 | 21 28 | 43 | 112 | 20 45 | -43 | 112 | 20 02 | -43 | 113 | 19 19 | -44 | 114 | 18 35 | -43 | 4 | 119 | 12 43 | -45 | 120 | 11 58 | -44 | 121 | 300 |
| 59 | 22 52 | 42 | 112 | 22 10 | 43 | 112 | 21 27 | 44 | 113 | 20 43 | 43 | 114 | 20 00 | 44 | 115 | 19 16 | 43 | | 120 | 13 22 | 45 | 121 | 12 37 | 45 | 122 | 301 |
| 58 | 23 34 | 43 | 112 | 22 51 | 43 | 113 | 22 08 | 43 | 114 | 21 25 | 44 | 115 | 20 41 | 44 | 115 | 19 57 | 44 | | 121 | 14 01 | 45 | 122 | 13 16 | 46 | 122 | 302 |
| 57 | 24 16 | 43 | 113 | 23 33 | 44 | 114 | 22 49 | 44 | 115 | 22 06 | 44 | 115 | 21 22 | 44 | 116 | 20 38 | 45 | | 122 | 14 39 | 45 | 122 | 13 54 | 46 | 123 | 303 |
| 56 | 24 58 | 44 | 114 | 24 14 | 45 | 115 | 23 31 | 44 | 115 | 22 47 | 45 | 116 | 22 02 | 44 | 117 | 21 18 | 45 | | 123 | 15 17 | 46 | 123 | 14 31 | 45 | 124 | 304 |
| 55 | 25 39 | -44 | 115 | 24 55 | -44 | 115 | 24 11 | -44 | 116 | 23 27 | -44 | 117 | 22 43 | -45 | 118 | 21 58 | -45 | | 123 | 15 55 | -46 | 124 | 15 09 | -44 | 125 | 305 |
| 54 | 26 20 | 44 | 116 | 25 36 | 44 | 116 | 24 52 | 45 | 117 | 24 07 | 44 | 118 | 23 23 | 45 | 119 | 22 38 | 45 | 47 | 124 | 16 32 | 46 | 125 | 15 46 | 46 | 125 | 306 |
| 53 | 27 01 | 44 | 116 | 26 17 | 45 | 117 | 25 32 | 45 | 118 | 24 47 | 45 | 119 | 24 02 | 45 | 119 | 23 17 | 45 | 47 | 125 | 17 09 | 46 | 126 | 16 23 | 47 | 126 | 307 |
| 52 | 27 41 | 44 | 117 | 26 57 | 45 | 118 | 26 12 | 46 | 119 | 25 27 | 45 | 119 | 24 42 | 46 | 120 | 23 56 | 46 | 47 | 126 | 17 46 | 47 | 126 | 16 59 | 47 | 127 | 308 |
| 51 | 28 21 | 44 | 118 | 27 37 | 46 | 119 | 26 51 | 45 | 120 | 26 06 | 45 | 120 | 25 21 | 46 | 121 | 24 35 | 46 | 48 | 126 | 18 22 | 47 | 127 | 17 35 | 47 | 128 | 309 |

*Figure 20–4.* Excerpt from Pub. No. 249, Volume III, showing the values for Latitude 41°N, Declination 3°S, and LHA 305 to be: Hc 23°27′, d −44′, Z 117°.

for 3° declination, and, opposite the LHA of 305°, extract the three values: Hc 23°27′, d −44′, and Z 117°. The tabular value for Hc needs to be adjusted for the incremental minutes of declination (here, 01.3′), and this is done in Table 5, excerpted in Figure 20–5. In our practical example, the altitude differential, d, of −44′, applied to 1′ of declination, yields a correction of −01′ to the tabular altitude, making the final Hc 23°26.0′. This Hc is then compared with the observed altitude, Ho, which we determined earlier, to arrive at the intercept, a. Since Hc in our example is greater than Ho, the intercept of 4.6′ is "away." Applying the rule in the upper corner of the sight reduction table (Figure 20–4), with an LHA of 305°, the true azimuth, Zn, is equal to the azimuth angle, Z, so our azimuth line for plotting is 117°.

The final step is to plot the intercept from the as-

## TABLE 5.—Correction to Tabulated Altitude

| 41 42 | 43 44 45 | 46 47 48 | 49 50 51 | 52 53 54 | 55 56 57 | 58 59 60 | $\dfrac{d}{\prime}$ |
|---|---|---|---|---|---|---|---|
| 0  0 | 0  0  0 | 0  0  0 | 0  0  0 | 0  0  0 | 0  0  0 | 0  0  0 | 0 |
| 1  1 | 1  1  1 | 1  1  1 | 1  1  1 | 1  1  1 | 1  1  1 | 1  1  1 | 1 |
| 1  1 | 1  1  2 | 2  2  2 | 2  2  2 | 2  2  2 | 2  2  2 | 2  2  2 | 2 |
| 2  2 | 2  2  2 | 2  2  2 | 2  2  3 | 3  3  3 | 3  3  3 | 3  3  3 | 3 |
| 3  3 | 3  3  3 | 3  3  3 | 3  3  3 | 3  4  4 | 4  4  4 | 4  4  4 | 4 |
| 3  4 | 4  4  4 | 4  4  4 | 4  4  4 | 4  4  4 | 5  5  5 | 5  5  5 | 5 |
| 4  4 | 4  4  4 | 5  5  5 | 5  5  5 | 5  5  5 | 6  6  6 | 6  6  6 | 6 |
| 5  5 | 5  5  5 | 5  5  6 | 6  6  6 | 6  6  6 | 6  7  7 | 7  7  7 | 7 |
| 5  6 | 6  6  6 | 6  6  6 | 7  7  7 | 7  7  7 | 7  7  8 | 8  8  8 | 8 |
| 6  6 | 6  7  7 | 7  7  7 | 7  8  8 | 8  8  8 | 8  8  9 | 9  9  9 | 9 |
| 7  7 | 7  7  8 | 8  8  8 | 8  8  8 | 9  9  9 | 9  9 10 | 10 10 10 | 10 |
| 8  8 | 8  8  8 | 8  9  9 | 9  9  9 | 10 10 10 | 10 10 10 | 11 11 11 | 11 |
| 8  8 | 9  9  9 | 9  9 10 | 10 10 10 | 10 11 11 | 11 11 11 | 12 12 12 | 12 |
| 9  9 | 9 10 10 | 10 10 10 | 11 11 11 | 11 11 12 | 12 12 12 | 13 13 13 | 13 |
| 10 10 | 10 10 10 | 11 11 11 | 11 12 12 | 12 12 13 | 13 13 13 | 14 14 14 | 14 |

*Figure 20–5.* **Excerpt from Table 5, Pub. No. 249, showing a correction of 01′ for *d* of 44, and incremental minutes of declination, 01.**

sumed position; in our example in the direction opposite the azimuth ("away"). At the end of the intercept, the line of position is constructed at right angles to the azimuth line. Label the position line, and your moon sight is recorded for posterity.

Many present-day navigators find moon sights to be second only to sun lines, so forget the problems of the ancients, and try the moon yourself. The reward is well worth the few extra steps this valuable body requires.

# 21 The Planets

Four major planets are of interest to celestial navigators: Venus, Mars, Jupiter, and Saturn. As for the sun and moon, the *Nautical Almanac*'s daily pages present the complete astronomical data for each of these planets for each whole hour of Greenwich mean time. Planet information is found on the left-hand page, or "star side" of the almanac, an example of which is shown in Figure 21–1.

Of the four planets, Venus is the most distinctive. Not only is it the brightest body in the heavens besides the sun and moon, but it is also easy to identify as a morning or evening "star," never far from the sun. Under ideal conditions, Venus can be seen in the daytime, offering an opportunity for a simultaneous fix by the observation of two celestial bodies. Jupiter is also quite brilliant, often being brighter than Sirius, the brightest of the stars, but while it can occasionally be observed in daylight, Jupiter frequently provides excellent sights at morning or evening twilight. Mars and Saturn are more difficult to distinguish from the stars at twilight, and you may find it best to work through a quick trial reduction, obtaining an approximate altitude and azimuth to help find them.

As we did with the sun and moon, let's work through

204       1984 OCTOBER 18, 19, 20 (THURS., FRI., SAT.)

| G.M.T | ARIES | VENUS −3.4 | | MARS +0.6 | | JUPITER −1.7 | | SATURN +0.8 | | STARS | | |
|---|---|---|---|---|---|---|---|---|---|---|---|---|
| | G.H.A. | G.H.A. | Dec. | G.H.A. | Dec. | G.H.A. | Dec. | G.H.A. | Dec. | Name | S.H.A. | Dec. |
| 18 00 | 26 39.8 | 151 53.2 | S20 24.2 | 106 47.4 | S25 08.9 | 109 21.6 | S23 25.4 | 162 18.7 | S14 42.6 | Acamar | 315 34.5 | S40 21.8 |
| 01 | 41 42.3 | 166 52.6 | 25.0 | 121 47.9 | 08.7 | 124 23.6 | 25.4 | 177 20.9 | 42.7 | Achernar | 335 42.2 | S57 18.8 |
| 02 | 56 44.8 | 181 51.9 | 25.8 | 136 48.4 | 08.6 | 139 25.7 | 25.4 | 192 23.1 | 42.8 | Acrux | 173 34.8 | S63 00.6 |
| 03 | 71 47.2 | 196 51.2 | .. 26.6 | 151 48.9 | .. 08.4 | 154 27.8 | .. 25.3 | 207 25.3 | .. 42.8 | Adhara | 255 29.7 | S28 56.7 |
| 04 | 86 49.7 | 211 50.6 | 27.4 | 166 49.4 | 08.3 | 169 29.9 | 25.3 | 222 27.4 | 42.9 | Aldebaran | 291 14.3 | N16 28.9 |
| 05 | 101 52.2 | 226 49.9 | 28.2 | 181 49.9 | 08.1 | 184 32.0 | 25.3 | 237 29.6 | 43.0 | | | |
| 06 | 116 54.6 | 241 49.2 | S20 29.0 | 196 50.4 | S25 08.0 | 199 34.1 | S23 25.3 | 252 31.8 | S14 43.1 | Alioth | 166 40.2 | N56 02.6 |
| 07 | 131 57.1 | 256 48.6 | 29.9 | 211 50.9 | 07.8 | 214 36.2 | 25.3 | 267 34.0 | 43.2 | Alkaid | 153 16.5 | N49 23.5 |
| T 08 | 146 59.5 | 271 47.9 | 30.7 | 226 51.4 | 07.7 | 229 38.3 | 25.3 | 282 36.2 | 43.3 | Al Na'ir | 28 10.8 | S47 02.4 |
| H 09 | 162 02.0 | 286 47.2 | .. 31.5 | 241 51.9 | .. 07.5 | 244 40.3 | .. 25.3 | 297 38.3 | .. 43.3 | Alnilam | 276 08.4 | S 1 12.5 |
| U 10 | 177 04.5 | 301 46.5 | 32.3 | 256 52.4 | 07.4 | 259 42.4 | 25.2 | 312 40.5 | 43.4 | Alphard | 218 17.8 | S 8 35.2 |
| R 11 | 192 06.9 | 316 45.9 | 33.1 | 271 52.9 | 07.2 | 274 44.5 | 25.2 | 327 42.7 | 43.5 | | | |
| S 12 | 207 09.4 | 331 45.2 | S20 33.9 | 286 53.4 | S25 07.1 | 289 46.6 | S23 25.2 | 342 44.9 | S14 43.6 | Alphecca | 126 29.9 | N26 46.1 |
| D 13 | 222 11.9 | 346 44.5 | 34.7 | 301 53.9 | 06.9 | 304 48.7 | 25.2 | 357 47.1 | 43.7 | Alpheratz | 358 06.0 | N29 00.5 |
| A 14 | 237 14.3 | 1 43.8 | 35.5 | 316 54.4 | 06.8 | 319 50.8 | 25.2 | 12 49.3 | 43.8 | Altair | 62 31.4 | N 8 49.7 |
| Y 15 | 252 16.8 | 16 43.2 | .. 36.3 | 331 54.9 | .. 06.6 | 334 52.9 | .. 25.2 | 27 51.4 | .. 43.9 | Ankaa | 353 36.7 | S42 23.4 |
| 16 | 267 19.3 | 31 42.5 | 37.1 | 346 55.4 | 06.5 | 349 55.0 | 25.2 | 42 53.6 | 43.9 | Antares | 112 53.5 | S26 24.0 |
| 17 | 282 21.7 | 46 41.8 | 37.9 | 1 55.9 | 06.3 | 4 57.0 | 25.1 | 57 55.8 | 44.0 | | | |
| 18 | 297 24.2 | 61 41.1 | S20 38.7 | 16 56.4 | S25 06.1 | 19 59.1 | S23 25.1 | 72 58.0 | S14 44.1 | Arcturus | 146 16.0 | N19 15.8 |
| 19 | 312 26.6 | 76 40.5 | 39.5 | 31 56.9 | 06.0 | 35 01.2 | 25.1 | 88 00.2 | 44.2 | Atria | 108 15.5 | S69 00.3 |
| 20 | 327 29.1 | 91 39.8 | 40.3 | 46 57.4 | 05.8 | 50 03.3 | 25.1 | 103 02.3 | 44.3 | Avior | 234 27.2 | S59 27.2 |
| 21 | 342 31.6 | 106 39.1 | .. 41.1 | 61 57.9 | .. 05.7 | 65 05.4 | .. 25.1 | 118 04.5 | .. 44.4 | Bellatrix | 278 55.3 | N 6 20.4 |
| 22 | 357 34.0 | 121 38.4 | 41.9 | 76 58.4 | 05.5 | 80 07.5 | 25.1 | 133 06.7 | 44.5 | Betelgeuse | 271 24.9 | N 7 24.5 |
| 23 | 12 36.5 | 136 37.7 | 42.7 | 91 58.9 | 05.4 | 95 09.5 | 25.1 | 148 08.9 | 44.5 | | | |
| 19 00 | 27 39.0 | 151 37.1 | S20 43.5 | 106 59.4 | S25 05.2 | 110 11.6 | S23 25.0 | 163 11.1 | S14 44.6 | Canopus | 264 05.7 | S52 40.8 |
| 01 | 42 41.4 | 166 36.4 | 44.3 | 121 59.9 | 05.0 | 125 13.7 | 25.0 | 178 13.3 | 44.7 | Capella | 281 06.6 | N45 59.0 |
| 02 | 57 43.9 | 181 35.7 | 45.1 | 137 00.4 | 04.9 | 140 15.8 | 25.0 | 193 15.4 | 44.8 | Deneb | 49 46.4 | N45 13.7 |
| 03 | 72 46.4 | 196 35.0 | .. 45.9 | 152 00.9 | .. 04.7 | 155 17.9 | .. 25.0 | 208 17.6 | .. 44.9 | Denebola | 182 56.2 | N14 39.6 |
| 04 | 87 48.8 | 211 34.3 | 46.7 | 167 01.5 | 04.6 | 170 20.0 | 25.0 | 223 19.8 | 45.0 | Diphda | 349 17.5 | S18 04.2 |
| 05 | 102 51.3 | 226 33.7 | 47.5 | 182 02.0 | 04.4 | 185 22.0 | 25.0 | 238 22.0 | 45.1 | | | |
| 06 | 117 53.8 | 241 33.0 | S20 48.3 | 197 02.5 | S25 04.2 | 200 24.1 | S23 25.0 | 253 24.2 | S14 45.1 | Dubhe | 194 18.7 | N61 50.0 |
| 07 | 132 56.2 | 256 32.3 | 49.1 | 212 03.0 | 04.1 | 215 26.2 | 24.9 | 268 26.3 | 45.2 | Elnath | 278 40.1 | N28 35.8 |
| 08 | 147 58.7 | 271 31.6 | 49.8 | 227 03.5 | 03.9 | 230 28.3 | 24.9 | 283 28.5 | 45.3 | Eltanin | 90 56.6 | N51 29.6 |
| F 09 | 163 01.1 | 286 30.9 | .. 50.6 | 242 04.0 | .. 03.8 | 245 30.4 | .. 24.9 | 298 30.7 | .. 45.4 | Enif | 34 08.5 | N 9 48.3 |
| R 10 | 178 03.6 | 301 30.2 | 51.4 | 257 04.5 | 03.6 | 260 32.4 | 24.9 | 313 32.9 | 45.5 | Fomalhaut | 15 47.8 | S29 42.3 |
| I 11 | 193 06.1 | 316 29.6 | 52.2 | 272 05.0 | 03.4 | 275 34.5 | 24.9 | 328 35.1 | 45.6 | | | |
| D 12 | 208 08.5 | 331 28.9 | S20 53.0 | 287 05.5 | S25 03.3 | 290 36.6 | S23 24.8 | 343 37.2 | S14 45.6 | Gacrux | 172 26.2 | S57 01.4 |
| A 13 | 223 11.0 | 346 28.2 | 53.8 | 302 06.0 | 03.1 | 305 38.7 | 24.8 | 358 39.4 | 45.7 | Gienah | 176 15.2 | S17 27.2 |
| Y 14 | 238 13.5 | 1 27.5 | 54.6 | 317 06.5 | 02.9 | 320 40.8 | 24.8 | 13 41.6 | 45.8 | Hadar | 149 20.0 | S60 17.9 |
| 15 | 253 15.9 | 16 26.8 | .. 55.3 | 332 07.0 | .. 02.8 | 335 42.8 | .. 24.8 | 28 43.8 | .. 45.9 | Hamal | 328 25.3 | N23 23.5 |
| 16 | 268 18.4 | 31 26.1 | 56.1 | 347 07.5 | 02.6 | 350 44.9 | 24.8 | 43 46.0 | 46.0 | Kaus Aust. | 84 13.0 | S34 23.7 |
| 17 | 283 20.9 | 46 25.4 | 56.9 | 2 08.0 ' | 02.4 | 5 47.0 | 24.8 | 58 48.1 | 46.1 | | | |
| 18 | 298 23.3 | 61 24.7 | S20 57.7 | 17 08.5 | S25 02.3 | 20 49.1 | S23 24.8 | 73 50.3 | S14 46.2 | Kochab | 137 19.8 | N74 13.2 |
| 19 | 313 25.8 | 76 24.1 | 58.5 | 32 09.0 | 02.1 | 35 51.2 | 24.8 | 88 52.5 | 46.2 | Markab | 14 00.0 | N15 07.5 |
| 20 | 328 28.3 | 91 23.4 | 20 59.2 | 47 09.5 | 01.9 | 50 53.2 | 24.7 | 103 54.7 | 46.3 | Menkar | 314 37.7 | N 4 01.5 |
| 21 | 343 30.7 | 106 22.7 | 21 00.0 | 62 10.0 | .. 01.8 | 65 55.3 | .. 24.7 | 118 56.9 | .. 46.4 | Menkent | 148 34.0 | S36 17.6 |
| 22 | 358 33.2 | 121 22.0 | 00.8 | 77 10.5 | 01.6 | 80 57.4 | 24.7 | 133 59.0 | 46.5 | Miaplacidus | 221 44.9 | S69 38.8 |
| 23 | 13 35.6 | 136 21.3 | 01.6 | 92 11.0 | 01.4 | 95 59.5 | 24.7 | 149 01.2 | 46.6 | | | |
| 20 00 | 28 38.1 | 151 20.6 | S21 02.3 | 107 11.5 | S25 01.3 | 111 01.5 | S23 24.7 | 164 03.4 | S14 46.7 | Mirfak | 309 11.5 | N49 48.5 |
| 01 | 43 40.6 | 166 19.9 | 03.1 | 122 12.0 | 01.1 | 126 03.6 | 24.7 | 179 05.6 | 46.8 | Nunki | 76 25.5 | S26 19.1 |
| 02 | 58 43.0 | 181 19.2 | 03.9 | 137 12.5 | 00.9 | 141 05.7 | 24.7 | 194 07.8 | 46.8 | Peacock | 53 53.4 | S56 47.4 |
| 03 | 73 45.5 | 196 18.5 | .. 04.6 | 152 13.0 | .. 00.8 | 156 07.8 | .. 24.6 | 209 09.9 | .. 46.9 | Pollux | 243 54.5 | N28 03.9 |
| 04 | 88 48.0 | 211 17.8 | 05.4 | 167 13.5 | 00.6 | 171 09.9 | 24.6 | 224 12.1 | 47.0 | Procyon | 245 22.6 | N 5 16.1 |
| 05 | 103 50.4 | 226 17.1 | 06.2 | 182 14.0 | 00.4 | 186 11.9 | 24.6 | 239 14.3 | 47.1 | | | |
| 06 | 118 52.9 | 241 16.4 | S21 06.9 | 197 14.4 | S25 00.3 | 201 14.0 | S23 24.6 | 254 16.5 | S14 47.2 | Rasalhague | 96 27.0 | N12 34.3 |
| S 07 | 133 55.4 | 256 15.7 | 07.7 | 212 14.9 | 25 00.1 | 216 16.1 | 24.6 | 269 18.7 | 47.3 | Regulus | 208 07.0 | N12 02.7 |
| A 08 | 148 57.8 | 271 15.1 | 08.5 | 227 15.4 | 24 59.9 | 231 18.2 | 24.6 | 284 20.8 | 47.4 | Rigel | 281 32.9 | S 8 12.9 |
| T 09 | 164 00.3 | 286 14.4 | .. 09.2 | 242 15.9 | .. 59.7 | 246 20.2 | .. 24.5 | 299 23.0 | .. 47.4 | Rigil Kent. | 140 22.6 | S60 46.3 |
| U 10 | 179 02.8 | 301 13.7 | 10.0 | 257 16.4 | 59.6 | 261 22.3 | 24.5 | 314 25.2 | 47.5 | Sabik | 102 37.9 | S15 42.4 |
| V 11 | 194 05.2 | 316 13.0 | 10.8 | 272 16.9 | 59.4 | 276 24.4 | 24.5 | 329 27.4 | 47.6 | | | |
| R 12 | 209 07.7 | 331 12.3 | S21 11.5 | 287 17.4 | S24 59.2 | 291 26.5 | S23 24.5 | 344 29.6 | S14 47.7 | Schedar | 350 05.3 | N56 27.3 |
| D 13 | 224 10.1 | 346 11.6 | 12.3 | 302 17.9 | 59.0 | 306 28.5 | 24.5 | 359 31.7 | 47.8 | Shaula | 96 51.9 | S37 05.8 |
| A 14 | 239 12.6 | 1 10.9 | 13.0 | 317 18.4 | 58.9 | 321 30.6 | 24.5 | 14 33.9 | 47.9 | Sirius | 258 53.0 | S16 41.4 |
| Y 15 | 254 15.1 | 16 10.2 | .. 13.8 | 332 18.9 | .. 58.7 | 336 32.7 | .. 24.5 | 29 36.1 | .. 48.0 | Spica | 158 54.7 | S11 04.7 |
| 16 | 269 17.5 | 31 09.5 | 14.6 | 347 19.4 | 58.5 | 351 34.7 | 24.4 | 44 38.3 | 48.0 | Suhail | 223 08.8 | S43 21.8 |
| 17 | 284 20.0 | 46 08.8 | 15.3 | 2 19.9 | 58.3 | 6 36.8 | 24.4 | 59 40.5 | 48.1 | | | |
| 18 | 299 22.5 | 61 08.1 | S21 16.1 | 17 20.4 | S24 58.2 | 21 38.9 | S23 24.4 | 74 42.6 | S14 48.2 | Vega | 80 54.0 | N38 46.3 |
| 19 | 314 24.9 | 76 07.4 | 16.8 | 32 20.9 | 58.0 | 36 41.0 | 24.4 | 89 44.8 | 48.3 | Zuben'ubi | 137 30.1 | S15 58.6 |
| 20 | 329 27.4 | 91 06.7 | 17.6 | 47 21.4 | 57.8 | 51 43.0 | 24.4 | 104 47.0 | 48.4 | | S.H.A. | Mer. Pass. |
| 21 | 344 29.9 | 106 06.0 | .. 18.3 | 62 21.9 | .. 57.6 | 66 45.1 | .. 24.4 | 119 49.2 | .. 48.5 | Venus | 123 58.1 | 13 54 |
| 22 | 359 32.3 | 121 05.3 | 19.1 | 77 22.4 | 57.5 | 81 47.2 | 24.3 | 134 51.4 | 48.5 | Mars | 79 20.5 | 16 51 |
| 23 | 14 34.8 | 136 04.6 | 19.8 | 92 22.9 | 57.3 | 96 49.3 | 24.3 | 149 53.5 | 48.6 | Jupiter | 82 32.7 | 16 37 |
| Mer. Pass. 22 05.8 | | v −0.7 | d 0.8 | v 0.5 | d 0.2 | v 2.1 | d 0.0 | v 2.2 | d 0.1 | Saturn | 135 32.1 | 13 05 |

*Figure 21–1.* Typical daily page from the *Nautical Almanac* showing the astronomical data for the 4 major planets and 57 navigational stars.

a practical example of a planet sight, following the six standard steps of the celestial process as before, and noting the minor procedural exceptions as we progress. As navigator, this time you are on an Atlantic crossing, and just after sunset on October 18, 1984, at DR position Latitude 41°04′N, Longitude 60°41′W, you make an observation of Venus at a sextant altitude of 12°29.9′. Your watch reads 21:20:03 GMT, and has no error; the index correction is −2.4′, and the height of eye, 9 feet. The workform for planet sights is similar to those you have worked with in the earlier exercises. Completed for this example, and to be used to follow the explanation, the workbook looks like this:

| DATE | Oct. 18, 1984 |
|---|---|
| BODY | Venus |
| hs | 12-29.9 |
| IC | -2.4 |
| D | -2.9 |
| ha | 12-24.6 |
| R | -4.3 |
| add'l corr | +0.1 |
| Ho | 12-20.4 |
| W | 21-20-03 |
| corr | 00 |
| GMT | 21-20-03 |
| gha ⌐v | 106-39.1 ⌐0.7 |
| incr | 5-00.8 |
| v corr | -0.2 |
| GHA | 111-39.7 |
| | |
| aλ | 60-39.7 |
| LHA | 51 |
| dec ⌐d | 20-41.1 ⌐0.8 |
| d corr | +0.3 |
| Dec | 20-41.4 |
| a L | 41 N |
| Tab Hc | 12-49 |
| corr | -33 |
| Hc | 12-16.0 |
| Ho | 12-20.4 |
| a | 4.4 T |
| Zn | 228° |

The first exception that applies to planet sights is the most important. In observing planets with your sextant, you must be sure to bring the *center* of the body to the horizon. Unlike stars, which show only a pinpoint of light, planets exhibit a visible disc when viewed through a magnifying eyepiece, and for accurate sights, it is essential that the center of the body, and not one of its limbs, be bisected by the horizon. The index correction and the correction for height of eye are found and applied in the same way as for other sights. Using our IC of −2.4′, and the correction of −2.9′ found in the dip table (Figure 21–2), the apparent altitude of Venus becomes 12°24.6′. The R-correction is then obtained from the PLANETS column

## ALTITUDE CORRECTION TABLES 10°–90°

| STARS AND PLANETS | | | | DIP | | | |
|---|---|---|---|---|---|---|---|
| App. Alt. | Corrⁿ | App. Alt. | Additional Corrⁿ | Ht. of Eye | Corrⁿ | Ht. of Eye | Ht. of Eye Corrⁿ |

| App. Alt. | Corrⁿ | App. Alt. | Additional Corrⁿ | Ht. of Eye (m) | Corrⁿ | Ht. of Eye (ft.) | Ht. of Eye (m) | Corrⁿ |
|---|---|---|---|---|---|---|---|---|
| 9 56 | −5·3 | **1984** | | 2·4 | −2·8 | 8·0 | 1·0 − | 1·8 |
| 10 08 | −5·2 | **VENUS** | | 2·6 | −2·9 | 8·6 | 1·5 − | 2·2 |
| 10 20 | −5·1 | Jan. 1-Dec. 12 | | 2·8 | −3·0 | 9·2 | 2·0 − | 2·5 |
| 10 33 | −5·0 | | | 3·0 | −3·1 | 9·8 | 2·5 − | 2·8 |
| 10 46 | −4·9 | 0 / | | 3·2 | −3·2 | 10·5 | 3·0 − | 3·0 |
| 11 00 | −4·8 | 60 + 0·1 | | 3·4 | −3·3 | 11·2 | See table | |
| 11 14 | −4·7 | Dec. 13-Dec. 31 | | 3·6 | −3·4 | 11·9 | ← | |
| 11 29 | −4·6 | | | 3·8 | −3·5 | 12·6 | m | |
| 11 45 | −4·5 | 0 / | | 4·0 | −3·6 | 13·3 | 20 − | 7·9 |
| 12 01 | −4·4 | 41 + 0·2 | | 4·3 | −3·7 | 14·1 | 22 − | .8·3 |
| 12 18 | −4·3 | 76 + 0·1 | | 4·5 | −3·8 | 14·9 | 24 − | 8·6 |
| 12 35 | −4·2 | | | 4·7 | −3·9 | 15·7 | 26 − | 9·0 |
| 12 54 | | | | 5·0 | | 16·5 | | |

*Figure 21–2.* Portion of the *Nautical Almanac's* Altitude Correction Tables for stars and planets. The dip correction is −2.9′ for a 9-foot height of eye; the R-correction for Venus's apparent altitude of 12°24.6′ is −4.3′; there is an additional correction for Venus, +0.1′, for the date of the observation.

of the altitude correction tables inside the front cover of the *Nautical Almanac*, which are excerpted in Figure 21–2. For an ha of 12°24.6′, the R-correction is −4.3′; for both planets and stars, it is always negative. In the case of certain planets, usually Venus and Mars, there may be a small additional correction like the one shown for Venus in Figure 21–2 of +0.1′. Applying both of these corrections to the apparent altitude, we arrive at the observed altitude, Ho, of 12°20.4′.

The Greenwich hour angle and the declination for our sight are taken from the almanac's daily page, shown in Figure 21–1. Figure 21–3 is a portion of this page cover-

## 1984 OCTOBER 18, 19, 20

| G.M.T. | ARIES G.H.A. | VENUS −3.4 G.H.A. | Dec. | MARS +0.6 G.H.A. | Dec. |
|---|---|---|---|---|---|
| **18** 00 | 26 39.8 | 151 53.2 | S20 24.2 | 106 47.4 | S25 08.9 |
| 01 | 41 42.3 | 166 52.6 | 25.0 | 121 47.9 | 08.7 |
| 02 | 56 44.8 | 181 51.9 | 25.8 | 136 48.4 | 08.6 |
| 03 | 71 47.2 | 196 51.2 ·· | 26.6 | 151 48.9 ·· | 08.4 |
| 04 | 86 49.7 | 211 50.6 | 27.4 | 166 49.4 | 08.3 |
| 05 | 101 52.2 | 226 49.9 | 28.2 | 181 49.9 | 08.1 |
| 06 | 116 54.6 | 241 49.2 | S20 29.0 | 196 50.4 | S25 08.0 |
| 07 | 131 57.1 | 256 48.6 | 29.9 | 211 50.9 | 07.8 |
| T 08 | 146 59.5 | 271 47.9 | 30.7 | 226 51.4 | 07.7 |
| H 09 | 162 02.0 | 286 47.2 ·· | 31.5 | 241 51.9 ·· | 07.5 |
| U 10 | 177 04.5 | 301 46.5 | 32.3 | 256 52.4 | 07.4 |
| R 11 | 192 06.9 | 316 45.9 | 33.1 | 271 52.9 | 07.2 |
| S 12 | 207 09.4 | 331 45.2 | S20 33.9 | 286 53.4 | S25 07.1 |
| D 13 | 222 11.9 | 346 44.5 | 34.7 | 301 53.9 | 06.9 |
| A 14 | 237 14.3 | 1 43.8 | 35.5 | 316 54.4 | 06.8 |
| Y 15 | 252 16.8 | 16 43.2 ·· | 36.3 | 331 54.9 ·· | 06.6 |
| 16 | 267 19.3 | 31 42.5 | 37.1 | 346 55.4 | 06.5 |
| 17 | 282 21.7 | 46 41.8 | 37.9 | 1 55.9 | 06.3 |
| 18 | 297 24.2 | 61 41.1 | S20 38.7 | 16 56.4 | S25 06.1 |
| 19 | 312 26.6 | 76 40.5 | 39.5 | 31 56.9 | 06.0 |
| 20 | 327 29.1 | 91 39.8 | 40.3 | 46 57.4 | 05.8 |
| 21 | 342 31.6 | 106 39.1 ·· | 41.1 | 61 57.9 ·· | 05.7 |
| 22 | 357 34.0 | 121 38.4 | 41.9 | 76 58.4 | 05.5 |
| 23 | 12 36.5 | 136 37.7 | 42.7 | 91 58.9 | 05.4 |
| Mer. Pass. | 22 05.8 ʰ ᵐ | v −0.7 | d 0.8 | v 0.5 | d 0.2 |

*Figure 21–3.* Excerpt from the *Nautical Almanac* showing the astronomical data for Venus on October 18, 1984. At 21ʰ GMT, Venus's GHA is 106°39.1′, and the Dec 20°41.1′S. Note the *v* and *d* values at the bottom of the table, which apply for the entire day.

ing the particular data we need. You will note that the tabulations are similar to those for the sun and moon, except that the values of v and d are given only at the bottom of the table and apply for the whole day. For our sight, the GHA of Venus at 21 hours GMT is seen to be 106°39.1′, with a v of −0.7′. The tabular declination at the same hour is 20°41.1′S, and the value of d is 0.8′; positive, because the declination is increasing. The corrections to the tabular Greenwich hour angle are found, as usual, in the tables in the back of the almanac; an excerpt for 20 minutes of time is seen in Figure 21–4. Be sure to use the PLANETS column, which is shared with the sun, and to extract the v- and d-corrections at the same time. For our example, the GHA increment for 20$^m$03$^s$ is 5°00.8′, and the v-correction, −0.2′ (remember that the v-value was negative in this case). Applying the hour-angle corrections to the tabular value, Venus's final GHA becomes

## 20$^m$ INCREMENTS AND CORRECTIONS

| 20$^m$ | SUN PLANETS | ARIES | MOON | v or Corr$^n$ d | v or Corr$^n$ d | v or Corr$^n$ d |
|---|---|---|---|---|---|---|
| s | ° ′ | ° ′ | ° ′ | ′ ′ | ′ ′ | ′ ′ |
| 00 | 5 00·0 | 5 00·8 | 4 46·3 | 0·0 0·0 | 6·0 2·1 | 12·0 4·1 |
| 01 | 5 00·3 | 5 01·1 | 4 46·6 | 0·1 0·0 | 6·1 2·1 | 12·1 4·1 |
| 02 | 5 00·5 | 5 01·3 | 4 46·8 | 0·2 0·1 | 6·2 2·1 | 12·2 4·2 |
| 03 | 5 00·8 | 5 01·6 | 4 47·0 | 0·3 0·1 | 6·3 2·2 | 12·3 4·2 |
| 04 | 5 01·0 | 5 01·8 | 4 47·3 | 0·4 0·1 | 6·4 2·2 | 12·4 4·2 |
| 05 | 5 01·3 | 5 02·1 | 4 47·5 | 0·5 0·2 | 6·5 2·2 | 12·5 4·3 |
| 06 | 5 01·5 | 5 02·3 | 4 47·8 | 0·6 0·2 | 6·6 2·3 | 12·6 4·3 |
| 07 | 5 01·8 | 5 02·6 | 4 48·0 | 0·7 0·2 | 6·7 2·3 | 12·7 4·3 |
| 08 | 5 02·0 | 5 02·8 | 4 48·2 | 0·8 0·3 | 6·8 2·3 | 12·8 4·4 |
| 09 | 5 02·3 | 5 03·1 | 4 48·5 | 0·9 0·3 | 6·9 2·4 | 12·9 4·4 |

*Figure 21–4.* **Excerpt from the *Increments and Corrections* tables showing the GHA increment for 20$^m$03$^s$, and the appropriate *v*- and *d*- corrections.**

| | N. Lat. {LHA greater than 180°....Zn=Z; LHA less than 180°....Zn=360—Z} | | LAT 41° | | DECLINATION (15°-29°) | | | | | | | | | | | | | | | |
|---|---|---|---|---|---|---|---|---|---|---|---|---|---|---|---|---|---|---|---|---|
| | 15° | | | 16° | | | 17° | | | 18° | | | 19° | | | 20° | | | 21° | | |
| LHA | Hc | d | Z | Hc | d | Z | Hc | d | Z | Hc | d | Z | Hc | d | Z | Hc | d | Z | Hc | d | Z |
| 69 | 0515 | 43 | 115 | 0432 | 42 | 116 | 0350 | 43 | 117 | 0307 | 42 | 117 | 0225 | 43 | 118 | 0142 | 42 | 119 | 0100 | 43 | 119 |
| 68 | 0556 | 43 | 116 | 0513 | 43 | 117 | 0430 | 42 | 117 | 0348 | 43 | 118 | 0305 | 43 | 119 | 0222 | 43 | 119 | 0139 | 43 | 120 |
| 67 | 0636 | 43 | 117 | 0553 | 42 | 117 | 0511 | 44 | 118 | 0427 | 43 | 119 | 0344 | 43 | 119 | 0301 | 43 | 120 | 0218 | 43 | 121 |
| 66 | 0717 | 43 | 117 | 0634 | 44 | 118 | 0550 | 43 | 119 | 0507 | 43 | 119 | 0424 | 44 | 120 | 0340 | 43 | 121 | 0257 | 43 | 121 |
| 65 | 0757 | -43 | 118 | 0714 | -44 | 119 | 0630 | -43 | 119 | 0547 | -44 | 120 | 0503 | -44 | 121 | 0419 | -43 | 121 | 0336 | -44 | 122 |
| 64 | 0837 | 44 | 119 | 0753 | 44 | 119 | 0709 | 43 | 120 | 0626 | 44 | 121 | 0542 | 44 | 121 | 0458 | 44 | 122 | 0414 | 44 | 123 |
| 63 | 0916 | 43 | 119 | 0833 | 44 | 120 | 0749 | 45 | 121 | 0704 | 44 | 121 | 0620 | 44 | 122 | 0536 | 44 | 123 | 0452 | 45 | 123 |
| 62 | 0956 | 44 | 120 | 0912 | 45 | 121 | 0827 | 44 | 121 | 0743 | 45 | 122 | 0658 | 44 | 123 | 0614 | 45 | 123 | 0529 | 44 | 124 |
| 61 | 1035 | 45 | 121 | 0950 | 44 | 121 | 0906 | 45 | 122 | 0821 | 45 | 123 | 0736 | 44 | 124 | 0652 | 45 | 124 | 0607 | 45 | 125 |
| 60 | 1114 | -45 | 122 | 1029 | -45 | 122 | 0944 | -45 | 123 | 0859 | -45 | 124 | 0814 | -45 | 124 | 0729 | -45 | 125 | 0644 | -45 | 126 |
| 59 | 1152 | 45 | 122 | 1107 | 45 | 123 | 1022 | 45 | 124 | 0937 | 45 | 124 | 0851 | 45 | 125 | 0806 | 45 | 126 | 0721 | 46 | 126 |
| 58 | 1230 | 45 | 123 | 1145 | 46 | 124 | 1059 | 45 | 124 | 1014 | 46 | 125 | 0928 | 45 | 126 | 0843 | 46 | 126 | 0757 | 46 | 127 |
| 57 | 1308 | 46 | 124 | 1222 | 45 | 124 | 1137 | 46 | 125 | 1051 | 46 | 126 | 1005 | 46 | 126 | 0919 | 46 | 127 | 0833 | 46 | 128 |
| 56 | 1346 | 46 | 125 | 1300 | 44 | 125 | 1214 | 47 | 126 | 1127 | 46 | 126 | 1041 | 46 | 127 | 0955 | 46 | 128 | 0909 | 47 | 128 |
| 55 | 1423 | -46 | 125 | 1337 | -47 | 126 | 1250 | -46 | 127 | 1204 | -47 | 127 | 1117 | -46 | 128 | 1031 | -47 | 129 | 0944 | -47 | 129 |
| 54 | 1500 | 47 | 126 | 1413 | 47 | 127 | 1326 | 46 | 127 | 1240 | 47 | 128 | 1153 | 47 | 129 | 1106 | 47 | 129 | 1019 | 47 | 130 |
| 53 | 1536 | 47 | 127 | 1449 | 47 | 127 | 1402 | 47 | 128 | 1315 | 47 | 129 | 1228 | 47 | 129 | 1141 | 48 | 130 | 1053 | 47 | 131 |
| 52 | 1612 | 47 | 128 | 1525 | 47 | 128 | 1438 | 47 | 129 | 1350 | 47 | 130 | 1303 | 46 | 130 | 1215 | 47 | 131 | 1128 | 48 | 131 |
| 51 | 1648 | 48 | 128 | 1600 | 47 | 129 | 1513 | 48 | 130 | 1425 | 48 | 130 | 1337 | 48 | 131 | 1249 | 48 | 132 | 1201 | 48 | 132 |
| 50 | 1723 | -48 | 129 | 1635 | -48 | 130 | 1547 | -48 | 130 | 1459 | -48 | 131 | 1411 | -48 | 132 | 1323 | -48 | 132 | 1235 | -49 | 133 |
| 49 | 1758 | 48 | 130 | 1710 | 48 | 131 | 1622 | 49 | 131 | 1533 | 48 | 132 | 1445 | 49 | 132 | 1356 | 48 | 133 | 1308 | 49 | 134 |
| 48 | 1833 | 49 | 131 | 1744 | 48 | 131 | 1656 | 49 | 132 | 1607 | 49 | 133 | 1518 | 49 | 133 | 1429 | 49 | 134 | 1340 | 49 | 134 |
| 47 | 1907 | 49 | 132 | 1818 | 49 | 132 | 1729 | 49 | 133 | 1640 | 49 | 133 | 1551 | 49 | 134 | 1502 | 50 | 135 | 1412 | 49 | 135 |

*Figure 21–5.* Excerpt from Pub. No. 249, Volume III, showing the values for Latitude 41°N, declination 20°S, and LHA 51° to be: Hc 12°49', d −48', Z 132°.

111°39.7'. The d-correction amounts to 0.3', and that added to the tabular Dec produces a declination of 20° 41.1'S.

By now you will have selected an assumed longitude of 60°39.7'W, near your DR position, and suitable for making the local hour angle a whole number. The selection of an assumed latitude at 41°N is equally obvious if you remember that we want the whole degree nearest our DR. The remainder of the procedure for reducing your planet sight follows the same routine you learned for the sun and the moon. The appropriate page of the sight reduction table, Pub. No. 249, is entered with the assumed latitude, 41°, the local hour angle, 51°, and the degrees of declination, 20°. The excerpt in Figure 21–5 is from the page that includes Venus's calculated declination, with its name contrary to that of the latitude; the declination in our example is South, and the assumed latitude North. From the table, opposite LHA 51°, and

| CONTRARY NAME TO LATITUDE | | | | | | | | | | | | |
|---|---|---|---|---|---|---|---|---|---|---|---|---|
| 22° | | | 23° | | | 24° | | | 25° | | | |
| Hc | d | Z | Hc | d | Z | Hc | d | Z | Hc | d | Z | Hc |
| 00 17 | 42 | 120 | −0 25 | 43 | 121 | −1 08 | 43 | 121 | −1 51 | 42 | 122 | −2 3: |
| 00 56 | 43 | 121 | 00 13 | 42 | 121 | −0 29 | 43 | 122 | −1 12 | 43 | 123 | −1 5: |
| 01 35 | 43 | 121 | 00 52 | 43 | 122 | 00 09 | 43 | 123 | −0 34 | 44 | 123 | −1 1: |
| 02 14 | 44 | 122 | 01 30 | 43 | 123 | 00 47 | 44 | 123 | 00 03 | 43 | 124 | −0 4: |
| 02 52 | −44 | 123 | 02 08 | −44 | 123 | 01 24 | −43 | 124 | 00 41 | −44 | 125 | −0 0: |
| 03 30 | 44 | 123 | 02 46 | 44 | 124 | 02 02 | 44 | 125 | 01 18 | 44 | 125 | 00 3: |
| 04 07 | 44 | 124 | 03 23 | 44 | 125 | 02 39 | 45 | 125 | 01 54 | 44 | 126 | 01 1: |
| 04 45 | 45 | 125 | 04 00 | 44 | 125 | 03 16 | 45 | 126 | 02 31 | 45 | 127 | 01 4: |
| 05 22 | 45 | 126 | 04 37 | 45 | 126 | 03 52 | 45 | 127 | 03 07 | 45 | 127 | 02 2: |
| 05 59 | −44 | 126 | 05 13 | −45 | 127 | 04 28 | −45 | 127 | 03 43 | −46 | 128 | 02 5: |
| 06 35 | 46 | 127 | 05 49 | 46 | 128 | 05 04 | 46 | 128 | 04 18 | 46 | 129 | 03 3: |
| 07 11 | 46 | 128 | 06 25 | 46 | 128 | 05 39 | 46 | 129 | 04 53 | 46 | 130 | 04 0: |
| 07 47 | 46 | 128 | 07 01 | 47 | 129 | 06 14 | 46 | 130 | 05 28 | 46 | 130 | 04 4: |
| 08 22 | 46 | 129 | 07 36 | 47 | 130 | 06 49 | 47 | 130 | 06 02 | 46 | 131 | 05 1: |
| 08 57 | −47 | 130 | 08 10 | −47 | 130 | 07 23 | −47 | 131 | 06 36 | −47 | 132 | 05 4: |
| 09 32 | 47 | 131 | 08 45 | 48 | 131 | 07 57 | 47 | 132 | 07 10 | 47 | 132 | 06 2: |
| 10 06 | 47 | 131 | 09 19 | 48 | 132 | 08 31 | 48 | 133 | 07 43 | 47 | 133 | 06 5: |
| 10 40 | 48 | 132 | 09 52 | 48 | 133 | 09 04 | 48 | 133 | 08 16 | 48 | 134 | 07 2: |
| 11 13 | 48 | 133 | 10 25 | 48 | 133 | 09 37 | 48 | 134 | 08 49 | 49 | 135 | 08 0: |
| 11 46 | −48 | 134 | 10 58 | −49 | 134 | 10 09 | −48 | 135 | 09 21 | −49 | 135 | 08 3: |
| 12 19 | 49 | 134 | 11 30 | 49 | 135 | 10 41 | 49 | 135 | 09 52 | 48 | 136 | 09 0: |
| 12 51 | 49 | 135 | 12 02 | 49 | 136 | 11 13 | 49 | 136 | 10 24 | 50 | 137 | 09 3: |
| 13 23 | 49 | 136 | 12 34 | 50 | 136 | 11 44 | 50 | 137 | 10 54 | 49 | 138 | 10 0: |

under declination 20°, we extract the tabular Hc of 12°49′, the altitude differential, d, of –48′, and the azimuth angle, Z, 132°. Note that d in this instance bears no relation to the d representing hourly change, which we used in figuring the declination; don't be confused, they are entirely separate. The tabular Hc is corrected with Table 5 (Figure 21–6) in the regular way. For a d of –48, and minutes of declination of 41.4, the adjustment amounts to –33′, resulting in a final computed altitude, Hc, of 12° 16.0′. Comparing this with the previously calculated Ho, the intercept works out to 4.4′, "toward," because Ho is greater.

The rule for finding true azimuth is in the corner of the sight reduction table. With an LHA less than 180° (ours is 51°), Zn = 360° − Z, so our true azimuth for plotting, which is done in exactly the same way as for your other sights, is 228°. We can turn now to the last category of celestial bodies, the stars.

## Table 5.—Correction to Tabulated Altitude for Minutes of Declination

| 43 44 45 | 46 47 48 | 49 50 51 | 52 53 54 | 55 56 57 | 58 59 60 | $\dfrac{d}{\prime}$ |
|---|---|---|---|---|---|---|
| 0 0 0 | 0 0 0 | 0 0 0 | 0 0 0 | 0 0 0 | 0 0 0 | 0 |
| 1 1 1 | 1 1 1 | 1 1 1 | 1 1 1 | 1 1 1 | 1 1 1 | 1 |
| 1 1 2 | 2 2 2 | 2 2 2 | 2 2 2 | 2 2 2 | 2 2 2 | 2 |
| 2 2 2 | 2 2 2 | 2 2 3 | 3 3 3 | 3 3 3 | 3 3 3 | 3 |
| 3 3 3 | 3 3 3 | 3 3 3 | 3 4 4 | 4 4 4 | 4 4 4 | 4 |
| 4 4 4 | 4 4 4 | 4 4 4 | 4 4 4 | 5 5 5 | 5 5 5 | 5 |
| 4 4 4 | 5 5 5 | 5 5 5 | 5 5 5 | 6 6 6 | 6 6 6 | 6 |
| 5 5 5 | 5 5 6 | 6 6 6 | 6 6 6 | 6 7 7 | 7 7 7 | 7 |
| 6 6 6 | 6 6 6 | 7 7 7 | 7 7 7 | 7 7 8 | 8 8 8 | 8 |
| 6 7 7 | 7 7 7 | 7 8 8 | 8 8 8 | 8 8 9 | 9 9 9 | 9 |
| 7 7 8 | 8 8 8 | 8 8 8 | 9 9 9 | 9 9 10 | 10 10 10 | 10 |
| 8 8 8 | 8 9 9 | 9 9 9 | 10 10 10 | 10 10 10 | 11 11 11 | 11 |
| 9 9 9 | 9 9 10 | 10 10 10 | 10 11 11 | 11 11 11 | 12 12 12 | 12 |
| 9 10 10 | 10 10 10 | 11 11 11 | 11 11 12 | 12 12 12 | 13 13 13 | 13 |
| 10 10 10 | 11 11 11 | 11 12 12 | 12 12 13 | 13 13 13 | 14 14 14 | 14 |
| 11 11 11 | 12 12 12 | 12 12 13 | 13 13 14 | 14 14 14 | 14 15 15 | 15 |
| 11 12 12 | 12 13 13 | 13 13 14 | 14 14 14 | 15 15 15 | 15 16 16 | 16 |
| 12 12 13 | 13 13 14 | 14 14 14 | 15 15 15 | 16 16 16 | 16 17 17 | 17 |
| 13 13 14 | 14 14 14 | 15 15 15 | 16 16 16 | 16 17 17 | 17 18 18 | 18 |
| 14 14 14 | 15 15 15 | 16 16 16 | 16 17 17 | 17 18 18 | 18 19 19 | 19 |
| 14 15 15 | 15 16 16 | 16 17 17 | 17 18 18 | 18 19 19 | 19 20 20 | 20 |
| 15 15 16 | 16 16 17 | 17 18 18 | 18 19 19 | 19 20 20 | 20 21 21 | 21 |
| 16 16 16 | 17 17 18 | 18 18 19 | 19 19 20 | 20 21 21 | 21 22 22 | 22 |
| 16 17 17 | 18 18 18 | 19 19 20 | 20 20 21 | 21 21 22 | 22 23 23 | 23 |
| 17 18 18 | 18 19 19 | 20 20 20 | 21 21 22 | 22 22 23 | 23 24 24 | 24 |
| 18 18 19 | 19 20 20 | 20 21 21 | 22 22 22 | 23 23 24 | 24 25 25 | 25 |
| 19 19 20 | 20 20 21 | 21 22 22 | 23 23 23 | 24 24 25 | 25 26 26 | 26 |
| 19 20 20 | 21 21 22 | 22 22 23 | 23 24 24 | 25 25 26 | 26 27 27 | 27 |
| 20 21 21 | 21 22 22 | 23 23 24 | 24 25 25 | 26 26 27 | 27 28 28 | 28 |
| 21 21 22 | 22 23 23 | 23 24 25 | 25 26 26 | 27 27 28 | 28 29 29 | 29 |
| 22 22 22 | 23 24 24 | 24 25 26 | 26 26 27 | 28 28 28 | 29 30 30 | 30 |
| 22 23 23 | 24 24 25 | 25 26 26 | 27 27 28 | 28 29 29 | 30 30 31 | 31 |
| 23 23 24 | 25 25 26 | 26 27 27 | 28 28 29 | 29 30 30 | 31 31 32 | 32 |
| 24 24 25 | 25 26 26 | 27 28 28 | 29 29 30 | 30 31 31 | 32 32 33 | 33 |
| 24 25 26 | 26 27 27 | 28 28 29 | 29 30 31 | 31 32 32 | 33 33 34 | 34 |
| 25 26 26 | 27 27 28 | 29 29 30 | 30 31 32 | 32 33 33 | 34 34 35 | 35 |
| 26 26 27 | 28 28 29 | 29 30 31 | 31 32 32 | 33 34 34 | 35 35 36 | 36 |
| 27 27 28 | 28 29 30 | 30 31 31 | 32 33 33 | 34 35 35 | 36 36 37 | 37 |
| 27 28 28 | 29 30 30 | 31 32 32 | 33 34 34 | 35 35 36 | 37 37 38 | 38 |
| 28 29 29 | 30 31 31 | 32 32 33 | 34 34 35 | 36 36 37 | 38 38 39 | 39 |
| 29 29 30 | 31 31 32 | 33 33 34 | 35 35 36 | 37 37 38 | 39 39 40 | 40 |
| 29 30 31 | 31 32 33 | 33 34 35 | 36 36 37 | 38 38 39 | 40 40 41 | 41 |
| 30 31 32 | 32 33 34 | 34 35 36 | 36 37 38 | 38 39 40 | 41 41 42 | 42 |
| 31 32 32 | 33 34 34 | 35 36 37 | 37 38 39 | 39 40 41 | 42 42 43 | 43 |

*Figure 21–6.* Excerpt from Table 5, Pub. No. 249, showing a correction of −33′ for *d* of −48′ and incremental minutes of declination, 41.

# 22 | The Stars

Most laymen, when they think about celestial navigation, think first of the stars, but for experienced yacht navigators, this is not usually the case. Stars do offer the attractive possibility of being able to make observations of several of them within a short period of time, thus producing lines of position that can be crossed for a simultaneous fix, and certain stars are particularly easy to reduce with Volume I of Pub. No. 249. On the other hand, shooting the stars from the deck of a small boat is much more demanding than sights of the sun or moon, and the quality of the results is not as good. Let's talk about the easy part first—solving a star sight for its line of position—and follow that process by means of a practical example; then we will return to the special problems in making the actual sextant observation.

A navigator in DR position Latitude 40°53′N, Longitude 67°49′W, takes a sight of Arcturus during evening twilight on June 8, 1984. The sextant reads 63°03.2′, the index correction is –2.4′, and the height of eye, 9 feet. The watch is set to GMT, with no error, and reads 00:20:09, June 9, because the new day has already started in Greenwich. (This is a point to look out for in evening sights in west longitudes; be sure you have Greenwich mean time on the right day.)

The six standard steps that you have followed with all the other celestial bodies apply equally to the stars, but when you come to the sight reduction step, you have a choice between the volumes of Pub. No. 249. To illustrate the procedure and your two options, the respective workforms, completed for our practical example, are displayed here in parallel. We will discuss the differences, which first appear at the almanac step, as we proceed.

*Stars—Vol. I Pub. No. 249*

| DATE | June 9, 1984 |
|------|--------------|
| BODY | Arcturus |
| hs | 63 - 03.2 |
| IC | - 2.4 |
| D | - 2.9 |
| ha | 62 - 57.9 |
| R | - 0.5 |
| Ho | 62 - 57.4 |
| W | 00 - 20 - 09 |
| corr | 00 |
| GMT | 00 - 20 - 09 |
| gha ♈ | 257 - 32.6 |
| incr | 5 - 03.1 |
| GHA ♈ | 262 - 35.7 |
| | |
| | |
| aλ | 67 - 35.7 |
| LHA ♈ | 195 |
| a L | 41 N |
| Hc | 63 - 01.0 |
| Ho | 62 - 57.4 |
| a | 3.6 A |
| Zn | 138° |

*Stars—Vol. II/III Pub. No. 249*

| DATE | June 9, 1984 |
|------|--------------|
| BODY | Arcturus |
| hs | 63 - 03.2 |
| IC | - 2.4 |
| D | - 2.9 |
| ha | 62 - 57.9 |
| R | - 0.5 |
| Ho | 62 - 57.4 |
| W | 00 - 20 - 09 |
| corr | 00 |
| GMT | 00 - 20 - 09 |
| gha ♈ | 257 - 32.6 |
| incr | 5 - 03.1 |
| GHA ♈ | 262 - 35.7 |
| SHA★ | 146 - 15.7 |
| | - 360 |
| GHA★ | 48 - 51.4 |
| | + 360 |
| | 408 - 51.4 |
| a λ | 67 - 51.4 |
| LHA★ | 341 |
| Dec | 19 - 15.9 N |
| a L | 41 N |
| Tab Hc | 62 - 40 |
| corr | + 13 |
| Hc | 62 - 53.0 |
| Ho | 62 - 57.4 |
| a | 4.4 T |
| Zn | 138° |

The sextant observation of a star is similar to that of a planet; the point-source of light should appear to bisect the horizon. Corrections for index error and dip are made in the usual way, and the refraction, or R-correction, is taken from the STARS column of the almanac's altitude correction tables, Figure 22–1. In our example, the index correction of –2.4', and the –2.9'-dip correction, found in the dip table for the 9-foot height of eye, are applied to the sextant altitude of 63°03.2' to produce the apparent altitude, 62°57.9'. Entering the STARS column of Figure 22–1, the R-correction for the apparent altitude we calculated is –0.5'. For the stars there is always just a single R-correction, and as it is for the planets, the correction is

| STARS AND PLANETS | | | | DIP | | | |
|---|---|---|---|---|---|---|---|
| App. Alt. | Corrⁿ | App. Alt. | Additional Corrⁿ | Ht. of Eye | Corrⁿ | Ht. of Eye | Ht. of Eye | Corrⁿ |

| App. Alt. | Corrⁿ | | Ht. of Eye | Corrⁿ | Ht. of Eye | Ht. of Eye | Corrⁿ |
|---|---|---|---|---|---|---|---|
| ° ' | | | m | | ft. | m | |
| 9 56 | −5·3 | **1984** | 2·4 | −2·8 | 8·0 | 1·0 − 1·8 | |
| 10 08 | −5·2 | **VENUS** | 2·6 | −2·9 | 8·6 | 1·5 − 2·2 | |
| 10 20 | −5·1 | Jan. 1-Dec. 12 | 2·8 | −3·0 | 9·2 | 2·0 − 2·5 | |
| 10 33 | −5·0 | ° ' | 3·0 | −3·1 | 9·8 | 2·5 − 2·8 | |
| 10 46 | | ° + 0·1 | 3·2 | | 10·5 | 3·0 − 3·0 | |

| App. Alt. | Corrⁿ | Ht. of Eye | Corrⁿ | Ht. of Eye | Ht. of Eye | Corrⁿ |
|---|---|---|---|---|---|---|
| 52 18 | −0·7 | 17·4 | −7·4 | 57·4 | 120 − 10·6 | |
| 56 11 | −0·6 | 17·9 | −7·5 | 58·9 | 125 − 10·8 | |
| 60 28 | −0·5 | 18·4 | −7·6 | 60·5 | | |
| 65 08 | −0·4 | 18·8 | −7·7 | 62·1 | 130 − 11·1 | |
| 70 11 | −0·3 | 19·3 | −7·8 | 63·8 | 135 − 11·3 | |
| 75 34 | −0·2 | 19·8 | −7·9 | 65·4 | 140 − 11·5 | |
| 81 13 | −0·1 | 20·4 | −8·0 | 67·1 | 145 − 11·7 | |
| 87 03 | 0·0 | 20·9 | −8·1 | 68·8 | 150 − 11·9 | |
| 90 00 | | 21·4 | | 70·5 | 155 − 12·1 | |

*Figure 22–1.* **Portion of Altitude Correction Tables from the** *Nautical Almanac* **showing the dip correction of − 2.9' for a height of eye of 9 feet, and the star's refraction correction of − 0.5' for an apparent altitude of 62°57.9'.**

always negative. When the R-correction is applied in our exercise, the observed altitude, Ho, of Arcturus becomes 62°57.4′. Timing a star sight is also identical to timing any other celestial observation; just be sure, as we have mentioned, that you have identified the correct Greenwich day. In our practical example, the time was 00:20:09, after midnight in Greenwich although it was only evening, local time, in the longitude where the observation was made.

In the third step, obtaining the astronomical data from the almanac, you will see a slight difference in star sights in the process of determining the Greenwich hour angle from the almanac's daily pages. Figure 21–1 illustrates a typical left-hand daily page from the *Nautical Almanac*. It is called the "star side," because it contains all the information for the 57 navigational stars as well as the planet data. An excerpt of the page covering our observation of Arcturus is shown in Figure 22–2. Since the stars change position with respect to each other only at a very slow rate, the almanac designers, in order to simplify the presentation, have chosen to show the data for an arbitrary, single point on the celestial sphere, and relate all the stars' positions to it. The arbitrary point, which is called the First Point of Aries, or Vernal Equinox, and is indicated by the symbol, ♈, is tabulated in the almanac as if it were a celestial body. All the stars are positioned from Aries by their sidereal hour angle, a measurement similar to Greenwich hour angle, but reckoned westward from the First Point of Aries instead of from Greenwich. Thus the simple formula:

$$\text{GHA Aries} + \text{SHA star} = \text{GHA star}$$

Returning to our practical example, from the ARIES column in the almanac excerpt in Figure 22–2, you will see that the GHA ♈ at 00 hours on June 9, is 257°32.6′. The incremental minutes and seconds of time are dealt

## 1984 JUNE 8, 9, 10

| G.M.T. | ARIES G.H.A. | STARS Name | S.H.A. | Dec. |
|---|---|---|---|---|
| 8 00 | 256 33.5 | Acamar | 315 35.5 | S40 21.9 |
| 01 | 271 36.0 | Achernar | 335 43.4 | S57 18.8 |
| 02 | 286 38.4 | Acrux | 173 34.2 | S63 01.0 |
| 03 | 301 40.9 | Adhara | 255 30.3 | S28 57.0 |
| 04 | 316 43.4 | Aldebaran | 291 15.2 | N16 28.7 |
| 05 | 331 45.8 | | | |
| 06 | 346 48.3 | Alioth | 166 39.7 | N56 03.0 |
| 07 | 1 50.7 | Alkaid | 153 15.9 | N49 23.7 |
| 08 | 16 53.2 | Al Na'ir | 28 11.2 | S47 02.1 |
| F 09 | 31 55.7 | Alnilam | 276 09.2 | S 1 12.6 |
| R 10 | 46 58.1 | Alphard | 218 18.1 | S 8 35.4 |
| I 11 | 62 00.6 | | | |
| D 12 | 77 03.1 | Alphecca | 126 29.4 | N26 46.1 |
| A 13 | 92 05.5 | Alpheratz | 358 06.7 | N29 00.0 |
| Y 14 | 107 08.0 | Altair | 62 29.6 | N 8 49.4 |
| 15 | 122 10.5 | Ankaa | 353 37.6 | S42 23.3 |
| 16 | 137 12.9 | Antares | 112 53.2 | S26 24.0 |
| 17 | 152 15.4 | | | |
| 18 | 167 17.9 | Arcturus | 146 15.7 | N19 15.9 |
| 19 | 182 20.3 | Atria | 108 14.5 | S69 00.1 |
| 20 | 197 22.8 | Avior | 234 27.7 | S59 27.7 |
| 21 | 212 25.2 | Bellatrix | 278 56.2 | N 6 20.2 |
| 22 | 227 27.7 | Betelgeuse | 271 25.7 | N 7 24.3 |
| 23 | 242 30.2 | | | |
| 9 00 | 257 32.6 | Canopus | 264 06.6 | S52 41.2 |
| 01 | 272 35.1 | Capella | 281 07.8 | N45 59.0 |
| 02 | 287 37.6 | Deneb | 49 46.4 | N45 13.1 |

*Figure 22–2.* **Extract from the** *Nautical Almanac* **daily page showing the astronomical data for the star Arcturus on June 9 at 00ʰ GMT.**

with in the *Increments and Corrections* tables, Figure 22–3, in the usual manner, making certain that you use only the ARIES column. The tabular Greenwich hour angle of Aries (257°32.6′) plus the increment of 5°03.1′ for the 20 minutes and 09 seconds of time, produce the GHA♈, shown on the workforms to be 262°35.7′.

Having found Aries's Greenwich hour angle, you now have the choice of volumes mentioned earlier. The first and simplest is Volume I of Pub. No. 249, provided you have selected one of the seven stars listed for your local hour angle. It is quite likely that your star will be one appearing in the table, since you probably will have

## 20ᵐ INCREMENTS AND CORRECTIONS

| 20 | SUN PLANETS | ARIES | MOON | v or Corrⁿ d | v or Corrⁿ d | v or Corrⁿ d |
|---|---|---|---|---|---|---|
| s | ° ′ | ° ′ | ° ′ | ′ ′ | ′ ′ | ′ ′ |
| 00 | 5 00·0 | 5 00·8 | 4 46·3 | 0·0 0·0 | 6·0 2·1 | 12·0 4·1 |
| 01 | 5 00·3 | 5 01·1 | 4 46·6 | 0·1 0·0 | 6·1 2·1 | 12·1 4·1 |
| 02 | 5 00·5 | 5 01·3 | 4 46·8 | 0·2 0·1 | 6·2 2·1 | 12·2 4·2 |
| 03 | 5 00·8 | 5 01·6 | 4 47·0 | 0·3 0·1 | 6·3 2·2 | 12·3 4·2 |
| 04 | 5 01·0 | 5 01·8 | 4 47·3 | 0·4 0·1 | 6·4 2·2 | 12·4 4·2 |
| 05 | 5 01·3 | 5 02·1 | 4 47·5 | 0·5 0·2 | 6·5 2·2 | 12·5 4·3 |
| 06 | 5 01·5 | 5 02·3 | 4 47·8 | 0·6 0·2 | 6·6 2·3 | 12·6 4·3 |
| 07 | 5 01·8 | 5 02·6 | 4 48·0 | 0·7 0·2 | 6·7 2·3 | 12·7 4·3 |
| 08 | 5 02·0 | 5 02·8 | 4 48·2 | 0·8 0·3 | 6·8 2·3 | 12·8 4·4 |
| 09 | 5 02·3 | 5 03·1 | 4 48·5 | 0·9 0·3 | 6·9 2·4 | 12·9 4·4 |
| 10 | 5 02·5 | 5 03·3 | 4 48·7 | 1·0 0·3 | 7·0 2·4 | 13·0 4·4 |
| 11 | 5 02·8 | 5 03·6 | 4 49·0 | 1·1 0·4 | 7·1 2·4 | 13·1 4·5 |

*Figure 22–3.* Excerpt from the *Increments and Corrections* tables, showing an increment of 5°03.1′ to Aries's GHA for 20 minutes, 09 seconds of time.

chosen it in advance for that very reason. On the other hand, if the declination of any star observed is less than 30°, you may elect to work the sight by Volume II or III, in the same way as for all the bodies of the solar system. To put the choice in perspective, of the 57 navigational stars listed in the almanac's daily pages, 7 stars are selected in Volume I for each degree of LHA♈; 41 are used altogether. Thirty of the 57 navigational stars, including 7 of the lesser ones, which do not appear in Volume I, can be worked with Volumes II or III. Thus, only 9, and those all minor stars, cannot be reduced with one or the other of the volumes of Pub. No. 249. Never, in my experience, has this been of consequence in the choice of Pub. No. 249 as the sight reduction table for yachtsmen. With normal preplanning you will probably use Volume I for most of your star sights, but since an even dozen of the 19 first-magnitude (brightest) stars in the almanac list can be worked with either volume, it is worthwhile to understand the procedure for each.

Looking first at Volume I, you will notice in the specimen page shown in Figure 22–4 a somewhat different arrangement from the Volume III reduction table page illustrated in Figure 17–1. Volume I requires only the latitude, the local hour angle of Aries, and the name of the star as entering arguments; the computed altitude, with no need for correction, and the true azimuth are read out directly. You don't have to concern yourself with the star's declination, or whether it is the same or contrary to the name of the latitude; you don't have to calculate the local hour angle of the star; you don't have to adjust the computed altitude for fractional degrees of declination; you don't have to convert azimuth angle to true azimuth; and it's all done with a single opening of the book.

Let's complete our practical example, which you can follow in the shorter of the workforms, using Volume I. Starting with the Greenwich hour of Aries, the assumed longitude is applied in the usual manner to obtain the local hour angle of Aries; here, an $a\lambda$ of 67°35.7'W, applied to the GHA ♈ of 262°35.7', produces an LHA ♈ of 195°. The assumed latitude is selected as for any sight, and Volume I opened to the corresponding page. The latitude assumed for our sight should be 41°N, the whole degree nearest to our DR latitude of 40°53'N. An excerpt of the appropriate page from Volume I appears in Figure 22–5. Descend the leftmost column to the LHA ♈ of the sight, 195°, and opposite it, under the name of the star, Arcturus, extract the computed altitude, 63°01', and the true azimuth, 138°. The comparison between Hc and Ho is made in the usual way; in our example, it yields an intercept of 3.6' to be plotted from the assumed position Latitude 41°N, Longitude 67°35.7'W, in the direction "away" from the true azimuth—the reciprocal of 138°. That is all there is to it.

While no corrections or interpolations are required with the figures from Volume I, you should notice that your copy of the table will be for a certain "epoch" year.

## LAT 41°N

| LHA ♈ | Hc | Zn | Hc | Zn | Hc | Zn | Hc | Zn | Hc | Zn | Hc | Zn | Hc | Zn |
|---|---|---|---|---|---|---|---|---|---|---|---|---|---|---|
| | Kochab | | •VEGA | | ARCTURUS | | •SPICA | | REGULUS | | •POLLUX | | CAPELLA | |
| 180 | 51 28 | 017 | 18 31 | 054 | 53 59 | 117 | 34 24 | 155 | 52 00 | 228 | 36 59 | 277 | 21 46 | 313 |
| 181 | 51 41 | 017 | 19 08 | 055 | 54 39 | 118 | 34 43 | 156 | 51 25 | 230 | 36 14 | 278 | 21 13 | 313 |
| 182 | 51 54 | 017 | 19 45 | 055 | 55 19 | 119 | 35 01 | 157 | 50 50 | 231 | 35 29 | 278 | 20 40 | 314 |
| 183 | 52 07 | 016 | 20 23 | 056 | 55 58 | 120 | 35 18 | 158 | 50 15 | 232 | 34 45 | 279 | 20 07 | 314 |
| 184 | 52 20 | 016 | 21 00 | 056 | 56 37 | 122 | 35 35 | 159 | 49 39 | 233 | 34 00 | 280 | 19 35 | 315 |
| 185 | 52 32 | 016 | 21 38 | 057 | 57 15 | 123 | 35 50 | 160 | 49 02 | 235 | 33 15 | 280 | 19 03 | 315 |
| 186 | 52 45 | 016 | 22 16 | 057 | 57 53 | 124 | 36 05 | 162 | 48 25 | 236 | 32 31 | 281 | 18 31 | 316 |
| 187 | 52 57 | 015 | 22 54 | 058 | 58 30 | 126 | 36 19 | 163 | 47 47 | 237 | 31 46 | 281 | 17 59 | 316 |
| 188 | 53 09 | 015 | 23 33 | 058 | 59 07 | 127 | 36 32 | 164 | 47 09 | 238 | 31 02 | 282 | 17 28 | 317 |
| 189 | 53 20 | 015 | 24 11 | 059 | 59 42 | 128 | 36 44 | 165 | 46 31 | 239 | 30 18 | 282 | 16 57 | 317 |
| 190 | 53 31 | 014 | 24 50 | 059 | 60 18 | 130 | 36 55 | 166 | 45 52 | 240 | 29 34 | 283 | 16 26 | 317 |
| 191 | 53 42 | 014 | 25 29 | 060 | 60 52 | 131 | 37 05 | 168 | 45 12 | 241 | 28 49 | 283 | 15 56 | 318 |
| 192 | 53 53 | 014 | 26 08 | 060 | 61 25 | 133 | 37 15 | 169 | 44 32 | 242 | 28 05 | 284 | 15 26 | 318 |
| 193 | 54 04 | 013 | 26 48 | 061 | 61 58 | 135 | 37 23 | 170 | 43 52 | 243 | 27 22 | 285 | 14 56 | 319 |
| 194 | 54 14 | 013 | 27 27 | 061 | 62 30 | 136 | 37 30 | 171 | 43 12 | 244 | 26 38 | 285 | 14 26 | 319 |
| | •VEGA | | Rasalhague | | ARCTURUS | | •SPICA | | REGULUS | | •POLLUX | | Dubhe | |
| 195 | 28 07 | 062 | 24 20 | 094 | 63 01 | 138 | 37 37 | 172 | 42 31 | 245 | 25 54 | 286 | 62 45 | 330 |
| 196 | 28 47 | 062 | 25 05 | 095 | 63 30 | 140 | 37 42 | 174 | 41 49 | 246 | 25 11 | 286 | 62 22 | 329 |
| 197 | 29 27 | 062 | 25 50 | 096 | 63 59 | 142 | 37 47 | 175 | 41 08 | 247 | 24 27 | 287 | 61 59 | 329 |
| 198 | 30 07 | 063 | 26 35 | 096 | 64 26 | 144 | 37 50 | 176 | 40 26 | 248 | 23 44 | 287 | 61 35 | 328 |
| 199 | 30 47 | 063 | 27 20 | 097 | 64 53 | 146 | 37 53 | 177 | 39 44 | 249 | 23 01 | 288 | 61 11 | 327 |
| 200 | 31 28 | 064 | 28 05 | 098 | 65 18 | 148 | 37 54 | 179 | 39 02 | 250 | 22 18 | 288 | 60 46 | 327 |
| 201 | 32 09 | 064 | 28 50 | 099 | 65 41 | 150 | 37 55 | 180 | 38 19 | 250 | 21 35 | 289 | 60 21 | 327 |
| 202 | 32 50 | 065 | 29 35 | 099 | 66 04 | 152 | 37 55 | 181 | 37 36 | 251 | 20 52 | 290 | 59 56 | 326 |
| 203 | 33 31 | 065 | 30 19 | 100 | 66 24 | 154 | 37 53 | 182 | 36 53 | 252 | 20 10 | 290 | 59 31 | 326 |
| 204 | 34 12 | 066 | 31 04 | 101 | 66 43 | 156 | 37 51 | 184 | 36 10 | 253 | 19 27 | 291 | 59 05 | 325 |
| 205 | 34 53 | 066 | 31 48 | 102 | 67 01 | 158 | 37 48 | 185 | 35 27 | 254 | 18 45 | 291 | 58 39 | 325 |
| 206 | 35 35 | 067 | 32 33 | 102 | 67 17 | 161 | 37 43 | 186 | 34 43 | 255 | 18 03 | 292 | 58 13 | 325 |
| 207 | 36 16 | 067 | 33 17 | 103 | 67 31 | 163 | 37 38 | 187 | 34 00 | 255 | 17 21 | 292 | 57 47 | 324 |
| 208 | 36 58 | 067 | 34 01 | 104 | 67 43 | 166 | 37 32 | 189 | 33 16 | 256 | 16 39 | 293 | 57 20 | 324 |
| 209 | 37 40 | 068 | 34 45 | 105 | 67 53 | 168 | 37 24 | 190 | 32 32 | 257 | 15 58 | 294 | 56 54 | 324 |
| | •DENEB | | VEGA | | Rasalhague | | ANTARES | | •ARCTURUS | | REGULUS | | •Dubhe | |
| 210 | 21 48 | 048 | 38 22 | 068 | 35 28 | 105 | 14 19 | 146 | 68 02 | 171 | 31 47 | 258 | 56 27 | 323 |
| 211 | 22 22 | 049 | 39 04 | 069 | 36 12 | 106 | 14 44 | 147 | 68 08 | 173 | 31 03 | 258 | 56 00 | 323 |
| 212 | 22 56 | 049 | 39 46 | 069 | 36 55 | 107 | 15 09 | 148 | 68 13 | 176 | 30 19 | 259 | 55 32 | 323 |
| 213 | 23 30 | 050 | 40 29 | 070 | 37 39 | 108 | 15 32 | 149 | 68 15 | 178 | 29 34 | 260 | 55 05 | 323 |
| 214 | 24 05 | 050 | 41 11 | 070 | 38 22 | 109 | 15 56 | 149 | 68 16 | 181 | 28 50 | 261 | 54 37 | 322 |
| 215 | 24 40 | 051 | 41 54 | 070 | 39 04 | 110 | 16 19 | 150 | 68 14 | 183 | 28 05 | 261 | 54 10 | 322 |
| 216 | 25 15 | 051 | 42 36 | 071 | 39 47 | 110 | 16 41 | 151 | 68 10 | 186 | 27 20 | 262 | 53 42 | 322 |
| 217 | 25 50 | 051 | 43 19 | 071 | 40 29 | 111 | 17 02 | 152 | 68 05 | 188 | 26 35 | 263 | 53 14 | 322 |
| 218 | 26 26 | 052 | 44 02 | 072 | 41 11 | 112 | 17 23 | 153 | 67 57 | 191 | 25 50 | 263 | 52 46 | 322 |
| 219 | 27 01 | 052 | 44 45 | 072 | 41 53 | 113 | 17 44 | 154 | 67 48 | 193 | 25 05 | 264 | 52 18 | 322 |
| 220 | 27 37 | 053 | 45 28 | 073 | 42 35 | 114 | 18 03 | 155 | 67 37 | 196 | 24 20 | 265 | 51 50 | 322 |
| 221 | 28 13 | 053 | 46 12 | 073 | 43 16 | 115 | 18 23 | 155 | 67 24 | 198 | 23 35 | 266 | 51 22 | 322 |
| 222 | 28 50 | 053 | 46 55 | 073 | 43 57 | 116 | 18 41 | 156 | 67 09 | 200 | 22 50 | 266 | 50 54 | 321 |
| 223 | 29 26 | 054 | 47 38 | 074 | 44 37 | 117 | 18 59 | 157 | 66 52 | 203 | 22 05 | 267 | 50 26 | 321 |
| 224 | 30 03 | 054 | 48 22 | 074 | 45 17 | 118 | 19 16 | 158 | 66 34 | 205 | 21 19 | 268 | 49 58 | 321 |
| | DENEB | | •ALTAIR | | Rasalhague | | ANTARES | | •ARCTURUS | | Denebola | | •Dubhe | |
| 225 | 30 40 | 055 | 18 57 | 095 | 45 57 | 119 | 19 33 | 159 | 66 14 | 207 | 40 56 | 252 | 49 29 | 321 |
| 226 | 31 17 | 055 | 19 42 | 095 | 46 37 | 120 | 19 49 | 160 | 65 52 | 209 | 40 13 | 253 | 49 01 | 321 |
| 227 | 31 54 | 055 | 20 27 | 096 | 47 16 | 121 | 20 04 | 161 | 65 29 | 211 | 39 30 | 254 | 48 33 | 321 |
| 228 | 32 31 | 056 | 21 12 | 097 | 47 54 | 122 | 20 18 | 162 | 65 05 | 213 | 38 46 | 254 | 48 04 | 321 |
| 229 | 33 09 | 056 | 21 57 | 098 | 48 32 | 123 | 20 32 | 163 | 64 39 | 215 | 38 03 | 255 | 47 36 | 321 |
| 230 | 33 47 | 057 | 22 42 | 098 | 49 10 | 124 | 20 45 | 164 | 64 13 | 217 | 37 19 | 256 | 47 08 | 321 |
| 231 | 34 24 | 057 | 23 27 | 099 | 49 47 | 126 | 20 58 | 165 | 63 44 | 219 | 36 35 | 257 | 46 39 | 321 |
| 232 | 35 02 | 057 | 24 12 | 100 | 50 24 | 127 | 21 09 | 165 | 63 15 | 221 | 35 51 | 258 | 46 11 | 321 |
| 233 | 35 41 | 058 | 24 56 | 100 | 51 00 | 128 | 21 20 | 166 | 62 45 | 223 | 35 06 | 258 | 45 43 | 321 |
| 234 | 36 19 | 058 | 25 41 | 101 | 51 35 | 129 | 21 31 | 167 | 62 14 | 225 | 34 22 | 259 | 45 15 | 321 |
| 235 | 36 58 | 058 | 26 25 | 102 | 52 10 | 130 | 21 40 | 168 | 61 41 | 226 | 33 37 | 260 | 44 46 | 322 |
| 236 | 37 36 | 059 | 27 09 | 103 | 52 44 | 132 | 21 49 | 169 | 61 08 | 228 | 32 53 | 261 | 44 18 | 322 |
| 237 | 38 15 | 059 | 27 53 | 103 | 53 17 | 133 | 21 57 | 170 | 60 34 | 229 | 32 08 | 261 | 43 50 | 322 |
| 238 | 38 54 | 060 | 28 37 | 104 | 53 50 | 134 | 22 04 | 171 | 60 00 | 231 | 31 23 | 262 | 43 22 | 322 |
| 239 | 39 33 | 060 | 29 21 | 105 | 54 22 | 136 | 22 11 | 172 | 59 24 | 232 | 30 38 | 263 | 42 54 | 322 |
| | •DENEB | | ALTAIR | | Rasalhague | | •ANTARES | | ARCTURUS | | Denebola | | •Dubhe | |
| 240 | 40 12 | 060 | 30 05 | 106 | 54 53 | 137 | 22 17 | 173 | 58 48 | 234 | 29 53 | 264 | 42 26 | 322 |
| 241 | 40 52 | 061 | 30 48 | 106 | 55 23 | 139 | 22 22 | 174 | 58 11 | 235 | 29 08 | 264 | 41 58 | 322 |
| 242 | 41 31 | 061 | 31 32 | 107 | 55 53 | 140 | 22 26 | 175 | 57 34 | 236 | 28 23 | 265 | 41 31 | 322 |
| 243 | 42 11 | 061 | 32 15 | 108 | 56 21 | 142 | 22 30 | 176 | 56 56 | 238 | 27 38 | 266 | 41 03 | 322 |
| 244 | 42 51 | 062 | 32 58 | 109 | 56 49 | 143 | 22 32 | 177 | 56 17 | 239 | 26 53 | 266 | 40 35 | 323 |
| 245 | 43 30 | 062 | 33 41 | 110 | 57 15 | 145 | 22 34 | 178 | 55 38 | 240 | 26 08 | 267 | 40 08 | 323 |
| 246 | 44 10 | 062 | 34 23 | 110 | 57 41 | 147 | 22 36 | 179 | 54 59 | 241 | 25 22 | 268 | 39 40 | 323 |
| 247 | 44 50 | 062 | 35 06 | 111 | 58 05 | 148 | 22 36 | 180 | 54 19 | 243 | 24 37 | 268 | 39 13 | 323 |
| 248 | 45 31 | 063 | 35 48 | 112 | 58 28 | 150 | 22 36 | 181 | 53 38 | 244 | 23 52 | 269 | 38 46 | 323 |
| 249 | 46 11 | 063 | 36 30 | 113 | 58 51 | 152 | 22 35 | 182 | 52 57 | 245 | 23 07 | 270 | 38 19 | 323 |
| 250 | 46 51 | 063 | 37 11 | 114 | 59 11 | 153 | 22 33 | 183 | 52 16 | 246 | 22 21 | 270 | 37 52 | 323 |
| 251 | 47 32 | 064 | 37 52 | 115 | 59 31 | 155 | 22 30 | 184 | 51 35 | 247 | 21 36 | 271 | 37 25 | 324 |
| 252 | 48 13 | 064 | 38 33 | 116 | 59 49 | 157 | 22 27 | 185 | 50 53 | 248 | 20 51 | 272 | 36 58 | 324 |
| 253 | 48 53 | 064 | 39 14 | 117 | 60 06 | 159 | 22 23 | 186 | 50 11 | 249 | 20 06 | 272 | 36 31 | 324 |
| 254 | 49 34 | 065 | 39 54 | 118 | 60 22 | 161 | 22 18 | 187 | 49 29 | 250 | 19 20 | 273 | 36 05 | 324 |
| | •DENEB | | ALTAIR | | Nunki | | •ANTARES | | ARCTURUS | | •Alkaid | | Kochab | |
| 255 | 50 15 | 065 | 40 34 | 118 | 17 39 | 153 | 22 12 | 188 | 48 46 | 251 | 55 36 | 301 | 53 36 | 346 |
| 256 | 50 56 | 065 | 41 14 | 119 | 17 59 | 154 | 22 06 | 189 | 48 03 | 252 | 54 57 | 301 | 53 24 | 345 |
| 257 | 51 37 | 065 | 41 53 | 120 | 18 18 | 155 | 21 59 | 190 | 47 20 | 253 | 54 18 | 301 | 53 13 | 345 |
| 258 | 52 18 | 066 | 42 32 | 121 | 18 37 | 156 | 21 51 | 190 | 46 37 | 254 | 53 39 | 301 | 53 01 | 345 |
| 259 | 53 00 | 066 | 43 10 | 122 | 18 55 | 157 | 21 42 | 191 | 45 53 | 254 | 53 00 | 301 | 52 49 | 345 |
| 260 | 53 41 | 066 | 43 48 | 124 | 19 13 | 158 | 21 33 | 192 | 45 09 | 255 | 52 22 | 301 | 52 37 | 344 |
| 261 | 54 23 | 066 | 44 26 | 125 | 19 30 | 159 | 21 23 | 193 | 44 25 | 256 | 51 43 | 301 | 52 25 | 344 |
| 262 | 55 04 | 067 | 45 03 | 126 | 19 46 | 159 | 21 12 | 194 | 43 41 | 257 | 51 04 | 302 | 52 12 | 344 |
| 263 | 55 46 | 067 | 45 40 | 127 | 20 02 | 160 | 21 01 | 195 | 42 57 | 258 | 50 26 | 302 | 51 59 | 343 |
| 264 | 56 27 | 067 | 46 16 | 128 | 20 16 | 161 | 20 48 | 196 | 42 13 | 259 | 49 48 | 302 | 51 46 | 343 |
| 265 | 57 09 | 067 | 46 51 | 129 | 20 31 | 162 | 20 35 | 197 | 41 29 | 259 | 49 09 | 302 | 51 33 | 343 |
| 266 | 57 51 | 067 | 47 26 | 130 | 20 44 | 163 | 20 22 | 198 | 40 44 | 260 | 48 31 | 302 | 51 19 | 343 |
| 267 | 58 33 | 068 | 48 00 | 131 | 20 57 | 164 | 20 07 | 199 | 39 59 | 261 | 47 53 | 303 | 51 06 | 342 |
| 268 | 59 14 | 068 | 48 34 | 133 | 21 09 | 165 | 19 52 | 200 | 39 15 | 262 | 47 15 | 303 | 50 52 | 342 |
| 269 | 59 56 | 068 | 49 07 | 134 | 21 20 | 166 | 19 37 | 201 | 38 30 | 262 | 46 37 | 303 | 50 38 | 342 |

| LHA ♈ | Hc | Zn | Hc | Zn | Hc | Zn | Hc | Zn | Hc | Zn | Hc | Zn | Hc | Zn |
|---|---|---|---|---|---|---|---|---|---|---|---|---|---|---|
| | •Alpheratz | | ALTAIR | | Nunki | | •ANTARES | | ARCTURUS | | •Alkaid | | Kochab | |
| 270 | 17 14 | 066 | 49 39 | 135 | 21 31 | 167 | 19 20 | 202 | 37 45 | 263 | 45 59 | 303 | 50 24 | 342 |
| 271 | 17 55 | 067 | 50 11 | 136 | 21 41 | 168 | 19 03 | 203 | 37 00 | 264 | 45 21 | 303 | 50 10 | 342 |
| 272 | 18 37 | 067 | 50 41 | 138 | 21 50 | 169 | 18 45 | 203 | 36 15 | 265 | 44 43 | 304 | 49 55 | 341 |
| 273 | 19 19 | 068 | 51 11 | 139 | 21 58 | 170 | 18 27 | 204 | 35 30 | 265 | 44 05 | 304 | 49 41 | 341 |
| 274 | 20 01 | 068 | 51 41 | 141 | 22 06 | 171 | 18 08 | 205 | 34 45 | 266 | 43 28 | 304 | 49 26 | 341 |
| 275 | 20 43 | 069 | 52 09 | 142 | 22 13 | 172 | 17 49 | 206 | 33 59 | 267 | 42 51 | 304 | 49 11 | 341 |
| 276 | 21 26 | 070 | 52 36 | 143 | 22 19 | 173 | 17 28 | 207 | 33 14 | 267 | 42 13 | 305 | 48 56 | 341 |
| 277 | 22 08 | 070 | 53 03 | 145 | 22 24 | 174 | 17 07 | 208 | 32 29 | 268 | 41 36 | 305 | 48 41 | 340 |
| 278 | 22 51 | 071 | 53 29 | 146 | 22 29 | 175 | 16 46 | 209 | 31 44 | 269 | 40 59 | 305 | 48 26 | 340 |
| 279 | 23 34 | 071 | 53 53 | 148 | 22 33 | 176 | 16 24 | 210 | 30 58 | 269 | 40 22 | 306 | 48 10 | 340 |
| 280 | 24 16 | 072 | 54 17 | 149 | 22 36 | 177 | 16 01 | 210 | 30 13 | 270 | 39 45 | 306 | 47 55 | 340 |
| 281 | 25 00 | 072 | 54 39 | 151 | 22 38 | 177 | 15 38 | 211 | 29 28 | 271 | 39 09 | 306 | 47 40 | 340 |
| 282 | 25 43 | 073 | 55 01 | 153 | 22 40 | 178 | 15 14 | 212 | 28 42 | 271 | 38 32 | 306 | 47 24 | 340 |
| 283 | 26 26 | 073 | 55 21 | 154 | 22 41 | 179 | 14 50 | 213 | 27 57 | 272 | 37 56 | 307 | 47 08 | 340 |
| 284 | 27 10 | 074 | 55 40 | 156 | 22 41 | 180 | 14 25 | 214 | 27 12 | 273 | 37 20 | 307 | 46 52 | 340 |
| | •Mirfak | | Alpheratz | | •ALTAIR | | Rasalhague | | •ARCTURUS | | Alkaid | | Kochab | |
| 285 | 12 29 | 032 | 27 53 | 075 | 55 58 | 158 | 55 56 | 220 | 26 27 | 273 | 36 43 | 307 | 46 37 | 339 |
| 286 | 12 54 | 033 | 28 37 | 075 | 56 15 | 159 | 55 27 | 221 | 25 42 | 274 | 36 08 | 308 | 46 21 | 339 |
| 287 | 13 18 | 033 | 29 21 | 076 | 56 30 | 161 | 54 57 | 223 | 24 56 | 274 | 35 32 | 308 | 46 05 | 339 |
| 288 | 13 43 | 034 | 30 05 | 076 | 56 44 | 163 | 54 26 | 224 | 24 11 | 275 | 34 56 | 308 | 45 49 | 339 |
| 289 | 14 09 | 034 | 30 49 | 077 | 56 57 | 164 | 53 54 | 225 | 23 26 | 276 | 34 21 | 309 | 45 33 | 339 |
| 290 | 14 35 | 035 | 31 33 | 077 | 57 09 | 166 | 53 21 | 227 | 22 41 | 276 | 33 45 | 309 | 45 16 | 339 |
| 291 | 15 01 | 035 | 32 17 | 078 | 57 19 | 168 | 52 48 | 228 | 21 56 | 277 | 33 10 | 309 | 45 00 | 339 |
| 292 | 15 27 | 036 | 33 01 | 078 | 57 28 | 170 | 52 14 | 229 | 21 11 | 278 | 32 35 | 310 | 44 44 | 339 |
| 293 | 15 54 | 036 | 33 46 | 079 | 57 35 | 172 | 51 39 | 231 | 20 26 | 278 | 32 01 | 310 | 44 28 | 339 |
| 294 | 16 21 | 037 | 34 30 | 080 | 57 41 | 173 | 51 04 | 232 | 19 42 | 279 | 31 26 | 310 | 44 12 | 339 |
| 295 | 16 48 | 037 | 35 15 | 080 | 57 45 | 175 | 50 28 | 233 | 18 57 | 279 | 30 52 | 311 | 43 55 | 339 |
| 296 | 17 16 | 038 | 35 59 | 081 | 57 48 | 177 | 49 51 | 234 | 18 12 | 280 | 30 17 | 311 | 43 39 | 339 |
| 297 | 17 44 | 038 | 36 44 | 081 | 57 49 | 179 | 49 14 | 235 | 17 28 | 281 | 29 43 | 311 | 43 23 | 339 |
| 298 | 18 12 | 039 | 37 29 | 082 | 57 50 | 181 | 48 37 | 237 | 16 43 | 281 | 29 09 | 312 | 43 06 | 339 |
| 299 | 18 40 | 039 | 38 14 | 082 | 57 48 | 183 | 47 59 | 238 | 15 59 | 282 | 28 36 | 312 | 42 50 | 339 |
| | Mirfak | | •Alpheratz | | Enif | | •ALTAIR | | Rasalhague | | Alphecca | | •Kochab | |
| 300 | 19 09 | 040 | 38 59 | 083 | 51 21 | 137 | 57 45 | 185 | 47 20 | 239 | 34 21 | 277 | 42 34 | 339 |
| 301 | 19 38 | 040 | 39 44 | 084 | 51 52 | 138 | 57 41 | 186 | 46 41 | 240 | 33 36 | 278 | 42 17 | 339 |
| 302 | 20 08 | 041 | 40 29 | 084 | 52 22 | 139 | 57 35 | 188 | 46 02 | 241 | 32 51 | 279 | 42 01 | 339 |
| 303 | 20 37 | 041 | 41 14 | 085 | 52 51 | 141 | 57 28 | 190 | 45 22 | 242 | 32 07 | 279 | 41 45 | 339 |
| 304 | 21 07 | 041 | 41 59 | 085 | 53 19 | 142 | 57 19 | 192 | 44 42 | 243 | 31 22 | 280 | 41 29 | 339 |
| 305 | 21 37 | 042 | 42 44 | 086 | 53 46 | 144 | 57 09 | 194 | 44 02 | 244 | 30 37 | 280 | 41 12 | 339 |
| 306 | 22 08 | 042 | 43 29 | 086 | 54 13 | 145 | 56 58 | 196 | 43 21 | 245 | 29 53 | 281 | 40 56 | 339 |
| 307 | 22 38 | 043 | 44 14 | 087 | 54 38 | 147 | 56 45 | 197 | 42 40 | 246 | 29 08 | 281 | 40 40 | 339 |
| 308 | 23 09 | 043 | 45 00 | 088 | 55 03 | 148 | 56 31 | 199 | 41 58 | 247 | 28 24 | 282 | 40 24 | 339 |
| 309 | 23 40 | 044 | 45 45 | 088 | 55 26 | 150 | 56 15 | 201 | 41 16 | 248 | 27 40 | 283 | 40 08 | 339 |
| 310 | 24 12 | 044 | 46 30 | 089 | 55 48 | 151 | 55 59 | 202 | 40 34 | 249 | 26 56 | 283 | 39 52 | 339 |
| 311 | 24 43 | 044 | 47 15 | 090 | 56 09 | 153 | 55 41 | 204 | 39 52 | 249 | 26 12 | 284 | 39 36 | 339 |
| 312 | 25 15 | 045 | 48 01 | 090 | 56 29 | 155 | 55 22 | 206 | 39 09 | 250 | 25 28 | 284 | 39 20 | 339 |
| 313 | 25 47 | 045 | 48 46 | 091 | 56 48 | 156 | 55 01 | 207 | 38 27 | 251 | 24 44 | 285 | 39 04 | 339 |
| 314 | 26 19 | 046 | 49 31 | 092 | 57 05 | 158 | 54 40 | 209 | 37 44 | 252 | 24 00 | 285 | 38 48 | 340 |
| | CAPELLA | | •Alpheratz | | FOMALHAUT | | •ALTAIR | | Rasalhague | | VEGA | | •Kochab | |
| 315 | 10 20 | 036 | 50 16 | 092 | 14 19 | 154 | 54 17 | 211 | 37 01 | 253 | 62 34 | 277 | 38 32 | 340 |
| 316 | 10 47 | 036 | 51 02 | 093 | 14 38 | 155 | 53 54 | 212 | 36 17 | 254 | 61 49 | 278 | 38 17 | 340 |
| 317 | 11 14 | 037 | 51 47 | 094 | 14 57 | 156 | 53 29 | 214 | 35 34 | 255 | 61 04 | 278 | 38 01 | 340 |
| 318 | 11 41 | 038 | 52 32 | 094 | 15 15 | 157 | 53 04 | 215 | 34 50 | 255 | 60 19 | 279 | 37 45 | 340 |
| 319 | 12 09 | 038 | 53 17 | 095 | 15 33 | 157 | 52 37 | 217 | 34 06 | 256 | 59 34 | 279 | 37 30 | 340 |
| 320 | 12 37 | 039 | 54 02 | 096 | 15 50 | 158 | 52 10 | 218 | 33 22 | 257 | 58 50 | 280 | 37 15 | 340 |
| 321 | 13 05 | 039 | 54 47 | 097 | 16 06 | 159 | 51 41 | 219 | 32 38 | 258 | 58 05 | 280 | 36 59 | 340 |
| 322 | 13 34 | 040 | 55 32 | 098 | 16 22 | 160 | 51 12 | 221 | 31 53 | 258 | 57 21 | 280 | 36 44 | 340 |
| 323 | 14 03 | 040 | 56 17 | 098 | 16 37 | 161 | 50 42 | 222 | 31 09 | 259 | 56 36 | 281 | 36 29 | 341 |
| 324 | 14 32 | 041 | 57 02 | 099 | 16 52 | 162 | 50 11 | 224 | 30 25 | 260 | 55 52 | 281 | 36 14 | 341 |
| 325 | 15 02 | 041 | 57 46 | 100 | 17 06 | 163 | 49 40 | 225 | 29 40 | 261 | 55 07 | 282 | 35 59 | 341 |
| 326 | 15 32 | 042 | 58 31 | 101 | 17 19 | 163 | 49 08 | 226 | 28 55 | 261 | 54 23 | 282 | 35 44 | 341 |
| 327 | 16 02 | 042 | 59 15 | 102 | 17 32 | 164 | 48 35 | 227 | 28 10 | 262 | 53 39 | 283 | 35 29 | 341 |
| 328 | 16 33 | 043 | 60 00 | 103 | 17 43 | 165 | 48 01 | 229 | 27 26 | 263 | 52 55 | 283 | 35 15 | 341 |
| 329 | 17 04 | 043 | 60 44 | 104 | 17 55 | 166 | 47 27 | 230 | 26 41 | 263 | 52 11 | 283 | 35 00 | 341 |
| | •CAPELLA | | Hamal | | Diphda | | •FOMALHAUT | | ALTAIR | | •VEGA | | Kochab | |
| 330 | 17 35 | 044 | 36 10 | 089 | 19 54 | 139 | 18 05 | 167 | 46 52 | 231 | 51 27 | 284 | 34 46 | 342 |
| 331 | 18 06 | 044 | 36 55 | 090 | 20 24 | 140 | 18 15 | 168 | 46 16 | 232 | 50 43 | 284 | 34 32 | 342 |
| 332 | 18 38 | 045 | 37 41 | 090 | 20 53 | 140 | 18 24 | 169 | 45 40 | 233 | 49 59 | 285 | 34 18 | 342 |
| 333 | 19 09 | 045 | 38 26 | 091 | 21 21 | 141 | 18 32 | 170 | 45 04 | 234 | 49 15 | 285 | 34 04 | 342 |
| 334 | 19 42 | 045 | 39 11 | 092 | 21 49 | 142 | 18 40 | 171 | 44 27 | 235 | 48 31 | 286 | 33 50 | 342 |
| 335 | 20 14 | 046 | 39 56 | 092 | 22 17 | 143 | 18 47 | 172 | 43 49 | 236 | 47 48 | 286 | 33 36 | 342 |
| 336 | 20 47 | 046 | 40 42 | 093 | 22 44 | 144 | 18 53 | 172 | 43 11 | 238 | 47 04 | 286 | 33 22 | 343 |
| 337 | 21 20 | 047 | 41 27 | 094 | 23 10 | 145 | 18 59 | 173 | 42 33 | 239 | 46 21 | 287 | 33 09 | 343 |
| 338 | 21 53 | 047 | 42 12 | 094 | 23 36 | 146 | 19 04 | 174 | 41 54 | 240 | 45 38 | 287 | 32 56 | 343 |
| 339 | 22 26 | 048 | 42 57 | 095 | 24 01 | 147 | 19 08 | 175 | 41 15 | 241 | 44 55 | 288 | 32 42 | 343 |
| 340 | 23 00 | 048 | 43 42 | 096 | 24 25 | 148 | 19 11 | 176 | 40 35 | 242 | 44 11 | 288 | 32 29 | 34 |
| 341 | 23 34 | 049 | 44 27 | 097 | 24 49 | 149 | 19 14 | 177 | 39 55 | 242 | 43 28 | 289 | 32 16 | 34 |
| 342 | 24 08 | 049 | 45 12 | 097 | 25 12 | 150 | 19 16 | 178 | 39 15 | 243 | 42 46 | 289 | 32 04 | 344 |
| 343 | 24 42 | 050 | 45 57 | 098 | 25 35 | 151 | 19 17 | 179 | 38 34 | 244 | 42 03 | 289 | 31 51 | 344 |
| 344 | 25 17 | 050 | 46 42 | 099 | 25 56 | 152 | 19 18 | 180 | 37 53 | 245 | 41 20 | 290 | 31 39 | 344 |
| | •CAPELLA | | ALDEBARAN | | Diphda | | •FOMALHAUT | | ALTAIR | | •VEGA | | Kochab | |
| 345 | 25 52 | 050 | 15 21 | 081 | 26 18 | 153 | 19 18 | 181 | 37 12 | 246 | 40 38 | 290 | 31 26 | 34 |
| 346 | 26 27 | 051 | 16 06 | 082 | 26 38 | 154 | 19 17 | 182 | 36 31 | 247 | 39 55 | 291 | 31 14 | 34 |
| 347 | 27 02 | 051 | 16 51 | 083 | 26 58 | 155 | 19 15 | 183 | 35 49 | 248 | 39 13 | 291 | 31 02 | 34 |
| 348 | 27 37 | 052 | 17 36 | 083 | 27 17 | 156 | 19 13 | 183 | 35 07 | 249 | 38 31 | 292 | 30 50 | 34 |
| 349 | 28 13 | 052 | 18 21 | 084 | 27 35 | 157 | 19 10 | 184 | 34 24 | 250 | 37 49 | 292 | 30 39 | 34 |
| 350 | 28 49 | 052 | 19 06 | 084 | 27 53 | 158 | 19 06 | 185 | 33 42 | 250 | 37 07 | 292 | 30 27 | 34 |
| 351 | 29 25 | 053 | 19 51 | 085 | 28 10 | 159 | 19 01 | 186 | 32 59 | 251 | 36 25 | 293 | 30 16 | 34 |
| 352 | 30 01 | 053 | 20 36 | 086 | 28 26 | 160 | 18 56 | 187 | 32 16 | 252 | 35 44 | 293 | 30 05 | 34 |
| 353 | 30 37 | 054 | 21 21 | 086 | 28 41 | 161 | 18 50 | 188 | 31 33 | 253 | 35 02 | 294 | 29 54 | 34 |
| 354 | 31 14 | 054 | 22 06 | 087 | 28 56 | 162 | 18 43 | 189 | 30 50 | 254 | 34 21 | 294 | 29 43 | 34 |
| 355 | 31 51 | 054 | 22 51 | 088 | 29 09 | 163 | 18 36 | 190 | 30 06 | 254 | 33 39 | 295 | 29 33 | 34 |
| 356 | 32 27 | 055 | 23 37 | 088 | 29 22 | 164 | 18 28 | 191 | 29 22 | 255 | 32 58 | 295 | 29 22 | 34 |
| 357 | 33 05 | 055 | 24 22 | 089 | 29 35 | 165 | 18 19 | 192 | 28 39 | 256 | 32 18 | 296 | 29 12 | 34 |
| 358 | 33 42 | 056 | 25 07 | 090 | 29 46 | 166 | 18 09 | 193 | 27 55 | 257 | 31 37 | 296 | 29 02 | 34 |
| 359 | 34 19 | 056 | 25 53 | 090 | 29 56 | 167 | 17 59 | 193 | 27 10 | 257 | 30 56 | 297 | 28 52 | 34 |

***Figure 22–4.*** **Specimen page from Volume I *(Selected Stars)*, Pub. No. 249, Epoch 1985.0. Only latitude, LHA ♈, and the name of the star are required to obtain Hc and Zn directly.**

## LAT 41°N

| LHA ϒ | Hc  Zn | Hc  Zn | Hc  Zn | Hc  Zn | Hc  Zn | Hc  Zn | Hc  Zn |
|---|---|---|---|---|---|---|---|
|  | Kochab | ◆VEGA | ARCTURUS | ◆SPICA | REGULUS | ◆POLLUX | CAPELLA |
| 180 | 51 28 017 | 18 31 054 | 53 59 117 | 34 24 155 | 52 00 228 | 36 59 277 | 21 46 313 |
| 181 | 51 41 017 | 19 08 055 | 54 39 118 | 34 43 156 | 51 25 230 | 36 14 278 | 21 13 313 |
| 182 | 51 54 017 | 19 45 055 | 55 19 119 | 35 01 157 | 50 50 231 | 35 29 278 | 20 40 314 |
| 183 | 52 07 016 | 20 23 056 | 55 58 120 | 35 18 158 | 50 15 232 | 34 45 279 | 20 07 314 |
| 184 | 52 20 016 | 21 00 056 | 56 37 122 | 35 35 159 | 49 39 233 | 34 00 280 | 19 35 315 |
| 185 | 52 32 016 | 21 38 057 | 57 15 123 | 35 50 160 | 49 02 235 | 33 15 280 | 19 03 315 |
| 186 | 52 45 016 | 22 16 057 | 57 53 124 | 36 05 162 | 48 25 236 | 32 31 281 | 18 31 316 |
| 187 | 52 57 015 | 22 54 058 | 58 30 126 | 36 19 163 | 47 47 237 | 31 46 281 | 17 59 316 |
| 188 | 53 09 015 | 23 33 058 | 59 07 127 | 36 32 164 | 47 09 238 | 31 02 282 | 17 28 317 |
| 189 | 53 20 015 | 24 11 059 | 59 42 128 | 36 44 165 | 46 31 239 | 30 18 282 | 16 57 317 |
| 190 | 53 31 014 | 24 50 059 | 60 18 130 | 36 55 166 | 45 52 240 | 29 34 283 | 16 26 317 |
| 191 | 53 42 014 | 25 29 060 | 60 52 131 | 37 05 168 | 45 12 241 | 28 49 283 | 15 56 318 |
| 192 | 53 53 014 | 26 08 060 | 61 25 133 | 37 15 169 | 44 32 242 | 28 05 284 | 15 26 318 |
| 193 | 54 04 013 | 26 48 061 | 61 58 135 | 37 23 170 | 43 52 243 | 27 22 285 | 14 56 319 |
| 194 | 54 14 013 | 27 27 061 | 62 30 136 | 37 30 171 | 43 12 244 | 26 38 285 | 14 26 319 |
|  | ◆VEGA | Rasalhague | ARCTURUS | ◆SPICA | REGULUS | ◆POLLUX | Dubhe |
| 195 | 28 07 062 | 24 20 094 | 63 01 138 | 37 37 172 | 42 31 245 | 25 54 286 | 62 45 330 |
| 196 | 28 47 062 | 25 05 095 | 63 30 140 | 37 42 174 | 41 49 246 | 25 11 286 | 62 22 329 |
| 197 | 29 27 062 | 25 50 096 | 63 59 142 | 37 47 175 | 41 08 247 | 24 27 287 | 61 59 329 |
| 198 | 30 07 063 | 26 35 096 | 64 26 144 | 37 50 176 | 40 26 248 | 23 44 287 | 61 35 328 |
| 199 | 30 47 063 | 27 20 097 | 64 53 146 | 37 53 177 | 39 44 249 | 23 01 288 | 61 11 327 |
| 200 | 31 28 064 | 28 05 098 | 65 18 148 | 37 54 179 | 39 02 250 | 22 18 288 | 60 46 327 |
| 201 | 32 09 064 | 28 50 099 | 65 41 150 | 37 55 180 | 38 19 250 | 21 35 289 | 60 21 327 |
| 202 | 32 50 065 | 29 35 099 | 66 04 152 | 37 55 181 | 37 36 251 | 20 52 290 | 59 56 326 |

*Figure 22–5.* **Excerpt from main tables of Volume I, Pub. No. 249 for Latitude 41°N. At LHA ϒ 195°, Arcturus's Hc is 63°01′, and Zn 138°.**

The table used in our excerpts is for Epoch 1985.0, and the volume is updated every five years. If you are more than a year either side of the epoch year, you may wish to adjust your position line or fix, by means of Table 5 in the back of Volume I, for *precession* and *nutation*. These technical terms simply mean that while the stars' positions can be considered fixed for short periods, they do wander slowly over a period of years, and this should be taken into account. The majority of small-boat navigators ignore this correction, which only applies to sights worked with Volume I, but that can admit errors of two or three miles in the distant years, a matter of significance if you are counting on precise results.

If you choose to perform your star-sight reduction with Volumes II or III of Pub. No. 249, you can see the procedure outlined in the longer of the workforms, which has been completed for the same observation of Arcturus.

After having established the Greenwich hour angle of Aries, 262°35.7′, you next calculate the Greenwich hour angle of the star. This is accomplished, in accordance with the formula described earlier, by adding the sidereal hour angle of the star to GHA Aries. The sidereal hour angle of Arcturus is found in the almanac list (Figure 22–2); for either June 8, 9, or 10, the SHA is 146°15.7′. That value is added to Aries's GHA (then subtracting 360° because the total exceeds 360°) to produce the Greenwich hour angle of Arcturus, 48°51.4′. At the same time that Arcturus's SHA is being taken from the almanac, you can also extract the declination—in this case, 19°15.9′N—for use in the sight reduction table. Like the SHA, the declination of a star is changing so slowly that no correction is needed for any of the three days included on the same page. On the other hand, you may have noticed in the lower right-hand corner of the daily page (Figure 21–1), the sidereal hour angles of the principal planets. These values are only for 00 hours on the middle day of the three, and if you try to find the GHA of a planet by adding its sidereal hour angle to GHA Aries, a correction is necessary. It is much better to use the regular planet tables.

To the star's GHA, the assumed longitude must be applied to obtain the local hour angle of the star. In our example, we assumed a longitude of 67°51.4′W, near our DR longitude, and one that would allow the local hour angle to be a whole degree, 341°. Since the longitude assumed is greater than the star's Greenwich hour angle, 360° must first be added to the GHA to make the subtraction called for by the West longitude possible. You will notice in this particular case that in combining SHA★ with GHA♈, it was necessary to subtract 360°, and then, in the next step, when applying aλ to GHA★, it was necessary to add it back again. By inspection, the navigator probably would have realized that by omitting the subtraction and later readdition of 360°, the result would have been the identical LHA★, and he might have skipped the extra steps, which I included for clarity. You should also note that we used a somewhat different assumed longitude than we did in the Volume I solution; in each case it was selected to make the local hour angle come out to a whole degree, but in one instance you have calculated the local hour angle of Aries, and in the other, the local hour angle of the star itself. As you will see if you plot the position lines, the two lines will be virtually coincident, as long as you remember to plot each one from its respective assumed position.

In the Volume II/III method, after calculating the local hour angle of the star, and having already found the star's declination in the almanac list, and assumed a latitude (41°) near your DR position, you are ready to enter the sight reduction tables in the regular way. The excerpt in Figure 22–6 shows the data we seek. At Latitude 41°, with the declination of the same name, North, descend the LHA column to 341°, the value we had found for Arcturus's local hour angle. Opposite the LHA, in the column containing the whole degrees, 19°, of Arcturus's declination (19°15.9′N), you find the tabular Hc, 62°40′, and the azimuth angle, Z, 138°. The altitude differential, d, you will note, is +50′. Turning to Table 5, Figure 22–7, the correction to the tabulated altitude for 15.9′ of declination at a d-value of +50, is 13′. This correction, added to the tabular value, produces a computed altitude of 62° 53′, which when compared with the observed altitude, yields an intercept of 4.4′ "toward." Since the LHA of 341° is greater than 180°, the rule in this case is that Zn equals Z, and the true azimuth is 138°. Except for the rounding off that is inherent in the process and may create minor differences, Arcturus's line of position, properly plotted, will be the same line as the one derived in the Volume I solution, as has been explained.

By now, you will have correctly concluded that reducing star sights is no more difficult than reducing any

N. Lat. {LHA greater than 180°....... Zn=Z
{LHA less than 180°........... Zn=360–Z

## DECLINATION (15°–29°)  SAME NAME AS LATITUDE   LAT 41°

| LHA | 15'<br>Hc d Z | 16'<br>Hc d Z | 17'<br>Hc d Z | 18'<br>Hc d Z | 19'<br>Hc d Z | 20'<br>Hc d Z | 23'<br>Hc d Z | 24'<br>Hc d Z | LHA |
|---|---|---|---|---|---|---|---|---|---|
| 0 | 64 00 +60 180 | 65 00 +60 180 | 66 00 +60 180 | 67 00 +60 180 | 68 00 +60 180 | 69 00 +60 180 | 7( J0+60 180 | 73 00+60 180 | 360 |
| 1 | 63 59 60 .178 | 64 59 60 178 | 65 59 60 178 | 66 59 60 178 | 67 59 60 178 | 68 59 60 177 | 6' 39 60 177 | 72 59 60 177 | 359 |
| 2 | 63 57 59 176 | 64 56 60 176 | 65 56 60 175 | 66 56 60 175 | 67 56 60 175 | 68 56 60 175 | 6 55 60 174 | 72 55 60 174 | 358 |
| 3 | 63 52 60 173 | 64 52 60 173 | 65 52 59 173 | 66 51 60 173 | 67 51 60 173 | 68 51 59 172 | ' 50 59 171 | 72 49 59 171 | 357 |
| 4 | 63 46 60 171 | 64 46 59 171 | 65 45 60 171 | 66 45 59 170 | 67 44 60 170 | 68 44 59 170 | ( 41 59 168 | 72 40 59 168 | 356 |
| 5 | 63 38 +60 169 | 64 38 +59 169 | 65 37 +59 168 | 66 36 +59 168 | 67 35 +59 168 | 68 34 +59 167 | 6 31+59 165 | 72 30+58 165 | 355 |
| 6 | 63 29 59 167 | 64 28 59 167 | 65 27 59 166 | 66 26 59 166 | 67 25 58 165 | 68 23 59 165 | 8 59 163 | 72 17 57 162 | 354 |
| 7 | 63 18 59 165 | 64 17 58 164 | 65 15 59 164 | 66 14 58 163 | 67 12 58 163 | 68 10 58 162 | 69 1 57 160 | 72 01 57 159 | 353 |
| 8 | 63 05 59 163 | 64 04 58 162 | 65 02 58 162 | 66 00 58 161 | 66 58 57 161 | 67 55 58 160 | 68. 57 157 | 71 44 56 156 | 352 |
| 9 | 62 51 58 161 | 63 49 58 160 | 64 47 57 159 | 65 44 58 159 | 66 42 57 158 | 67 39 57 157 | 68: 56 155 | 71 25 55 153 | 351 |
| 10 | 62 35 +58 159 | 63 33 +57 158 | 64 30 +57 157 | 65 27 +57 157 | 66 24 +56 156 | 67 20 +57 155 | 68: +55 152 | 71 03+55 151 | 350 |
| 11 | 62 18 57 157 | 63 15 57 156 | 64 12 56 155 | 65 08 57 154 | 66 05 55 154 | 67 00 56 153 | 67 54 150 | 70 40 54 148 | 349 |
| 12 | 61 59 57 155 | 62 56 56 154 | 63 52 56 153 | 64 48 56 152 | 65 44 55 151 | 66 39 55 151 | 67 54 147 | 70 16 52 146 | 348 |
| 13 | 61 39 56 153 | 62 35 56 152 | 63 31 55 151 | 64 26 55 150 | 65 21 55 149 | 66 16 54 148 | 67 / 52 145 | 69 49 52 143 | 347 |
| 14 | 61 18 55 151 | 62 13 55 150 | 63 08 55 149 | 64 03 54 148 | 64 57 54 147 | 65 51 54 146 | 6' 0 52 143 | 69 22 51 141 | 346 |
| 15 | 60 55 +55 149 | 61 50 +55 148 | 62 45 +54 147 | 63 39 +53 146 | 64 32 +54 145 | 65 26 +52 144 | ( i2+51 140 | 68 53+50 139 | 345 |
| 16 | 60 31 55 147 | 61 26 53 146 | 62 19 54 145 | 63 13 53 144 | 64 06 52 143 | 64 58 52 142 | ( i2 50 138 | 68 22 49 137 | 344 |
| 17 | 60 06 54 146 | 61 00 53 145 | 61 53 53 144 | 62 46 52 143 | 63 38 52 142 | 64 30 51 140 | 6. 2 49 136 | 67 51 48 135 | 343 |
| 18 | 59 40 53 144 | 60 33 53 143 | 61 26 52 142 | 62 18 52 141 | 63 10 51 140 | 64 01 50 139 | 64 48 135 | 67 18 48 133 | 342 |
| 19 | 59 13 52 142 | 60 05 52 141 | 60 57 52 140 | 61 49 51 139 | 62 40 50 138 | 63 30 50 137 | 64. 48 133 | 66 45 46 131 | 341 |
| 20 | 58 45 +51 141 | 59 36 +52 140 | 60 28 +51 138 | 61 19 +50 137 | 62 09 +50 136 | 62 59 +49 135 | 634 47 131 | 66 10+46 129 | 340 |
| 21 | 58 15 51 139 | 59 06 51 138 | 59 57 50 137 | 60 47 50 136 | 61 37 49 135 | 62 26 48 133 | 631 46 129 | 65 35 44 128 | 339 |
| 22 | 57 45 51 137 | 58 36 50 136 | 59 26 49 135 | 60 15 49 134 | 61 04 49 133 | 61 53 47 132 | 62' 45 128 | 64 58 44 126 | 338 |
| 23 | 57 14 50 136 | 58 04 49 135 | 58 53 49 134 | 59 42 47 133 | 60 31 47 131 | 61 18 47 130 | 62 44 126 | 64 21 44 124 | 337 |
| 24 | 56 42 49 134 | 57 31 49 133 | 58 20 49 132 | 59 09 47 131 | 59 56 47 130 | 60 43 47 129 | 6' , 44 124 | 63 44 42 123 | 336 |

*Figure 22–6.* Excerpt from Volume III, Pub. No. 249, showing that at Latitude 41°, same name as declination, at LHA 341°, and declination 19°, Hc is 62°40', d is +50', and Z, 138°.

other observation—with Volume I, perhaps, stars are even easier—so why all the concern expressed earlier? The problem lies in the process of taking, timing, and recording star sights, and when you first try to do it by yourself, you will understand the challenge in getting precise results.

First, of course, you have to identify the star you are shooting. Unlike the familiar bodies in the solar system, a star's identification is not obvious, especially during twilight when the constellations, by which most observers relate a star's position in the sky, may not be totally visible. Unless you have been observing the same body night after night, the most practical solution is preplanning. To do this, you need to estimate the approximate time you expect to be taking your sights, and that can be done either by knowing the time of twilight by previous observation, or by calculating it from the auxiliary tables in the almanac's daily pages (Figure 16–2). With the estimated time of observation converted to Greenwich mean time, you can find the Greenwich hour angle of Aries, just as you do in working a star sight, and by applying an estimate of your expected longitude at twilight, you can calculate the approximate local hour angle of Aries. Then, you can follow one of two recommended routes: You can enter Volume I of Pub. No. 249 (Figure 22–4), and opposite the approximate LHA♈, read out the seven selected stars and their altitudes and azimuths; or you can use a device called a star finder.

| 43 | 44 | 45 | 46 | 47 | 48 | 49 | 50 | 51 | 52 | 53 | 54 | 55 | 56 | 57 | 58 | 59 | 60 | $\frac{d}{'}$ |
|---|---|---|---|---|---|---|---|---|---|---|---|---|---|---|---|---|---|---|
| 0 | 0 | 0 | 0 | 0 | 0 | 0 | 0 | 0 | 0 | 0 | 0 | 0 | 0 | 0 | 0 | 0 | 0 | 0 |
| 1 | 1 | 1 | 1 | 1 | 1 | 1 | 1 | 1 | 1 | 1 | 1 | 1 | 1 | 1 | 1 | 1 | 1 | 1 |
| 1 | 1 | 2 | 2 | 2 | 2 | 2 | 2 | 2 | 2 | 2 | 2 | 2 | 2 | 2 | 2 | 2 | 2 | 2 |
| 2 | 2 | 2 | 2 | 2 | 2 | 2 | 2 | 3 | 3 | 3 | 3 | 3 | 3 | 3 | 3 | 3 | 3 | 3 |
| 3 | 3 | 3 | 3 | 3 | 3 | 3 | 3 | 3 | 3 | 3 | 3 | 4 | 4 | 4 | 4 | 4 | 4 | 4 |
| 4 | 4 | 4 | 4 | 4 | 4 | 4 | 4 | 4 | 4 | 4 | 4 | 5 | 5 | 5 | 5 | 5 | 5 | 5 |
| 4 | 4 | 4 | 5 | 5 | 5 | 5 | 5 | 5 | 5 | 5 | 5 | 6 | 6 | 6 | 6 | 6 | 6 | 6 |
| 5 | 5 | 5 | 5 | 5 | 6 | 6 | 6 | 6 | 6 | 6 | 6 | 6 | 7 | 7 | 7 | 7 | 7 | 7 |
| 6 | 6 | 6 | 6 | 6 | 6 | 7 | 7 | 7 | 7 | 7 | 7 | 7 | 7 | 8 | 8 | 8 | 8 | 8 |
| 6 | 7 | 7 | 7 | 7 | 7 | 7 | 8 | 8 | 8 | 8 | 8 | 8 | 8 | 9 | 9 | 9 | 9 | 9 |
| 7 | 7 | 8 | 8 | 8 | 8 | 8 | 8 | 8 | 9 | 9 | 9 | 9 | 9 | 10 | 10 | 10 | 10 | 10 |
| 8 | 8 | 8 | 8 | 9 | 9 | 9 | 9 | 9 | 10 | 10 | 10 | 10 | 10 | 10 | 11 | 11 | 11 | 11 |
| 9 | 9 | 9 | 9 | 9 | 10 | 10 | 10 | 10 | 10 | 11 | 11 | 11 | 11 | 11 | 12 | 12 | 12 | 12 |
| 9 | 10 | 10 | 10 | 10 | 10 | 11 | 11 | 11 | 11 | 11 | 12 | 12 | 12 | 12 | 13 | 13 | 13 | 13 |
| 10 | 10 | 10 | 11 | 11 | 11 | 11 | 12 | 12 | 12 | 12 | 13 | 13 | 13 | 13 | 14 | 14 | 14 | 14 |
| 11 | 11 | 11 | 12 | 12 | 12 | 12 | 12 | 13 | 13 | 13 | 14 | 14 | 14 | 14 | 14 | 15 | 15 | 15 |
| 11 | 12 | 12 | 12 | 13 | 13 | 13 | 13 | 14 | 14 | 14 | 14 | 15 | 15 | 15 | 15 | 16 | 16 | 16 |
| 12 | 12 | 13 | 13 | 13 | 14 | 14 | 14 | 14 | 15 | 15 | 15 | 16 | 16 | 16 | 16 | 17 | 17 | 17 |
| 13 | 13 | 14 | 14 | 14 | 14 | 15 | 15 | 15 | 16 | 16 | 16 | 16 | 17 | 17 | 17 | 18 | 18 | 18 |
| 14 | 14 | 14 | 15 | 15 | 15 | 16 | 16 | 16 | 16 | 17 | 17 | 17 | 18 | 18 | 18 | 19 | 19 | 19 |
| 14 | 15 | 15 | 15 | 16 | 16 | 16 | 17 | 17 | 17 | 18 | 18 | 18 | 19 | 19 | 19 | 20 | 20 | 20 |
| 15 | 15 | 16 | 16 | 16 | 17 | 17 | 18 | 18 | 18 | 19 | 19 | 19 | 20 | 20 | 20 | 21 | 21 | 21 |
| 16 | 16 | 16 | 17 | 17 | 18 | 18 | 18 | 19 | 19 | 19 | 20 | 20 | 21 | 21 | 21 | 22 | 22 | 22 |
| 16 | 17 | 17 | 18 | 18 | 18 | 19 | 19 | 20 | 20 | 20 | 21 | 21 | 21 | 22 | 22 | 23 | 23 | 23 |
| 17 | 18 | 18 | 18 | 19 | 19 | 20 | 20 | 20 | 21 | 21 | 22 | 22 | 22 | 23 | 23 | 24 | 24 | 24 |

*Figure* 22–7. Excerpt from Table 5, Pub. No. 249, showing a correction of 13′ for *d* of 50, and incremental minutes of declination, 16.

The first way is the simplest and quickest and is particularly to be recommended if you intend to work your sights with Volume I. If you prefer to predict the positions of all the visible stars, to give yourself the widest possible choice, the best device, in my opinion, is the Rude Star Finder. Originally developed for the Navy and now offered commercially, the star finder consists of a base and a series of transparent templates for each 10° of latitude. The appropriate template is placed over the circular base and oriented to the estimated local hour angle of Aries. The altitudes and azimuths of all the visible navigational stars can then be found by inspection. However you choose to do your star finding, adopt the technique of the most experienced navigators, and prepare ahead of time a list of the approximate altitudes and azimuths of the stars you expect to shoot. It will simplify matters considerably when you go on deck.

The idea behind star observations is no more complicated than for any other sight. You measure the altitude by centering the reflected image on the horizon, immediately record it along with the exact time, and then move on to the next star. On small boats, and especially in a seaway, the problem is that you have to perform all the operations and hold on at the same time; with only two hands, it is not so easy. The problem is magnified by the narrow span between the time the sky is too bright to see the stars, and the time it is too dark to see the horizon; and the low level of luminosity, which makes a star's image indistinct, doesn't help. The finer optics and larger field of view of the better sextants alleviate the problem somewhat, but star sights are seldom as easy as those of the sun.

You can usually find a star in the sextant's field of view by presetting the estimated altitude from your prepared list, and panning along the horizon at the star's approximate azimuth. Alternatively, you can hold the sextant upside down with your left hand, aim it directly at the star, and having located the star through the eye-piece, move the index arm with your right hand to bring the horizon up to the star. This done, reverse the sextant, and the star's image should be close to the visible horizon. This latter technique is easiest with a straight telescope for an eyepiece, but if you prefer to use a monocular like the one illustrated in Figure 14–1, it will require some practice.

Should you be fortunate enough to have a shipmate available to help you, the task of taking star sights will be immeasurably easier. He can read off the estimated altitudes and azimuths from your prepared list and can take and record the exact time of each observation as you call out, "Mark." Your night vision won't be affected by having to use a light, you can concentrate fully on the sextant manipulation, and you will have the best opportunity to complete a round of good sights within the narrow twilight period. Even under these happy circumstances, however, I reiterate my comment made at the onset: Under the normal conditions aboard a small boat at sea, the sun is a more constant companion to a conscientious navigator.

# 23 | Special Celestial Cases

Although the majority of celestial observations are converted to lines of position by means of the techniques described in the preceding chapters, you can also take advantage of two special situations: shortcut solutions for finding the latitude by observation of the sun at local apparent noon (LAN), or by observation of Polaris, the pole star.

The most common of these special cases is the noon sight of the sun. Technically called "latitude by meridian altitude," the process of obtaining a quick and reliable latitude check by means of a single reduction of a sun sight at the moment the sun's path crosses the meridian of the observer and reaches its highest point of the day is a mariner's tradition. No one knows with certainty when the technique was first practiced, but the concept was well understood by the time the astrolabe appeared in the third century B.C., and as increasingly accurate altitude-measuring instruments evolved, the use of noon latitudes became universal. By the fifteenth century, it was common practice on long passages to run down to the latitude of a destination, to a point well to seaward of it, and then to shape the course east or west until a landfall was made, using noon sights all the way. Even today, the noon observation is a ritual, performed as it has been for years, aboard Navy and merchant ships.

For a navigator, the special appeal of a noon sight is that the sun's altitude is changing very slowly at the time, thereby reducing the need for precise time measurement. Then, too, after an observation has been made, the calculation needed to determine the latitude is simple and rapid—whether done manually or with a calculator—and the only piece of astronomical information required is the sun's declination. While, for the reasons given, the *exact* time of local apparent noon is not essential, as it is in normal sights, it is useful to predict the approximate time when LAN will occur, so that the navigator can come on deck a few minutes early for an unhurried series of observations. There are a number of ways to predict the time of local apparent noon, three of which are commonly used by yacht navigators.

The first way, called the "GHA method," is based on the fact that at the moment of meridian passage, the local hour angle of the sun is zero. Remembering the formula,

$$\text{LHA} = \text{GHA} \begin{array}{c} -\text{West} \\ +\text{East} \end{array} \text{Longitude}$$

the Greenwich hour angle of the sun at LAN must be the same as your longitude if West, or 360° minus the longitude if East. Accordingly, the procedure is first to estimate what you expect your longitude to be about the time of local apparent noon—this can be done simply by running your position ahead by dead reckoning—and then, entering the SUN column of the almanac's correct daily page, find the GHA *next smaller* than your longitude, and note the hours of Greenwich mean time opposite that GHA. Next, subtract the selected GHA from the longitude, and use that difference to enter the *Increments and Corrections* tables in reverse—that is, you enter the body of the table to locate the increment in the SUN column equal to the difference you just calculated and read out the minutes and seconds of time that correspond to that increment. The hours you noted on the daily page, and the minutes and seconds of time from the increment table, represent the time of LAN expressed as Greenwich mean time. It is a simple matter to convert that to local watch time by applying the zone description.

Let's look at a practical example. On June 8, 1984, a navigator estimates that his longitude about the time of LAN will be 70°07.5′W. Entering the SUN column of the *Nautical Almanac* with this estimated longitude (Figure 23–1), he finds that the next smaller GHA is 60°14.0′ at 16 hours GMT. Subtracting the tabular GHA from the longitude produces a difference of 9°53.5′, and turning to the *Increments and Corrections* tables in the back of the

| 1984 JUNE 8 | | |
|---|---|---|
| | **SUN** | |
| G.M.T. | G.H.A. | Dec. |
| **8** 00 | 180 15.9 | N22 50.6 |
| 01 | 195 15.8 | 50.9 |
| 02 | 210 15.7 | 51.1 |
| 03 | 225 15.5 ·· | 51.3 |
| 04 | 240 15.4 | 51.5 |
| 05 | 255 15.3 | 51.8 |
| 06 | 270 15.2 | N22 52.0 |
| 07 | 285 15.1 | 52.2 |
| 08 | 300 14.9 | 52.4 |
| F 09 | 315 14.8 ·· | 52.6 |
| R 10 | 330 14.7 | 52.9 |
| I 11 | 345 14.6 | 53.1 |
| D 12 | 0 14.5 | N22 53.3 |
| A 13 | 15 14.3 | 53.5 |
| Y 14 | 30 14.2 | 53.7 |
| 15 | 45 14.1 ·· | 54.0 |
| 16 | 60 14.0 | 54.2 |
| 17 | 75 13.9 | 54.4 |
| 18 | 90 13.7 | N22 54.6 |
| 19 | 105 13.6 | 54.8 |
| 20 | 120 13.5 | 55.0 |
| 21 | 135 13.4 ·· | 55.2 |
| 22 | 150 13.3 | 55.4 |
| 23 | 165 13.1 | 55.7 |

*Figure 23–1.* Excerpt from the *Nautical Almanac* for June 8, 1984, showing GHA of 60°14′ opposite GMT 16 hours. At 1639 GMT, the declination is found to be 22°54.3′N.

almanac, Figure 23–2, he finds the equivalent increment in the SUN column for 39 minutes and 34 seconds of time. The estimated time of LAN, therefore, is 16:39:34, or if the ship is keeping Eastern Daylight Saving Time (ZD + 4), the local time would read 12:39:34.

A second, even quicker solution can be found by the "meridian passage method." If you are good at mental arithmetic and can accept a little more of an approximation, the local time of LAN can be determined virtually by inspection. In this method, you take the time of the sun's meridian passage from the box on the lower right-hand side of the almanac's daily page (Figure 23–3) and adjust it by the difference, expressed in time, between the estimated noon longitude and the nearest standard, or

## INCREMENTS AND CORRECTIONS 39ᵐ

| 39ᵐ | SUN PLANETS | ARIES | MOON | v or Corrⁿ d | | v or Corrⁿ d | | v or Corrⁿ d | |
|---|---|---|---|---|---|---|---|---|---|
| s | ° ′ | ° ′ | ° ′ | ′ | ′ | ′ | ′ | ′ | ′ |
| 00 | 9 45·0 | 9 46·6 | 9 18·4 | 0·0 | 0·0 | 6·0 | 4·0 | 12·0 | 7·9 |
| 01 | 9 45·3 | 9 46·9 | 9 18·6 | 0·1 | 0·1 | 6·1 | 4·0 | 12·1 | 8·0 |
| 02 | 9 45·5 | 9 47·1 | 9 18·8 | 0·2 | 0·1 | 6·2 | 4·1 | 12·2 | 8·0 |
| 03 | 9 45·8 | 9 47·4 | 9 19·1 | 0·3 | 0·2 | 6·3 | 4·1 | 12·3 | 8·1 |
| 28 | 9 52·0 | 9 53·6 | 9 25·0 | 2·8 | 1·8 | 8·8 | 5·8 | 14·8 | 9·7 |
| 29 | 9 52·3 | 9 53·9 | 9 25·3 | 2·9 | 1·9 | 8·9 | 5·9 | 14·9 | 9·8 |
| 30 | 9 52·5 | 9 54·1 | 9 25·5 | 3·0 | 2·0 | 9·0 | 5·9 | 15·0 | 9·9 |
| 31 | 9 52·8 | 9 54·4 | 9 25·7 | 3·1 | 2·0 | 9·1 | 6·0 | 15·1 | 9·9 |
| 32 | 9 53·0 | 9 54·6 | 9 26·0 | 3·2 | 2·1 | 9·2 | 6·1 | 15·2 | 10·0 |
| 33 | 9 53·3 | 9 54·9 | 9 26·2 | 3·3 | 2·2 | 9·3 | 6·1 | 15·3 | 10·1 |
| 34 | 9 53·5 | 9 55·1 | 9 26·5 | 3·4 | 2·2 | 9·4 | 6·2 | 15·4 | 10·1 |
| 35 | 9 53·8 | 9 55·4 | 9 26·7 | 3·5 | 2·3 | 9·5 | 6·3 | 15·5 | 10·2 |
| 36 | 9 54·0 | 9 55·6 | 9 26·9 | 3·6 | 2·4 | 9·6 | 6·3 | 15·6 | 10·3 |
| 37 | 9 54·3 | 9 55·9 | 9 27·2 | 3·7 | 2·4 | 9·7 | 6·4 | 15·7 | 10·3 |
| 38 | 9 54·5 | 9 56·1 | 9 27·4 | 3·8 | 2·5 | 9·8 | 6·5 | 15·8 | 10·4 |
| 39 | 9 54·8 | 9 56·4 | 9 27·7 | 3·9 | 2·6 | 9·9 | 6·5 | 15·9 | 10·5 |

*Figure 23–2.* Excerpt from the *Nautical Almanac Increments and Corrections* tables, showing the increment 9°53.5′ corresponding to 39 minutes, 34 seconds of time.

| Day | SUN | | |
|---|---|---|---|
| | Eqn. of Time | | Mer. Pass. |
| | 00ʰ | 12ʰ | |
| | m   s | m   s | h   m |
| **8** | 01 04 | 00 58 | 11 59 |
| 9 | 00 52 | 00 46 | 11 59 |
| 10 | 00 41 | 00 35 | 11 59 |

*Figure 23–3.* Excerpt from the *Nautical Almanac* daily page June 8, 1984, showing sun's meridian passage to occur at 1159, and Equation of Time at 12ʰ to be 00 minutes, 58 seconds.

zone meridian. In our practical example, the difference between the estimated longitude, 70°07.5′W, and the nearest standard meridian, 75°W, is 4°52.5′. Since the sun moves 15° per hour, or 1° every 4 minutes, 4°52.5′ represents an adjustment of just under 20 minutes in time, and because the estimated longitude is east of the standard meridian, the correction must be subtracted from the tabular time of meridian passage, 1159, to produce the local time of LAN, 1139. The adjustment can be made more precise by taking the exact longitude difference, 4° 52.5′, and by means of the arc-to-time conversion table in the back of the almanac (Figure 23–4), find the exact time correction, 19 minutes, 30 seconds. This would mean a local time of LAN of 11:39:30, or 12:39:30 if daylight time is being kept.

A third method for finding the time of local apparent noon, the "equation-of-time method," is based on the Equation of Time, which is the difference between the time of the fictitious, mean sun and the apparent solar, or "sundial" time. The equation of time for 12 hours, as seen

*Figure 23–4.* Table from the *Nautical Almanac* for converting arc to time. 4°52.5′ is the equivalent of 19 minutes, 30 seconds of time.

# CONVERSION OF ARC TO TIME

| 0°–59° | | 60°–119° | | 120°–179° | | 180°–239° | | 240°–299° | | 300°–359° | | 0'.00 | | 0'.25 | 0'.50 | 0'.75 |
|---|---|---|---|---|---|---|---|---|---|---|---|---|---|---|---|---|
| ° | h m | ° | h m | ° | h m | ° | h m | ° | h m | ° | h m | ' | m s | m s | m s | m s |
| 0 | 0 00 | 60 | 4 00 | 120 | 8 00 | 180 | 12 00 | 240 | 16 00 | 300 | 20 00 | 0 | 0 00 | 0 01 | 0 02 | 0 03 |
| 1 | 0 04 | 61 | 4 04 | 121 | 8 04 | 181 | 12 04 | 241 | 16 04 | 301 | 20 04 | 1 | 0 04 | 0 05 | 0 06 | 0 07 |
| 2 | 0 08 | 62 | 4 08 | 122 | 8 08 | 182 | 12 08 | 242 | 16 08 | 302 | 20 08 | 2 | 0 08 | 0 09 | 0 10 | 0 11 |
| 3 | 0 12 | 63 | 4 12 | 123 | 8 12 | 183 | 12 12 | 243 | 16 12 | 303 | 20 12 | 3 | 0 12 | 0 13 | 0 14 | 0 15 |
| 4 | 0 16 | 64 | 4 16 | 124 | 8 16 | 184 | 12 16 | 244 | 16 16 | 304 | 20 16 | 4 | 0 16 | 0 17 | 0 18 | 0 19 |
| 5 | 0 20 | 65 | 4 20 | 125 | 8 20 | 185 | 12 20 | 245 | 16 20 | 305 | 20 20 | 5 | 0 20 | 0 21 | 0 22 | 0 23 |
| 6 | 0 24 | 66 | 4 24 | 126 | 8 24 | 186 | 12 24 | 246 | 16 24 | 306 | 20 24 | 6 | 0 24 | 0 25 | 0 26 | 0 27 |
| 7 | 0 28 | 67 | 4 28 | 127 | 8 28 | 187 | 12 28 | 247 | 16 28 | 307 | 20 28 | 7 | 0 28 | 0 29 | 0 30 | 0 31 |
| 8 | 0 32 | 68 | 4 32 | 128 | 8 32 | 188 | 12 32 | 248 | 16 32 | 308 | 20 32 | 8 | 0 32 | 0 33 | 0 34 | 0 35 |
| 9 | 0 36 | 69 | 4 36 | 129 | 8 36 | 189 | 12 36 | 249 | 16 36 | 309 | 20 36 | 9 | 0 36 | 0 37 | 0 38 | 0 39 |
| 10 | 0 40 | 70 | 4 40 | 130 | 8 40 | 190 | 12 40 | 250 | 16 40 | 310 | 20 40 | 10 | 0 40 | 0 41 | 0 42 | 0 43 |
| 11 | 0 44 | 71 | 4 44 | 131 | 8 44 | 191 | 12 44 | 251 | 16 44 | 311 | 20 44 | 11 | 0 44 | 0 45 | 0 46 | 0 47 |
| 12 | 0 48 | 72 | 4 48 | 132 | 8 48 | 192 | 12 48 | 252 | 16 48 | 312 | 20 48 | 12 | 0 48 | 0 49 | 0 50 | 0 51 |
| 13 | 0 52 | 73 | 4 52 | 133 | 8 52 | 193 | 12 52 | 253 | 16 52 | 313 | 20 52 | 13 | 0 52 | 0 53 | 0 54 | 0 55 |
| 14 | 0 56 | 74 | 4 56 | 134 | 8 56 | 194 | 12 56 | 254 | 16 56 | 314 | 20 56 | 14 | 0 56 | 0 57 | 0 58 | 0 59 |
| 15 | 1 00 | 75 | 5 00 | 135 | 9 00 | 195 | 13 00 | 255 | 17 00 | 315 | 21 00 | 15 | 1 00 | 1 01 | 1 02 | 1 03 |
| 16 | 1 04 | 76 | 5 04 | 136 | 9 04 | 196 | 13 04 | 256 | 17 04 | 316 | 21 04 | 16 | 1 04 | 1 05 | 1 06 | 1 07 |
| 17 | 1 08 | 77 | 5 08 | 137 | 9 08 | 197 | 13 08 | 257 | 17 08 | 317 | 21 08 | 17 | 1 08 | 1 09 | 1 10 | 1 11 |
| 18 | 1 12 | 78 | 5 12 | 138 | 9 12 | 198 | 13 12 | 258 | 17 12 | 318 | 21 12 | 18 | 1 12 | 1 13 | 1 14 | 1 15 |
| 19 | 1 16 | 79 | 5 16 | 139 | 9 16 | 199 | 13 16 | 259 | 17 16 | 319 | 21 16 | 19 | 1 16 | 1 17 | 1 18 | 1 19 |
| 20 | 1 20 | 80 | 5 20 | 140 | 9 20 | 200 | 13 20 | 260 | 17 20 | 320 | 21 20 | 20 | 1 20 | 1 21 | 1 22 | 1 23 |
| 21 | 1 24 | 81 | 5 24 | 141 | 9 24 | 201 | 13 24 | 261 | 17 24 | 321 | 21 24 | 21 | 1 24 | 1 25 | 1 26 | 1 27 |
| 22 | 1 28 | 82 | 5 28 | 142 | 9 28 | 202 | 13 28 | 262 | 17 28 | 322 | 21 28 | 22 | 1 28 | 1 29 | 1 30 | 1 31 |
| 23 | 1 32 | 83 | 5 32 | 143 | 9 32 | 203 | 13 32 | 263 | 17 32 | 323 | 21 32 | 23 | 1 32 | 1 33 | 1 34 | 1 35 |
| 24 | 1 36 | 84 | 5 36 | 144 | 9 36 | 204 | 13 36 | 264 | 17 36. | 324 | 21 36 | 24 | 1 36 | 1 37 | 1 38 | 1 39 |
| 25 | 1 40 | 85 | 5 40 | 145 | 9 40 | 205 | 13 40 | 265 | 17 40 | 325 | 21 40 | 25 | 1 40 | 1 41 | 1 42 | 1 43 |
| 26 | 1 44 | 86 | 5 44 | 146 | 9 44 | 206 | 13 44 | 266 | 17 44 | 326 | 21 44 | 26 | 1 44 | 1 45 | 1 46 | 1 47 |
| 27 | 1 48 | 87 | 5 48 | 147 | 9 48 | 207 | 13 48 | 267 | 17 48 | 327 | 21 48 | 27 | 1 48 | 1 49 | 1 50 | 1 51 |
| 28 | 1 52 | 88 | 5 52 | 148 | 9 52 | 208 | 13 52 | 268 | 17 52 | 328 | 21 52 | 28 | 1 52 | 1 53 | 1 54 | 1 55 |
| 29 | 1 56 | 89 | 5 56 | 149 | 9 56 | 209 | 13 56 | 269 | 17 56 | 329 | 21 56 | 29 | 1 56 | 1 57 | 1 58 | 1 59 |
| 30 | 2 00 | 90 | 6 00 | 150 | 10 00 | 210 | 14 00 | 270 | 18 00 | 330 | 22 00 | 30 | 2 00 | 2 01 | 2 02 | 2 03 |
| 31 | 2 04 | 91 | 6 04 | 151 | 10 04 | 211 | 14 04 | 271 | 18 04 | 331 | 22 04 | 31 | 2 04 | 2 05 | 2 06 | 2 07 |
| 32 | 2 08 | 92 | 6 08 | 152 | 10 08 | 212 | 14 08 | 272 | 18 08 | 332 | 22 08 | 32 | 2 08 | 2 09 | 2 10 | 2 11 |
| 33 | 2 12 | 93 | 6 12 | 153 | 10 12 | 213 | 14 12 | 273 | 18 12 | 333 | 22 12 | 33 | 2 12 | 2 13 | 2 14 | 2 15 |
| 34 | 2 16 | 94 | 6 16 | 154 | 10 16 | 214 | 14 16 | 274 | 18 16 | 334 | 22 16 | 34 | 2 16 | 2 17 | 2 18 | 2 19 |
| 35 | 2 20 | 95 | 6 20 | 155 | 10 20 | 215 | 14 20 | 275 | 18 20 | 335 | 22 20 | 35 | 2 20 | 2 21 | 2 22 | 2 23 |
| 36 | 2 24 | 96 | 6 24 | 156 | 10 24 | 216 | 14 24 | 276 | 18 24 | 336 | 22 24 | 36 | 2 24 | 2 25 | 2 26 | 2 27 |
| 37 | 2 28 | 97 | 6 28 | 157 | 10 28 | 217 | 14 28 | 277 | 18 28 | 337 | 22 28 | 37 | 2 28 | 2 29 | 2 30 | 2 31 |
| 38 | 2 32 | 98 | 6 32 | 158 | 10 32 | 218 | 14 32 | 278 | 18 32 | 338 | 22 32 | 38 | 2 32 | 2 33 | 2 34 | 2 35 |
| 39 | 2 36 | 99 | 6 36 | 159 | 10 36 | 219 | 14 36 | 279 | 18 36 | 339 | 22 36 | 39 | 2 36 | 2 37 | 2 38 | 2 39 |
| 40 | 2 40 | 100 | 6 40 | 160 | 10 40 | 220 | 14 40 | 280 | 18 40 | 340 | 22 40 | 40 | 2 40 | 2 41 | 2 42 | 2 43 |
| 41 | 2 44 | 101 | 6 44 | 161 | 10 44 | 221 | 14 44 | 281 | 18 44 | 341 | 22 44 | 41 | 2 44 | 2 45 | 2 46 | 2 47 |
| 42 | 2 48 | 102 | 6 48 | 162 | 10 48 | 222 | 14 48 | 282 | 18 48 | 342 | 22 48 | 42 | 2 48 | 2 49 | 2 50 | 2 51 |
| 43 | 2 52 | 103 | 6 52 | 163 | 10 52 | 223 | 14 52 | 283 | 18 52 | 343 | 22 52 | 43 | 2 52 | 2 53 | 2 54 | 2 55 |
| 44 | 2 56 | 104 | 6 56 | 164 | 10 56 | 224 | 14 56 | 284 | 18 56 | 344 | 22 56 | 44 | 2 56 | 2 57 | 2 58 | 2 59 |
| 45 | 3 00 | 105 | 7 00 | 165 | 11 00 | 225 | 15 00 | 285 | 19 00 | 345 | 23 00 | 45 | 3 00 | 3 01 | 3 02 | 3 03 |
| 46 | 3 04 | 106 | 7 04 | 166 | 11 04 | 226 | 15 04 | 286 | 19 04 | 346 | 23 04 | 46 | 3 04 | 3 05 | 3 06 | 3 07 |
| 47 | 3 08 | 107 | 7 08 | 167 | 11 08 | 227 | 15 08 | 287 | 19 08 | 347 | 23 08 | 47 | 3 08 | 3 09 | 3 10 | 3 11 |
| 48 | 3 12 | 108 | 7 12 | 168 | 11 12 | 228 | 15 12 | 288 | 19 12 | 348 | 23 12 | 48 | 3 12 | 3 13 | 3 14 | 3 15 |
| 49 | 3 16 | 109 | 7 16 | 169 | 11 16 | 229 | 15 16 | 289 | 19 16 | 349 | 23 16 | 49 | 3 16 | 3 17 | 3 18 | 3 19 |
| 50 | 3 20 | 110 | 7 20 | 170 | 11 20 | 230 | 15 20 | 290 | 19 20 | 350 | 23 20 | 50 | 3 20 | 3 21 | 3 22 | 3 23 |
| 51 | 3 24 | 111 | 7 24 | 171 | 11 24 | 231 | 15 24 | 291 | 19 24 | 351 | 23 24 | 51 | 3 24 | 3 25 | 3 26 | 3 27 |
| 52 | 3 28 | 112 | 7 28 | 172 | 11 28 | 232 | 15 28 | 292 | 19 28 | 352 | 23 28 | 52 | 3 28 | 3 29 | 3 30 | 3 31 |
| 53 | 3 32 | 113 | 7 32 | 173 | 11 32 | 233 | 15 32 | 293 | 19 32 | 353 | 23 32 | 53 | 3 32 | 3 33 | 3 34 | 3 35 |
| 54 | 3 36 | 114 | 7 36 | 174 | 11 36 | 234 | 15 36 | 294 | 19 36 | 354 | 23 36 | 54 | 3 36 | 3 37 | 3 38 | 3 39 |
| 55 | 3 40 | 115 | 7 40 | 175 | 11 40 | 235 | 15 40 | 295 | 19 40 | 355 | 23 40 | 55 | 3 40 | 3 41 | 3 42 | 3 43 |
| 56 | 3 44 | 116 | 7 44 | 176 | 11 44 | 236 | 15 44 | 296 | 19 44 | 356 | 23 44 | 56 | 3 44 | 3 45 | 3 46 | 3 47 |
| 57 | 3 48 | 117 | 7 48 | 177 | 11 48 | 237 | 15 48 | 297 | 19 48 | 357 | 23 48 | 57 | 3 48 | 3 49 | 3 50 | 3 51 |
| 58 | 3 52 | 118 | 7 52 | 178 | 11 52 | 238 | 15 52 | 298 | 19 52 | 358 | 23 52 | 58 | 3 52 | 3 53 | 3 54 | 3 55 |
| 59 | 3 56 | 119 | 7 56 | 179 | 11 56 | 239 | 15 56 | 299 | 19 56 | 359 | 23 56 | 59 | 3 56 | 3 57 | 3 58 | 3 59 |

The above table is for converting expressions in arc to their equivalent in time ; its main use in this Almanac is for the conversion of longitude for application to L.M.T. (*added if west, subtracted if east*) to give G.M.T. or vice versa, particularly in the case of sunrise, sunset, etc.

in Figure 23–3, is 00 minutes, 58 seconds on June 8, and the formula is:

GMT of LAN = Estimated longitude ÷ 15 + 12 ± Equation of time

The equation of time is subtracted if the listed meridian passage occurs before 1200, as in our case, or it is added if the meridian passage takes place after noon. Applying the formula to our practical example, the Greenwich mean time of LAN works out to be 16:39:32.

In any of the methods described, the accuracy of the predicted time of LAN is only as good as your estimate of the longitude. As a consequence, if the time you calculate for LAN turns out to be quite different from the time you used for estimating the longitude originally, it is a good idea to reestimate the longitude at a time closer to your calculated LAN and then run through the procedure a second time.

The technique in making the actual noon observation of the sun consists of measuring the sun's altitude (usually the lower limb) at the highest point of its arc. In practice, the navigator begins shooting several minutes before the predicted time of LAN and, through a series of observations, follows the sun's altitude up until it appears to "hang" at the highest point before starting to descend. Some navigators plot each successive altitude on a graph in order to be certain of the highest reading, but I have never found this to be necessary. On the other hand, if the sky is at all obscured, it is a good idea to record the time and altitude of one or more of your good sights, so that if you miss the noon shot, you can still work out the sight by the regular method. Most of the time, however, a simple series of observations is all that is needed, recording only the maximum altitude, and then calculating the latitude directly by the following steps:

• The sextant altitude is corrected in exactly the same way as any normal sun sight, obtaining the observed altitude, Ho, which is marked with the sun's bearing from you, North or South.

- The observed altitude is subtracted from 90°, arriving at an intermediate value, zenith distance, z, which is marked with the name *opposite* to the sun's bearing.
- The sun's declination for the estimated time of LAN (expressed as Greenwich mean time) is taken from the almanac and added to z if of the same name, or the difference is taken if the names are opposite. The result is the observer's latitude, with the name of the larger of z or declination.

Let's return to our practical example and assume that at local apparent noon on June 8, 1984, the sun's maximum altitude measures 71°58.0′, its bearing is South, the sextant's index correction is −2.4′, and the dip correction is −2.9′ for a height of eye of 9 feet. The completed workform, with which you can follow the noon-sight solution, looks like this:

| DATE | June 8, 1984 |
|---|---|
| Est. λ | 70 - 07.5 w |
| Std. Mer. | 75 w |
| Corr in time | -19 - 30 |
| Mer. Pass. | 11 - 59 - 00 |
| LAN | 11 - 39 - 30 |
| GMT | 16 - 39 - 30 |
| hs | 71 - 58.0 |
| IC | - 2.4 |
| D | - 2.9 |
| ha | 71 - 52.7 |
| R | + 15.6 |
| Ho | 72 - 08.3 s |
| 90° | 89 - 60.0 |
| - Ho | 72 - 08.3 s |
| z | 17 - 51.7 N |
| Dec | 22 - 54.3 N |
| L | 40 - 46.0 ° |
| (name) | N |

Starting with the estimated longitude of 70°07.5′W, the meridian passage method is used to predict the time of LAN. The almanac's arc-to-time table, Figure 23–4, shows the difference in time, corresponding to the 4° 52.5′-difference in longitude between the estimated longitude and the standard meridian, to be 19 minutes, 30 seconds. Because the observer's longitude is east of the standard meridian, the time difference is subtracted from the 1159 time of meridian passage listed in the almanac (Figure 23–3), producing a Greenwich mean time of LAN at 16:39:30. The sextant altitude is corrected for index error and dip in the usual way, arriving at an apparent altitude, ha, of 71°52.7′, and the apparent altitude is further adjusted for the refraction, or R-correction, of +15.6′ found in the regular sun-altitude correction table (Figure 23–5). The resulting observed altitude, Ho, of 72°98.3′ is marked South (from the sun's bearing) and is subtracted from 90° to obtain the zenith distance, z, of 17° 51.7′, which is marked North, the name opposite the sun's bearing. In the SUN column of the almanac's daily page, Figure 23–1, the sun's declination for the predicted time of LAN is found to be 22°54.3′N. Since declination and z are of the same name, the rule calls for them to be added, yielding the latitude, 40°46.0′, which is North, the name of the declination, which is larger than z.

As you can see, this is a very easy way to produce a good latitude line, and it works well in all circumstances, with the possible exception of a vessel on a northerly or southerly course traveling at high speed. In that situation, the sun's measured altitude may still appear to be changing at the predicted time of meridian passage, and to avoid error, it is better to measure one good altitude, time it precisely, and work the sight for a regular line of position.

Since, as we have discussed, the sun's Greenwich hour angle is equal to your West longitude (or 360° minus East longitude) at local apparent noon, it should be possi-

## A2 ALTITUDE CORRECTION TABLES 10°-90°

| OCT.—MAR. SUN APR.—SEPT. | | | | | | DIP | | |
|---|---|---|---|---|---|---|---|---|
| App. Alt. | Lower Limb | Upper Limb | App. Alt. | Lower Limb | Upper Limb | Ht. of Eye Corrⁿ | Ht. of Eye | Ht. of Eye Corrⁿ |
| 50 46 | +15·5 | - 16·8 | 52 44 | +15·3 | ·· 16·5 | m | ft. | m |
| 54 49 | +15·6 | - 16·7 | 57 02 | ·| 15·4 | - 16·4 | 2·4 | 8·0 | 1·0 -- 1·8 |
| 59 23 | +15·7 | - 16·6 | 61 51 | +15·5 | - 16·3 | 2·6 −2·8 | 8·6 | 1·5 -- 2·2 |
| 64 30 | +15·8 | 16·5 | 67 17 | +15·6 | - 16·2 | 2·8 −2·9 | 9·2 | 2·0 -- 2·5 |
| 70 12 | +15·9 | · 16·4 | 73 16 | +15·7 | - 16·1 | 3·0 −3·0 | 9·8 | 2·5 -- 2·8 |
| 76 26 | +16·0 | - 16·3 | 79 43 | +15·8 | - 16·0 | 3·2 −3·1 | 10·5 | 3·0 - 3·0 |
| 83 05 | +16·1 | 16·2 | 86 32 | +15·9 | - 15·9 | 3·4 −3·2 | 11·2 | See table |
| 90 00 | | | 90 00 | | | 3·6 −3·3 | 11·9 | ← |

*Figure 23–5.* Excerpt from the *Nautical Almanac*'s altitude correction tables showing a dip correction of −2.9′ for a height of eye of 9 feet, and an R-correction of +15.6′ for the apparent altitude, 71°52.7′.

ble in theory, given the *exact* time of LAN, to look up the sun's Greenwich hour angle for that moment, and to use that GHA to make a direct determination of your longitude. The difficulty, however, lies in obtaining a sufficiently precise timing of the instant that the sun attains its maximum altitude, because, as you will observe, the altitude changes almost imperceptibly for a short time before or after its peak. Some navigators try by beginning their series of observations 15 minutes or more prior to the predicted time of LAN, recording or plotting the time and altitude of each sight as the sun ascends, and then, as the readings start to decrease, taking the time of each matching altitude. In concept, the actual time of LAN can then be calculated by averaging the times of common altitudes, but the procedure requires a lot of time and effort. Should clouds or sea conditions, or the vessel's own movement during the series, introduce an error into some of the sights, the results are apt to be inconclusive. With accurate time available, it is usually better to use the LAN observation just for latitude, and to rely on regular sun lines at other times during the day.

A second special case allowing the direct determination of latitude is an observation of Polaris, the pole star, at morning or evening twilight. Although you may not use the technique as often as the noon sight, a Polaris observation works anywhere in the Northern Hemisphere and shares with the noon sun the distinction of being one of the earliest exercises in nautical astronomy—possibly because the star is so easy to identify. Despite the fact that Polaris is a second magnitude star (Mag. 2.1, to be exact), anyone at all familiar with the night sky knows how to find it by following the pointers from the Big Dipper. More sophisticated observers can also spot Polaris's position in relation to the constellation Cassiopeia, the flattened "W" opposite the Dipper. The special quality of Polaris, which makes the solution for latitude so easy, is its constant position within a degree or so of the North Celestial Pole. Since the altitude of the celestial pole is equivalent to the observer's latitude, it is only a question of correcting the sextant altitude, and adjusting for the exact position of the star, to obtain a precise latitude. The steps are simple and straightforward.

- Correct the sextant altitude, hs, in the same manner as for any star sight, to obtain the observed altitude, Ho.
- Calculate LHA of Aries by applying your estimated longitude to GHA Aries found in the almanac for the time of observation.
- Enter the Polaris tables (at the back of the *Nautical Almanac*) and extract the value of $a_0$, for the corresponding LHA♈; $a_1$, for the estimated latitude; and $a_2$, for the month of observation.

- Then, Ho $-1° + a_0 + a_1 + a_2$ = latitude, and since Polaris is visible only in the Northern Hemisphere, the latitude is always North.

Let's review the Polaris procedure with a practical example. Returning from the Bahamas on March 16, 1984, a navigator estimates his position at evening twilight to be at Latitude 26°41.2'N, Longitude 79°31.9'W. At 18:51:09 local time (23:51:09 GMT), he observes Polaris on the starboard beam at an altitude of 27°16.8'. The sextant's index correction is −2.4', and the observer's height of eye is 9 feet. What is his precise latitude? As with our other sights, we will use a workform to follow the solution step by step.

| DATE | March 16, 1984 |
|------|----------------|
| hs | 27-16.8 |
| IC | -2.4 |
| D | -2.9 |
| ha | 27-11.5 |
| R | -1.9 |
| Ho | 27-09.6 |
| W | 23-51-09 |
| corr | 00 |
| GMT | 23-51-09 |
| gha $\Upsilon$ | 159-42.5 |
| incr | 12-49.4 |
| GHA $\Upsilon$ | 172-31.9 |
| | |
| | |
| a λ | 79-31.9 |
| LHA $\Upsilon$ | 93-00 |
| a L | 26-41 N |
| Ho | 27-09.6 |
| −1° | 26-09.6 |
| +$a_0$ | 34.3 |
| +$a_1$ | 0.4 |
| +$a_2$ | 0.9 |
| L | 26-45.2 N |

In the regular way, applicable to all observations, the IC and D-corrections adjust our sextant altitude of 27° 16.8′ to an apparent altitude of 27°11.5′, and the R-correction, found in the STARS column of the almanac tables to be −1.9′ (Figure 23–6), then produces an observed altitude of 27°09.6′. Polaris's position is presented in the almanac as a function of the local hour angle of Aries, so we must next determine LHA♈, again following the procedure for any normal star sight. The Greenwich hour angle of Aries is found in the usual way in the almanac's daily pages and increment tables. Figure 23–7 shows a tabular GHA Aries at 23ʰ GMT on March 16 of 159°42.5′, and Figure 23–8 shows an increment of

## ALTITUDE CORRECTION TABLES 10 -90

| STARS AND PLANETS | | DIP | | |
|---|---|---|---|---|
| App. Alt.   Corrⁿ | App.  Additional Alt.   Corrⁿ | Ht. of Eye  Corrⁿ  Ht. of Eye | | Ht. of Eye  Corrⁿ |
| | | m    ft. | | m    , |
| 9 56 , | 1984 | 2·4 ,  8·0 | | 1·0 —  1·8 |
| 10 08 −5·3 | VENUS | 2·6 −2·8  8·6 | | 1·5 —  2·2 |
| 10 20 −5·2 | Jan. 1-Dec. 12 | 2·8 −2·9  9·2 | | 2·0 —  2·5 |
| 10 33 −5·1 | | 3·0 −3·0  9·8 | | 2·5 —  2·8 |
| 10 46 −5·0 | °  °  , | 3·2 −3·1  10·5 | | 3·0 —  3·0 |
| ʈʈ ᴏᴏ −4·9 | 60  + 0·1 | ᴀ  −3·2  --- | | |
| ʈʈ ᴧᴏ −2·4 | 41  + 0·1 | 10·3 −5·7  33·9 | | 8 —  2·7 |
| 22 19 −2·3 | 76 | 10·6 −5·8  35·1 | | 10— 3·1 |
| 23 13 −2·2 | Aug. 28-Dec. 31 | 11·0 −5·9  36·3 | | See table |
| 24 11 −2·1 | | 11·4 −6·0  37·6 | | ← |
| 25 14 −2·0 | °  , | 11·8 −6·1  38·9 | | |
| 26 22 −1·9 | 60  + 0·1 | 12·2 −6·2  40·1 | | ft.  , |
| 27 36 −1·8 | | 12·6 −6·3  41·5 | | 70 —  8·1 |
| 28 56 −1·7 | | 13·0 −6·4  42·8 | | 75 —  8·4 |
| 30 24 −1·6 | | 13·4 −6·5  44·2 | | 80 —  8·7 |
| ᴈᴈ ᴏᴏ | | ᴠᴀ ᴏ  ᴀᴀ  ᴀ | | ᴏ᷄  ᴏ  ᴀ |

*Figure 23–6.* Excerpt from the *Nautical Almanac's* altitude correction tables showing a dip correction of −2.9′ for a height of eye of 9 feet, and an R-correction of −1.9′ for a star altitude of 27°11.5′.

## 1984 MARCH 16

| G.M.T. | ARIES | |
|---|---|---|
| | G.H.A. | |
| | ° | ′ |
| 16 00 | 173 | 45.8 |
| 01 | 188 | 48.3 |
| 02 | 203 | 50.8 |
| 03 | 218 | 53.2 |
| 04 | 233 | 55.7 |
| 05 | 248 | 58.2 |
| 06 | 264 | 00.6 |
| 07 | 279 | 03.1 |
| 08 | 294 | 05.5 |
| F 09 | 309 | 08.0 |
| R 10 | 324 | 10.5 |
| I 11 | 339 | 12.9 |
| D 12 | 354 | 15.4 |
| A 13 | 9 | 17.9 |
| Y 14 | 24 | 20.3 |
| 15 | 39 | 22.8 |
| 16 | 54 | 25.3 |
| 17 | 69 | 27.7 |
| 18 | 84 | 30.2 |
| 19 | 99 | 32.7 |
| 20 | 114 | 35.1 |
| 21 | 129 | 37.6 |
| 22 | 144 | 40.0 |
| 23 | 159 | 42.5 |

*Figure 23–7.* Excerpt from the *Nautical Almanac's* daily pages showing GHA Aries at 23ʰ on March 16, 1984, to be 159°42.5′.

## INCREMENTS AND CORRECTIONS 51ᵐ

| 51ᵐ | SUN PLANETS | ARIES | MOON | $v$ or Corrⁿ $d$ | | $v$ or Corrⁿ $d$ | | $v$ or Corrⁿ $d$ | |
|---|---|---|---|---|---|---|---|---|---|
| s | ° ′ | ° ′ | ° ′ | ′ | ′ | ′ | ′ | ′ | ′ |
| 00 | 12 45·0 | 12 47·1 | 12 10·2 | 0·0 | 0·0 | 6·0 | 5·2 | 12·0 | 10·3 |
| 01 | 12 45·3 | 12 47·3 | 12 10·4 | 0·1 | 0·1 | 6·1 | 5·2 | 12·1 | 10·4 |
| 02 | 12 45·5 | 12 47·6 | 12 10·6 | 0·2 | 0·2 | 6·2 | 5·3 | 12·2 | 10·5 |
| 03 | 12 45·8 | 12 47·8 | 12 10·9 | 0·3 | 0·3 | 6·3 | 5·4 | 12·3 | 10·6 |
| 04 | 12 46·0 | 12 48·1 | 12 11·1 | 0·4 | 0·3 | 6·4 | 5·5 | 12·4 | 10·6 |
| 05 | 12 46·3 | 12 48·3 | 12 11·3 | 0·5 | 0·4 | 6·5 | 5·6 | 12·5 | 10·7 |
| 06 | 12 46·5 | 12 48·6 | 12 11·6 | 0·6 | 0·5 | 6·6 | 5·7 | 12·6 | 10·8 |
| 07 | 12 46·8 | 12 48·8 | 12 11·8 | 0·7 | 0·6 | 6·7 | 5·8 | 12·7 | 10·9 |
| 08 | 12 47·0 | 12 49·1 | 12 12·1 | 0·8 | 0·7 | 6·8 | 5·8 | 12·8 | 11·0 |
| 09 | 12 47·3 | 12 49·4 | 12 12·3 | 0·9 | 0·8 | 6·9 | 5·9 | 12·9 | 11·1 |

*Figure 23–8.* Excerpt from the *Nautical Almanac's* Increments and Corrections tables, showing the GHA increment for Aries to be 12°49.4′ for 51 minutes, 09 seconds of time.

12°49.4′ for 51 minutes and 09 seconds of time. The sum of the two is the GHA Aries at 23:51:09, 172°31.9′. Applying the estimated longitude of 79°31.9′W (remembering to add if East and subtract if West), the local hour angle of Aries works out to a convenient 93°. Because the longitude is a determining factor in the accuracy of the Polaris procedure, you should always use your best estimate, even if LHA ♈ comes out to fractional degrees.

Having found the local hour angle of Aries, turn to the special Polaris tables in the back of the *Nautical Almanac*, Figure 23–9, to find the three corrections to the observed altitude that will produce the latitude. Entering the upper part of the table with the LHA ♈ of 93°, the first correction, $a_0$ is found to be 34.3′. The second correction, $a_1$, depends on the latitude; here, using the same column, it is 0.4′ for our estimated position between 26° and 27°N. The third correction, $a_2$, is a function of the month; in March 1984, the correction is 0.9′. The formula for calculating latitude is:

$$\text{Latitude} = \text{Ho} - 1° + a_0 + a_1 + a_2$$

If you follow the final four entries on the workform, you will see that the total adjustment nets out to −24.4′, which, when applied to the observed altitude of 27°09.6′, produces the observer's latitude, 26°45.2′, or some four miles north of the vessel's estimated position.

If you prefer and are using Pub. No. 249, Volume I, for your star sights, the Polaris corrections can also be obtained by a single entry of LHA ♈ in Table 6, illustrated in Figure 23–10. Here you will see that for 93° the correction is −25′, very close to the net of the *Nautical Almanac* table, although the latter is usually the more accurate.

Latitude is not the only useful determination that can

---

*Figure 23–9.* Polaris tables from the *Nautical Almanac.* Used for the determination of latitude by an observation of Polaris.

## POLARIS (POLE STAR) TABLES, 1984
### FOR DETERMINING LATITUDE FROM SEXTANT ALTITUDE AND FOR AZIMUTH

| L.H.A. ARIES | 0°–9° | 10°–19° | 20°–29° | 30°–39° | 40°–49° | 50°–59° | 60°–69° | 70°–79° | 80°–89° | 90°–99° | 100°–109° | 110°–119° |
|---|---|---|---|---|---|---|---|---|---|---|---|---|
| | $a_0$ | $a_0$ | $a_0$ | $a_0$ | $a_0$ | $a_0$ | $a_0$ | $a_0$ | $a_0$ | $a_0$ | $a_0$ | $a_0$ |
| ° | ° ′ | ° ′ | ° ′ | ° ′ | ° ′ | ° ′ | ° ′ | ° ′ | ° ′ | ° ′ | ° ′ | ° ′ |
| 0 | 0 18.8 | 0 14.7 | 0 11.9 | 0 10.6 | 0 10.8 | 0 12.4 | 0 15.5 | 0 19.9 | 0 25.5 | 0 32.2 | 0 39.6 | 0 47.6 |
| 1 | 18.3 | 14.4 | 11.7 | 10.6 | 10.9 | 12.7 | 15.9 | 20.4 | 26.2 | 32.9 | 40.4 | 48.4 |
| 2 | 17.9 | 14.0 | 11.5 | 10.5 | 11.0 | 12.9 | 16.3 | 21.0 | 26.8 | 33.6 | 41.2 | 49.3 |
| 3 | 17.4 | 13.7 | 11.4 | 10.5 | 11.1 | 13.2 | 16.7 | 21.5 | 27.4 | 34.3 | 42.0 | 50.1 |
| 4 | 17.0 | 13.4 | 11.2 | 10.5 | 11.3 | 13.5 | 17.1 | 22.0 | 28.1 | 35.1 | 42.8 | 50.9 |
| 5 | 0 16.6 | 0 13.1 | 0 11.1 | 0 10.5 | 0 11.4 | 0 13.8 | 0 17.6 | 0 22.6 | 0 28.7 | 0 35.8 | 0 43.6 | 0 51.8 |
| 6 | 16.2 | 12.9 | 11.0 | 10.5 | 11.6 | 14.1 | 18.0 | 23.2 | 29.4 | 36.6 | 44.4 | 52.6 |
| 7 | 15.8 | 12.6 | 10.9 | 10.6 | 11.8 | 14.5 | 18.5 | 23.8 | 30.1 | 37.3 | 45.2 | 53.4 |
| 8 | 15.4 | 12.4 | 10.8 | 10.6 | 12.0 | 14.8 | 19.0 | 24.3 | 30.8 | 38.1 | 46.0 | 54.3 |
| 9 | 15.0 | 12.1 | 10.7 | 10.7 | 12.2 | 15.2 | 19.4 | 24.9 | 31.5 | 38.8 | 46.8 | 55.1 |
| 10 | 0 14.7 | 0 11.9 | 0 10.6 | 0 10.8 | 0 12.4 | 0 15.5 | 0 19.9 | 0 25.5 | 0 32.2 | 0 39.6 | 0 47.6 | 0 56.0 |

| Lat. | $a_1$ | $a_1$ | $a_1$ | $a_1$ | $a_1$ | $a_1$ | $a_1$ | $a_1$ | $a_1$ | $a_1$ | $a_1$ | $a_1$ |
|---|---|---|---|---|---|---|---|---|---|---|---|---|
| ° | ′ | ′ | ′ | ′ | ′ | ′ | ′ | ′ | ′ | ′ | ′ | ′ |
| 0 | 0.5 | 0.6 | 0.6 | 0.6 | 0.6 | 0.5 | 0.5 | 0.4 | 0.4 | 0.3 | 0.2 | 0.2 |
| 10 | .5 | .6 | .6 | .6 | .6 | .6 | .5 | .5 | .4 | .3 | .3 | .3 |
| 20 | .5 | .6 | .6 | .6 | .6 | .6 | .5 | .5 | .4 | .4 | .3 | .3 |
| 30 | .6 | .6 | .6 | .6 | .6 | .6 | .5 | .5 | .5 | .4 | .4 | .4 |
| 40 | 0.6 | 0.6 | 0.6 | 0.6 | 0.6 | 0.6 | 0.6 | 0.5 | 0.5 | 0.5 | 0.5 | 0.5 |
| 45 | .6 | .6 | .6 | .6 | .6 | .6 | .6 | .6 | .6 | .6 | .5 | .5 |
| 50 | .6 | .6 | .6 | .6 | .6 | .6 | .6 | .6 | .6 | .6 | .6 | .6 |
| 55 | .6 | .6 | .6 | .6 | .6 | .6 | .6 | .6 | .6 | .7 | .7 | .7 |
| 60 | .6 | .6 | .6 | .6 | .6 | .6 | .6 | .7 | .7 | .7 | .8 | .8 |
| 62 | 0.7 | 0.6 | 0.6 | 0.6 | 0.6 | 0.6 | 0.7 | 0.7 | 0.7 | 0.8 | 0.8 | 0.8 |
| 64 | .7 | .6 | .6 | .6 | .6 | .6 | .7 | .7 | .8 | .8 | .9 | .9 |
| 66 | .7 | .6 | .6 | .6 | .6 | .6 | .7 | .8 | .8 | .9 | 0.9 | 0.9 |
| 68 | 0.7 | 0.6 | 0.6 | 0.6 | 0.6 | 0.7 | 0.7 | 0.8 | 0.9 | 0.9 | 1.0 | 1.0 |

| Month | $a_2$ | $a_2$ | $a_2$ | $a_2$ | $a_2$ | $a_2$ | $a_2$ | $a_2$ | $a_2$ | $a_2$ | $a_2$ | $a_2$ |
|---|---|---|---|---|---|---|---|---|---|---|---|---|
| | ′ | ′ | ′ | ′ | ′ | ′ | ′ | ′ | ′ | ′ | ′ | ′ |
| Jan. | 0.7 | 0.7 | 0.7 | 0.7 | 0.7 | 0.7 | 0.7 | 0.7 | 0.7 | 0.7 | 0.6 | 0.6 |
| Feb. | .6 | .6 | .7 | .7 | .7 | .7 | .8 | .8 | .8 | .8 | .8 | .8 |
| Mar. | .5 | .5 | .6 | .6 | .7 | .7 | .8 | .8 | .8 | .9 | .9 | .9 |
| Apr. | 0.3 | 0.4 | 0.4 | 0.5 | 0.5 | 0.6 | 0.7 | 0.7 | 0.8 | 0.9 | 0.9 | 0.9 |
| May | .2 | .2 | .3 | .3 | .4 | .5 | .5 | .6 | .7 | .8 | .8 | .9 |
| June | .2 | .2 | .2 | .2 | .3 | .3 | .4 | .5 | .5 | .6 | .7 | .8 |
| July | 0.2 | 0.2 | 0.2 | 0.2 | 0.2 | 0.3 | 0.3 | 0.3 | 0.4 | 0.5 | 0.5 | 0.6 |
| Aug. | .4 | .3 | .3 | .3 | .3 | .2 | .3 | .3 | .3 | .3 | .4 | .4 |
| Sept. | .5 | .5 | .4 | .4 | .3 | .3 | .3 | .3 | .3 | .3 | .3 | .3 |
| Oct. | 0.7 | 0.7 | 0.6 | 0.5 | 0.5 | 0.4 | 0.4 | 0.3 | 0.3 | 0.3 | 0.3 | 0.3 |
| Nov. | 0.9 | 0.9 | 0.8 | .7 | .7 | .6 | .5 | .5 | .4 | .4 | .3 | .3 |
| Dec. | 1.0 | 1.0 | 1.0 | 0.9 | 0.8 | 0.8 | 0.7 | 0.6 | 0.6 | 0.5 | 0.4 | 0.4 |

| Lat. | AZIMUTH | | | | | | | | | | | |
|---|---|---|---|---|---|---|---|---|---|---|---|---|
| ° | ° | ° | ° | ° | ° | ° | ° | ° | ° | ° | ° | ° |
| 0 | 0.4 | 0.3 | 0.1 | 0.0 | 359.8 | 359.7 | 359.6 | 359.5 | 359.4 | 359.3 | 359.2 | 359.2 |
| 20 | 0.4 | 0.3 | 0.1 | 0.0 | 359.8 | 359.7 | 359.6 | 359.4 | 359.3 | 359.2 | 359.2 | 359.2 |
| 40 | 0.5 | 0.3 | 0.2 | 0.0 | 359.8 | 359.6 | 359.5 | 359.3 | 359.2 | 359.1 | 359.0 | 359.0 |
| 50 | 0.6 | 0.4 | 0.2 | 0.0 | 359.8 | 359.5 | 359.3 | 359.2 | 359.0 | 358.9 | 358.8 | 358.8 |
| 55 | 0.7 | 0.5 | 0.2 | 0.0 | 359.7 | 359.5 | 359.3 | 359.1 | 358.9 | 358.8 | 358.7 | 358.6 |
| 60 | 0.8 | 0.5 | 0.3 | 0.0 | 359.7 | 359.4 | 359.1 | 358.9 | 358.7 | 358.6 | 358.5 | 358.4 |
| 65 | 0.9 | 0.6 | 0.3 | 0.0 | 359.6 | 359.3 | 359.0 | 358.7 | 358.5 | 358.3 | 358.2 | 358.1 |

Latitude = Apparent altitude (corrected for refraction) − 1° + $a_0$ + $a_1$ + $a_2$

The table is entered with L.H.A. Aries to determine the column to be used; each column refers to a range of 10°. $a_0$ is taken, with mental interpolation, from the upper table with the units of L.H.A. Aries in degrees as argument; $a_1$, $a_2$ are taken, without interpolation, from the second and third tables with arguments latitude and month respectively. $a_0$, $a_1$, $a_2$ are always positive. The final table gives the azimuth of *Polaris*.

# TABLE 6—CORRECTION (Q) FOR *POLARIS*

| LHA ♈ | Q | LHA ♈ | Q | LHA ♈ | Q | LHA ♈ | Q | LHA ♈ | Q | LHA ♈ | Q | LHA ♈ | Q | LHA ♈ | Q |
|---|---|---|---|---|---|---|---|---|---|---|---|---|---|---|---|
| 359 40 | −40 | 84 18 | −30 | 118 16 | −4 | 150 19 | +22 | 205 44 | +48 | 276 27 | +22 | 308 39 | −4 | 342 18 | −30 |
| 1 49 | −41 | 85 49 | −29 | 119 28 | −3 | 151 19 | +23 | 222 23 | +47 | 277 48 | +21 | 309 51 | −5 | 343 49 | −31 |
| 4 06 | −42 | 87 18 | −28 | 120 40 | −2 | 153 02 | +24 | 228 31 | +46 | 279 08 | +20 | 311 03 | −6 | 345 23 | −32 |
| 6 33 | −43 | 88 46 | −27 | 121 52 | −1 | 154 25 | +25 | 232 45 | +45 | 280 27 | +19 | 312 15 | −7 | 346 59 | −33 |
| 9 14 | −44 | 90 13 | −26 | 123 03 | 0 | 155 49 | +26 | 236 13 | +44 | 281 45 | +18 | 313 27 | −8 | 348 37 | −34 |
| 12 12 | −45 | 91 37 | −25 | 124 16 | +1 | 157 14 | +27 | 239 14 | +43 | 283 03 | +17 | 314 40 | −9 | 350 18 | −35 |
| 15 37 | −46 | 93 01 | −24 | 125 27 | +2 | 158 41 | +28 | 241 56 | +42 | 284 19 | +16 | 315 52 | −10 | 352 02 | −36 |
| 19 48 | −47 | 94 23 | −23 | 126 39 | +3 | 160 10 | +29 | 244 25 | +41 | 285 35 | +15 | 317 06 | −11 | 353 50 | −37 |
| 25 51 | −48 | 95 45 | −22 | 127 51 | +4 | 161 40 | +30 | 246 44 | +40 | 286 51 | +14 | 318 19 | −12 | 355 41 | −38 |
| 42 16 | −47 | 97 05 | −21 | 129 03 | +5 | 163 12 | +31 | 248 54 | +39 | 288 06 | +13 | 319 33 | −13 | 357 38 | −39 |
| 48 19 | −46 | 98 24 | −20 | 130 15 | +6 | 164 47 | +32 | 250 58 | +38 | 289 21 | +12 | 320 47 | −14 | 359 40 | −40 |
| 52 30 | −45 | 99 43 | −19 | 131 27 | +7 | 166 23 | +33 | 252 56 | +37 | 290 35 | +11 | 322 02 | −15 | 1 49 | −41 |
| 55 55 | −44 | 101 01 | −18 | 132 40 | +8 | 168 02 | +34 | 254 49 | +36 | 291 48 | +10 | 323 17 | −16 | 4 06 | −42 |
| 58 53 | −43 | 102 18 | −17 | 133 52 | +9 | 169 44 | +35 | 256 38 | +35 | 293 02 | +9 | 324 33 | −17 | 6 33 | −43 |
| 61 34 | −42 | 103 34 | −16 | 135 05 | +10 | 171 29 | +36 | 258 23 | +34 | 294 15 | +8 | 325 49 | −18 | 9 14 | −44 |
| 64 01 | −41 | 104 50 | −15 | 136 19 | +11 | 173 18 | +37 | 260 05 | +33 | 295 27 | +7 | 327 06 | −19 | 12 12 | −45 |
| 66 18 | −40 | 106 05 | −14 | 137 32 | +12 | 175 11 | +38 | 261 44 | +32 | 296 40 | +6 | 328 24 | −20 | 15 37 | −46 |
| 68 27 | −39 | 107 20 | −13 | 138 46 | +13 | 177 09 | +39 | 263 20 | +31 | 297 52 | +5 | 329 43 | −21 | 19 48 | −47 |
| 70 29 | −38 | 108 34 | −12 | 140 01 | +14 | 179 13 | +40 | 264 55 | +30 | 299 04 | +4 | 331 02 | −22 | 25 51 | −48 |
| 72 26 | −37 | 109 48 | −11 | 141 16 | +15 | 181 23 | +41 | 266 27 | +29 | 300 16 | +3 | 332 22 | −23 | 42 16 | −47 |
| 74 17 | −36 | 111 01 | −10 | 142 32 | +16 | 183 42 | +42 | 267 57 | +28 | 301 28 | +2 | 333 44 | −24 | 48 19 | −46 |
| 76 05 | −35 | 112 15 | −9 | 143 48 | +17 | 186 11 | +43 | 269 26 | +27 | 302 40 | +1 | 335 06 | −25 | 52 30 | −45 |
| 77 49 | −34 | 113 27 | −8 | 145 04 | +18 | 188 53 | +44 | 270 53 | +26 | 303 51 | 0 | 336 30 | −26 | 55 55 | −44 |
| 79 30 | −33 | 114 40 | −7 | 146 22 | +19 | 191 54 | +45 | 272 18 | +25 | 305 04 | −1 | 337 54 | −27 | 58 53 | −43 |
| 81 08 | −32 | 115 52 | −6 | 147 40 | +20 | 195 22 | +46 | 273 42 | +24 | 306 15 | −2 | 339 21 | −28 | 61 34 | −42 |
| 82 44 | −31 | 117 04 | −5 | 148 59 | +21 | 199 36 | +47 | 275 05 | +23 | 307 27 | −3 | 340 49 | −29 | 64 01 | −41 |
| 84 18 | | 118 16 | | 150 19 | | 205 44 | | 276 27 | | 308 39 | | 342 18 | | 66 18 | |

The above table, which does *not* include refraction, gives the quantity Q to be applied to the corrected sextant altitude of *Polaris* to give the latitude of the observer. In critical cases ascend.

*Polaris*: Mag. 2·1, SHA 325° 56′, Dec. N 89° 12′·0

# TABLE 7—AZIMUTH OF *POLARIS*

| LHA ♈ | Latitude | | | | | | |
|---|---|---|---|---|---|---|---|
| | 0 | 30 | 50 | 55 | 60 | 65 | 70 |
| 0 | 0·4 | 0·5 | 0·7 | 0·8 | 0·9 | 1·1 | 1·4 |
| 10 | 0·3 | 0·4 | 0·5 | 0·6 | 0·7 | 0·8 | 1·0 |
| 20 | 0·2 | 0·2 | 0·3 | 0·3 | 0·4 | 0·5 | 0·6 |
| 30 | 0·1 | 0·1 | 0·1 | 0·1 | 0·1 | 0·1 | 0·2 |
| 40 | 359·9 | 359·9 | 359·9 | 359·9 | 359·8 | 359·8 | 359·7 |
| 50 | 359·8 | 359·7 | 359·7 | 359·6 | 359·6 | 359·5 | 359·3 |
| 60 | 359·7 | 359·6 | 359·4 | 359·4 | 359·3 | 359·1 | 358·9 |
| 70 | 359·5 | 359·3 | 359·2 | 359·0 | 358·9 | 358·6 | 358·6 |
| 80 | 359·4 | 359·3 | 359·1 | 359·0 | 358·8 | 358·6 | 358·3 |
| 90 | 359·3 | 359·2 | 359·0 | 358·8 | 358·7 | 358·4 | 358·0 |
| 100 | 359·3 | 359·2 | 358·9 | 358·6 | 358·5 | 358·3 | 357·8 |
| 110 | 359·2 | 359·1 | 358·8 | 358·6 | 358·4 | 358·2 | 357·7 |
| 120 | 359·2 | 359·1 | 358·8 | 358·6 | 358·4 | 358·1 | 357·7 |
| 130 | 359·2 | 359·1 | 358·8 | 358·6 | 358·5 | 358·1 | 357·7 |
| 140 | 359·2 | 359·1 | 358·8 | 358·7 | 358·5 | 358·2 | 357·8 |
| 150 | 359·3 | 359·2 | 358·9 | 358·8 | 358·6 | 358·3 | 357·9 |
| 160 | 359·4 | 359·3 | 359·0 | 358·9 | 358·7 | 358·5 | 358·1 |
| 170 | 359·4 | 359·4 | 359·1 | 359·0 | 358·9 | 358·7 | 358·4 |
| 180 | 359·6 | 359·5 | 359·3 | 359·2 | 359·1 | 359·0 | 358·7 |
| 180 | 359·6 | 359·5 | 359·3 | 359·2 | 359·1 | 359·0 | 358·7 |
| 190 | 359·7 | 359·6 | 359·5 | 359·4 | 359·4 | 359·2 | 359·1 |
| 200 | 359·8 | 359·8 | 359·7 | 359·7 | 359·6 | 359·6 | 359·5 |
| 210 | 359·9 | 359·9 | 359·9 | 359·9 | 359·9 | 359·9 | 359·8 |
| 220 | 0·1 | 0·1 | 0·1 | 0·1 | 0·2 | 0·2 | 0·2 |
| 230 | 0·2 | 0·3 | 0·3 | 0·4 | 0·4 | 0·5 | 0·6 |
| 240 | 0·3 | 0·4 | 0·5 | 0·6 | 0·7 | 0·8 | 1·0 |
| 250 | 0·5 | 0·5 | 0·7 | 0·8 | 0·9 | 1·1 | 1·3 |
| 260 | 0·6 | 0·7 | 0·9 | 1·0 | 1·1 | 1·3 | 1·6 |
| 270 | 0·7 | 0·8 | 1·0 | 1·1 | 1·3 | 1·5 | 1·9 |
| 280 | 0·7 | 0·8 | 1·1 | 1·3 | 1·4 | 1·7 | 2·1 |
| 290 | 0·8 | 0·9 | 1·2 | 1·3 | 1·5 | 1·8 | 2·2 |
| 300 | 0·8 | 0·9 | 1·2 | 1·4 | 1·6 | 1·9 | 2·3 |
| 310 | 0·8 | 0·9 | 1·2 | 1·3 | 1·5 | 1·8 | 2·3 |
| 320 | 0·8 | 0·9 | 1·2 | 1·3 | 1·5 | 1·8 | 2·3 |
| 330 | 0·7 | 0·8 | 1·1 | 1·3 | 1·5 | 1·7 | 2·1 |
| 340 | 0·6 | 0·8 | 1·0 | 1·1 | 1·3 | 1·6 | 1·9 |
| 350 | 0·6 | 0·6 | 0·9 | 1·0 | 1·1 | 1·3 | 1·7 |
| 360 | 0·4 | 0·5 | 0·7 | 0·8 | 0·9 | 1·1 | 1·4 |

When Cassiopeia is left (right), *Polaris* is west (east).

be made by Polaris observations; its proximity to the true pole allows accurate azimuths to be read from the same tables, and in either one you can see that the true azimuth at the time of our sight is 359.2°.

Celestial azimuths may be used for comparison with the compass bearing of a body to determine compass error. Since there are no terrestrial references available at sea by which to perform a compass check, calculated azimuths are the accepted method. Besides Polaris, any celestial body can be used for the purpose—the sun is actually the most common one—and the azimuth is determined by a regular sight reduction as described in Chapter 17. If you only want the azimuth, however, you need not bother with the sextant observation; all you need is the local hour angle at the time you take the bearing of a body, its declination, and your assumed latitude to enter the sight reduction tables and extract the true azimuth.

Before concluding the subject of sight reduction by tables, it is useful to compare the six types of sights we have discussed in the preceding chapters—sun, moon, planets, stars, LAN sun, and Polaris—and to review the similarities and differences in the procedures for dealing with each. Since most of the steps are similar in each instance, navigators find it easiest to remember one general procedure, and to think of the small differences as exceptions peculiar to a certain type of observation. The table on pages 234–235 shows each of the headings used in a standard sight reduction, the source of the information needed, and for each type of sight, the measurement involved. The Appendix contains standardized workbook forms for each of the procedures, and with these tools, the almanac, and Pub. No. 249, you should be able to solve any sight you take.

---

*Figure 23–10.* Tables 6 and 7 from Pub. No. 249, Volume I, showing the "Q" correction for LHA ♈ 93° to be − 25′. The true azimuth is 359.2°.

## COMPARISON OF PROCEDURES

| VALUE SOUGHT | SOURCE | SUN | MOON |
|---|---|---|---|
| **hs** | Sextant | Lower or Upper Limb | Lower or Upper Limb |
| **IC** | Measurement | Pretrial | Pretrial |
| **D** | Dip table | Almanac, front cover | Almanac, back cover |
| **ha** | Calculation | hs + IC + D | hs + IC + D |
| **R** | Almanac table | Front cover, SUN column | Back cover, two parts: R, HP |
| **Ho** | Calculation | ha + R | ha + R + HP |
| | | | |
| **GMT** | Watch (+ZD) | Greenwich mean time | Greenwich mean time |
| **gha$^h$** | Almanac daily pages | SUN column, hours | MOON column, hours |
| **incr$^{ms}$** | Increments & corrections tables | SUN column, min., sec. | MOON column, min., sec. |
| **add'l corr** | Increments & corrections tables | (none required) | v-correction |
| **GHA** | Calculation | gha + incr | gha + incr + v-corr. |
| **aλ** | Assumed | Near DR, to make LHA whole degree | Near DR, to make LHA whole degree |
| **LHA** | Calculation | GHA + aλ | GHA + aλ |
| **Dec** | Almanac daily pages | SUN column, interpol. | MOON column + d corr. |
| **aL** | Assumed | Whole degree near DR | Whole degree near DR |
| | | | |
| **Tab Hc** | Pub. No. 249 | Vol. II/III | Vol. II/III |
| **Corr** | Pub. No. 249 | Table 5 | Table 5 |
| **Hc** | Calculation | Tab Hc + corr. | Tab Hc + corr. |
| **Ho** | Earlier calculation | (From above) | (From above) |
| **a** | Calculation | Ho − Hc | Ho − Hc |
| **Zn** | Pub. No. 249 | Z + rules | Z + rules |

(Note: Plus sign indicates algebraic sum; minus sign indicates take difference.)

## — CELESTIAL OBSERVATIONS

| PLANETS | STARS | LAN-SUN | POLARIS |
|---------|-------|---------|---------|
| Center of disc | Center light source | Lower limb—Max. altitude | Center light source |
| Pretrial | Pretrial | Pretrial | Pretrial |
| Almanac, front cover | Almanac, front cover | Almanac, front cover | Almanac, front cover |
| hs + IC + D | hs + IC + D | hs + IC + D | hs + IC + D |
| Front cover, PLANET columns | Front cover, STAR column | Front cover, SUN column | Front cover, STAR column |
| ha + R | ha + R | ha + R | ha + R |
| | | | |
| Greenwich mean time | Greenwich mean time | Max. altitude; approx. Greenwich mean time | Greenwich mean time |
| Name of PLANET column, hours | ARIES column, hours | (not required) | ARIES column, hours |
| PLANETS column, min., sec. | ARIES column, min., sec. | (not required) | ARIES column, min., sec. |
| *v*-correction | SHA★ (Vol. II/III) | (not required) | (not required) |
| gha + incr + *v*-corr. | gha + incr (+ SHA★) | (not required) | gha + incr |
| Near DR, to make LHA whole degree | Near DR, to make LHA whole degree | (not required except for estimating time of LAN) | Best estimate of present longitude |
| GHA + aλ | GHA + aλ | (not required) | GHA + est. λ |
| PLANET column + *d* corr. | Almanac STAR list | SUN column, interpol. | (not required) |
| Whole degree near DR | Whole degree near DR | (not required) | Best estimate of present latitude |
| | | | |
| Vol. II/III | Vol. I, II, or III | (not required) | (not required, use Polaris table) |
| Table 5 | Vol. I—not required Vol. II/III—Table 5 | (not required) | (not required) |
| Tab Hc + corr. | Vol. I—read directly Vol. II/III—Tab Hc + corr. | (not required) | (not required) |
| (From above) | (From above) | Calculate latitude | Calculate latitude |
| Ho — Hc | Ho — Hc | Read latitude | Read latitude |
| Z + rules | Vol. I—read directly Vol. II/III—Z + rules | North or South | Polaris table |

# 24 | Celestial Theory

In the introductory remarks, I proposed to concentrate first on the practical technique, leaving celestial theory until later. Having done so, let's look now at some of the underlying mechanics involved in modern celestial navigation. In a century that has seen the development of electric light, the automobile, air travel, and even space exploration, it is remarkable that celestial navigation, except for timekeeping, has changed only by refinement since its last major breakthrough—the discovery, in 1837, of the line-of-position concept by an American captain, Thomas Sumner, and the altitude-intercept method of computation developed a few years later by a French commander, Marcq St.-Hilaire. This is not to suggest that the science has been allowed to become obsolete; on the contrary, the methods have withstood the test of time.

Each of the regular celestial procedures described in the preceding chapters is comprised of three key operations, identified for the sake of simplicity as "shoot," "compute," and "compare." "Shoot" refers to the measurement of the altitude of a celestial body with a precision instrument such as a marine sextant. In concept, the measurement is of the angle between the true horizontal and a line from the center of the earth to the celestial body, but in practice, the measurement is of the angle between the line of sight to the visible horizon and the line of sight from the observer to the body, and it is made from a position on the earth's surface. As a result, adjustments have to be made to the measured altitude in order to arrive at the true altitude desired.

The normal altitude corrections are the three seen in each of our practical examples: an adjustment for instrument error (the index correction), primarily due to lack of parallelism of the index and horizon mirrors; an adjustment for the observer's elevated position, which causes the visible horizon to appear below the true horizontal (the dip correction); and an adjustment to compensate for the bending of light rays as they pass through the earth's atmosphere (the refraction correction). In the case of the moon, an additional adjustment is needed for parallax— the difference in the body's apparent position as viewed from the surface instead of from the center of the earth. All the other celestial bodies are so far distant from the earth that the parallax correction is negligible, and the few other minor adjustments that might apply are incorporated in the almanac tables. After correction, the sextant altitude becomes the true, or "observed" altitude, Ho, and is the value used in the subsequent calculations.

Turning to celestial mechanics, at any moment in time there is a single point on the earth's surface that is directly beneath a given celestial body. Known, variously, as the subsolar, sublunar, or substellar point, depending upon the body observed, the point is commonly referred to as the body's geographical position, or GP. It is the one location where the body, at that particular moment, is at the zenith—vertically overhead. In piloting, you learned that if you can locate a point precisely, and can determine your distance from it, your position must be somewhere on the circumference of the circle whose center is at the designated point, and whose radius is your distance from it. At the same time, if you know your exact direction from the point, you know where you are on the circumference. In celestial navigation, we can determine the precise location of a body's geographical position by means of the almanac and can determine our distance from that GP by our altitude measurement, as will be explained in a moment. The problem, however, is that the distance, though accurate, is usually so great that it is not practical to plot the circle of position; and shipboard bearing-measurements are not precise enough to be able to pinpoint your location on it. As a consequence, St.-Hilaire's indirect method of approach was developed.

Visualize, if you will, the right angle formed at the geographical position of a body, between the horizontal line to the observer and the perpendicular line to the body, and you can see that it is but one element of a right triangle whose three points are the observer, the GP, and the body at the zenith. The outermost triangle in Figure 24–1 illustrates the relationship. The second angle of the right triangle is the altitude of the body as measured at the observer's position (angle Ho in the figure), and the third is the angle formed at the zenith. Because the triangle is a right triangle, the third angle is the complement of the second, and for this reason, it is known as the coaltitude (90°–altitude). In the figure, you can also see that the coaltitude is subtended by the line between the GP and the observer, and it is a measure of the angular distance (arc distance) between the two points. For this reason, the coaltitude is often referred to as the zenith distance, although "zenith angle" might be more descriptive and less confusing.

For any given angle at the zenith (or for the altitude angle that complements it), the locus of all points on earth where the angle remains the same is the circle, previously mentioned, whose center is the GP, and whose radius is the distance between the GP and the point from

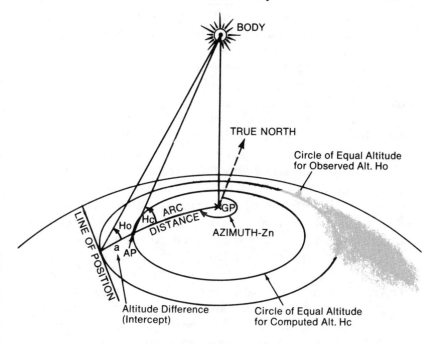

*Figure 24–1.* Elements of the horizon system, showing how the difference between the observed altitude, Ho, and the computed altitude, Hc, establishes the intercept, a.

which the altitude is measured. This circle, illustrated in Figure 24–1, is called a circle of equal altitude—everywhere on its circumference, the altitude of the celestial body will be the same. As I have explained, even though we can find the information necessary to describe the circle of equal altitude for a given observation, it usually isn't practical to plot it because the circle is so large. The alternative, then, is to "compute," St.-Hilaire's ingenious idea of constructing a simultaneous, second circle of equal altitude from a *known* position (the assumed position, AP) by computing the altitude of the body as it would be at the assumed position. In the final, "compare" phase, that computed altitude, Hc, can be compared with the altitude measured by the observer, Ho, to determine the difference in arc distance from the GP between the actual and assumed altitude circles. The altitude difference is the intercept, a, shown in Figure 24–1, and you can also see that if the computed altitude is greater than the observed altitude, as it appears in the figure, the observer's position will be farthest away from the GP.

Although you know now how far the observer is from the assumed position, it is still necessary to know in exactly which direction. This is found by calculating the bearing of the GP from the assumed position at the same time the altitude is computed. That direction, expressed in compass degrees from true North, is known as the azimuth, Zn. While the intercept method adopts the convention that the same azimuth will apply to the bearing of the GP from the observer's actual position, it is not exactly true, but since the positions are so close in global terms, any small difference is immaterial.

As you can see in Figure 24–1, the intersection of the azimuth line with the observer's circle of equal altitude identifies the portion of the circumference on which the observer is located. Because the circumference is usually so large, and since the azimuth may not be exact, for the reason explained, the line of position is constructed as a short, straight line at right angles to the azimuth at the point of intersection. It is virtually coincident with the circumference, and for practical purposes, the line can be used just as is any other line of position.

In discussing the "compute" phase, we passed over the technique of making the actual calculation of the computed altitude and azimuth. It employs the methods of trigonometry, and you may recall, if you have ever studied the subject, that if you are given certain parts—sides and angles—of triangles, you can, by using established formulas, find the missing elements. The same concept applies to a triangle on a sphere, as well as to one on a plane surface, and it is a spherical triangle that is used in celestial navigation. Appropriately named the navigational triangle, its various elements are illustrated in Figure 24–2.

For computing the altitude and azimuth from an assumed position, we predetermine two of the sides, the polar distance (90° minus the body's declination), and the colatitude (90° minus the assumed latitude), and the included angle, the local hour angle, LHA. The triangle is then solved for the third side, the coaltitude, and its adjacent angle, the azimuth angle, Z. The first side, polar distance, is obtained by finding the body's declination in the almanac for the time of the observation, and subtracting that value from 90°. The colatitude is determined directly by subtracting the latitude of the assumed position from 90°. The local hour angle is found by applying the longitude of the assumed position to the Greenwich

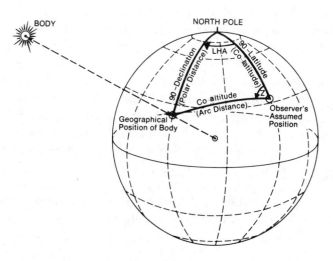

*Figure 24–2.* **The Elements of the Navigational Triangle Projected on Earth.**

hour angle of the body from the almanac. The relationship between Greenwich hour angle, local hour angle, and longitude has been explained in Chapter 16, and is illustrated in Figure 16–1.

While the methods of spherical trigonometry are used in the solution, the manual computation is tedious, and two alternatives are available to the modern navigator: the use of inspection tables, such as Pub. No. 249, recommended in this book; and by means of an electronic calculator, discussed in Chapter 25. The process, however worked, is called sight reduction, and the special tables for the purpose are known as sight reduction tables.

Once the missing elements of the navigational triangle have been found, the side identified as the coaltitude is subtracted from 90° to obtain the computed altitude, Hc, and the azimuth angle, Z, is converted to the true azimuth by applying the quadrant rules that appear in the sight reduction tables. In the final plot, the intercept is stepped off from the assumed position in the proper direction along the azimuth line to locate the point at which the right-angled line of position is constructed.

If you refer to our practical examples and their accompanying workforms, you will see that "shoot" (the sextant observation, its correction and timing) occupies the first part of the exercise; "compute" (using the almanac for the astronomical data, and the sight reduction table to reduce it) occupies the second portion; and "compare," at the conclusion, produces the information needed to complete the plot. Whether or not you become a student of celestial theory, "shoot," "compute," and "compare" will help you to remember the routine, and a well-rehearsed routine is the very best way to avoid mistakes.

# 25 | Celestial Navigation by Calculator

The principal procedures in celestial navigation, just as in piloting, can be expressed in numerical terms, and the solutions to them obtained by the application of conventional mathematical precepts. Historically, however, mathematical solutions have been avoided by celestial navigators because of the tedious computations involved and the inherent opportunity for error. The advent of the electronic calculator has had an effect on this posture, since it is now possible to deal rapidly and accurately with quite complex computations. As a result, it is not unusual to find a calculator as part of a modern navigator's kit.

For discussion purposes, the celestial procedure can be divided into three categories: *arithmetic operations*, normally performed by hand, and exemplified by the correction process for sextant altitudes; *astronomical calculations*, normally extracted from the almanac, and based on long and complex formulas; and *sight reductions*, usually resolved by means of sight reduction tables, which provide solutions to exercises in spherical trigonometry.

How each operational category is handled by calculator is largely a function of the type of calculator used. A manual, scientific-level calculator represents the minimum for practical celestial navigation, but with manual operation there is little time to be saved against that of an experienced navigator using modern inspection tables like the *Nautical Almanac* and Pub. No. 249. For that reason, if a calculator is to be used regularly for celestial navigation, most navigators prefer the more advanced, programmable types. General-purpose, scientific-level, programmable calculators, such as the Hewlett-Packard Series 40, not only have the capability to be programmed by the operator, but they can also accept modular memories that have been preprogrammed by the manufacturer to perform a variety of procedures, including celestial navigation. Specialized navigational calculators are the other class that has found particular favor with yacht navigators. These instruments, exemplified by the Tamaya NC-series, are prewired specifically to perform navigational computations. Since this is their primary purpose, they are called dedicated, or hard-wired calculators, and their keyboards and displays are all designed to facilitate navigation solutions. For yachtsmen who use celestial navigation only occasionally, the specialized navigation calculator is probably the easiest and most convenient to use, but for navigators who wish to make a variety of other types of calculations, the general-purpose calculators, with specialized modules, are the logical choice.

As explained in Chapter 11, a calculator accepts input data, and through a stepped sequence—executed either by a series of individual keystrokes in a manual machine, or automatically in a programmed model—arrives at the solution. The formula applied determines the steps in the sequence. If an operator develops a sequence himself, it must be stored in a program memory before entering the variable data and running the program; in the case of the dedicated instruments and modules, such a program has already been established by the manufacturer, and the operator need only enter the input and command the machine to execute. The technique of programming a particular calculator is a function of the model and its design, but any program involves identifying the input information available, the output solution desired, and the formula that will be applied. It is an absorbing exercise if one is mathematically inclined, but it does require knowledge of both the mathematical basis of the problem and the machine's programming procedure, and, if you are to be good at it, lots of practice.

Let's review the principal celestial operations that we have studied in earlier chapters and look at the approach to solving them by calculator. The first category includes the process of finding and applying the regular corrections to the sextant altitude. The index correction, you will recall, is found by trial, while the dip and refraction corrections are normally extracted from the almanac tables. The last two corrections can also be calculated. The formula for finding dip correction, in minutes of arc, is:

$$0.97\sqrt{\text{Height of eye (in feet)}}$$

and the formula for finding the refraction correction, in decimal degrees, where the apparent altitude, ha, is given in decimal degrees is:

$$\frac{0.97 \tan[\text{ha} - \tan^{-1} 12(\text{ha} + 3)]}{60}$$

You will notice that the last formula is expressed in decimal degrees, while the first formula and the index correction normally use minutes of arc. In determining the algebraic sum by calculator, it is necessary to express all the values in the same terms—decimal degrees—then perform the arithmetic, and then reconvert the total to the sexagesimal system (60 seconds equals 1 minute, and 60 minutes equals 1 degree), the way in which navigators usually state angular measurement. On certain calculators, the conversion function is programmed into the instrument, but if it is not, the formula to convert minutes and seconds of arc to decimal degrees is as given in Chapter 11:

$$\frac{(\text{Minutes} \times 60) + \text{Seconds}}{3600}$$

In the case of sun or moon sights worked by calculator, an additional correction for semidiameter—it is already incorporated in the almanac's refraction tables—must be included because the formula given applies only to the center of the body. Unless the sextant corrections are performed as part of a complete celestial program, even though they are relatively easy to compute by calculator, many navigators find it just as quick to take the values from the almanac tables. The technique of performing sexagesimal/decimal conversions, then performing the addition or subtraction, and finally, returning the result to the sexagesimal system, can also be used in arithmetical routines such as finding the latitude by an observation of the sun at local apparent noon, or the latitude-by-Polaris procedure. It can be used in a similar manner to convert Greenwich hour angle to local hour angle by the application of longitude, but the process of determining the Greenwich hour angle, itself, by calculator is quite another matter.

The fundamental equations of dynamic astronomy are far too complex for direct use in the majority of applications, and even the simplified formulas used in the Naval Observatory's *Almanac for Computers* are beyond the practical reach of any manual calculator. As a consequence, the navigator has two main choices for deriving the necessary astronomical data to solve a sight. Either he can extract the data from the almanac in the conventional way and use his calculator to combine it, or he can use one of the dedicated calculators or modules that are programmed to compute the Greenwich hour angle and declination of the celestial bodies for any moment in time. Ofttimes, these dedicated devices are capable of incorporating the astronomical data they produce in an entire celestial sequence; that is where their real time advantage appears.

Sight reduction is a much less complicated exercise in spherical trigonometry and lends itself well to electronic calculation. There are two basic formulas that apply, in which $L$ is the latitude, and $d$ the declination, both expressed in decimal degrees. To find the computed altitude, Hc, in decimal degrees, the formula is:

$$\text{Sin}^{-1}[(\sin L \sin d) + (\cos L \cos d \cos LHA)]$$

Then, the azimuth angle, Z, may be calculated from the formula:

$$\text{Cos}^{-1}\left[\frac{\sin d - (\sin L \sin Hc)}{(\cos L \cos Hc)}\right]$$

In either formula, when the latitude and declination are of contrary name, declination is treated as a negative quantity.

When you try these formulas on a manual calculator, you may find, as you have in similar instances, that there is not a great time saving over the use of sight reduction tables, but the calculator does have one big advantage over the tables; since the calculator does not require that the latitude and local hour angle be in whole degrees, the dead-reckoning position may be used as the assumed position, greatly simplifying the plot.

Unless you are a calculator buff and are capable of programming your own calculator, you will probably share the conclusion of most yacht navigators that the preprogrammed instruments are the most convenient for celestial navigation. Even if you decide to use one regularly, you will still want to carry your almanac and sight reduction tables with you on every voyage and *know how to use them*. The environment aboard a small boat at sea is notoriously inhospitable to delicate electronic equipment, and it would be foolhardy if, because of equipment failure, you lost the major advantage that celestial navigation enjoys over all other offshore navigation systems: it is completely passive and self-contained.

# 26 | Wrinkles in Celestial Navigation

Now that you have had an opportunity to learn what celestial navigation is all about, it is time to introduce some of the practical wrinkles that experienced yacht navigators have found helpful, both in easing their burdens and improving their performance. Mine is by no means an all-inclusive list; as you gain experience yourself, you will discover a number of tricks of your own, and that is part of the pleasure to be found in the navigational art.

Planning ahead is useful in any navigational exercise, and this is particularly true in celestial navigation. One very good wrinkle, applicable to beginners and old hands alike, is to do as much preparation as possible before going on deck to take sights. This can include getting out the almanac and the appropriate volume of the sight reduction tables, checking the watch for the correct time, and in the case of star sights, preparing a list of the approximate altitudes and azimuths of the bodies you intend to shoot. If you are in an area with considerable magnetic variation, you may want to convert your azimuths to magnetic readings; it will be much easier to locate the star by the yacht's compass. It is also good practice to run up your dead-reckoning position on the chart or plotting sheet, so that there will be no delay in selecting the appropriate assumed latitude and longitude when it comes time to work the sight reduction. Because the sight reduction process requires the most time in the celestial procedure, if you are planning on using visual or electronic bearings to cross with your celestial line of position, it is often advantageous to take your bearings first, so there will not be an inordinate delay between supposedly "simultaneous" lines of position. All of these preparations are designed to allow the navigator to make his observations rapidly and with a minimum of distraction, and especially, to be able to work out the sights expeditiously, without being pressured by his shipmates' insistent, "You're the navigator. Where are we?"

As we have seen, the accuracy of any celestial line of position depends in large part on the accuracy of the original observation, and it is here that the navigator plays the major personal role. Anything that can contribute to improved performance is worth trying, and the simple effect of practice will improve most of your results. Some navigators get less accurate results than they should by being careless about their sextant's index error. A few professionals prefer to determine their index correction following a series of sights, but I have always found it best to get into the habit of checking it each time I go on deck and am setting up to make my observations. With a good sextant, properly cared for, the index error may change infrequently, but conditions on a small boat are never ideal for delicate equipment, and I have been surprised more than once by an unexpected change in the index error. Checking an index error takes a little practice; even the best navigators admit that they often make several tests to make sure of their findings.

Once on deck, finding a place on a small yacht from

which to take sights can be a challenge. When sailing, it is often necessary to use several stations in order to avoid having the observation blanketed by the sails or interfered with by the rigging. In heavy weather, it is desirable to station yourself as high as possible above the water surface without jeopardizing your stability or safety. This is both to avoid a false horizon created by the crests of nearby seas and to keep the sextant's optics from becoming clouded with spray. Since both hands are needed for the fine sextant adjustment, it can be helpful to hook on to the standing rigging with a safety harness, so that you can concentrate on the sight instead of fighting the motion of the boat. In any kind of a seaway, sights should be timed to take place as the vessel rises to the top of a wave, since the true horizon will also be at the distant wavetops. To overlook this point is to invite a significant error in the altitude you measure.

Earlier I explained the advantage of having a digital watch set to Greenwich mean time, and this advantage will be clearly apparent the first time you try to make an observation and take your own time from a bouncing deck. Rather than expose a fine timepiece to the elements, especially in wet conditions, I have found that a cheap, quartz wristwatch does the trick nicely, and it is only necessary to check it against an accurate timepiece once before you come on deck. If it is necessary to spend much time on deck in stormy weather, before or between sights, I have found it worthwhile to protect my sextant with a light, plastic bag. I used to use a lanyard attached to the sextant, and many navigators swear by the practice, but I found it to be one more thing to get in the way. I never let go of my sextant, nor set it down, except in its box, but even with all this care, I have succeeded in knocking it out of adjustment once or twice. If a sextant is unavoidably exposed to salt spray, it is good to remove the salt from the optical surfaces with a soft cloth dampened in fresh water. Be careful not to use coarse material, or to wipe the surfaces with a dry cloth as long as salt remains; it is very easy to scratch the lens or mirror faces.

A completely overcast sky makes it impossible to obtain workable sights, but one should never give up just because it's partly cloudy or hazy, or if the horizon is partially obscured. By lowering the height of eye as much as practicable—I have even done this by lying on deck—your horizon is brought closer; often close enough to gain adequate definition. By use of the sextant's shades, the fuzzy image of the sun may be seen well enough through the eyepiece to bring one limb to the horizon, even though it doesn't appear possible to the naked eye. In broken clouds, a common condition at sea, it is a good idea to be on deck and at the ready for that short interval when a body appears from behind a cloud, and you get off a quick shot. The three things to remember in these kinds of conditions are height of eye, sextant shades, and patience—the latter being the test of the experienced celestial navigator.

You have been cautioned about the potential eye damage that can occur if an index shade is not used for sun sights, particularly on a bright, sunny day. It is rare that at least the lightest shade isn't needed for a sun sight, so many careful navigators automatically swing a selected shade into place before even starting to locate the sun's image in the horizon mirror.

In Chapter 22, we discussed some of the problems involved in taking star sights, and the same problems also apply to the lesser planets. At either morning or evening twilight, objects near the eastern horizon should be observed first—in the evening, the eastern horizon darkens first, and in the morning, it becomes visible first. With all the celestial bodies, especially the planets and stars, it is desirable, when you have a choice, to concentrate on sights in the middle band of altitudes, between 15° and 70°. The problem with low-altitude sights is that the refraction is more critical, as a glance at the almanac table will confirm, and that the attenuated light passing through the earth's atmosphere at an oblique angle results in fainter images. At high altitudes, as a body approaches the zenith, it is difficult to find the point on the horizon directly beneath the observed body. When the sextant is rocked, the arc that the reflected image makes is so shallow that it is hard to determine the lowest point and to know that the sextant has been held absolutely vertically.

With regard to the horizontal dispersal of sights, you will recall that fixes resulting from lines of position that intersect at small angles are generally less reliable than those in which the angle of intersection approaches the ideal right angle. Because of this, it is preferable, whenever practical, to select bodies 30° or more apart. This objective should not be carried to extremes, however; it should apply when you have a free choice. With modern equipment and extra care, the results that can be obtained from observations near the limits are far more useful than none at all.

On the matter of extremes, the altitude correction tables in the *Nautical Almanac* (Figure 14–4) are based on average conditions of temperature (50°F.) and barometric pressure (29.83 inches) at sea level. This need only concern you in cases of major deviation from these norms, and then, principally for low-altitude observations. Table A4, at the front of the almanac, provides the additional refraction correction for nonstandard conditions, but it is seldom necessary to use it in normal yachting weather.

In making stellar observations, some navigators prefer morning to evening stars, the argument being that the sea is often calmer at dawn, and since you start with all the stars visible, identification is easier. There is also an advantage in having daylight in which to work the sights after you go below, but generally speaking, if you routinely plan your round of stars in advance and have

developed an average skill in taking star sights, the difference between observations at dawn and dusk is not of
great importance. The best way to identify stars, as we
have discussed, is to locate them beforehand by means of
Pub. No. 249 or the star-finder. In either case, you need to
calculate the local hour angle of Aries, and a quick way to
do this is to enter the ARIES column in the almanac's
daily page, substituting your local time for Greenwich
mean time, and reading the corresponding GHA Aries as
LHA Aries. The local hour angle, figured this way, is only
as accurate as your proximity to the standard meridian of
your time zone, and the wrinkle works easiest in West
longitudes, but the method is fast, and sufficiently accurate for star identification.

We have talked about thinking of the celestial procedure as a standard routine, with the minor variations
required for different bodies as exceptions. One advantage in doing this is that you develop a regular pattern for
using the tables. The correct page becomes easier to find
in a hurry, and you are much more likely to find all the
information required in a particular page opening
quicker, and with less chance of error. Some navigators
like to use bookmarks, or, in the almanac, to pencil out or
cut off the corners of the pages as they are used.

You may recall from Chapter 8 the technique in piloting for advancing lines of position to obtain a running fix.
The process works equally well with celestial position
lines, and it is the basis of a favorite routine of mine. The
routine is to take forenoon sights of the sun, within an
hour or two of local apparent noon, and to advance the
resulting lines of position to LAN in order to produce a
three-line, running fix. Figure 26–1 illustrates a typical
morning's work. A sun sight is taken at 1100, another at
1200, and a latitude line determined at local apparent
noon, at 1241. Since the vessel is traveling at 15 knots,
the 1100–line is advanced an estimated 25.3 nautical
miles along the course, and the 1200-line, an estimated

# POSITION PLOTTING SHEET

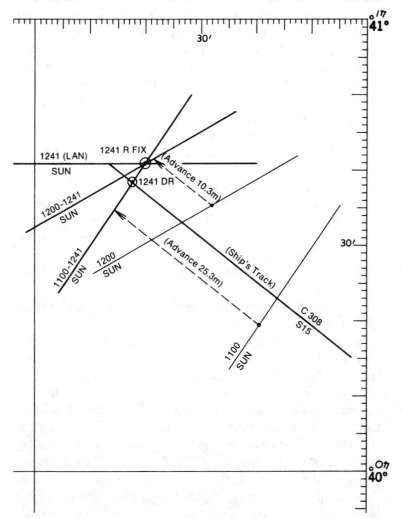

*Figure 26–1.* Morning sun lines, advanced and combined with a latitude observation at local apparent noon, produce a running fix.

10.3 miles. The intersection of the three position lines results in a 1241 running fix, located, in this case, about three miles northeast of the corresponding DR position.

The accuracy of any running fix is only as good as the estimate of the vessel's movement during the elapsed period, so a yacht navigator has to compromise between a short time interval between sights, and a longer interval, which allows a greater change in the sun's azimuth and produces a better angle of intersection at the fix.

Other useful sun lines—and this can apply to sights of other celestial bodies as well—are lines taken when the body's bearing is nearly ahead or astern of the vessel, with the resulting position line at right angles to the track. As in piloting, these are called "speed lines" because they determine the ship's progress along her track. The 1100-line in Figure 26–1 is an example of such a speed line. Similarly, sights taken when a body is abeam produce "course lines" because those position lines indicate whether you are to the right or left, or directly on your intended course. The valuable information such single lines of position can provide, short of a fix, should not be overlooked.

If you are using a calculator for sight reduction, and your dead-reckoning position as the assumed position, a single sight, by the length of its intercept, will give you an idea as to how close you are to your DR. If this is done at several DR positions, you can plot all the position lines from any one DR, creating, in effect, a running fix. A similar technique can be applied to positions obtained by Loran or other electronic means. If you use the electronic fix as your assumed position, a quick celestial observation can provide a good indication of the accuracy of the fix. If there is a large discrepancy, as indicated by large intercepts, it is a good idea to start a series of sights in order to determine whether you made a mistake in your observation, or if the electronic data are in error.

The two signs that are the mark of a proficient navigator are a neat, carefully labeled plot, and a well-organized workbook. There are many choices of workforms, as we have discussed, and as a guide, sample forms for the sights we have examined are included in the Appendix. Forms such as these may be combined into one universal form, they may be prepared in pads, or in a looseleaf notebook, or placed on strips to be used as bookmarks in the margins of a blank notebook. The choice, as well as the opportunity to make improvements of your own, is up to you.

At the risk of sounding contradictory, I should like to suggest that an accomplished navigator resists the temptation to overnavigate. By this I mean engaging the entire ship's company in the act, or making a large-scale production out of a routine exercise. The objective is not to impress the crew with your own navigational acumen, nor to overdramatize the procedures; your fellow crew members will become bored, if not annoyed, and may not take you seriously in time of need. The calm, professional approach is always best.

Throughout this book the emphasis has been on the practice and methods for navigating in a thoroughly competent manner, and the disciplines for doing this have been stressed. Yet one should never lose sight of the crowning personal satisfaction and pride that comes from a job well done—a demanding passage at sea made safely and according to plan.

# Glossary

**Almanac**—A publication containing the astronomical data required for the practice of celestial navigation, arranged by calendar date and time interval. The *Nautical Almanac*, recommended in this text, supplies the information from which the Greenwich hour angle and declination of the principal celestial bodies can be determined for any instant of time.

**Altitude Difference** (a)—The difference between the observed altitude (Ho) and the computed altitude (Hc); commonly called the intercept.

**Apparent Altitude** *(App. Alt.* or ha)—The sextant altitude (hs) corrected for index error and dip.

**Arc Distance**—The distance measured along a curve; in celestial navigation usually a portion of a great circle.

**Assumed Latitude** (aL)—The latitude at which the observer is assumed to be for the purpose of calculating the computed altitude (Hc) of a celestial body. Usually selected to the nearest whole degree.

**Assumed Longitude** (aλ)—The longitude at which the observer is assumed to be for the purpose of calculating the computed altitude (Hc) of a celestial body.

Usually selected so that the local hour angle (LHA) works out to a whole degree.

**Assumed Position** (AP)—The position assumed for calculating the computed altitude (Hc) of a celestial body, and the point from which the altitude difference, or intercept (a) is plotted.

**Azimuth** (Z and Zn)—The uncorrected azimuth (Z), also called azimuth angle, is measured from North (0°) or South (180°), clockwise or counterclockwise, through 180°. The corrected, or true, azimuth (Zn) is measured from North (0°) clockwise through 360°.

**Bearing**—The horizontal direction of a line between two points on the surface of the earth.

**Binnacle**—The base or stand in which a compass is housed.

**Celestial Sphere**—An imaginary sphere, concentric with the earth and with the earth at its center, on which all the celestial bodies are presumed to be projected.

**Characteristic**—The identifying color and period of a light; the identifying signal of a sound device or radiobeacon.

**Chart Sounding Datum**—The state or level of the tide to which all charted soundings are referenced.

**Coaltitude**—90° minus the altitude; also called the zenith distance (z).

**Colatitude**—90° minus the latitude.

**Computed Altitude** (Hc)—The altitude of a celestial body at a given time and position as determined by computation.

**Course**—The direction of travel, also called the track, usually stated as a compass direction.

**Critical Table**—A table in which a single value is tabulated for the limiting increments of the entry values as, for example, the *Nautical Almanac's* dip and altitude correction tables.

**Current**—The sum of the elements diverting a vessel

from its intended track; the hypothetical set and drift accounting for the difference between the dead-reckoning position and a concurrent fix.

**Danger Angle**—The bearing, as observed from a vessel, that limits the safe approach to an off-lying danger.

**Dead Reckoning** (DR)—The process of establishing a position by applying courses and distances sailed from the last known position.

**Declination** (Dec or dec)—The angular distance north or south of the celestial equator, corresponding to latitude on earth. The abbreviation $d$ is used in the almanac to indicate the hourly change in declination.

**Departure**—The point or position from which a voyage, and the dead-reckoning plot, commences.

**Deviation**—The difference between the magnetic direction and the compass reading; a function of the vessel's magnetic field.

**Dip** (D)—The angle between the true horizontal and the observer's line of sight to the visible horizon.

**Drift**—The rate of flow of a current.

**Equation of Time**—The difference between the time of the mean sun and the apparent solar, or sundial time. While the equation of time may be positive or negative, it never exceeds 16.4 minutes.

**Estimated Position** (EP)—The most probable position of a vessel, short of a fix, determined by applying current data or other correcting information to the position determined by dead reckoning.

**Estimated Time of Arrival** (ETA)—The time of arrival of a vessel at a designated destination, as determined by projecting the speed of advance of the vessel.

**First Point of Aries**(♈)—The point at which the sun's path intersects the celestial equator as it changes from south to north declination at the Vernal Equinox. Values for the Greenwich hour angle of Aries are tabulated in the daily pages of the almanac as if it

were a celestial body, and the positions of all the stars
are measured westward from that point by their Sidereal hour angles.

**Fix**—A position, determined without reference to a previous position, usually resulting from the intersection of two or more lines of position. A *running fix* is
a position derived from lines of position taken at
different times and advanced (or retired) to a common time.

**Geographical Position** (GP)—The point on earth directly
beneath a celestial body.

**Great Circle**—The circle formed by the intersection of a
plane passing through the center of a sphere with the
surface of the sphere.

**Greenwich Hour Angle** (GHA)—The angular distance
measured westward from the meridian of Greenwich
(0°) on the celestial sphere. Corresponds to longitude
on earth. The small case abbreviation (gha) is often
used to identify the uncorrected tabular value extracted from the GHA column in the almanac's daily
pages.

**Greenwich Mean Time** (GMT)—Local mean time at the
meridian of Greenwich (0°). Time signals, broadcast
as Coordinated Universal Time (UTC), may vary by a
fraction of a second from GMT as a result of irregular
rotation of the earth. For practical purposes, navigators use the two times interchangeably.

**Horizon Glass**—The half-mirrored glass, attached to the
frame of a sextant, through which the horizon is
viewed.

**Horizon Shades**—The darkened glass that can be moved
into place to reduce the intensity of light passing
through the clear portion of the horizon glass.

**Horizontal Parallax** (H.P.)—The difference in altitude
between that measured from the observer's position
on the surface of the earth and that measured from

the center of the earth. Of primary interest to the navigator in correcting altitudes of the moon, where the value is of significance because of the relative closeness of the moon to the earth, an additional correction for it must be taken from the almanac.

**Index Arm**—The movable arm of a sextant.

**Index Correction** (IC)—The value that must be applied to correct the index error (failure to read exactly zero when the true and reflected images are in coincidence) of a sextant. Usually confirmed before or after each series of observations.

**Index Shades**—The darkened glass that can be moved into place between the mirror on the index arm and the eyepiece to reduce the intensity of the reflected image of a celestial body. It is essential that the reflection of the sun's image be reduced in intensity by use of the index shades as, otherwise, injury can result to the unprotected eye.

**Inspection Tables**—A volume of tabulated solutions from which an answer can be extracted by simple inspection.

**Intercept** (a)—The difference between the observed altitude (Ho) and the computed altitude (Hc).

**Interpolation**—The process of determining intermediate values between given, tabular values.

**Latitude**—The angular distance north or south of the equator.

**Leading Light**—A light so located that vessels may steer directly for it until close aboard (when a new course is taken). Also called a leading mark.

**Limb** (of a celestial body)—The body's circular, outer edge.

**Line of Position**—"A line on some point of which a vessel may be presumed to be located as a result of observation or measurement"—Bowditch.

**Local Apparent Noon** (LAN)—That moment when the

sun crosses the observer's meridian and is at its
maximum altitude for the day.

**Local Hour Angle** (LHA)—The angular distance measured westward from the observer's meridian on the
celestial sphere.

**Longitude**—The angular distance east or west of the
Prime Meridian, (0°), located at Greenwich, England.

**Loran**—A radio-navigation system operating on the principle that the difference in the time of arrival of radio
pulses from two precisely synchronized transmitting
stations describes a hyperbolic line of position.

**Lubber's Line**—The index, aligned with the ship's head,
against which the compass card is read.

**Main Arc**—That part of a sextant upon which the readings in degrees are inscribed. Sometimes called "the
limb."

**Mercator Projection**—A projection, named after its in-
ventor, a Flemish geographer of the sixteenth century, in which the coordinates on earth are conceived
as projected on a cylinder tangent to the earth at the
equator. Classified by type, it is an *equatorial cylindrical orthomorphic* projection.

**Meridian**—A great circle through the geographical poles
of the earth. The meridian of Greenwich (0°) is called
the *Prime Meridian.*

**Meridian Passage** (Mer Pass)—The time of meridian passage; when a celestial body crosses a given meridian.

**Micrometer Drum**—A device for making precise, small
measurements on a sextant. The mechanism is also
referred to as an endless tangent screw, and a sextant
so equipped is an ETS sextant.

**Navigational Triangle**—The spherical triangle whose
points are the elevated pole, the celestial body, and
the zenith of the observer projected on earth, which is
solved in determining computed altitude (Hc) and
azimuth.

**Noon Sight**—Observation of the sun's altitude at local apparent noon.

**Observed Altitude** (Ho)—The apparent altitude (ha) corrected for refraction (R), and in the case of the moon, additionally for Horizontal Parallax (H.P.).

**Parallel**—A common name for a circle on earth, parallel with the equator, connecting all points of equal latitude.

**Piloting**—"Navigation involving frequent or continuous determination of position or a line of position relative to geographical points, to a high degree of accuracy"—Bowditch.

**Pilot Waters**—Waters, usually inshore, in which navigation is performed by piloting.

**Polar Distance**—The angular distance from the celestial pole; in celestial navigation, 90° minus the declination.

**Polaris**—The Pole Star, located less than 1° from the North Celestial Pole in the constellation Ursa Minor. Useful for a special-case latitude determination.

**Radar**—A radio-location system in which transmission and reception take place at the same location, and which utilizes the radio-reflecting properties of objects to determine their positions.

**Range**—Two or more objects in line, or the distance of an object from an observer.

**Refraction** (R)—The correction due to the bending of light rays passing obliquely through the earth's atmosphere. The refraction correction in the *Nautical Almanac* includes, for the convenience of a single-entry solution, other elements such as semidiameter.

**Rhumb Line**—A line on the earth's surface that makes the same oblique angle with all the meridians.

**Semidiameter** (SD)—The angular distance from the center of a celestial body of finite diameter (e.g. the sun) to its outer edge or limb.

**Set**—The direction toward which a current flows.

**Sextant Altitude** (hs)—The uncorrected altitude of a celestial body as measured directly by sextant observation.

**Sidereal Hour Angle** (SHA)—The angular distance measured westward on the celestial sphere, from the First Point of Aries through 360°.

**Sight Reduction Tables**—Tables for solving the navigational triangle for computed altitude (Hc) and azimuth (Zn). Pub. No. 249, *Sight Reduction Tables for Air Navigation,* is used in this text.

**Soundings**—The measured or charted depths of the water.

**Speed Made Good**—The speed actually made good over the track, regardless of the speed through the water.

**Standard Meridian**—A central meridian selected for a time zone, located at multiples of 15° longitude east or west of Greenwich (0°).

**Tabular Difference** (d) The difference between the tabulated altitudes in a sight reduction table for successive degrees of declination. Used for purposes of interpolation.

**Tabulated Altitude** (Tab Hc)—The uncorrected value of Hc as extracted from the sight reduction table.

**Variable Correction** (v)—Small, additional corrections due to excesses of actual movement over the constant rates used in the body of the *Increments and Corrections* tables in the almanac.

**Variation**—The difference between true and magnetic direction.

**Vector**—A straight line representing direction by its orientation and magnitude by its length.

**Vernier**—A scale for precise, small readings on a sextant.

**Watch Time** (W)—The time registered on the navigator's watch or clock.

**Zenith**—That point on the celestial sphere directly over the observer.

**Zenith Distance** (z)—The angular distance from the zenith. In celestial navigation: 90° minus the altitude—also called coaltitude.

**Zone Description** (ZD)—The number of whole hours that are added to or subtracted from the zone time to obtain Greenwich mean time.

# Appendix I

# Chart No. 1

United States of America

# Nautical Chart Symbols and Abbreviations

Eighth Edition
NOVEMBER 1984

Prepared jointly by

**DEPARTMENT OF COMMERCE**
**National Oceanic and Atmospheric Administration**
National Ocean Service

**DEPARTMENT OF DEFENSE**
**Defense Mapping Agency**
Hydrographic/Topographic Center

Published at Washington, D.C.
**DEPARTMENT OF COMMERCE**
National Oceanic and Atmospheric Administration
National Ocean Service
Washington, D.C. 20230

# INTRODUCTION

**General Remarks**—This publication (Chart No. 1) contains symbols and abbreviations that have been approved for use on nautical charts published by the United States of America. A Glossary of Terms used on the charts of various nations is also included. The user should refer to DMAHTC Pub. No. 9, **American Practical Navigator** (Bowditch), Volume I, for the use of the chart in the practice of navigation and more detailed information pertaining to the chart sounding datum, tides and currents, visual and audible aids to navigation, etc.

**Numbering**—Terms, symbols, and abbreviations are numbered in accordance with a standard format approved by a 1952 resolution of the International Hydrographic Organization (IHO). Although the use of IHO-approved symbols and abbreviations is not mandatory, the United States has adopted many IHO-approved symbols for standard use. Style differences of the alphanumeric identifiers in the first column of the following pages show the status of symbols and abbreviations.

VERTICAL FIGURES indicate those items for which the symbols and abbreviations are in accordance with resolutions of IHO.

SLANTING FIGURES indicate those symbols for which no IHO resolution has been adopted.

SLANTING FIGURES ASTERISKED indicate IHO and U.S. symbols do not agree.

SLANTING LETTERS IN PARENTHESIS indicate that the items are in addition to those appearing in the IHO STANDARD LIST OF SYMBOLS AND ABBREVIATIONS.

**Metric Charts and Feet/Fathom Charts**—In January 1972 the United States began producing certain new nautical charts in meters. Since then many charts have been issued with soundings and contours in meters; however, for some time to come there will still be many charts on issue depicting sounding units in feet or fathoms. Modified reproductions of foreign charts are being produced retaining the native sounding unit value. The sounding unit is stated in bold type outside the border of every chart and in the chart title.

**Chart Modernization**—Chart symbols and labeling are brought into reasonable agreement with uniform international charting standards and procedures as quickly as opportunity affords. An example of this is the trend toward using vertical type for labeling items referred to the shoreline plane of reference, and slant type for all items referred to the sounding datum. This is not completely illustrated in this publication but is reflected in new charts produced by this country in accordance with international practices.

**Soundings**—The sounding datum reference is stated in the chart title. In all cases the unit of depth used is shown in the chart title and in the border of the chart in bold type.

**Drying Heights**—On rocks and banks that cover and uncover the elevations are above the sounding datum as stated in the chart title.

**Shoreline**—Shoreline shown on charts represents the line of contact between the land and a selected water elevation. In areas affected by tidal fluctuation, this line of contact is usually the mean high-water line. In confined coastal waters of diminished tidal influence, a mean water level line may be used. The shoreline of interior waters (rivers, lakes) is usually a line representing a specified elevation above a selected datum. Shoreline is symbolized by a heavy line (A9).

Apparent Shoreline is used on charts to show the outer edge of marine vegetation where that limit would reasonably appear as the shoreline to the mariner or where it prevents the shoreline from being clearly defined. Apparent shoreline is symbolized by a light line (A7, C17).

**Landmarks**—A conspicuous feature on a building may be shown by a landmark symbol with a descriptive label. (See I 8b, 36, 44, 72.) Prominent buildings that are of assistance to the mariner may be shown by actual shape as viewed from above (See I 3a, 19, 47, 66). Legends associated with landmarks when shown in capital letters, indicate conspicuous or the landmarks may be labeled "CONSPIC" or "CONSPICUOUS."

**Buoys**—The buoyage systems used by other countries often vary from that used by the United States. U.S. Charts show the colors, lights and other characteristics in use for the area of the individual chart. Certain U.S. distributed modified reproduction charts of foreign waters may show shapes and other distinctive features that vary from those illustrated in this chart.

In the U.S. system, on entering a channel from seaward, buoys on the starboard side are red with even numbers, on the port side, black or green with odd numbers. Lights on buoys on the starboard side of the channel are red or white, on the port side, white or green. Mid-channel buoys have red and white or black and white vertical stripes and may be passed on either side. Junction or obstruction buoys have red and green or red and black horizontal bands, the top band color indicating the preferred side of passage. This system does not apply to foreign waters.

**IALA Buoyage System**—The International Association of Lighthouse Authorities (IALA) Maritime Buoyage System (combined Cardinal-Lateral System) is being implemented by nearly every maritime buoyage jurisdiction worldwide as either REGION A buoyage (red to port) or REGION B buoyage (red to starboard). The terms "REGION A" and "REGION B" will be used to determine which type of buoyage is in effect or undergoing conversion in a particular area. The major difference in the two buoyage regions will be in the lateral marks. In REGION A they will be red to port; in REGION B they will be red to starboard. Shapes of lateral marks will be the same in both REGIONS, can to port; cone (nun) to starboard. Cardinal and other marks will continue to follow current guidelines and may be found in both REGIONS. A modified lateral mark, indicating the preferred channel where a channel divides, will be introduced for use in both REGIONS.

**Aids to Navigation Positioning**—The aids to navigation depicted on charts comprise a system consisting of fixed and floating aids with varying degrees of reliability. Therefore, prudent mariners will not rely solely on any single aid to navigation, particularly a floating aid.

The buoy symbol is used to indicate the approximate position of the buoy body and the sinker which secures the buoy to the seabed. The approximate position is used because of practical limitations in positioning and maintaining buoys and their sinkers in precise geographical locations. These limitations include, but are not limited to, inherent imprecisions in position fixing methods, prevailing atmospheric and sea conditions, the slope of and the material making up the seabed, the fact that buoys are moored to sinkers by varying lengths of chain, and the fact that buoy body and/or sinker positions are not under continuous surveillance but are normally checked only during periodic maintenance visits which often occur more than a year apart. The position of the buoy body can be expected to shift inside and outside the charting symbol due to the forces of nature. The mariner is also cautioned that buoys are liable to be carried away, shifted, capsized, sunk, etc. Lighted buoys may be extinguished or sound signals may not function as the result of ice, running ice, other natural causes, collisions, or other accidents.

For the foregoing reasons a prudent mariner must not rely completely upon the position or operation of floating aids to navigation, but will also utilize bearings from fixed objects and aids to navigation on shore. Further, a vessel attempting to pass close aboard always risks collision with a yawing buoy or with the obstruction the buoy marks.

**Colors**—Colors are optional for characterizing various features and areas on the charts. For instance the land tint in this publication is gold as used on charts of the National Ocean Service; however, charts of the DMA show land tint as gray.

**Heights**—Heights of lights, landmarks, structures, etc. are referred to the shoreline plane of reference. Heights of small islets or offshore rocks, which due to space limitations must be placed in the water area, are bracketed. The unit of height used is shown in the chart title.

**Conversion Scales**—Depth conversion scales are provided on all charts to enable the user to work in meters, fathoms, or feet.

**Improved Channels**—Improved channels are shown by dashed limit lines with the depth and date of the latest examination placed adjacent to the channel or in a channel tabulation.

**Longitudes**—Longitudes are referred to the meridian of Greenwich.

**Traffic Separation Schemes**—Traffic separation schemes show established routes to increase safety of navigation, particularly in areas of high density shipping. These schemes were established by the International Maritime Organization (IMO) and are described in the IMO publication "Ships Routing".

Traffic separation schemes are generally shown on nautical charts at scales of 1:600,000, and larger. When possible, traffic separation schemes are plotted to scale and shown as depicted in Section P.

**Names**—Names on nautical charts compiled and published by the United States of America are in accordance with the principles of the Board of Geographic Names.

**Correction Dates**—The dates of New Editions are shown below the lower left border of the chart. These include the date of the latest Notice to Mariners applied to the charts.

**U.S. Coast Pilots, Sailing Directions, Light Lists, Lists of Lights**—These related publications furnish information required by the navigator that cannot be shown conveniently on the nautical charts.

**U.S. Nautical Chart Catalogs and Indexes**—These list nautical charts, auxiliary maps, and related publications and include general information relative to the use and ordering of charts.

# TABLE OF CONTENTS

## A   The Coastline

1  Coast, inadequately surveyed (Approximate shoreline)

•7  Mangroves; Apparent shoreline and mangrove vegetation limit

11d  Rock (uncovers at sounding datum)

high   low
•2  Steep coast

8  Surveyed coastline

•11e  Sand and Mud

2a  Flat coast

9  Shoreline

•11f  Sand and gravel

3  Cliffy coast

Uncovers
10  Chart sounding datum line

11g  Coral (uncovers at sounding datum)

3a  Rocky coast

(Aa)  Approximate sounding datum line

Breakers   Breakers
(if extensive)
12  Breakers along a shore

4  Sandhills; Dunes

11  Foreshore; Strand (in general)

Mud
•11a  Mud

Unsurveyed
12   13   11
17
14  Limit of unsurveyed areas

5  Stony or shingly shore

Sand
•11b  Sand

(Ab)  Rubble

6  Sandy shore

Gravel
•11c  Stones; Shingle; Gravel

## B Coast Features

| | | |
|---|---|---|
| 1 | G | Gulf |
| 2 | B | Bay |
| (Ba) | B | Bayou |
| 3 | Fd | Fjord |
| 4 | L | Loch; Lough; Lake |
| 5 | Cr | Creek |
| 5a | C | Cove |
| 6 | In | Inlet |
| 7 | Str | Strait |
| 8 | Sd | Sound |
| 9 | Pass | Passage; Pass |
| | Thoro | Thoroughfare |
| 10 | Chan | Channel |
| 10a | | Narrows |
| 11 | Entr | Entrance |
| 12 | Est | Estuary |
| 12a | | Delta |
| 13 | Mth | Mouth |
| 14 | Rd | Road; Roadstead |
| 15 | Anch | Anchorage |
| 16 | Hbr | Harbor |
| 16a | Hn | Haven |
| 17 | P | Port |
| (Bb) | P | Pond |
| 18 | I | Island |
| 19 | It | Islet |
| 20 | Arch | Archipelago |
| 21 | Pen | Peninsula |
| 22 | C | Cape |
| 23 | Prom | Promontory |
| 24 | Hd | Head; Headland |
| 25 | Pt | Point |
| 26 | Mt | Mountain; Mount |
| 27 | Rge | Range |
| 27a | | Valley |
| 28 | | Summit |
| 29 | Pk | Peak |
| 30 | Vol | Volcano |
| 31 | | Hill |
| 32 | Bld | Boulder |
| 33 | Ldg | Landing |
| | Lndg | Landing |
| 34 | | Tableland |
| | | Plateau |
| 35 | R, Rk, Rks | Rock, Rocks |
| 36 | | Isolated rock |
| (Bc) | Str | Stream |
| (Bd) | R | River |
| (Be) | Slu | Slough |
| (Bf) | Lag | Lagoon |
| (Bg) | Apprs | Approaches |
| (Bh) | Rky | Rocky |
| (Bi) | Is | Islands |
| (Bj) | Ma | Marsh |
| (Bk) | Mg | Mangrove |
| (Bl) | Sw | Swamp |

## C The Land

1 Contour lines (Contours)

1a Contour lines, approximate (Contours)

2 Hachures

2a Form lines, no definite interval

2b Shading

3 Glacier

4 Saltpans

5 Isolated trees

5a Deciduous; of unknown or unspecified type

5b Coniferous

5c Palm tree

5d Nipa palm

5e Filao

5f Casuarina

5g Evergreen tree (other than coniferous)

6 Cultivated fields

6a Grass fields

7 Paddy (rice) fields

7a Park; Garden

8 Bushes

8a Tree plantation in general

9 Deciduous woodland

10 Coniferous woodland

10a Woods in general

11 Tree top elevation (above shoreline datum)

12 Lava flow

13 River; Stream

14 Intermittent stream

15 Lake; Pond

16 Lagoon (Lag)

17 Marsh; Swamp

18 Slough (Slu.)

19 Rapids

20 Waterfalls

21 Spring

## D    Control Points

| | | | | | | |
|---|---|---|---|---|---|---|
| 1 | ▲ | Triangulation point (station) | 4 | ● Obs Spot | Observation spot | |
| 1a | | Astronomic station | 5 | ⊤ o BM | Bench mark | |
| 2 | ⊙ | Fixed point (landmark, position accurate) | 6 | View X | View point | |
| | | | 7 | | Datum point for grid of a plan | |
| (Da) | o | Fixed point (landmark, position approximate) | 8 | | Graphical triangulation point | |
| 3 | · 256 | Summit of height (Peak) (when not a landmark) | 9 | Astro | Astronomical | |
| | | | 10 | Tri | Triangulation | |
| (Db) | ◉ 256 | Peak, accentuated by contours | (Df) | C of E | Corps of Engineers | |
| (Dc) | ✺ 256 | Peak, accentuated by hachures | 12 | | Great trigonometrical survey station | |
| (Dd) | ◊ | Peak, elevation not determined | 13 | | Traverse station | |
| | | | 14 | Bdy Mon | Boundary monument | |
| (De) | ⊙ 256 | Peak, when a landmark | (Dg) | ◈ | International boundary monument | |

## E    Units

| | | | | | | | | | |
|---|---|---|---|---|---|---|---|---|---|
| 1 | hr, h | Hour | 11 | M, Mi / NMi, NM | Nautical mile(s) | 21 | ′ | Minute (of arc) | |
| 2 | m, min | Minute (of time) | 12 | kn | Knot(s) | 22 | ″ | Second (of arc) | |
| 3 | sec, s | Second (of time) | 12a | t | Tonne (metric ton equals 2,204.6 lbs) | 23 | No | Number | |
| 4 | m | Meter | | | | (Ea) | St M, St Mi | Statute mile | |
| 4a | dm | Decimeter | 12b | cd | Candela (new candle) | (Eb) | μsec, μs | Microsecond | |
| 4b | cm | Centimeter | 13 | lat | Latitude | (Ec) | Hz | Hertz (cps) | |
| 4c | mm | Millimeter | 14 | long | Longitude | (Ed) | kHz | Kilohertz (kc) | |
| 4d | m² | Square meter | 14a | | Greenwich | (Ee) | MHz | Megahertz (Mc) | |
| 4e | m³ | Cubic meter | 15 | pub | Publication | (Ef) | cps, c/s | Cycles/second (Hz) | |
| 5 | km | Kilometer(s) | 16 | Ed | Edition | (Eg) | kc | Kilocycle (kHz) | |
| 6 | in, ins | Inch(es) | 17 | corr | Correction | (Eh) | Mc | Megacycle (MHz) | |
| 7 | ft | Foot, feet | 18 | alt | Altitude | (Ei) | T | Ton (U.S. short ton equals 2,000 lbs) | |
| 8 | yd, yds | Yard(s) | 19 | ht; elev | Height; Elevation | | | | |
| 9 | fm, fms | Fathom(s) | 20 | ° | Degree | | | | |
| 10 | cbl | Cable length | | | | | | | |

## F    Adjectives, Adverbs, Nouns, and Other Words

| | | | | | | | | |
|---|---|---|---|---|---|---|---|---|
| 1 | gt | Great | 25 | discontd | Discontinued | (Fe) | cor | Corner |
| 2 | lit | Little | 26 | prohib | Prohibited | (Ff) | concr | Concrete |
| 3 | Lrg | Large | 27 | explos | Explosive | (Fg) | fl | Flood |
| 4 | sml | Small | 28 | estab | Established | (Fh) | mod | Moderate |
| 5 | | Outer | 29 | elec | Electric | (Fi) | bet | Between |
| 6 | | Inner | 30 | priv | Private, Privately | (Fj) | 1st | First |
| 7 | mid | Middle | 31 | prom | Prominent | (Fk) | 2nd, 2d | Second |
| 8 | | Old | 32 | std | Standard | (Fl) | 3rd, 3d | Third |
| 9 | anc | Ancient | 33 | subm | Submerged | (Fm) | 4th | Fourth |
| 10 | | New | 34 | approx | Approximate | (Fn) | DW | Deep Water |
| 11 | St | Saint | 35 | | Maritime | (Fo) | min | Minimum |
| 12 | CONSPIC | Conspicuous | 36 | maintd | Maintained | (Fp) | max | Maximum |
| 13 | | Remarkable | 37 | aband | Abandoned | (Fq) | N'ly | Northerly |
| 14 | D, Destr | Destroyed | 38 | temp | Temporary | (Fr) | S'ly | Southerly |
| 15 | | Projected | 39 | occas | Occasional | (Fs) | E'ly | Easterly |
| 16 | dist | Distant | 40 | extr | Extreme | (Ft) | W'ly | Westerly |
| 17 | abt | About | 41 | | Navigable | (Fu) | Sk | Stroke |
| 18 | | See chart | 42 | N M | Notice to Mariners | (Fv) | Restr | Restricted |
| 18a | | See plan | (Fa) | L N M | Local Notice to Mariners | (Fw) | Bl | Blast |
| 19 | | Lighted, Luminous | | | | (Fx) | CFR | Code of Federal Regulations |
| 20 | sub | Submarine | 43 | | Sailing Directions | (Fy) | COLREGS | Int'l Regulations for Preventing Collisions at Sea, 1972 |
| 21 | | Eventual | 44 | | List of Lights | | | |
| 22 | AERO | Aeronautical | (Fb) | unverd | Unverified | | | |
| 23 | | Higher | (Fc) | AUTH | Authorized | (Fz) | IWW | Intracoastal Waterway |
| 23a | | Lower | (Fd) | CL | Clearance | | | |
| 24 | exper | Experimental | | | | | | |

## G    Ports and Harbors

| | | | |
|---|---|---|---|
| 1 | | Anch | Anchorage (large vessels) |
| 2 | | Anch | Anchorage (small vessels) |
| 3 | | Hbr | Harbor |
| 4 | | Hn | Haven |
| 5 | | P | Port |
| 6 | | Bkw | Breakwater |
| 6a | | | Dike |
| 7 | | | Mole |
| 8 | | | Jetty (partly below MHW) |
| 8a | | | Submerged jetty |
| (Ga) | | | Jetty (small scale) |
| 9 | | Pier | Pier |
| 10 | | | Spit |
| 11 | | | Groin (partly below MHW) |
| •12 | ANCH PROHIBITED | ANCH PROHIB | Anchorage prohibited (Screen optional) |
| 12a | | | Anchorage reserved |
| 12b | QUARANTINE ANCHORAGE | QUAR ANCH | Quarantine anchorage |
| •12c | | | Quarantine Anchorage |
| •12d | | | Quarantine Anchorage |
| •12e | | FISH PROHIB | Fishing prohibited |
| 13 | Spoil Area | | Spoil ground (Dump Site) |
| (Gb) | Dumping Ground | | Dumping ground (depths may be less than indicated) (Dump Site) |
| (Gc) | Disposal Area 92 depths from survey of JUNE 1972 85 90    87 | | Disposal area (Dump Site) |
| (Gd) | ℗ | | Pump-out facilities |

| | | | |
|---|---|---|---|
| 14 | | Fsh stks | Fisheries; Fishing stakes |
| 14a | | | Fish trap; Fish weirs (actual shape charted) |
| 14b | | | Duck blind |
| 15 | | | Tunny nets |
| 15a | | Oys | Oyster bed |
| 16 | | Ldg,Lndg | Landing place |
| 17 | | | Watering place |
| 18 | | Whf | Wharf |
| 19 | | | Quay |
| 20 | Ⓐ  ⑭ | | Berth |
| •20a | ⑭  ⑭  Ⓑ | | Anchoring berth |
| 20b | 3 | | Berth number |
| 21 | Dol | | Dolphin |
| 22 | | | Bollard |
| 22a | SPM | | Fixed single point mooring structure (lighted) |
| 23 | | | Mooring ring |
| 24 | ⊖ | | Crane |
| 25 | | | Landing stage |
| 25a | | | Landing stairs |
| 26 | Quar | | Quarantine |
| 27 | | | Lazaret |
| 28 | Harbor Master  Hbr Mr | | Harbormaster's office |
| 29 | ⊖ Cus Ho | | Customhouse |
| 30 | | | Fishing harbor |
| 31 | | | Winter harbor |
| 32 | | | Refuge harbor |
| 33 | B Hbr | | Boat harbor |
| 34 | | | Stranding harbor (uncovers at LW) |
| 35 | | | Dock |
| 36 | | | Drydock (actual shape on large scale charts) |
| 37 | | | Floating dock (actual shape on large scale charts) |
| 38 | | | Gridiron; Careening grid |

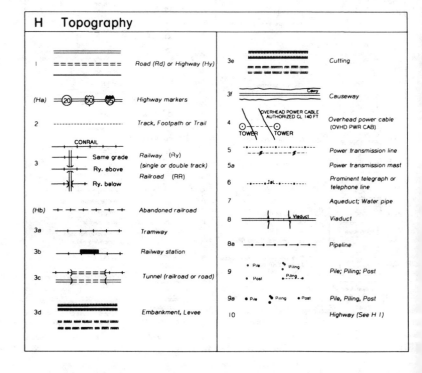

# G    Ports and Harbors

| | | |
|---|---|---|
| 39 | | Patent slip; Slipway; Marine railway |
| 39a | Ramp | Ramp |
| 40 | | Lock (point upstream) |
| 41 | | Wetdock |
| 42 | | Shipyard |
| 43 | | Lumber yard |
| 44 | Health Office | Health officer's office |
| 45 | Hk | Hulk (actual shape on large |
| 45a | | scale charts) |
| • 46 | PROHIBITED AREA / PROHIB AREA | Prohibited area (screen optional) |

| | | |
|---|---|---|
| 46a | 10 | Calling-in point for vessel traffic control |
| 47 | | Anchorage for seaplanes |
| 48 | | Seaplane landing area |
| • 49 / • 50 | Under construction | Work in progress / Under construction |
| 51 | | Work projected |
| (Ge) | Subm ruins | Submerged ruins |
| (Gf) | Dump site | Dump site |

# H    Topography

| | | |
|---|---|---|
| 1 | | Road (Rd) or Highway (Hy) |
| (Ha) | 20  50  95 | Highway markers |
| 2 | | Track, Footpath or Trail |
| 3 | CONRAIL — Same grade / Ry. above / Ry. below | Railway (Ry) (single or double track) / Railroad (RR) |
| (Hb) | | Abandoned railroad |
| 3a | | Tramway |
| 3b | | Railway station |
| 3c | | Tunnel (railroad or road) |
| 3d | | Embankment, Levee |

| | | |
|---|---|---|
| 3e | | Cutting |
| 3f | Cswy | Causeway |
| 4 | OVERHEAD POWER CABLE AUTHORIZED CL 140 FT / TOWER  TOWER | Overhead power cable (OVHD PWR CAB) |
| 5 | | Power transmission line |
| 5a | | Power transmission mast |
| 6 | Tel | Prominent telegraph or telephone line |
| 7 | | Aqueduct; Water pipe |
| 8 | Viaduct | Viaduct |
| 8a | | Pipeline |
| 9 | Pile / Piling / Post / Piling | Pile; Piling; Post |
| 9a | Pile  Piling  Post | Pile, Piling, Post |
| 10 | | Highway (See H 1) |

## H   Topography

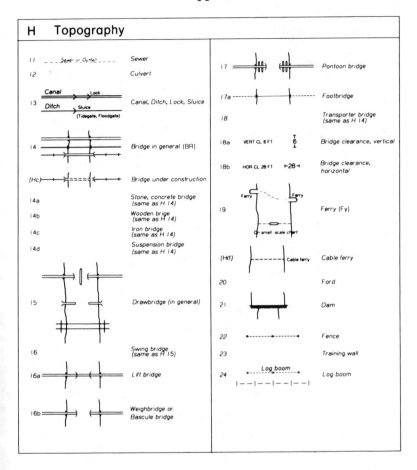

| | |
|---|---|
| 11 | Sewer |
| 12 | Culvert |
| 13 | Canal, Ditch, Lock, Sluice |
| 14 | Bridge in general (BR) |
| (Hc) | Bridge under construction |
| 14a | Stone, concrete bridge (same as H 14) |
| 14b | Wooden brige (same as H 14) |
| 14c | Iron bridge (same as H 14) |
| 14d | Suspension bridge (same as H 14) |
| 15 | Drawbridge (in general) |
| 16 | Swing bridge (same as H 15) |
| 16a | Lift bridge |
| 16b | Weighbridge or Bascule bridge |
| 17 | Pontoon bridge |
| 17a | Footbridge |
| 18 | Transporter bridge (same as H 14) |
| 18a | Bridge clearance, vertical |
| 18b | Bridge clearance, horizontal |
| 19 | Ferry (Fy) |
| (Hd) | Cable ferry |
| 20 | Ford |
| 21 | Dam |
| 22 | Fence |
| 23 | Training wall |
| 24 | Log boom |

## I  Buildings and Structures

| No. | Symbol | Description |
|---|---|---|
| 1 | | City or Town (large scale) |
| (1a) | | City or Town (small scale) |
| 1a | (30) | Height of a structure |
| 2 | | Suburb |
| 3 | Vil | Village |
| 3a | | Buildings in general |
| 4 | Cas | Castle |
| 5 | | House |
| 6 | | Villa |
| 7 | | Farm |
| 8 | Ch | Church |
| 8a | Cath | Cathedral |
| 8b | SPIRE Spire | Spire; Steeple |
| 9 | | Roman Catholic Church |
| 10 | | Temple |
| 11 | | Chapel |
| 12 | | Mosque |
| 12a | | Minaret |
| (1b) | | Moslem Shrine |
| 13 | | Marabout |
| 14 | Pag | Pagoda |
| 15 | | Buddhist Temple; Joss-House |
| 15a | | Shinto Shrine |
| 16 | | Monastery; Convent |
| 17 | | Calvary; Cross |
| 17a | Cem | Cemetery, Non-Christian |
| 18 | | Cemetery, Christian |
| 18a | | Tomb |
| 19 | | Fort (actual shape charted) |
| 20 | | Battery |
| 21 | | Barracks |
| 22 | | Powder magazine |
| • 23 | | Airplane landing field |
| • 24 | | Airport, large scale |

| No. | Symbol | Description |
|---|---|---|
| (1c) | | Airport, military (small scale) |
| (1d) | | Airport, civil (small scale) |
| 25 | | Mooring mast |
| 26 | St | Street |
| 26a | Ave | Avenue |
| 26b | Blvd | Boulevard |
| 27 | Tel | Telegraph |
| 28 | Tel Off | Telegraph office |
| 29 | PO | Post office |
| 30 | Govt Ho | Government house |
| 31 | | Town hall |
| 32 | Hosp | Hospital |
| 33 | | Slaughter house |
| 34 | Magz | Magazine |
| 34a | | Warehouse; Storehouse |
| 35 | MON Mon | Monument |
| 36 | CUP Cup | Cupola |
| 37 | ELEV Elev | Elevator |
| (1e) | Elev | Elevation; Elevated |
| 38 | | Shed |
| 39 | | Zinc roof |
| 40 | Ruins Ru | Ruins |
| 41 | TR Tr | Tower |
| (1f) | ABAND LT HO | Abandoned lighthouse |
| 42 | WINDMILL | Windmill |
| 43 | | Watermill |
| 43a | WINDMOTOR | Windmotor |
| 44 | CHY Chy | Chimney; Stack |
| • 45 | S'PIPE S'pipe | Water tower; Standpipe |
| 46 | | Oil tank; Gas tank; Gasholder; Gasometer |
| 47 | Facty | Factory |
| 48 | | Saw mill |
| 49 | | Brick kiln |
| 50 | | Mine; Quarry |
| 51 | Well | Well |
| 52 | | Cistern |
| 53 | TANK Tk | Tank |
| 54 | | Noria |
| 55 | | Fountain |
| 61 | Inst | Institute |
| 62 | | Establishment |
| 63 | | Bathing establishment |
| 64 | Ct Ho | Courthouse |

## I Buildings and Structures

| | | | | | | | | |
|---|---|---|---|---|---|---|---|---|
| 65 | | Sch | School | 74 | | | | Pyramid |
| (Ig) | | HS | High school | 75 | | | | Pillar |
| (Ih) | | Unlv | University | 76 | ⊙ | | ⊡ | Oil derrick |
| 66 | ■ ▨ | □ Bldg | Building | (Ii) | | Ltd | | Limited |
| | | | | (Ij) | | Apt | | Apartment |
| 67 | | Pav | Pavilion | (Ik) | | Cap | | Capitol |
| 68 | | | Hut | (Il) | | Co | | Company |
| 69 | | | Stadium | (Im) | | Corp | | Corporation |
| 70 | | T | Telephone | (In) | ⊙ | | | Landmark (position accurate) |
| 71 | ● ● ⊘ | | Gas tank; Gasometer | (Io) | o | | | Landmark (position approximate) |
| 72 | ⊙ GAB | o Gab | Gable | (Ip) | | | | Flare; Stack (on land) |
| 73 | | | Wall | | | | | |

## J Miscellaneous Stations

| | | | | | | |
|---|---|---|---|---|---|---|
| 1 | | Sta | Any kind of station | 15 | | Ice signal station |
| 2 | | Sta | Station | 16 | | Time signal station |
| 3 | ✦ C G | Coast Guard station (similar to Lifesaving station, J 6) | 16a | | Manned oceanographic station |
| | | | 16b | | Unmanned oceanographic station |
| (Ja) | ⊙ R TR / C G WALLIS SANDS | Coast Guard station (when landmark) | 17 | | Time ball |
| | | | 18 | | Signal mast |
| | | | 18a | o Mast | Mast |
| 4 | ⊙ LOOK TR ▲ | Lookout station; Watch tower | 19 | ⊙ FS o FP / ⊙ FP o FS | Flagstaff; Flagpole |
| 5 | ✦ | Lifeboat station | 19a | ⊙F TR oF Tr | Flag tower |
| 6 | ✦ LS S | Lifesaving station | 20 | | Signal |
| | | | 21 | Obsy | Observatory |
| | | | 22 | Off | Office |
| 7 | Rkt Sta | Rocket station | (Jc) | o BELL | Bell (on land) |
| 8 | Pilots / ⊙ PIL STA | Pilot station/Pilots | (Jd) | o HECP | Harbor entrance control post |
| | | | (Je) | o MARINE POLICE | Marine police station |
| | | | (Jf) | o FIREBOAT STATION | Fireboat station |
| 9 | ⊙ S S Sig Sta | Signal station | (Jg) | | Notice board |
| 10 | Sem | Semaphore | | | |
| 11 | S Sig Sta | Storm signal station | | | |
| 12 | | Weather signal station | | | |
| (Jb) | ⊙ NWS SIG STA | National Weather Service signal station | | | |
| 13 | | Tide signal station | | | |
| 14 | | Stream signal station | | | |

## K    Lights

| | | |
|---|---|---|
| 1 | ! ✦ ● ★ . | Position of light |
| •2 | Lt | Light |
| (Ka) | | Riprap surrounding light |
| 3 | Lt Ho | Lighthouse |
| 4 | AERO ✦AERO | Aeronautical light |
| 4a | | Marine and air navigation light |
| •5 | •Bn | Light beacon |
| 6 | | Light vessel; Lightship |
| 8 | | Lantern |
| 9 | | Street lamp |
| 10 | REF | Reflector |
| 11 | | Leading light |
| 11a | Lts in line 270° | Lighted range |
| 12 | | Sector light |
| 13 | RED GREEN | Directional light |
| 14 | | Harbor light |
| 15 | | Fishing light |
| 16 | | Tidal light |
| 17 | ! ★ ● Priv maintd | Private light (maintained by private interests; to be used with caution) |
| 21 | F | Fixed (steady light) |
| 22 | Oc; Occ | Occulting (total duration of light more than dark) |
| 23 | Fl | Single-Flashing (total duration of light less than dark) |
| (Kb) | L Fl | Long-Flashing (2 sec or longer) |
| | Fl (2+1) | Composite group-flashing |
| 23a | Iso; E Int | Isophase (light and dark equal) |
| 24 | Q; Qk Fl | Continuous Quick Flashing (50 to 79 per minute; 60 in US) |
| | Q(3) | Group Quick |
| 25 | IQ; Int Qk Fl; I Qk Fl | Interrupted Quick Flashing |

| | | |
|---|---|---|
| 25a | S Fl | Short Flashing |
| (Kc) | VQ; V Qk Fl | Continuous Very Quick Flashing (80 to 159 - usually either 100 or 120 per minute) |
| | VQ (3) | Group Very Quick |
| | IVQ | Interrupted Very Quick |
| | UQ | Continuous Ultra Quick (160 or more - usually 240 to 300 flashes per minute) |
| | IUQ | Interrupted Ultra Quick |
| 26 | Al; Alt | Alternating |
| 27 | Oc (2); Gp Occ | Group-Occulting |
| | Oc(2+3) | Composite group occulting |
| 28 | Fl (2); Gp Fl | Group Flashing |
| 28a | S-L Fl | Short-Long Flashing |
| 28b | | Group-Short Flashing |
| 29 | F Fl | Fixed and Flashing |
| 30 | F Gp Fl | Fixed and Group Flashing |
| 30a | Mo (A) | Morse Code light (with flashes grouped as in letter A) |
| 31 | Rot | Revolving or Rotating light |
| 41 | | Period |
| 42 | | Every |
| 43 | | With |
| 44 | | Visible (range) |
| (Kd) | M; Mi; N Mi | Nautical mile |
| (Ke) | m; min | Minutes |
| (Kf) | s; sec | Seconds |
| 45 | Fl | Flash |
| 46 | Oc; Occ | Occultation |
| 46a | | Eclipse |
| 47 | Gp | Group |
| 48 | Oc; Occ | Intermittent light |
| 49 | SEC | Sector |
| 50 | | Color of sector |
| 51 | Aux | Auxiliary light |
| 52 | | Varied |
| 61 | Vi | Violet |
| 62 | | Purple |
| 63 | Bu; Bl | Blue |
| 64 | G | Green |

## K    Lights

| | | | | | | | | | |
|---|---|---|---|---|---|---|---|---|---|
| 65 | Or; Y | Orange | 72 | Prov | Provisional light | 80 | Vert | Vertical lights |
| 66 | R | Red | 73 | Temp | Temporary light | 81 | Hor | Horizontal lights |
| 67 | W | White | (Kg) | D; Destr | Destroyed | (Kh) | VB | Vertical beam |
| 67a | Y  Am | Amber | 74 | Exting | Extinguished light | (Ki) | RGE | Range |
| (Ko) | Y | Yellow | 75 | | Faint light | (KJ) | Exper | Experimental light |
| 68 | OBSC | Obscured light | 76 | | Upper light | | | |
| 68a | Fog Det Lt | Fog detector light | 77 | | Lower light | (Kp) | | Lighted offshore platform |
| 70 | Occas | Occasional light | 78 | | Rear light | | | |
| 71 | Irreg | Irregular light | 79 | | Front light | (Kq) | | Flare  (Flame) |

## L    Buoys and Beacons

| | | | | | |
|---|---|---|---|---|---|
| ·1 | Approximate position of buoy | · 21 | Tel | Telegraph - cable buoy |
| ·2 | Light buoy | · 22 | | Mooring buoy (colors of mooring buoys never carried) |
| · 3 | BELL  BELL  Bell buoy | 22a | | Mooring |
| · 3a | GONG  GONG  Gong buoy | · 22b | Tel  Tel | Mooring buoy with telegraphic communications |
| · 4 | WHIS  WHIS  Whistle buoy | · 22c | T  T | Mooring buoy with telephonic communications |
| · 5 | C  Can or Cylindrical buoy | · 23 | | Warping buoy |
| · 6 | N  Nun or Conical buoy | · 24 | Y | Quarantine buoy |
| · 7 | SP  Spherical buoy | 24a | | Practice area buoy |
| · 8 | S  Spar buoy | · 25 | Explos Anch | Explosive anchorage buoy |
| · 8a | P  Pillar or Spindle buoy | · 25a | AERO | Aeronautical anchorage buoy |
| · 9 | Buoy with topmark (ball) | · 26 | Deviation | Compass adjustment buoy |
| · 10 | Barrel or Ton buoy | · 27 | BW | Fish trap (area) buoy (BWHB) |
| (La) | Color unknown | · 27a | | Spoil ground buoy |
| (Lb) | FLOAT  Float | · 28 | W | Anchorage buoy (marks limits) |
| · 12 | FLOAT  FLOAT  Lightfloat | · 29 | Priv maintd | Private aid to navigation (buoy) (maintained by private interests, use with caution) |
| 13 | Outer or Landfall buoy | 30 | | Temporary buoy |
| · 14 | RW  BW  Fairway buoy (RWVS; BWVS) | 30a | | Winter buoy |
| · 14a | RW  BW  Midchannel buoy (RWVS; BWVS) | · 31 | HB | Horizontal bands |
| · 15 | R/2  Starboard - hand buoy (entering from seaward - US waters) | · 32 | VS | Vertical stripes |
| · 16 | -1-  -1-  Port - hand buoy (entering from seaward - US waters) | · 33 | Chec | Checkered |
| · 17 | RB  BR  RG  GR  RB  Bifurcation buoy | · 33a | Diag | Diagonal bands |
| · 18 | RB  BR  RG  GR  BR  Junction buoy | 41 | W | White |
| · 19 | RB  BR  RG  GR  RG  Isolated danger buoy | 42 | B | Black |
| · 20 | RB  BR  RG  GR  G  Wreck buoy | 43 | R | Red |
| · 20a | RB  BR  RG  GR  G  Obstruction buoy | 44 | Y | Yellow |
| | | 45 | G | Green |
| | | 46 | Br | Brown |
| | | 47 | Gy | Gray |

# 286          Appendix

## L    Buoys and Beacons

| | | |
|---|---|---|
| 48 | Bu | Blue |
| 48a | Am | Amber |
| 48b | Or | Orange |
| • 51 | ∮ ⌂⌂⌂⌂⌂⌂ | Floating beacon (and variations) |
| • 52 | Fixed beacons (unlighted or daybeacons) | |
| | ▲R Bn   △RG Bn | Triangular beacon |
| | ▲Bn | Black beacon |
| | ■G Bn   □GR Bn   □W Bn | Square and other shaped beacons |
| | □Bn ✦ | Color unknown |
| | ↑ ↓ ⌂ ⌂ ⌂ | Variations |
| 53 | ↓ Bn □ ▲ | Beacon, in general |
| 54 | ♁ ✦ | Tower beacon |
| 55 | | Cardinal marking system |
| 56 | △Deviation Bn | Compass adjustment beacon |
| 57 | ⌂ ▲ ⦂ ∘ ✕ ▲ ▲ ▼ ⌂ | Topmarks |
| 58 | | Telegraph-cable (landing) beacon |

| | | |
|---|---|---|
| • 59 | ▪Piles   ∘Piles | Piles |
| | ▴Stumps | Stumps |
| | | Stakes, perches |
| (Lc) | ⊙MARKER ∘Marker | Private aid to navigation |
| 61 | ⊙CAIRN ⌂Cairn ▲ ⛫ | Cairn |
| 62 | | Painted patches |
| 63 | ⊙ | Landmark (position accurate) |
| (Ld) | ∘ | Landmark (position approximate) |
| 64 | REF | Reflector |
| 65 | ⊙MARKER ⊥ | Range targets, markers |
| (Le) | ⊙W Or ⊥ ⧆ Y Y | Special-purpose buoys |
| | ⊙W Or ⧊ ⧈ Y Y | |
| 66 | | Oil installation buoy |
| 67 | ⊡ | Drilling platform |
| 70 | NOTE: Refer to IALA Buoyage System    description on page 48 for aids used in certain foreign waters. | |
| 71 | ⬲ | LANBY (Large Auto. Nav. Buoy); Superbuoy |
| 72 | ⬱ | TANKER terminal buoy (mooring) |
| 73 | ⬲ODAS | ODAS (Oceanographic Data Aquisition System) |
| (Lg) | ⌀Art | Articulated light (floating light) |

## M    Radio and Radar Stations

| | | |
|---|---|---|
| 1 | ∘R Sta | Radio telegraph station |
| 2 | ∘RT | Radio telephone station |
| 3 | ⊙R Bn, Ro Bn | Radiobeacon |
| • 4 | ⊙R Bn, RC | Circular radiobeacon |
| 5 | ⊙RD 072°30′ RD | Directional radiobeacon; Radio range |
| 6 | ⊙RW | Rotating loop radiobeacon |
| • 7 | ⊙RDF, Ro DF, RG | Radio direction finding station |
| (Ma) | ⊙ANTENNA (TELEM) ⊙TELEM ANT | Telemetry antenna |
| (Mb) | ⊙R RELAY MAST | Radio relay mast |
| (Mc) | ⊙MICRO TR | Microwave tower |
| 9 | ⊙R MAST ⯭ | Radio mast |
| | ⊙R TR ⯭ | Radio tower |

| | | |
|---|---|---|
| 9a | ⊙TV TR ⯭Tr ⯭ | Television mast; Television tower |
| 10 | ⊙R TR (WBAL) 1090 kHz ⊕⊏ | Radio broadcasting station (commercial) |
| • 10a | ∘R Sta | QTG radio station |
| 11 | ⊙Ra | Radar station |
| 12 | ⊙Racon ∘Ra Sur | Radar responder beacon |
| 13 | ⌁Ra Ref | Radar reflector |
| 14 | ⊱Ra (conspic) | Radar conspicuous object |
| 14a | ⊙ | Ramark |
| 15 | DFS ⊙R Telem | Distance finding station (synchronized signals) |
| 16 | AERO R Bn ⊙302 ⌁ R C Aero | Aeronautical radiobeacon |
| 17 | ∘Decca Sta | Decca station |
| 18 | ∘Loran Sta Venice | Loran station (name) |

## M    Radio and Radar Stations

| | | | | | | |
|---|---|---|---|---|---|---|
| 19 | ⊚ | CONSOL Bn 190 kHz MMF ▐▐. | Consol (Consolan) station | (Mf) | ⊙ LORAN TR SPRING ISLAND | Loran tower (name) |
| (Md) | ⊚ | AERO R Rge 342 ▐▐▐. | Aeronautical radio range | (Mg) | ⊙ R TR F R Lt | Obstruction light |
| (Me) | ⊚ | Ra Ref Calibration Bn | Radar calibration beacon | (Mh) | ⊙RA DOME  ⊙DOME (RADAR) ⊙Ra Dome  ⊙Dome (Radar) | Radar dome |
| | | | | (Mi) | uhf | Ultrahigh frequency |
| | | | | (Mj) | vhf | Very high frequency |

## N    Fog Signals

| | | | | | | |
|---|---|---|---|---|---|---|
| 1 | Fog Sig | Fog-signal station | 13 | HORN | Air (foghorn) |
| 2 | | Radio fog-signal station | 13a | HORN | Electric (foghorn) |
| 3 | GUN | Explosive fog signal | 14 | BELL | Fog bell |
| 4 | | Submarine fog signal | 15 | WHIS | Fog whistle |
| 5 | SUB-BELL | Submarine fog bell (action of waves) | 16 | HORN | Reed horn |
| 6 | SUB-BELL | Submarine fog bell (mechanical) | 17 | GONG | Fog gong |
| 7 | SUB-OSC | Submarine oscillator | 18 | ◉ | Submarine sound signal not connected to the shore |
| 8 | NAUTO | Nautophone | 18a | ◉〜〜 | Submarine sound signal connected to the shore |
| 9 | DIA | Diaphone | | | |
| 10 | GUN | Fog gun | (Na) | HORN | Typhon |
| 11 | SIREN | Fog siren | (Nb) | Fog Det Lt | Fog detector light |
| 12 | HORN | Fog trumpet | (Nc) | Mo | Morse Code fog signal |

## O    Dangers

| | | | | | |
|---|---|---|---|---|---|
| 1 | ⊚ (21)  ▲ (4 m) | Rock which does not cover (height above MHW) | 6a | 2¹ Rk   2¹ Obstr | Sunken danger with depth cleared (swept) by wire drag |
| 2 | *Uncov 2 ft  ⊙Uncov 2 ft *(2)   (2) (4)   Dries 4 ft | Rock which covers and uncovers with height above chart sounding datum (see introduction) | | 3¹   3¹   5 | |
| | | | 7 | Reef | Reef of unknown extent |
| | | | 8 | )Sub vol | Submarine volcano |
| 3 | ⁂  ⊛  ⊚  (0) | Rock awash at (near) level of chart sounding datum | 9 | )Discol water | Discolored water |
| | ⁂ | Dotted line emphasizes danger to navigation | 10 | Coral  Co) Co   Co | Coral reef, detached (uncovers at sounding datum) |
| (Oa) | • | Rock awash (height unknown) | | | |
| | ⁂ | Dotted line emphasizes danger to navigation | | + Co + 3, + | Coral or Rocky reef, covered at sounding datum |
| 4 | + | Submerged rock (depth unknown) | | | |
| | ⁂ | Dotted line emphasizes danger to navigation | | | |
| 5 | 5 Rk  9 R  2 + 5 Rks  (+)(8)  2 P | Shoal sounding on isolated rock or rocks | 11 | | Wreck showing any portion of hull or superstructure (above sounding datum) |
| 6 | +  35 R.  35 R + (35) | Submerged rock not dangerous to surface navigation | 12 | +++ Masts  Mast (10 ft)  Funnel | Wreck with only masts (and other protruding objects) visible above sounding datum |

## O   Dangers

| | | |
|---|---|---|
| 13 | | Old symbols for wrecks |
| 13a | PA | Wreck always partially submerged |
| 14 | +++ | Sunken wreck dangerous to surface navigation (less than 11 fathoms over wreck) |
| 14a | +++ | Sunken wreck covered 20 to 30 meters |
| 15 | Wk   +++ (9) | Wreck over which depth is known |
| 15a | 2⌐ Wk   Wk   Wk | Wreck with depth cleared by wire drag |
| 15b | Wk   +++ 2⌐ Wk | Unsurveyed wreck over which the exact depth is unknown, but is considered to have a safe clearance to the depth shown |
| 16 | +++ | Sunken wreck, not dangerous to surface navigation |
| 17 | Foul  #  ⋒ | Foul ground, Foul bottom |
| 17a | ℳℳ | Mobil bottom (sand waves) |
| 18 | Tide rips  ∼∼∼ | Overfalls or Tide rips |
| 19 | Eddies | Eddies |
| 20 | Kelp | Kelp, Seaweed |
| 21 | Bk | Bank |
| 22 | Shl | Shoal |
| 23 | Rf | Reef |
| 23a | | Ridge |
| 24 | Le | Ledge |
| 25 | Br  or | Breakers |
| 26 | | Submerged rock |
| 27 | Obstr | Obstruction |
| (Ob) | Obstr  •Well  ✦ | Submerged well |
| | Obstr  Well | Submerged well (buoyed) |
| (Oc) | Obstruction (fish haven) | Fish haven (artificial fishing reef) |
| | | (actual shape) |

| | | |
|---|---|---|
| 28 | | Wreck |
| 29 | Wreckage  Wks | Wreckage |
| 29a | | Wreck remains (dangerous only for anchoring) |
| 30 | Subm piles  Subm piling | Submerged piling |
| | Subm piles  Stakes, Perches | |
| 30a | Snags  Stumps | Snags; Submerged stumps |
| 31 | | Lesser depth possible |
| 32 | Uncov | Dries |
| 33 | Cov | Covers |
| 34 | Uncov | Uncovers |
| 35 | Rep (1983) | Reported (with date) |
| | Eagle Rk (rep 1983) | Reported (with name and date) |
| 36 | Discol | Discolored |
| 37 | | Isolated danger |
| 38 | | Limiting danger line |
| 39 | + rky + | Limit of rocky area |
| 41 | PA | Position approximate |
| 42 | PD | Position doubtful |
| 43 | ED | Existance doubtful |
| 44 | P  Pos | Position |
| 45 | D | Doubtful |
| 46 | Unexam | Unexamined |
| (Od) | LD | Least Depth |
| (Oe) | Subm Crib | Crib |
| | Crib (above water) | |
| (Of) | Platform (lighted) HORN | Offshore platform (unnamed) |
| (Og) | Hazel (lighted) HORN | Offshore platform (named) |

## P    Various Limits, etc.

| | | |
|---|---|---|
| 1 | | Leading line; Range line |
| 2 | | Transit |
| 3 | | In line with |
| 4 | | Limit of sector |
| 5 | | Channel, Course, Track recommended (marked by buoys or beacons) |
| 5a | ◄► DW ◄► | Recommended track for deep draft vessels (defined by fixed marks) |
| 5b | ◄► DW83 ft ◄► DW76 ft | Depth is shown where it has been obtained by the cognizant authority |
| (Pa) | | Alternate course |
| 6 | — Ra —— Ra — | Radar - guided track |
| 6a | | Established traffic separation scheme. One - way traffic lanes (separated by line or zone) |
| 6b | | Established traffic separation scheme: Roundabout |
| | ◯ | If no separation zone exists, the center of the roundabout is shown by a circle |
| 6c | DW | Recommended direction of traffic flow |
| 7 | | Submarine cable (power telegraph, telephone, etc.) |
| 7a | Cable Area | Submarine cable area |
| 7b | ∧∧ ∧∧ ∧∧ ∧ ∧ | Abandoned submarine cable (includes disused cable) |
| 8 | | Submarine pipeline |
| 8a | Pipeline Area | Submarine pipeline area |
| 8b | | Abandoned submarine pipeline |
| 9 | | Maritime limit in general |
| (Pb) | RESTRICTED AREA | Limit of restricted area |
| • 10 | | Limits of national fishing zones |
| (Pc) | | U.S. Harbor Line |

| | | |
|---|---|---|
| 11 | | Limit of dumping ground, spoil ground |
| 12 | | Anchorage limit |
| • 13 | | Limit of airport |
| • 14 | | Limit of sovereignty (Territorial waters) |
| • 15 | | Customs boundary |
| • 16 | +++++++++ | International boundary (also State boundary) |
| 17 | | Stream limit |
| 18 | | Ice limit |
| 19 | | Limit of tide |
| 20 | | Limit of Navigation |
| 21 | -- ◄-- ►-- -- ◄-- ►-- | Recommended track (not marked by buoys or beacons) |
| 21a | -- ►-- ►-- -- DW __ DW | Recommended track for deep draft vessels (track not defined by fixed marks) |
| 21b | ►DW83 ft ► ►DW76 ft► DW83 ft DW76 ft | Depth is shown where it has been obtained by the cognizant authority |
| 22 | | District or province limit |
| 23 | —— · —— | Reservation line (Options) |
| 24 | COURSE 053° 00' TRUE MARKERS | Measured distance |
| 25 | PROHIBITED AREA | Prohibited area (Screen optional) |
| (Pd) | SAFETY FAIRWAY | Shipping safety fairway (two - way traffic) |
| (Pe) | | Limits of former mine danger area |
| (Pf) | 17386 | Reference larger scale chart |
| (Pg) | | Limit of fishing areas (fish trap areas) |
| (Ph) | | 3 - mile Territorial Sea Boundary 12 - mile Contiguous Zone Boundary; headland to headland line |
| (Pi) | | COLREGS demarcation line |

## Q　Soundings

| | | | | | | | |
|---|---|---|---|---|---|---|---|
| 1 | SD | | Doubtful sounding | 10 | | | Hairline depth figures |
| 2 | 85̄ | | No bottom found | | | | |
| 3 | (23) | 1036 | Out of position | 10a | 19　8₂　7½ | | Figures for ordinary soundings |
| 4 | (5) | | Least depth in narrow channels | 11 | | | Soundings taken from foreign charts |
| 5 | 30 FEET APR 1984 | | Dredged channel (with controlling depth indicated) | 12 | 8₂　19 | | Soundings taken from older surveys (or smaller scale charts) |
| 6 | 24 FEET OCT 1983 | | Dredged area | 13 | 8₂　19 | | Echo soundings |
| | | | | 14 | 8₂　19 | | Sloping figures |
| 7 | 6 | | Swept channel | 15 | 8₂　19 | | Upright figures |
| | | | | 16 | (25)　(2) | | Bracketed figures |
| 8 | 2₁ | | Drying (or uncovering) heights above chart sounding datum | 17 | | | Underlined sounding figures (drying) |
| 9 | 89　17　119　15 | | Swept area, not adequately sounded (shown by purple or green tint) | 18 | 3₂　6₁ | | Soundings expressed in fathoms and feet |
| 9a | 29　23　3　30　8　19　7　21 | | Swept area adequately sounded (swept by wire drag to depth indicated) | 22 | | | Unsounded area |
| | | | | (Qa) | 6—5　2 ft | | Stream |

## R　Depth Contours and Tints

| Feet | Fm/Meters | | | | Feet | Fm/Meters | |
|---|---|---|---|---|---|---|---|
| 0 | 0 | | | | 300 | 50 | |
| 6 | 1 | | | | 600 | 100 | |
| 12 | 2 | | | | 1,200 | 200 | |
| 18 | 3 | | | | 1,800 | 300 | |
| 24 | 4 | | | | 2,400 | 400 | |
| 30 | 5 | | | | 3,000 | 500 | |
| 36 | 6 | | | | 6,000 | 1,000 | |
| 60 | 10 | | | | Approximate depth contour | | |
| 120 | 20 | | | | Continuous lines, with values | | — 5 ——— (blue or |
| 180 | 30 | | | | | | black) ——— 100 —— |
| 240 | 40 | | | | | | |

## S　Quality of the Bottom

| | | | | | | | | | |
|---|---|---|---|---|---|---|---|---|---|
| 1 | Grd | Ground | 11 | Rk, rky | Rock; Rocky | (Sb) | Vol Ash | Volcanic ash |
| 2 | S | Sand | 11a | Blds | Boulders | 17 | La | Lava |
| 3 | M | Mud; Muddy | 12 | Ck | Chalk | 18 | Pm | Pumice |
| 4 | Oz | Ooze | 12a | Ca | Calcareous | 19 | T | Tufa |
| 5 | Ml | Marl | 13 | Qz | Quartz | 20 | Sc | Scoriae |
| 6 | Cl, Cy | Clay | 13a | Sch | Schist | 21 | Cn | Cinders |
| 7 | G | Gravel | 14 | Co | Coral | 21a | | Ash |
| 8 | Sn | Shingle | (Sa) | Co Hd | Coral head | 22 | Mn | Manganese |
| 9 | P | Pebbles | 15 | Mds | Madrepores | 23 | Sh | Shells |
| 10 | St | Stones | 16 | Vol | Volcanic | 24 | Oys | Oysters |

## S    Quality of the Bottom

| No. | Abbr. | Term | No. | Abbr. | Term | No. | Abbr. | Term |
|---|---|---|---|---|---|---|---|---|
| 25 | Ms | Mussels | 42 | h, hrd | Hard | 60 | gn | Green |
| 26 | Spg | Sponge | 43 | stf | Stiff | 61 | yl | Yellow |
| 27 | K | Kelp | 44 | sml | Small | 62 | or | Orange |
| 28 | Wd | Seaweed | 45 | lrg | Large | 63 | rd | Red |
|  | Grs | Grass | 46 | sy, stk | Sticky | 64 | br | Brown |
| 29 | Sta | Sea-tangle | 47 | bk, brk | Broken | 65 | ch | Chocolate |
| 31 | Sp. | Spicules | 47a | grd | Ground (Shells) | 66 | gy | Gray |
| 32 | Fr | Foraminifera | 48 | rt | Rotten | 67 | lt | Light |
| 33 | Gl | Globigerina | 49 | str | Streaky | 68 | dk | Dark |
| 34 | Di | Diatoms | 50 | spk | Speckled | 70 | vard | Varied |
| 35 | Rd | Radiolaria | 51 | gty | Gritty | 71 | unev | Uneven |
| 36 | Pt | Pteropods | 52 | dec | Decayed | (Sc) | S/M | Surface layer and Under layer |
| 37 | Po | Polyzoa | 53 | fly | Flinty | 76 | | Freshwater springs in seabed |
| 38 | Cir | Cirripedia | 54 | glac | Glacial | | | |
| 38a | Fu | Fucus | 55 | ten | Tenacious | (Sd) | 〰 | Mobile bottom (sand waves) |
| 38b | Ma | Mattes | 56 | wh | White | (Se) | Si | Silt |
| 39 | fne | Fine | 57 | bl, bk | Black | (Sf) | Cb | Cobbles |
| 40 | crs | Coarse | 58 | vi | Violet | (Sg) | m | Medium (used only before S (sand)) |
| 41 | so, sft | Soft | 59 | bu | Blue | | | |
| | | | | | | | Foreign Bottoms | See glossary |

## T    Tides and Currents

| No. | Abbr. | Term | No. | Abbr. | Term |
|---|---|---|---|---|---|
| 1 | HW | High water | 10 | ISLW | Indian spring low water |
| 1a | HHW | Higher high water | 11 | HWF&C | High-water full and change (vulgar establishment of the port) |
| 2 | LW | Low water | | | |
| (Ta) | LWD | Low-water datum | 12 | LWF&C | Low-water full and change |
| 2a | LLW | Lower low water | 13 | | Mean establishment of the port |
| 3 | MTL | Mean tide level | 13a | | Establishment of the port |
| 4 | MSL | Mean sea level | 14 | | Unit of height |
| 4a | | Elevation of mean sea level above chart (sounding) datum | 15 | | Equinoctial |
| 5 | | Chart datum (datum for sounding reduction) | 16 | | Quarter; Quadrature |
| | | | 17 | Str | Stream |
| 6 | Sp | Spring tide | 18 | → 2 kn | Current, general, with rate |
| 7 | Np | Neap tide | 19 | → 2 kn | Flood stream (current) with rate |
| 7a | MHW | Mean high water | 20 | → 2 kn | Ebb stream (current) with rate |
| 8 | MHWS | Mean high-water springs | 21 | ° Tide gauge | Tide gauge; Tidepole; Automatic tide gauge |
| 8a | MHWN | Mean high-water neaps | | | |
| 8b | MHHW | Mean higher high water | 23 | vel | Velocity; Rate |
| 8c | MLW | Mean low water | 24 | kn | Knots |
| 9 | MLWS | Mean low-water springs | 25 | ht | Height |
| 9a | MLWN | Mean low-water neaps | 26 | | Tide |
| 9b | MLLW | Mean lower low water | | | |

## T    Tides and Currents

| | | |
|---|---|---|
| 27 | 🙂 | New moon |
| 28 | ⚫ | Full moon |
| 29 | | Ordinary |
| 30 | | Syzygy |
| 31 | fl | Flood |
| 32 | | Ebb |
| 33 | | Tidal stream diagram |

| | | |
|---|---|---|
| 34 | Ⓐ Ⓑ | Place for which tabulated tidal stream data are given |
| 35 | | Range (of tide) |
| 36 | | Phase lag |
| (Tb) | | Current diagram, with explanatory note |
| (Tc) | CRD | Columbia River Datum |
| (Td) | GCLWD | Gulf Coast Low Water Datum |

## U    Compass

| | | |
|---|---|---|
| 1 | N | North |
| 2 | E | East |
| 3 | S | South |
| 4 | W | West |
| 5 | NE | Northeast |
| 6 | SE | Southeast |
| 7 | SW | Southwest |
| 8 | NW | Northwest |
| 9 | N | Northern |
| 10 | E | Eastern |
| 11 | S | Southern |
| 12 | W | Western |
| | | |
| 21 | brg; My | Bearing |
| 22 | T | True |
| 23 | mag | Magnetic |
| 24 | var | Variation |
| 25 | | Annual change |
| 25a | | Annual change nil |

| | | |
|---|---|---|
| 26 | +15° | Abnormal variation; Magnetic attraction |
| 27 | deg | Degrees |
| 28 | dev | Deviation |
| 29 | | Compass roses |

VAR 14° 45' W (1984)
ANNUAL INCREASE 2'

The outer circle is in degrees with zero at true north. The inner circles are in points and degrees with the arrow indicating magnetic north.

## Index of Abbreviations

## Index of Abbreviations

## Index of Abbreviations

## Index of Abbreviations

## Index of Abbreviations

| | | |
|---|---|---|
| unverd | Unverified | Fb |
| unev | Uneven | S 71 |
| μsec. μs | Microsecond (one millinoth) | Eb |
| UQ | Continuous Ultra Quick | Kc |

**V**

| | | |
|---|---|---|
| var | Variation | U 24 |
| vard | Varied | S 70 |
| VB | Vertical beam | Kh |
| vel | Velocity | T 23 |
| Vert | Vertical (lights) | K 80 |
| VERT CL | Vertical clearance | H 18a |
| vhf | Very high frequency | Mi |
| Vi, vi | Violet | K 61; S 58 |
| View X | View point | D 6 |
| Vil | Village | I 3 |
| Vol | Volcanic | S 16 |
| Vol Ash | Volcanic ash | Sb |
| VQ, V Qk Fl | Very quick flashing (light) | Kc |
| VS | Vertical stripes | L 32 |

**W**

| | | |
|---|---|---|
| W | West, Western | U 4, 12 |
| W, wh | White | K 67; L 41; S 56 |
| W Bn | White beacon | L 52 |
| Wd | Seaweed | S 28 |
| Whf | Wharf | G 18 |
| WHIS | Fog whistle | N 15 |
| Wk | Wreck | O 15, 15a, 28 |
| Wks | Wrecks, Wreckage | O 29 |
| W Or | White and orange | Le |
| W'ly | Westerly | Ft |

**Y**

| | | |
|---|---|---|
| Y, yl | Yellow | L 24, 44; S 61 |
| yd, yds | Yard(s) | E 8 |

| | | |
|---|---|---|
| 1st | First | Fj |
| 2nd, 2d | Second | Fk |
| 3rd, 3d | Third | Fl |
| 4th | Fourth | Fm |

| | | |
|---|---|---|
| ° | Degree | E 20 |
| ′ | Minute (of arc) | E 21 |
| ″ | Second (of arc) | E 22 |

# Appendix II

AIDS TO NAVIGATION

IN

UNITED STATES WATERS

## MODIFIED U.S. AID SYSTEM

### LATERAL AIDS AS SEEN ENTERING FROM SEAWARD

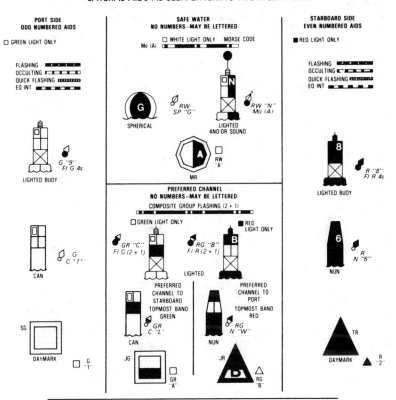

NOTE: WHEN USED ON THE INTRACOASTAL WATERWAY, THESE AIDS ARE ALSO EQUIPPED WITH SPECIAL YELLOW STRIPS, TRIANGLES, OR SQUARES. WHEN USED ON THE WESTERN RIVERS (MISSISSIPPI RIVER SYSTEM), THESE AIDS ARE NOT NUMBERED. (MISSISSIPPI RIVER SYSTEM ABOVE BATON ROUGE AND ALABAMA RIVERS)

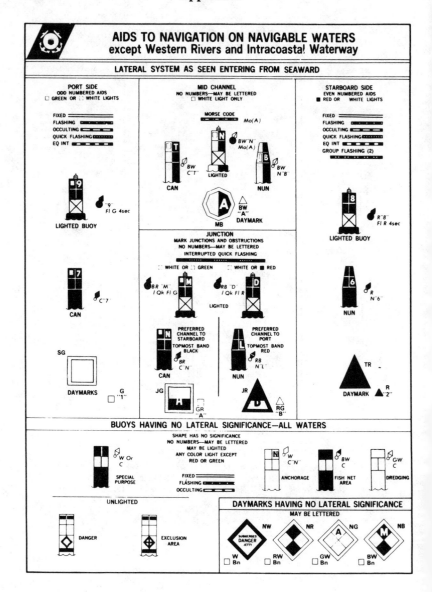

# AIDS TO NAVIGATION ON NAVIGABLE WATERS
## except Western Rivers and Intracoastal Waterway

### LATERAL SYSTEM AS SEEN ENTERING FROM SEAWARD

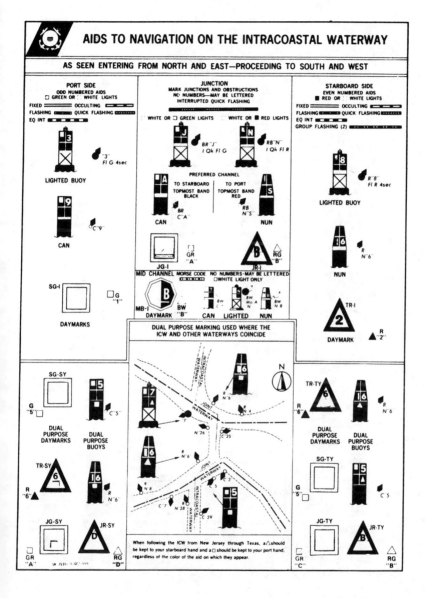

AIDS TO NAVIGATION ON THE INTRACOASTAL WATERWAY

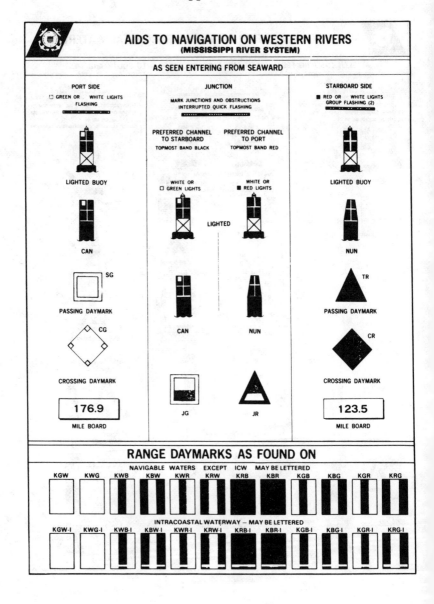

# UNIFORM STATE WATERWAY MARKING SYSTEM

**STATE WATERS AND DESIGNATED STATE WATERS FOR PRIVATE AIDS TO NAVIGATION**

## REGULATORY MARKERS

BOAT EXCLUSION AREA

SWIM AREA

EXPLANATION MAY BE PLACED OUTSIDE THE CROSSED DIAMOND SHAPE, SUCH AS DAM, RAPIDS, SWIM AREA, ETC.

DANGER

ROCK

THE NATURE OF DANGER MAY BE INDICATED INSIDE THE DIAMOND SHAPE, SUCH AS ROCK, WRECK, SHOAL, DAM, ETC.

CONTROLLED AREA

SLOW

NO WAKE

TYPE OF CONTROL IS INDICATED IN THE CIRCLE, SUCH AS SLOW, NO WAKE, ANCHORING, ETC.

MULLET LAKE

BLACK RIVER

INFORMATION

FOR DISPLAYING INFORMATION SUCH AS DIRECTIONS, DISTANCES, LOCATIONS, ETC.

BUOY USED TO DISPLAY REGULATORY MARKERS

MAY SHOW WHITE LIGHT
MAY BE LETTERED

5 MPH

## AIDS TO NAVIGATION

MAY SHOW WHITE REFLECTOR OR LIGHT

**MOORING BUOY**

WHITE WITH BLUE BAND

MAY SHOW WHITE REFLECTOR OR LIGHT

**RED-STRIPED WHITE BUOY**

MAY BE LETTERED
DO NOT PASS BETWEEN BUOY AND NEAREST SHORE

7

**BLACK-TOPPED WHITE BUOY**

MAY BE NUMBERED

PASS TO NORTH OR EAST OF BUOY

**RED-TOPPED WHITE BUOY**

PASS TO SOUTH OR WEST OF BUOY

**CARDINAL SYSTEM**

MAY SHOW GREEN REFLECTOR OR LIGHT

MAY SHOW RED REFLECTOR OR LIGHT

3

**SOLID RED AND SOLID BLACK BUOYS**

USUALLY FOUND IN PAIRS
PASS BETWEEN THESE BUOYS

4

PORT SIDE —— LOOKING UPSTREAM —— STARBOARD SIDE

**LATERAL SYSTEM**

SW 7630-01-GF2-5540

# Appendix III

# Celestial
# Workforms

## NAVIGATOR'S
## WORKBOOK

*Sun*

| DATE | |
|---|---|
| BODY | |
| hs | |
| IC | |
| D | |
| ha | |
| R | |
| Ho | |
| W | |
| corr | |
| GMT | |
| gha | |
| incr | |
| GHA | |
| | |
| aλ | |
| LHA | |
| Dec | |
| aL | |
| Tab. Hc | |
| corr | |
| Hc | |
| Ho | |
| a | |
| Zn | |

*LAN—Sun*

| DATE | |
|---|---|
| Est. λ | |
| Std. Mer. | |
| Corr in time | |
| Mer. Pass. | |
| LAN | |
| GMT | |
| hs | |
| IC | |
| D | |
| ha | |
| R | |
| Ho | |
| 90° | |
| − Ho | |
| z | |
| Dec | |
| L | |
| (name) | |

## NAVIGATOR'S
## WORKBOOK

| *Moon* | | | | *Planet* | | |
|---|---|---|---|---|---|---|
| DATE | | | | DATE | | |
| BODY | | | | BODY | | |
| hs | | | | hs | | |
| IC | | | | IC | | |
| D | | | | D | | |
| ha | | | | ha | | |
| R | | | | R | | |
| H.P. | H. P. | | ⌐ | add'l corr | | |
| ( − 30′) | | | | Ho | | |
| Ho | | | | W | | |
| W | | | | corr | | |
| corr | | | | GMT | | |
| GMT | | | | gha | v | ⌐ |
| gha | v | | ⌐ | incr | | |
| incr | | | | v corr | | |
| v corr | | | | GHA | | |
| GHA | | | | | | |
| | | | | aλ | | |
| aλ | | | | LHA | | |
| LHA | | | | dec | d | ⌐ |
| dec | d | | ⌐ | d corr | | |
| d corr | | | | Dec | | |
| Dec | | | | a L | | |
| a L | | | | Tab Hc | | |
| Tab Hc | | | | corr | | |
| corr | | | | Hc | | |
| Hc | | | | Ho | | |
| Ho | | | | a | | |
| a | | | | Zn | | |
| Zn | | | | | | |

## NAVIGATOR'S
## WORKBOOK

*Stars—Vol. I Pub. No. 249.*    *Stars—Vol. II/III Pub. No. 249*

| | | | | |
|---|---|---|---|---|
| DATE | | DATE | |
| BODY | | BODY | |
| hs | | hs | |
| IC | | IC | |
| D | | D | |
| ha | | ha | |
| R | | R | |
| Ho | | Ho | |
| W | | W | |
| corr | | corr | |
| GMT | | GMT | |
| gha ♈ | | gha ♈ | |
| incr | | incr | |
| GHA ♈ | | GHA ♈ | |
| | | SHA★ | |
| aλ | | GHA★ | |
| LHA ♈ | | | |
| a L | | | |
| Hc | | a λ | |
| Ho | | LHA★ | |
| a | | Dec | |
| Zn | | a L | |
| | | Tab Hc | |
| | | corr | |
| | | Hc | |
| | | Ho | |
| | | a | |
| | | Zn | |

## NAVIGATOR'S
## WORKBOOK

### *Polaris*

| DATE | |
|---|---|
| hs | |
| IC | |
| D | |
| ha | |
| R | |
| Ho | |
| W | |
| corr | |
| GMT | |
| gha ♈ | |
| incr | |
| GHA ♈ | |
| | |
| | |
| a λ | |
| LHA ♈ | |
| a L | |
| Ho | |
| $-1°$ | |
| $+a_0$ | |
| $+a_1$ | |
| $+a_2$ | |
| L | |

# Index

# Index